CW01508821

BACK AGAIN MR.BEGBIE

A Christian Man's Testimony of
Three Careers in One Life

REV. LT COL R.J.G. BEGBIE OBE

Sincerely yours

19ᵗ April 2001.

**ROSS
HOUSE
BOOKS**

Vallecito, California

Copyright 1992 by
Rev. Lt Col R.J.G. Begbie, OBE
and published privately by him
in South Africa from
P.O.Box 2771 George 6530.

All rights reserved

2000 A.D. Printing

No part of this publication maybe reproduced, stored in
a retrieval system, or transmitted, in any form or by any
means without the prior permission in writing of the
publisher, nor be otherwise circulated in any form of
binding or cover other than that in which it is published.

Library of Congress Catalog Card Number: 00-090842
ISBN: 1-879998-17-3

Printed in the United States of America

I dedicate this book to my dear wife, Win, who has supported me and looked after me with utter devotion while, without complaint, repeatedly sacrificing her career as an educationalist so that she could accompany me on my frequent moves in three different professions.

Table of Contents

Author's Preface 1

Preface 3

Introduction. 5

1. My Family 7

2. Boyhood. 17

3. "The Shop". 31

4. The War In England 39

5. Normandy To The Baltic 73

6. East Africa 113

7. Shrivenham To Camberley 141

8. The War Office 159

9. Germany 173

10. Chatham. 187

11. Pakistan 197

12. Carnival Night In Nurpur 229

13. In Business In South Africa 233

14. The Birth Of A Church. 247

15. Rhodesia. 269

16. Army Chaplain 281

17. Builder And Church Planter 299

18. Broadcaster. 315

19. Church Planter And Author 319

20. Service In Scotland. 343

Appendix A: Mabws 347

Appendix B: List of Abbreviations 351

Author's Preface

This book is published by Ross House Books, an affiliated but separate ministry of the Chalcedon Foundation, at the insistence of the Chairman, the Rev Rousas Rushdoony. The author wishes to thank him for giving the testimony of a very ordinary Christian such wide publicity, and also to express his deepest thanks to God for the teaching he has received from this dear brother which has so profoundly deepened his understanding of the sovereignty and will of Almighty God.

He also wishes to thank Mrs Andrea Schwartz, most sincerely, for all the time and care she has taken in preparing the book for publication.

Kilmacolm
Dick Begbie
Renfrewshire, Scotland
April 2000

Preface

by Rousas John Rushdoony

The life of Rev. Lt Col R.J.G. Begbie, OBE, is an important chronicle of the twentieth century, a key era in history. At the beginning of the century, European civilization dominated the world. Manufacturing was primarily limited to Europe and North America, and much of the world was commanded by the colonial powers. Two world wars shattered the Eurocentric world. By the latter half of the century, the world's economic power had shifted from the Atlantic to the Pacific basin. Perhaps no other century has seen an equivalent shift of power.

The shift of power began with Europe's and America's de-Christianization. The West moved from a religious to a racial center. Darwinism had by 1900 become the real faith of the West, and, as few are now ready to admit, Darwin's theory was a racist one.

The ancient Begbie family saw this great shaking occur. From a thousand year estate, the family was reduced to a scattered base. The family holding, a mansion, a village, and thirty-six farms, was lost, partly through bad planning and partly due to socialist taxes on inheritance.

But with decline came also renewal. In Dick Begbie, we have a distinguished military officer, a successful businessman, and then a Christian pastor and church builder who founded new congregations in South Africa.

In crisis came renewal. The story of Dick Begbie is a case in point, a marvellous one. We see old Christendom's son as a leader in the Christian revival of the West. His personal history is an example of what the Holy Spirit has begun to do. The next generation will see much more.

3

In itself, this is a very good personal history. But it is also part of a greater story now in its infancy, the story of the renewal of the Western world. The pre-Darwinian West began the evangelization of the world, and that mission is now being continued by others. Old Christendom is indeed in process of collapse, but it is also taking steps to Christianize the whole world and to make a new Christendom.

This work is a fragment of that story.

Introduction

"Baak agin, Misterr Begbee," ordered Quartermaster Sergeant Instructor Gordon of the Gordon Highlanders, as for the sixth time, I tried to execute a head flip in the gymnasium of the Royal Military Academy, Woolwich. I was a tall youth, heavily built, and although I could climb the rope and do horse work, I was not, in my opinion, built for being upside down. I always swear I did more gymnastics than anyone else in my class. Nevertheless, even after this sixth attempt, I still landed with a thump on my behind instead of on my feet, and all QMSI Gordon could say was, "Gie yer tew furra furrad rrole, go baak t'yer place." Back again, Mr. Begbie, seems to have become one of the themes of my life.

Seventeen years later, in 1955, I had become by several years the youngest temporary lieutenant colonel in the Royal Engineers, possibly in the entire British Army, yet I took early retirement in 1958. My first job in civvy street was as a petrol attendant in a service station before rising to become an oil company operations manager. Then, for reasons which will appear in this narrative, I had to start again as a lowly systems analyst in a fertilizer company before becoming head of its systems division. Then it was back again to become a humble curate and eventually a rector in the Church of England in South Africa.

It has been a wonderfully interesting and varied life, much of it lived in a world which has disappeared. This is why many people have urged me to record it before the memories, too, have vanished away.

Chapter One

My Family

I come from what, I suppose, used to be called an upper middle class family.

The Begbies hail from what is, today, no more than a large farm about twelve miles from Haddington in East Lothian, Scotland. Our family records go back to James Begbie, who was born in 1584 and died in 1621. Our family never occupied the Farm Begbie because, in generation after generation, our branch of the family descended from the youngest of several sons. In consequence, our ancestors were tenant farmers who worked such farms as Westfield, Nether Bolton, Phantassie, Prestonkirk, and Houston in the county of Haddington. George Begbie, who was born in 1656 and died in 1698, was ordained an elder in Bolton Kirk in 1681. In 1684 he subscribed ten merks, present equivalent about sixty pounds, towards a new "mortcloth" for the parish. The mortcloth covered the body of the deceased and was used in funeral after funeral.

Although we do not have family records further back, the family must have farmed in the same locality much earlier, for the area was known as "Begbie Lands" as early as 1178, when the Countess Ada granted some of these lands to the nuns of the Cistercian Nunnery in Haddington. Interestingly enough, the name was originally spelt Baigbie, meaning "little bay." So presumably the lands must originally have reached the coast.

My great-great-grandfather, Peter Begbie, who was born in 1768 and died in 1815, emigrated south and became a merchant in the City of London. He was granted a coat of arms with the motto "In Deo Confidentia," meaning, "Having confidence in God." I have miniatures of him and his wife Frances, daughter of Arthur Jones of Reigate Priory in Surrey. There is a lock of her hair perfectly preserved in the back of her miniature.

His son, who was born in 1810, was the Rev. Francis Richard Begbie, fellow of Pembroke College, Cambridge, and vicar of Diseworth in Leicestershire. He married Elizabeth Jane, daughter of Admiral Henry Richard Glynn of Glynn House near Liskeard, Cornwall. Beautifully framed, small, coloured pictures of Admiral and Mrs. Glynn are in my younger brother's possession. Tragically, the Rev. Begbie and his wife and all their children, except my grandfather and his sister, died in the same twelve month period. Admiral and Mrs. Glynn brought up the survivors, and Glynn has remained a family name ever since.

My grandfather, Alfred Glynn Begbie, was born with an exceptional ability for mathematics, and this gift has continued in the family ever since. My grandfather was commissioned into the Royal Engineers and served in the period between the Indian Mutiny and the South African War, and so, he saw no active service. But he became a railway engineer in India, and, after retiring as a lieutenant colonel, he became general manager of Burma Railways at the time of its construction. One of the family albums contains photographs of the massive trestle bridges which must have been built under his direction. Subsequently, he became managing director of Burma Railways in London and settled in Blackheath. In his later years, he used to submit solutions to the acrostic puzzles in the London *Times* under the pseudonym "Harmless Lunatic." He won the prize so regularly that eventually the *Times* published a notice stating that no more prizes would be given to Harmless Lunatic.

Harold Begbie, who at the beginning of this century wrote a number of novels warning of the inroads the Church of Rome was making into the Church of England, was his first cousin. The Smirnoff Begbies, who all became prominent Evangelical clergymen in Australia, were descended from another first cousin.

My grandfather married Henrietta Edith, younger daughter of Colonel John Allen Lloyd Philipps of Mabws in Cardiganshire and Dale Castle in Pembrokeshire. The Lloyd and Philipps families have pedigrees which go back to the kings of both North and South Wales and, perhaps in legend only, to Hu the Mighty, or Hisichon, the first Briton to come to Britain!

The Mabws Estate originally consisted of sixteen mountain farms for grazing sheep and sixteen valley farms for mixed agriculture.

The family lived in Ystrad Teilo, the largest farm on the estate, until the big house was built in 1600 by Richard Lloyd. He built at a time when such houses were erected as much for defence as for comfort. So the masonry walls of Mabws were four feet thick and the roof was covered with enormous, thick slates. When the new wing was added, another four feet of wall was added as well, so that one went through a door into a cupboard eight feet deep and then through another door to get into the new wing. The new wing had its own staircase and consisted of servants' rooms upstairs and domestic offices downstairs. The house was built on a slope with the kitchens facing the lower side. This meant that one went upstairs to the hall, dining room, and drawing room, all of which faced north up the slope.

Colonel Lloyd Philipps married twice, the second time to a lady who was considered to be below his station, and by her he had a son. When he died, he broke the male entail and left the Mabws Estate to my grandmother, and he left Dale Castle, which had recently come into the family by inheritance from the Allens, to the son of his second marriage. Consequently, the Glynn Begbie arms are now crossed with the Lloyd Philipps arms bearing the ducally gorged black lion of Rodri Mawr, the last king of North Wales.

When my grandmother inherited, the mountain farms had been sold off to pay death duties. The family used to spend the summer at Mabws and the winter in Blackheath. Blackheath is in southeast London, just up the hill from Greenwich and adjacent to Woolwich. Relationships with the tenant farmers were extremely good, and my grandparents and my father after them took care to see that everyone living on the estate, which included all of Llanrystyd village except the Red Lion pub, were provided for. This included allowing tenants to live rent free whenever work could not be found for them since the work load varied with the seasons in an agricultural community.

Relations between the family and the tenants were so good that my parents' wedding became the occasion for general rejoicing in the village, and a floral triumphal arch was erected across the village street. A report in *The Welsh Gazette* of Tuesday April 18th 1912 reads, "The happy event was the occasion of much rejoicing at Llanrystyd on Wednesday. The village was prettily decorated with flags and bunting, and a general holiday was observed. The tenants of the estate were entertained at the Red Lion Hotel, and an enjoyable time was spent with Major J. Lloyd Hughes, Attlwyd, in the chair. Mr. Hughes-Davies, Ystrad Teilo, proposed the toast of the "Bride and bridegroom," and this was drunk with enthusiasm. The toast of the health of Colonel Begbie was likewise honoured. Congratulatory speeches were also delivered by Mr. J.W. Morgan, Post Office; Mrs. Harris, Mabws Hen; Miss Griffiths, Glanrafon; and Mr. John Jones, Gwynfa. Subsequently, all the school children and the poor people of the district were entertained to tea. The rejoicings were kept up until the shades of night had fallen, when a bonfire was ignited on the Foel.

"Mr. Glynn Begbie is the heir of the Mabws estate, and comes of one of the oldest Cardiganshire families. He is well-known and greatly esteemed at Llanrystyd, which place he frequently visits. His father, Colonel Begbie, is an expert engineer, having taken a prominent part in the construction of the Burma Railways in India (sic), of which he is now chairman. The mansion of Mabws is one of the truly old dwellings of Cardiganshire. It was erected in the year 1600 by Richard Lloyd, Esq., of Ystrad Teilo, where they had resided for centuries. The house, which is built of grey stone, stands high, overlooking park like grounds with surrounding woods of much beauty. The motto of the Mabws family is "Ar Dduw i gyd." (On God depends everything.)"

Because my father's elder brother, Alfred Richard Glynn, was killed in the last week of the South African War, my father inherited Mabws when my grandfather died in 1921. Unfortunately, the income of the estate was divided under my grandmother's will, and that, with substantial mortgages arising from successive death duties, made it impossible for my father to retain the Mabws Estate, which had been in the family for hundreds of years. It was sold in 1923, and as I have only the vaguest memories of it, I have included my eldest sister's memory of it as an appendix to this book.

My father, Ronald Philipps Glynn Begbie, was born in Simla, India, on 18th July 1885, and was educated at Stratheden House, Blackheath, and at Cheltenham College. Having passed through the Royal Military Academy, Woolwich, he was commissioned into the Royal Artillery in 1904. After serving in various heavy artillery batteries, he became an instructor at the Royal Military Academy from 1909 to 1913.

In April 1912 he married Helen Gladys, daughter of James Dolphin, who was a member of Lloyds, and Jane, whose maiden name was Ommaney.

As far as can be established, the Dolphin family, from which I am descended, originated with Dolgfinnr, a viking from Scandinavia. King William II, during his campaign to capture Carlisle, drove Dolfin, son of the Northumbrian Earl Gospatrick, from Cumbria in AD 1092. This Dolphin's son, born in AD 1107, had a son Gilbert who was the founder of the Neville family of Raby Castle, Northumberland. One of his sons, Meldred, became the owner of the Staindrop Estate in nearby Durham. My branch of the family moved from there to Shenston Moss in Staffordshire and subsequently to Eyford House, near Upper Slaughter in Gloucestershire. The family arms are "Az, three dolphins naiant fesseways in pale or" with crest "A swan's head and neck between two swan's wings proper." The motto is "In coelo quies," meaning "Peace in Heaven." My earliest identified Dolphin ancestor was John Dolphin of Shenston Moss, who married Sarah some years before AD 1659, when their first child was born. Descended from him was my great-grandfather, James Dolphin, born 6th January 1810, who in 1841 married Agnes, daughter of William Crawshay, the founder of the giant steel works at Merthyr Tydfil in Wales (subsequently bought out by Guest, Keen, and Nettlefold) and builder of Cyfartha Castle there and Caversham House across the Thames from Reading. My grandfather, his eldest son, also James Dolphin, was born on 29th September 1842, and married Jane, daughter of Edward Ommanney, in 1844.

The Ommaneys were a distinguished army family one of whom was Captain Sir Charles Ommaney, Royal Engineers, and one time colonial secretary. His portrait hangs in the Royal Engineers Headquarter Mess at Chatham.

The outbreak of the Great War found my parents in South Africa, where my father commanded the coastal artillery at Lion Battery, Cape Town. My parents had been allotted a quarter in Wynberg Military Base. They arrived just in time to take part in the annual tennis tournament. Despite the unaccustomed heat, in the final, my mother, much to her satisfaction, beat the wife of the RAMC colonel who unduly prided herself on her skill.

On the 4th August 1914, a German freighter was in Cape Town docks feverishly getting up steam. In the meantime my father had the phone off the hook through to the Castle and was waiting for the war telegram to arrive from Whitehall. Half Cape Town were out on the foreshore waiting to see my father blow the freighter out of the water. But the German got away in time, and "good luck to him," my father used to say. One of my father's 9.2 inch coastal guns from Lion Battery is now preserved in Fort Vineyard in Cape Town.

My father served in the Southwest Africa campaign under General Louis Botha and was awarded the DSO and was mentioned in despatches. The Germans had one or two light aeroplanes, but the British and South Africans had none. So there was great concern amongst the Gunners, who improvised two guns to serve as anti-aircraft guns. Unfortunately, they fell apart each time they fired and took twenty minutes to put together again. One day one of these gun teams was out exercising in the desert outside Swakopmund when it came across a German cavalry patrol. The gun, called "Tinnie Lizzie," was hastily unlimbered, and a shell was fired in the general direction of the Germans, who, not knowing that there would be some delay before they could be fired on again, beat a hasty retreat. "Tinnie Lizzie" is now also in Fort Vineyard.

My father then returned to Cape Town to raise the 125th (South African) Siege Battery which he took to France and commanded through the battles on the Somme at Beaumont Hamel, during the German retreat in 1917, at Arras and Hill 70, and in Belgium. For these services he was awarded the MC, was again mentioned in despatches, and was decorated personally by King Albert of the Belgians with the Croix de Guerre with palms and made a chevalier of the Ordre de Couronne.

After the war, he was adjutant of the Artillery College of Science, Woolwich, and took early retirement in 1923 for family reasons. Throughout his life, he was immensely keen on all forms of outdoor sports, particularly rugby football, playing for Villagers in Cape Town, Blackheath, the Barbarians, Plymouth Albion, Old Cheltonians, Kent, and the Army.

From 1925 to 1932 he was honorary secretary of Blackheath and built it up into the side it was in its heyday, when it frequently provided the backbone of England's team. He was also the Kent representative on the Rugby Football Union, which meant we always got the best seats at the Internationals at Twickenham.

In 1932 we moved to Cheltenham. There my father became president of the Cheltenham Rugger Club and built the side up to eminence in club rugby. He also became a life member of the Cheltenham College council and a very active member of its executive committee.

Known affectionately as "Ronnie," he was admired and loved by a large circle in the rugby world, in the Gunners, amongst Cheltonians, and by the Woolwich cadets, so many of whom became the generals of the Second World War.

He was a man of the highest honour and integrity who by his kindness, humility, charm of manner, humour, and friendly interest, gave warmth to all with whom he came in contact. Despite his widespread interests he put his family first and was the most wonderful father to us all.

We could not have wished for a more loving and devoted mother either. In many ways she had never moved into the twentieth century, for her standards remained impeccably Victorian. If a naval captain runs a "tight" ship, my mother certainly ran a "tight" house. Everything had to be spotless, tiled passages scrubbed weekly, and the masses of brass and silver kept perfectly polished. The servants were kept up to the mark, and if any of them were away, my mother would get down on her hands and knees to do the work, and would require her daughters to do the same. Yet with all this, she was full of fun and joined in all our games. Once when we were playing "clumps" in the dark, she hid on the top of the dining room table, on which glasses were set for drinks at the other end. But the chinkling of the glasses set off by her barely restrained giggles gave her position away.

She was a notable hostess, particularly at the three-table bridge parties which she gave. The table suppers provided at these were lavish, and my mother never minded that my brother and I raided the food after the party had gone back to bridge in the drawing room.

She was a very good tennis player and bridge player and was tireless in teaching us how to play. When we were ill, or hurt in some minor accident, her warm-hearted sympathy soon made us forget our troubles.

It could possibly be said that the love and security which our parents gave us so cocooned us against the world outside that my brother and I were ill-prepared for its harshness when eventually we left the nest.

The mottoes which my father gave me have never left me and have stood me in good stead throughout my life. They are:

> Manners maketh man.
> Remember your station in life.
> Whatsoever thy hand findeth to do,
> do it with thy might.
> Be to their virtues ever kind
> and to their faults a little blind.

My eldest sister, Helen Joan Glynn, was born on 10th January 1913, my brother, Denys Lloyd Glynn, on 14th November 1921, my middle sister, Lorna Mary Glynn, on 7th June 1926, and my youngest sister, Sheila Rosemary Glynn, on 29th March 1931. Despite the age range, we were an exceedingly happy family. My parents joined in all the games, so we were never short of a four for tennis, or for bridge in the evenings once we were old enough to play.

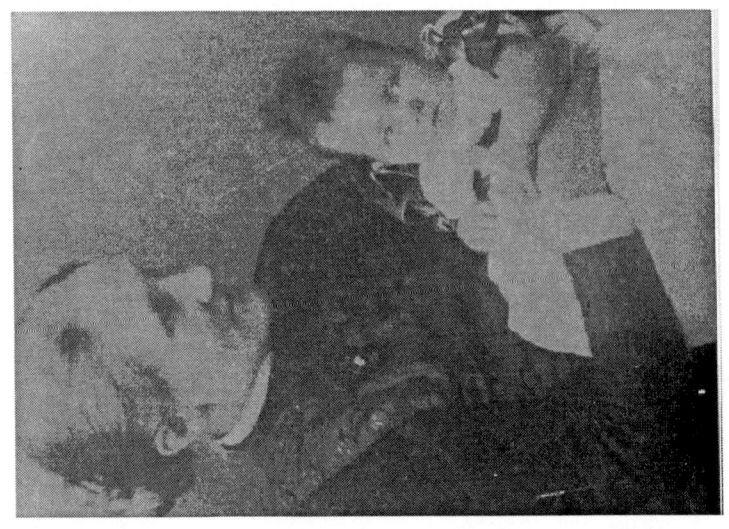

My grandmother, nee Henrietta Edith Lloyd Philipps,
with my father in 1885.

My grandfather,
Lt Col Alfred Glynn Begbie, RE (Retd).

My mother,
nee Helen Gladys Dolphin, in 1935.

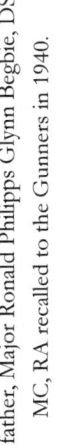

My father, Major Ronald Philipps Glynn Begbie, DSO,
MC, RA recalled to the Gunners in 1940.

Chapter Two

Boyhood

I was born on 2nd February 1920 at 40 Shooters Hill Road, Blackheath, London, and, despite the Second World War blitz, the house still stands today. I can only guess at what my mother endured, as I've been told that I weighed eleven and three-quarters pounds at birth. This latest addition to humanity, possibly out of complacency, but more likely because of prodigious obesity, did not condescend to open his eyes upon the world for three weeks, despite all the back slapping of his nurse, and of his seven year old sister, Joan, who had been waiting with some impatience for the arrival of a playmate.

When Grandfather Begbie became terminally ill, we moved into his house, 22 Kidbrooke Grove, so that my mother could look after him. He died shortly before my brother was born in November 1921.

My brother was born a sickly baby, and just when his life hung in the balance, my father received orders to proceed to India. He attempted to find a substitute, as was common practice in those days, but at the last moment his arrangement fell through and he had to send in his papers. So he retired in 1923 at the age of thirty-eight.

I can never remember my father ever expressing any bitterness, or even mentioning, his premature retirement from the army even though he would have gone far in it. Yet judging from his keenness to see me and my brother follow in his footsteps into the army, it must have been a bitter blow. As far back as I can remember, every birthday and every Christmas we were given soldiers, forts, and guns to play with, until we had a thousand soldiers between us. My brother had mostly Household Cavalry and Foot Guards, while I had Scots Greys, Dragoon Guards, Hussars, Lancers, Royal Scots, Argyll and Sutherland Highlanders, Norfolks, and Devons. We both had some Horse Artillery, but my brother had some Sappers and a pontoon bridge as well. I never thought my Sudan Camel Corps made up for the latter.

Sometimes we had highly organized set-piece battles in which we lined up an equal number, probably about 450, of soldiers along either side of the room. They were spaced so that when one fell, it would not knock another down. This usually meant about six ranks with the cavalry in the rear rank. Behind these ranks we left sufficient space for those playing to sit and fire marbles from mortars at the opposing army. My father and brother were usually on one side and a sister and I on the other. The winners were the first to knock the whole opposing army down, and they were lucky if they had more than two survivors left on their own side.

We also had Hornby trains and farms, and as we got older these were made to play their part in our wars. We became familiar with the problems of supplying and moving armies at an early age.

All this was fine until my middle sister, Lorna, reached an age at which she wanted to join in our games. Then there was trouble, only solved when we persuaded her to become the medical service for both armies. However, we still had occasional trouble when she became too greedy for casualties, and we were left with too few soldiers to play with. But this problem didn't arise until after we had moved to Cheltenham.

22 Kidbrooke Road was the family home for twelve years. It had three floors and a basement. As a little boy, I always found the basement dark and frightening, and the Irish cook quite terrifying. Down there, was a large, coal burning kitchen range with an oven on either side and hot plates right across the top of the fire and ovens. There was another large room with a baking oven in the corner which was never used. There was a dark larder with slab shelves, there being no such things as refrigerators in those days. Then there was a pantry and store room which my mother visited each morning to put out the food which was to be used that day. Underneath the stairs which led to the basement was the coal cellar, another mysterious place for a small boy.

One went up steps which were always kept white to the porch and front door. The rooms on the ground floor had very high ceilings and tall, drafty windows to match. The drawing room, which had a bay window looking out onto the road, was only used on Sundays and when there were parties. On Sunday evenings, we used to sing round the grand piano which my mother played. My father's favorite song was "Poor old Joe," and Joan used to sing "Coming down the Old Kent Road" in her idea of a cockney accent and in a very raucous voice.

The dining room had three tall windows looking out onto the garden at the back. The furniture consisted of huge mahogany pieces, and the dining table had three leaves so that fourteen people could sit round it with ease. The study, which looked out onto the road, was used most often. In it my father had a large, knee-hole desk with a black, leather covered top. The knee hole made an excellent room when we children played houses; we made further rooms and passages by draping rugs over and between the easy chairs. I can remember the first telephone arriving. It was one of those upright ones with the receiver hanging on the side.

Between the ground floor and the first floor, there was a landing off which led only the bathroom and lavatory. I can even remember my brother and I skidding round the bathroom floor on our potties instead of doing what we were supposed to do. He can't have been more than about two, but of course we were all "potty trained" before we were one year old in those days. I can also remember having "squeeze up baths" which ended up with my brother and I riding astride on Joan's back in the bath.

On the first floor were my parent's bedroom and dressing room, Joan's bedroom, the bedroom which Denys and I shared, and a spare bedroom. At the top of the house was our nursery and four bedrooms for the household staff. These consisted of, besides the Irish cook, a parlour maid, a house maid, and our nurse.

Down a couple of steps from the hall, there was a lobby were the dog slept and an enormous roll top desk in which my father kept his tools, nuts and bolts, etc. I think it was always in a bit of a muddle. On the same floor there was a conservatory over the garage, in which my father had hundreds of geranium cuttings of every conceivable colour ready to be planted out in the spring each year. My brother still has the descendants of some of these in his garden in Sussex.

Steps from there led down to a yard in which there was a very make-shift sort of shed in which were kept the garden tools, Joan's guinea pigs, and, when we were old enough to have them, our bicycles. There was a door from the yard into the garage which was under the conservatory. My father had a Vulcan tourer car which could seat six with ease. The windshield was divided horizontally in half, and the top half could be swung up for extra ventilation, the draft not being excessive because the absolute maximum speed was 45 mph. There was another screen which could be swung up on the back of the front seat to give protection for those in the back. When it rained, a canvas hood could be swung up from behind the back seat. The sides were closed with celluloid screens which were almost opaque. There were two spare wheels, one was on the back and the other on the running board beside the driver. For some reason the hand brake was out there as well. The hooter was operated by squeezing a rubber bulb. Mounted on the steering column were an advance and retard lever and a lever which controlled the mixture. There was also a brake on the prop-shaft, which occasionally used to catch fire. It was my job to slither under the car and blow the fire out. In the late twenties the Vulcan was replaced by a blue Hudson Essex. It was a saloon car, which was considered very modern for those days, though it didn't look much different from a Model T Ford.

From the yard, there was a gate through to the back garden which was largely taken up with a grass tennis court. There was a gravel path on the right side which led to a lilac tree in the corner at the end. To the left of that, there was a sandpit for us to play in. Then there was a little space where Joan, Denys, and I each had a garden about a yard square in which we mostly grew Virginia stock and Marigolds. Beyond that was the chicken run which always looked very ramshackle. My father's chickens frequently suffered from scaly foot and feather eating. But they kept us supplied with eggs, which were preserved in water glass in the basement. We gave all the chickens names, and when a couple were consigned to the pot we used to discuss whether it was Jenny or Jemima we were eating. We were quite callous in this respect.When I was five, I went to Shirley House Kindergarten School, which was opposite "The Sun in the Sands" public house in Shooters Hill Road. I remember being disappointed that I was never given anything more interesting to play in the band than the triangle. In those days the parents gave the prizes for the school sports. When I was six, my parents gave a clockwork tram which stopped automatically, then a bell rang, the doors opened, then shut, and the tram started automatically again. I was determined to win this, but I didn't know for which race it was the prize. So I won five prizes that day, including the tram. I have never won a race since.

I suppose it was a little over a mile walk to school, and my cousin Dorothy Christopherson, who was a few years older than me, used to see me safely there and back. This could be quite perilous when there was a fog. In those days winter fogs were a horrid pea green colour, and the soot from them got up your nose, making your nostrils filthy. Sometimes you could not see a yard in front of your face, and crossing a road in those circumstances, when in the fog you could not locate an oncoming vehicle from its noise, was quite hazardous.

Of course the traffic then, although not so heavy as now, was a great deal more messy. I can remember steam driven lorries and the glow of their fire boxes between their front wheels, and steam road rollers, and buses still running on solid tires.

After Mabws was sold, my parents would rent a house by the sea each year, usually at Sidmouth in Devon, for a six weeks holiday by the sea. The whole household went, including the staff, so there was a car party and a train party. One year, coming back and approaching Sparkford, the Vulcan ran a big end. So the car party had to leave the car at a garage for repair and continue the journey by train. After a while the Irish cook began to show acute signs of distress. It turned out that, in order to accommodate all her luggage, she was wearing no less than seven dresses, which was alright in an open tourer but not in a stuffy train! I wonder if she had been reading about the seven veils!

Our doctor used to come in a horse drawn coach and wearing a morning coat and grey silk top hat. He was rather corpulent and carried about him an aroma of alcohol. His cure for whooping cough, which my brother and I contracted together, was to put us both to bed in our parent's double bed with chopped garlic in our socks. The stench was awful, but we survived.

Denys and I always shared a room. He was troubled with eczema on his hands and with asthma. My poor brother had to have his hands bandaged and tied to his bed so that he would not scratch at night. Whenever he had an attack, I used to hear him wheezing and struggling for breath as he tried to get to sleep. I always think that the way he has suffered and endured has made him incredibly brave. The eczema eventually disappeared, but the asthma has never left him.

Joan used to delight in getting Denys and me to act with her in a play. For this purpose, she would put up curtains across the end of the dining room to form a stage, and then, after several rehearsals, my parents and some of the household staff would be invited to watch. We did "The Ghost Train" once, but when we did "The Monkey's Paw" I was so terrified by our own acting that I ran off the stage and found comfort in my mother's lap!

We used to have twenty or more children to our Christmas and birthday parties, when we would dance "Sir Roger de Coverley," play "Oranges and Lemons say the bells of St. Clement's," "Blind Man's Buff," and many other childish games. At tea-time there would be a paper hat at each place setting and crackers to be pulled afterwards. There were nice, thin sandwiches, lots of iced biscuits, cakes, jellies, and, of course, a super home-made cake with almond icing and candles to blow out. The party would always finish with the distribution of balloons all round and a gift for everyone.

When I was eight I went to Cherry Orchard Preparatory School, which must have been two or three miles away in Charlton, and I used to go on my bike. My uncle Colin, Mr. C.J.T. Robertson, OBE, was the headmaster, and he was especially strict with me, I think, in case he could be accused of favouring his nephew. I was caught cheating once, which didn't help, and was dealt with most severely.

I was never much good at team games, and I found cricket very boring. It was relieved sometimes by the slow, majestic flight of the Graf Zeppelin or the R100 making their ponderous way across the sky. They really looked magnificent with their silver envelopes glistening in the sun against

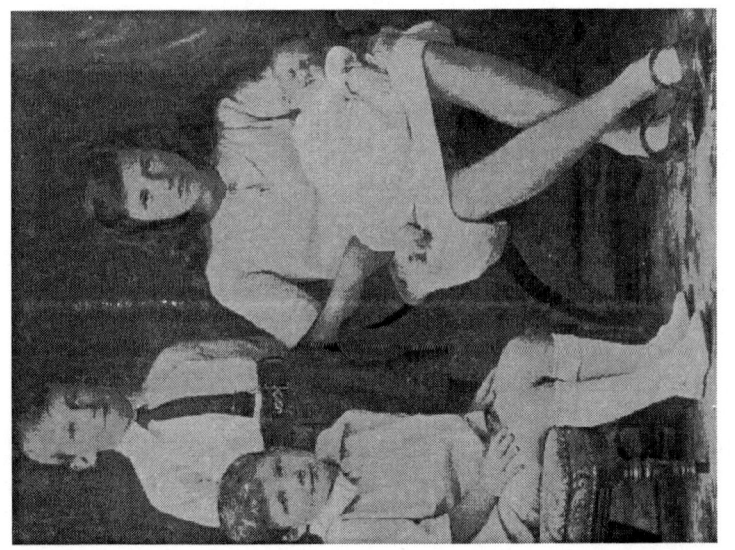

Joan aged 13, myself aged 6, Denys aged 4, and Lorna a few weeks old.

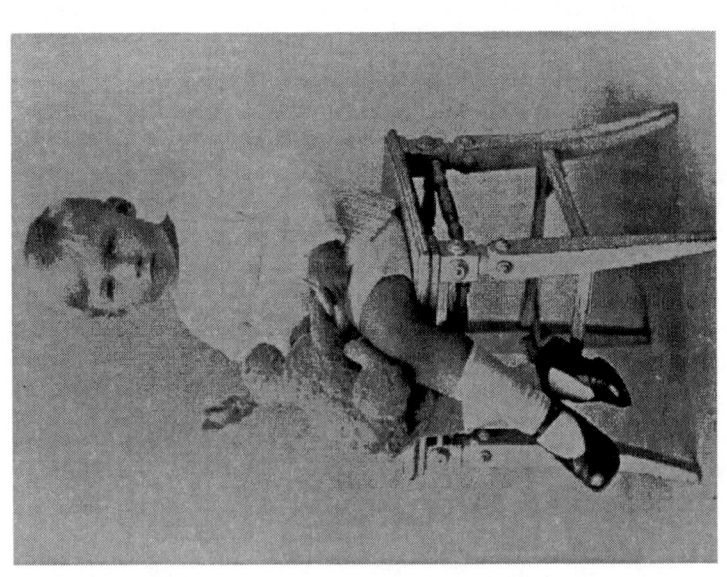

Myself aged two and a half in 1922.

the blue sky. The passengers must have had a wonderful view as they cruised along only a few thousand feet up.

In the summer term, 1929, a Dutch boy at the school died while being operated on for appendicitis. Soon after, I went into the Blackheath Cottage Hospital for the same operation. I remember my brother coming to visit with my mother. He blurted out that prayers were said for me during school prayers that morning. He was instantly hushed by mother in case I should be alarmed that matters were so serious that I had to be prayed for! The offending appendix was rather inefficiently removed, with the result that I'm left to this day with an enormous scar.

We always went to church on Sundays as a family. Everybody did, and the church used to be full. All the pews on both sides of the central aisle were rented, and there was a socket for a visiting card to show whose pew it was. The servants and work people sat in the pews in the side aisles, where they could hardly see what was going on because of the thickness of the pillars. I can remember my father lifting me up onto the pew when the hymns and psalms were sung so that I could see what was going on. I don't remember much about the services, but I do remember always being impressed by the shiny heads of the bald men and wondering whether they used floor polish on them! Sunday School was at three o'clock in the afternoon, but we were not expected to go regularly as Sunday school was for those poor children whose parents were so bad that they never went to church. But we did go about once a month to cheer up those poor children with the naughty parents.

For the summer holiday in 1929, my parents rented a house for six weeks on the sea front at Dale facing Milford Haven. My father's cousin, Lt Col Rodri Lloyd Philipps, owned Dale Castle, Dale peninsula, and the village of Dale itself. The whole estate was dreadfully run down. The castle leaked, and green mildew ran down the stone walls of the drawing room, where my brother and I played Hornby trains with our cousin John. The village cottages were badly in need of repair, there was no water-borne sewage, and the village women threw the contents of their slop buckets over the sea wall while shouting the Welsh equivalent of "Regardez la, sauve qui peut!"

The organ in the village church was pumped by hand by means of a large, wooden lever which projected from one side of it. The operator was the "village idiot," who faced the congregation with a wide grin on his face and operated the handle by bending his knees and straightening them for each stroke. His mother played the organ and led the choir with a loud, screechy voice. A cousin, Colonel George Rind, read the first lesson from Daniel 3. After he read "the sound of the cornet, flute, harp, sackbut, psaltery, dulcimer, and all kinds of musick" twice, he got fed up and substituted "the band as before" in such an aggressive tone of voice that the minister and congregation submitted, as no doubt his soldiers had always done before.

By and by the organist, who was the "idiot's" mother, had a fit, which apparently happened quite often as a mattress was provided by the organ stool for her to fall on. The "idiot" froze in mid-stroke in a squatting position, the organ stopped, and the choir stopped singing. Obviously following a routine which had become well established, a warden left his place and applied smelling salts to the unfortunate woman. She soon revived and returned to her stool, the "idiot" with an even more inane grin than before resumed his pumping, the organ started, the screechy voice resumed, and the choir began to sing again. Meanwhile, the congregation had remained quite unperturbed throughout. It was really all too much for a nine year old boy, and my brother and I giggled uncontrollably.

Worse was to come when the minister got into the pulpit. He had a permanent drip on the end of his nose but had an aversion to wiping or blowing his nose in the pulpit. He used to screw his handkerchief up into a ball and became remarkably adept at throwing the ball from one hand to the other so that it just brushed his nose in passage. Each point of his sermon was punctuated by this trick. It was altogether too much for me despite my father's threatening scowls.

But we had a super holiday visiting the lovely beaches in the area. One afternoon we children, coming back on the top of a hay wain, stopped in order to attend to nature. My cousin Sheila squatted, of course, while my brother and I stood to relieve ourselves. She, being interested in our performance, lifted her skirt and said, "Look I've got something different than you." This was the first I knew that there was something different about girls other than long hair and dresses. Our parents never did tell us about sex until one day, not long before I went to the Shop, my father said he supposed I knew about girls. At the age of eighteen, I was too embarrassed to say that I didn't know a thing.

When I was eleven, I had a painfully swollen knee and was put to bed with hot lamps over my knee three times a day. I think it all began from a scratch which turned septic. I was not long recovered from that when I became terribly ill. I had the most terrific nose bleeds which simply would not stop, very bad ear aches and head aches, and a high fever. Our family doctor apparently gave up on me, and I was dying. In desperation, my father contacted Bill Tucker, a London doctor who was playing for Blackheath. An ambulance came to collect me, and my sister always says I had begun to turn green when I left! We raced up through London, and I felt awfully important with all the traffic stopping to let us pass. Immediately on arrival at St. George's Hospital, I was rushed into the operating theatre, where both my eardrums were pierced to let the poison out. Apparently I had septicemia in the head, although I knew little about it at the time. I was in a coma for the first few days, and when I was

Myself aged 17, Denys 15, and our dog Bruce.

Myself aged 10.

conscious the pain was so intense that I imagined the bed had collapsed and all the broken iron was sticking into me.

I was in hospital for three weeks and had lost so much blood that I was fed on raw liver (ugh!), there being no such thing as blood transfusion in those days. I remember the nurses being quite amazed that I was strong enough to walk when eventually I got out of bed. I regained my strength quickly during our six week holiday down at Sidmouth that year.

I always hated coming back to Blackheath. The heath always looked so bleak and bare with the grass scorched brown by the autumn sun.

In November that same year, 1931, both my mother's parents died within a fortnight of one another, and my parents decided to move to Cheltenham. There my brother and I could go to the Junior School and then on to Cheltenham College as day boys, while my two younger sisters could go to the Ladies College as day girls.

My father bought an absolutely marvellous family house called Murvagh across the road from the college and alongside one of the playing fields. The house had two staircases, a number of interconnecting rooms both upstairs and downstairs, and was ideal for "Murder" and other games in the dark. The house also included rooms for a nurse, cook, parlour maid, and house maid, a menage symbolic of an age now long past.

The nurse and house maid used to join in the games in the dark. When I was about fifteen, I remember the house maid making "a pass" at me in the box room in the dark, but, being still more or less sexually unaware, I had no idea what she was after. In attempting to fondle her breast I pricked my finger on the pin which held up her apron and that ended the incident.

At about this time I started to develop back trouble and stopped growing. The family doctor put me to bed and that made it worse. So my father took me to a chiropractor in Brighton. His name was Dr. Drewitt, and he also owned the Brighton Greyhound Racing Stadium. The first thing he found was that my head "wasn't on the right way." So he lifted me up by my head, there was a crack, and he plonked me down again. From then on I could turn my head properly, which I had never been able to do before.

But he said my back ache was due to adhesions joining my vertebrae together. He used to break these down with a series of twists and cracks which were quite painful. This treatment gave me relief, but the treatment had to be repeated every three months or so.

The result was that from the age of fifteen to eighteen I was unable to play rugger, which, I think, was a big disappointment to my father. But I could row in the summer with the College Boat Club on the River Severn just downstream from Tewkesbury, to which we used to go over in four busses three afternoons a week. Being so small, I used to row bow and

Murvagh, Cheltenham--our family home 1932-1947.

Top: The drawing room.

Bottom: The south elevation with the tennis court in the foreground.

thoroughly enjoyed it, especially the bumping races at the end of the summer term.

In the winter, being unable to play rugger or hockey, I joined the College Debating Society and, with the house prefect, won the inter-house debating competition. In due course I became secretary of the society, and when we were playing rugger against other colleges, we used to take on the opposing school in a debate. I remember winning against Rugby School and Clifton College.

When I was fifteen, I remember my father and house master (Mr. S.H. Stevens) discussing whether I should be confirmed. As I was in my matric year, it was decided to postpone that event to the following year.

When that year came, the college chaplain, the Rev. Mr. Kemmis, had a group of us boys together for confirmation class. He was, as I now know, an Anglo-Catholic and quite monk-like. All I can remember of these classes was a white model of a cross with some steps leading up to it. He used this as an illustration to say that the Christian life was like climbing steps to get nearer to the cross. He was, as I now know, teaching us the heretical doctrine of salvation by works. I don't remember the Gospel ever being mentioned in College chapel. Certainly there was no attempt to discover whether or not I had been converted, nor was there any intimation that the idea of confirmation was for me to confirm my faith, whatever it might be, before the bishop and congregation.

I was left in such ignorance that I imagined that, in some remarkable way, when the Bishop of Gloucester (Dr. A.C. Headlam) placed his hand on my head, I would get up a better chap. When no such thing happened and I sensed no improvement by attending "Pie," as early communion was called, I became quite disillusioned and began to think the church was a sham.

I remember that soon after Joan was married to Dick Stead, Lord Lee of Fareham and Lady Lee came to lunch. Other guests were the headmaster, Mr. R.V.H. Roseveare, and his wife. Lord Lee, who had given Chequers to the nation for the prime minister's use, was the President of the College Council.

The conversation at lunch included a discussion over which retired colonels in Cheltenham were hen-pecked by their wives. Suddenly, Sheila, my youngest sister who was then only four years old and who evidently had been following the conversation with the closest interest, piped up and asked, in all innocence, whether any of the wives were ever cock-pecked! Looking across the table, I could see Dick Stead only restraining himself with difficulty, which caused me to guffaw, and then followed laughter from Dick and the rest of us children. My poor mother could hardly change the subject of conversation quickly enough.

I passed matric when I was fifteen and then sat for three years in the sixth form, during which time the Head of the Military and Engineering Side, Mr. P. Fletcher, known as Percy or "the pink flea" because of his initials and the colour of his hair and face, took several of us through the Cambridge Tripos Maths syllabus. Partly because I was unfit, I had ideas of becoming an aeronautical engineer, which might have been quite rewarding, but my father was adamant. "Do you think I've spent all this money on your education for you to become a box wallah? There are perfectly good engineers in the army, so into the army you'll go." And into the army I went.

Fortunately, six months before my eighteenth birthday, my parents took me to a specialist in Harley Street, a Mr. Montgomery Anderson, who discovered what was causing my back trouble and lack of growth. He put me on a six months course of injections and various pills. I began to shoot up like a beanstalk, and my back was cured just in time to pass the army medical exam.

The army entrance examination was run by the Civil Service Commissioners and was taken at the age of eighteen and a half. The top eighty would pass into the Royal Military Academy, Woolwich, "the Shop," and the next 200 or so would go to the Royal Military College, Sandhurst. The remainder could have another shot six months later if they felt so inclined. To get into the top eighty, one's standard had to be at least the equivalent of the Higher School Certificate. After passing the examination, one had to pass the medical, and an interview.

The interview took place in the head office of the Civil Service Commissioners in Burlington House, Piccadilly. We all gathered in the hall there in July 1938. Before getting there, we had all swotted up on current affairs, such as recent test match and international rugger results, the Spanish Civil War, the Japanese invasion of China, etc. Anxiously, we would ask the next one out what he had been asked and then feverishly consult our notes. The next man before me, Ian McNaughton, had been asked about the war in Spain. Desperately, I tried to remember the horribly long names of the rivers and mountains in Spain.

My turn came. I entered the door at the end of a long room which was thickly carpeted and darkly curtained. At the far end, facing me across an enormous table, sat four stern and menacing looking gentlemen. We knew they were a general, an air marshal, an admiral, and the head of the Civil Service Commissioners, but not which was which. "Don't stand there, boy, come over here and sit down." I did so. "Let's see now, Begbie, isn't it?" "Yes, Sir." "Any relation of Ronnie Begbie, by any chance?" "Yes, Sir, he is my father."

Then they began talking amongst themselves. "You remember Ronnie, don't you?" At least two of them, it appeared, had been taught by my father when he was an instructor at the Shop from 1910 to 1913, one of them had played rugger with him, and so they went on with their remembrances of him. Eventually I was asked, "By the way, how is your father now?" "He is fine, Sir, and is now living in Cheltenham." "Glad to hear it. That will be all. You can send the next fellow in." So I passed the oral examination purely on my father's reputation.

I passed into the Shop fifteenth in the order of merit which was a lot better than anyone expected, and it gave me confidence for what lay ahead.

My father drove me up from Sidmouth in August 1938 and delivered me to he Shop. We shook hands when he left me, and I always remember how work hardened his hand was. It was also the first of the few times I ever shook hands with my father, and I remember the pride in his eyes at my initiation into the career he had wanted for himself and which he had chosen for me.

I had been a prefect at college for my last year and a staff sergeant in the OTC. As such, I was a member of the colour party on ceremonial parade. The OTC had a King's colour and a regimental colour carried by two under officers, and I marched between them with a cork on the top of my bayonet so that it did not damage the colours. Now I was to become "a snooker," the term used to describe a cadet in his first term at the Shop. So it was indeed a case of "Baak agin, Mister Begbee."

Chapter Three

"The Shop"

On arrival at "The Shop" we became Gentlemen Cadets. The difference between GCs and all who have become Officer Cadets since the beginning of World War II, is that our parents contributed towards the cost of our education and paid for all our equipment and uniform. The latter must have been very expensive as all our uniform and even our boots were made to measure. Fifty years later my parade boots are still in excellent condition.

I was accommodated in K House, known as K-ouse, which was next to the staff house, known as "Stuffouse," facing the west end of the enormous parade ground. I found myself sharing a front room with David Benson, who was destined to become a Gunner. We got on well together, and we both played rugger for the Shop 2nd XV.

Strict discipline began that first night. We all stood to outside our rooms, standing rigidly at attention in our civilian suits. David and I faced Carr and Brennan across the passage, both of whom were also to become Gunners. Our house cadet corporal was Tony Babbington, another future Gunner in his third and final term of six months duration. There were altogether sixteen snookers in K-ouse.

We were told that we were in 4 Company, that our under officer was Stephen Crookenden, and that our Company Sergeant Major was RSM Langdale of the Warwickshire Regiment. We were told that we would have three weeks grace before being punished with extra drills, called "hoxters," for offences. In the morning we would be issued with white canvas jackets and trousers, and service caps, which we would wear till our uniforms arrived. We would always march whether on or off duty. We would not lounge, about but would stand easy when not otherwise engaged. We were to salute officers no matter how far away they might be. We would parade at 7am each morning for inspection before being marched to chapel and then breakfast.

After we had got our uniforms and after the three weeks grace were over, a typical daily programme would take this form:

7.00 — 7.15	Parade under the house corporal and march to chapel
7.20 — 7.35	Morning Service
7.40	Breakfast
8.30 — 9.15	Classroom lecture
9.30 — 10.15	Gymnasium
10.30 — 12.30	Horsemanship
13.00	Lunch parade
13.15	Lunch
14.00 — 16.30	Recreational training
17.00 — 19.00	Classroom lectures
19.30	Dinner
20.30 — 22.00	Cleaning kit as snookers, thereafter written work of some sort
22.00	Parade outside our rooms
22.30	Lights out

We were told that after three weeks at the Shop, we would all have to take part in the Snooker boxing competition whether we had ever boxed before or not. So in those first weeks we spent the recreational periods in the afternoons practicing boxing. I was by no means a natural boxer. But we knew beforehand that the object of the competition was to see what we were made of.

As it happened, I was drawn to box against A.G.I. Wells, who had boxed for Imperial Service College for the last three years and had been captain of boxing for his last year there. I reckoned that there was little chance that I would be able to prevent him hitting me, so the best thing to do would be to go all out to hit him. Wells became a Gunner and survived the war.

The evening arrived, and the commandant, Major General Phillip Neame, VC, who was an Old Cheltonian, and all the instructors, were there in mess kit, which was the first time I had seen it, and the two terms senior to us were in blue patrols, the customary wear for cadets in the evenings.

A number of bouts took place before mine. One or two chaps put up a bad show, particularly an Egyptian cadet who I don't think really understood what was going on. My turn came, and I could not for the life of me land a blow on Wells; he was so quick. In the meantime he rained blows on me more or less without interruption. But I must have a thick scull, for he could not knock me down. Eventually the fight was stopped in the first round to quite prolonged applause "for a gallant loser!" I tottered off to my corner in a daze, with a broken tooth and a prolific nose bleed. But I was quite happy in that I had evidently passed the test.

We very soon learned that the standard of drill which was expected was far superior to anything we had attained to in the OTC at college. We learned what it was to stand dead still without even moving our eyes, and how to keep our arms straight by bending our wrists back and with our thumbs to the front. I enjoyed drill and the team spirit it engendered in a squad who were all determined to do their best.

The classroom work was interesting and not too difficult. It included maths, all of which I had already done at Cheltenham, the chemistry of explosives, elementary survey, engineer drawing, military history, organization and tactics at battalion level, military law and King's Regulations, and double entry accounting and preparation of balance sheets.

There were several civilian instructors, of whom the senior was Mr. Roberts who taught maths. He not only remembered my father as an instructor in 1910-12, but also had taught him when he was a GC in 1902-4! At our first session with Roberts, he wanted to know what we all wanted to be. When I said, "Sapper," he said, "But your father was a Gunner." "Yes," I said, "but my grandfather was a Sapper." This amused the class because one seldom got the better of Roberts.

The military instructors were headed by two lieutenant colonels. One was Williams, a Gunner, who was relatively innocuous and taught us military history so well that I became a keen student of it for the rest of my service.

The other was Lt Col Caldwell, a Sapper, who was so ferocious that he was known as "Hindy," short for Hindenburg, because rumor had it that his strict discipline had almost caused a mutiny at Chatham where he was adjutant during the First World War. But he was a first rate teacher of tactics particularly.

We had to move quickly and smartly between periods. The worst one was between gym and riding. After doing a good deal more gymnastics than anyone else, as I have related in the introduction, we were dismissed as a rule at 10.15am. But if Sergeant Major Instructor Hartigan was in a bad mood, he would dismiss us at 10.17. We then had to rush down to the change room beneath the gym and there take off our gym shoes, put on our black walking shoes, tie a scarf round our necks so that there were no wrinkles in front, put on our blazers, and our pill-box hats at precisely the right angle, and then run like mad for the bike shed some 150 yards away. There, eighty cadets would all be trying to get their bikes out at the same moment. We would then ride as fast as possible to our house 400 yards away and rush up the stairs and strip off. We would then have to fold our gym clothes and put them away tidily in the cupboard. Then on went under pants and vest, shirt, tie with no flukes under the knot in front, tie pin under the tie and through the collar both sides without pricking your thumb, breeches with all those horrid little buttons to do up round the calf, braces, boots, lace them up, leather leggings with a lace to zig-zag between hooks all the way up, cap, and gloves with two buttons to do up on each. Then we'd run down stairs, mount our bicycles, and pedal like mad to get on parade 200 yards away at 10.30am. One morning Stanley Peploe got a hoxter because he'd pricked his thumb and got some blood on his collar.

We then rode on our bikes to the riding school which was in the Artillery Barracks about a mile away. After parking our bikes, we'd get the command, "Ride, fall in on your horses." These were lined up down the centre of the school. I could always recognize a horse from one day to the next, but some couldn't. So I got a wonderful, great chestnut mare, called Mufti, who was really an arm-chair ride and knew all the words of command. "Ride, trot," and she'd trot, "Ride, canter," and she'd canter, and so on, and all I had to do was sit comfortably on her.

One unfortunate cadet in our ride by the name of Rusher was quite incapable of recognizing a horse, and he'd always be left with a ferocious beast called, appropriately, "Vesuvius." We were never allowed to use our irons to mount. Instead, we were taught to vault up and swing our right leg over the horse's haunches. Poor Rusher used to get stuck halfway up as his arms were not strong enough for him to straighten them in order to get his leg over the horse's haunches. At this stage Vesuvius used to nibble the seat of Rusher's britches. The riding instructor, Sergeant Major Rorke, would rage at him, and between fear of Rorke and fear of the horse, Rusher would make a despairing attempt, only to over-balance and fall off the other side. Eventually he clocked up a phenomenal total of some sixty hoxters and had to leave the academy. Rumor had it that he finished up a clergyman.

My friend Stanley Peploe was a hopeless horseman and took some dreadful tumbles, including one when he was dragged along the length of the riding school jammed, between the horse and the wall. He never got any sympathy from Rorke, who would demand, "Who told you to dismount you b----r sir?"

Usually bad riders would be warned, "If you go on like that you'll ruin your matrimonial prospects, won't you?" We had a chap called Latimer in our ride who rode with such long leathers that it seemed his prospects must be ruined anyway, which rather left the instructor short on his usual comments. One day we were out on Woolwich Common doing cavalry drill when Latimer's horse ran away with him. Away he went up the common at full gallop in the general direction of the Herbert Hospital. "Never mind 'im," said Rorke, "I know where that 'oss 'ill take im."

A little later the ride trotted up the common in the same direction as Latimer's horse had taken him. Soon we saw the riderless horse standing on the sky-line on the edge of the town rubbish dump. If you've ever seen a horse laugh, well that horse was laughing. For there was Latimer spread-eagled amongst the rubbish at the bottom of the tip. He was unhurt, but apparently this was not the first time that horse had played that trick on a novice.

By this time most of the chaps in our ride had taken at least one tumble. But I had not, and my mare, Mufti, was such an easy and comfortable ride that I was never in any danger of coming off. Rorke had tried all his tricks, such as cracking his whip near Mufti when we were going over the jumps without stirrups or reins. But Mufti carried on quite unperturbed, much to Rorke's disappointment.

One morning we were down in the jumping field near the Artillery Rotunda when I was told to dismount from Mufti and mount Maesteg. I had watched Maesteg. She was a bad tempered little mare whose only ambition was to get off anyone who sat on her back. So as I walked across to her I thought, well it's either you or me, Maesteg, and it's not going to be me. So when I mounted her, I let my weight drop into the saddle from as high as I could get. Maesteg let out a grunt and escape of air, and from then on she was as quiet as a lamb. She had concluded that I was too heavy to budge.

Next time we went up to the jumping field near the Herbert Hospital. When we got there, Rorke told me to dismount from Mufti and mount a glorious mare which I had never seen before. I think her name was Venus. As soon as I was up, we were told, "Ride quit and cross your stirrups, drop your reins, hands crossed behind your backs. Now down this lane of jumps, Mr. Begbie leading." So I cantered up to the first jump, and Venus took off a full stride earlier than any other horse I had ridden. Off I came head first into the first jump, which consisted of a double wall of railway sleepers packed with cinders in between. I knocked myself out on the sleepers, but when I came to, I demanded of Sergeant Major Rorke that he let me ride this horse for the rest of my time at the Shop. This he conceded, and what a lovely ride she was once you knew her form.

Going back a little in time to mid-September 1938, about a month after we began at the Shop, it seemed that war was imminent. So one morning we were taken off our usual routine and told that the whole academy was to set to work digging air raid trenches opposite our houses. I was dressed in white canvas and was standing with the others on the steps of K House waiting for the spades to arrive. Being relaxed and the morning chilly, I put my hands in my pockets. That was when I got my first hoxter. One had to report to the company office in the lunch break to ask for a form which was an application to be put on extra drill. One had to fill out this form, being careful to dot the i's and cross the t's. If you made a mistake, you got another hoxter. I didn't make a mistake.

Hoxter parades took place before breakfast parade on the middle road. Dress was service dress, with breeches and properly rolled puttees, gloves, belt, rifle, and bayonet. We were subjected to a rigorous inspection by the orderly officer, and the smallest piece of fluff on one's jacket or movement of ones eyes would have meant the instant imposition of another hoxter.

After inspection we were marched up to the back square by the company sergeant major on duty. If one was lucky, this would be Langdale of the Warwickshires. Otherwise it would be one of two CSMs from the Guards or a CSM from the Black Watch. Everything was done at such a pace as would make the Rifle Brigade quick march a slow march by comparison. It was done with fixed bayonets and it went in rapid succession, "roight turn, left turn, roight turn, aboot turn," and so on for about a quarter of an hour, and then, "squad halt, order arms, stand at ease." Then within seconds would follow, "Roight, you've ad yer rest, attention, slope arms, quick march, roight turn, aboot turn, left turn," and so on for another quarter of an hour. Not only was it quite exhausting, but the worst thing about it was there wasn't time to shower before changing into slacks for breakfast parade.

After Mr. Chamberlain got back from Munich with his assurance of peace in our time, hoxters were spent filling in the trenches again, which was much easier than the drill. Of course in March 1939 we dug them all up again.

I used to reckon that if I could get as far as Tuesday without a hoxter, the chances were I would be able to work off any I did get before the weekend. I hated the thought of having to carry them over to the next week.

One awful Tuesday we had to hand our rifles into the armoury for inspection on our way into breakfast. SMI Hartigan was in a bad mood that day, so he dismissed us from gym two minutes late. So I didn't have time to fold my gym clothes neatly in the cupboard, and shoved them down inside my bed instead. At lunch parade there was a tap on my back from Crookenden, our company under officer, "Fluff, take an extra drill." After lunch I collected my rifle from the armoury to find a little note on it which read, "fluff in the gas escape, take an extra drill." When I got to my room there had been a room inspection, and my bed clothes were turned back with the inevitable note. That was three drills in the morning, and it was still only Tuesday! Such a run of drills was enough to have me marched in before the company commander, Major Stewart, a Sapper, for a dressing down, as such conduct almost amounted to mutiny!

I got eleven drills altogether in my first term but none in my second, which, I believe, was quite a creditable score.

In the spring of 1939 we had a visit from the secretary of state for war, Mr. Hore Belisha. For ceremonial parades, two companies would form up on each of the side roads of the Shop, and then we would march onto parade accompanied by the Royal Artillery band, which stood at the back of the centre of the parade ground. The command to halt was given exactly as the two halves of the battalion met in the middle in front of the band and as the music stopped. We would then get the commands, to face the front left and right turn, order arms, and stand at ease. At this stage during one of the rehearsals, the adjutant, Major Mansergh, later General Sir Robert Mansergh, shouted across the parade ground, "There are only 263 Gentlemen Cadets in the whole world, and yet you do it like that. Go back and do it again." I've always thought that was a most excellent rocket.

Anyway, we got it right on the day, and after the inspection we marched past in close column in quick and slow time to the music of the band. The drill at the Shop was the best in the world, and so it ought to have been as we were budding officers instructed by drill sergeants of the Brigade of Guards.

In the second term we had more freedom, and I spent several weekends with my eldest sister Joan and her husband Dick at Reigate. They were both very good tennis players and used to take me along to their club, but my standard of play was so bad I felt quite ashamed. I also had weekends with my Aunt Isabel and Bay Sandeman in their flat off Knightsbridge where I heard all the London gossip. Bay, who was already an old man, used to take me to Lords, where he would say, "I don't know anyone here any more as two generations of my friends have passed away, I can't see as far as the wicket, but I like the atmosphere of the place." I was also invited over to Grove House, Blackheath, the home of the Christopherson family. There my Aunt Gertrude was as vague as ever. I remember going up to a matinee in London with my cousins Marjorie and Dorothy once. We decided to pull Aunt Gertrude's leg on our return by giving her a copy of *Health and Efficiency*, the nudist magazine. She looked at it for a bit, and then in her vague way she said, "I'm not sure that this is very nice, is it?" Malcolm took me to Sunningdale one Saturday to watch Bobby Lock, the already famous South African golfer. I remember him playing in his enormously baggy plus-fours but cannot remember who his opponent was.

I also went up to the Windmill Theatre several times to see the girls in various states of undress or nothing at all. To my horror, on one occasion I found myself sitting next to Hindy Caldwell. I don't know which of us was the more embarrassed. I have never kept my eyes so strictly to the front before or since. Eventually he gave in first and left. So I enjoyed the rest of the show.

By May, the powers that be had evidently decided that war was now inevitable. So we were told that the present term would be cut short and finish at the end of June. The senior term would be commissioned on July 1st and we would be commissioned on July 3rd, but, after one week's leave, we would stay on at the Shop as 2nd Lieutenants for four weeks in order to learn in that time the essentials of what we would have learned in our third term.

I remember I caught a very heavy cold in the middle of the end of term exams and could hardly cope with the physics paper. But all was well. I passed out eighteenth, but fifteenth Sapper as three above me opted for Gunners. My relief was enormous as gunnery would have bored me to tears.

It was strange to come back to the Shop as an officer, being saluted by the fearsome non-commissioned instructors but not having to salute any officer below field rank, that is captain and below, and not having to march everywhere as if we were on parade. Several of us also managed to acquire cars. With war imminent, the bottom fell out of the second-hand car market, and I bought a Ford Popular saloon for £26.

The "essential" subjects covered in that month included the completion of our riding because it was firmly held at the time that if you couldn't manage a horse, you certainly couldn't manage a British private soldier. I think I was the first of our ride to win my spurs. We were also taught to drive a 15cwt truck, and we completed our study of infantry tactics.

So we left the Shop at the end of July. It closed down as soon as war broke out, and sadly it has never reopened.

Chapter Four

The War In England

We left the Shop in our cheaply acquired second hand cars and drove to Winterbourne Gunner on the edge of Salisbury Plain to do a fourteen day gas course. There we were joined by 42 Batch, the sappers of our erstwhile seniors at the Shop, and three commissioned directly from university, making thirty nine in all. Thankfully, as chemical warfare was not resorted to in the Second World War, we never had to make use of what we learned on this course.

But one day I drove over to Bulford to have lunch with my cousin Robert Loder Symmonds and his wife Merlin. Robert was a horse artilleryman and soon due to be promoted to captain. I was never to see him again. He had a most distinguished war career which included the retreat to Dunkirk, the Western Desert, and Arnhem. He was decorated repeatedly, and as a major general just after the war, he was killed when the Mosquito aircraft he was flying in to visit his command in the East Indies crashed. Having survived so much and with such a distinguished career, it was a tragedy that he should die in this way.

After the gas school, we joined the School of Military Engineering at Chatham where 42 and 43 Young Officer Batches were made up into a single class. As second lieutenants, we were the lowest of the low. It was indeed, "Back again, Mr. Begbie." Our mess kits, for which we had been fitted before leaving Woolwich, were now almost ready, and I went up to Hawkes in Saville Row for a final fitting and another visit to the Windmill.

Shortly after our arrival, we attended a formal guest night as guests of the Corps for our initiation into the Corps of Royal Engineers. Lieutenants were detailed to be host to each one of us. We all turned up in our scarlet mess bunny jackets with black facings, black waistcoats with brass buttons, stiff white shirts and black bow ties, blue trues with broad red stripes, and patent leather wellington boots and spurs. The idea seemed to be to ply us with as many drinks as possible before dinner. Dinner was accompanied by the orchestra of the R.E. Band in the magnificent Regency dining room. The top table and the twenty yard long side tables were decorated down their centres with a wonderful collection of silver trophies commemorating various campaigns and battles. There was a long, strip table cloth on either side of the trophies.

Dinner was served with a white and a red wine, and after the things were cleared away, I was amazed to find that the table in front of me, which had previously been white, was now mahogany, and in my hazy state I couldn't understand what had happened. Only afterwards, I discovered that the waiters standing at one end of the table had flicked the long strip cloth off without disturbing a single port glass in the act. I've always thought this to be a remarkable achievement.

Port was passed round several times, and the King's health was drunk with due solemnity. In the conservatory afterwards, we were offered a brandy, and then we in 42 and 43 Batches were sent off down the stairs to the wash room. From there, we were called up one at a time in seniority order to be initiated.

When my name was called, I charged through the door at the top of the stairs, where, after quite a struggle, I was tackled by four of my seniors and carried by hands and feet into the anteroom where I was shoved up on to a high mantlepiece. There I stood in somewhat unstable equilibrium with my back to the wall. "What is your name?," I was demanded. "Richard James Glynn Begbie," I yelled. "What a bloody awful name! Haul him down." I was then pulled down and shoved into the bottom shelf of a massive oak dinner wagon through which I was pulled backwards and forwards on my tummy. As my head and bottom alternately emerged from opposite ends of the trolley, they were thrashed with rolled up copies of *The Times*.

After that, I was hauled up and thrown over a settee into the hall, where mattresses had thoughtfully been laid on the floor to land on. Picking myself up, I was offered a drink of lemonade which was just what I needed. Unknown to me, of course, it was laced with methylated spirits. I managed to totter off to my room at the top of the furthest house on Brompton Barracks Square, where I was as sick as a dog and eventually passed out. I did not come to until about the middle of the next day, as was more or less the experience of us all. But the incident did us no harm, and certainly no one bore the slightest ill will about it.

Our work in the SME began with a course in construction which was soon to be terminated. All I remember of it were three diseases which afflict timber, namely foxiness, druxiness, and dotiness, together with cup shakes and heart shakes, and a visit to a cement factory.

We also visited the coastal defence battery on Sheppey Island where it was explained that the range of the guns was such that they interlaced with the guns on the Essex shore of the estuary. But the searchlights intersected at a different place. In consequence, when the guns could reach an enemy the searchlights wouldn't reveal it, and where the searchlights could reveal an enemy ship, the guns couldn't reach it. For the first time, our unquestioning faith in our superiors got a bit of a shock.

Coming back from that visit at the end of August, we saw newspaper placards announcing that general mobilization had been ordered. We listened on the wireless to Mr. Chamberlain declaring war at eleven o'clock on Sunday morning, 3rd September, and then were immediately ordered to take down all the oil paintings and other treasures and stow them away in the cellars under the mess. This was interrupted after a few minutes by the air raid sirens, which turned out to be sounding a false alarm.

Soon a number of us young officers were detailed to guard the railway line from London to Dover as it was being used at night by ammunition trains which it was thought the Germans might try to sabotage. I was given a platoon of sapper recruits from the training battalion under a Sgt. Fahy who had played cricket for the Corps. With these men, I was to guard the railway tunnels on either side of Chatham railway station.

We were accommodated in a platelayer's hut at Chatham sidings. At night, there was just room for all of us to lie down on the floor. All of us were strictly confined to the station, and meals were brought down to us each day. I don't know whether we brought them with us or not, but we were soon being eaten alive by fleas.

My orders were to post doubled sentries at each end of both tunnels. The sentries at the station ends of the tunnels were given whistles so that they could summon the rest of us if need be.

The sentries at the far ends of the tunnel were to fire a round into the bank opposite if they needed to summon help. Sgt. Fahy with half the platoon was then to dash through the tunnel, while I was to take the rest in a 15cwt truck and dash round to the other end of the tunnel to head off the enemy.

The sentries were issued with live ammunition and were to load their rifles with a round "up the spout." This was the first time these young soldiers had loaded live ammunition except on the range. Not surprisingly, perhaps, they were a little bit jittery.

The enormous, long ammunition trains used to come lumbering slowly through in the small hours of the night. We had several false alarms when the sentries at the far end of the tunnels fired their rifles when they heard a rat or something scrambling down a bank. One night I was summoned by the station master to deal with a train driver who was in a great rage. "I'm not going another bloody mile. I'm being shot at at every ruddy tunnel I come to. Core luv us!" Well, we cooled him down eventually, and on he went with his ammunition for the BEF.

After two weeks, we were relieved by the territorial army and were all heartily thankful that we had joined the regular army. When I got back to Brompton Barracks I was told to report to Ronnie Foster, who was the adjutant of the training battalion. The battalion, which had never moved before in living memory, was to move to Shorncliffe, and I was to be the transport officer working under Captain Foster. Fleets of motor coaches and lorries were requisitioned for the move, and I had to work to loading schedules prepared by Foster. My only real problem was with several senior bachelor majors who had far more baggage and furniture than Foster's schedules allowed. As a very raw 2nd Lt, I was faced with several very irate and, to me, very senior officers who had to be dealt with tactfully but firmly. It wasn't much fun.

As soon as that was done we began a shortened war course of six months duration. This included trying one's hand at every single sapper trade, from painting and decorating to bench fitting and engine driving. The latter was great fun as we were given Merryweather steam engines to stoke, and we soon had them rocking on their foundations. This exposure to all the trades has stood me in very good stead on a number of occasions since, as this narrative will show.

Our field engineering included tunneling, digging and revetting trenches of the 1914 type, semi-permanent bridging as well as training on equipment bridging, none of which was capable of carrying the tanks of the Second World War, and demolitions and mining. We also did a potted survey course and struggled with six figure logarithms.

We used to row across the Medway each morning for our folding boat and pontoon bridging training. The Medway has a very strong tidal current, and it was quite a pull to get across. My roommate, Bill Lucas, always managed to get hold of the boathook first, thus avoiding the rowing, and thereafter he was always known as Bill Boathook. As we rowed across, we got a good view of the dockyard, and I remember seeing a large cruiser in for repair of war damage, but I can't remember her name.

One of our number was a member of the House of Lords. Whenever we were on night work in the rain or cold, he would say he had to go and sit in the House. At the time this did not increase our respect either for him or the second chamber.

A Major Bennett taught us water supply. He was a chain smoker, and we used to run a shilling sweep on how many cigarettes he would smoke each morning. On one morning he needed one more to reach my number, and there were only a few minutes to go. From the back of the class, I went up and offered him one of mine. "No, thank you," he said, "I've got a taxi waiting to take me up to town." So I never did win the sweepstakes. He took a week to show us how to put in a water supply for a battalion camp, and then at the end he burbled through his walrus moustache, "And then some bloody ape of an infantryman will leave the tap running, and muck up the whole scheme."

When our course finished in January 1940, we were told that two of us would join field companies in France, four would go as class officers to Officer Cadet Training Units, and the rest as party officers to training battalions. I put first choice fd coy, second choice fd coy, third choice OCTU. The latter sounded more interesting than a training battalion. But if one was posted to a field company, it would more or less guarantee joining the BEF in France, which is what we all wanted.

So in February, David Willison, later to become Lt. Gen. Sir David, and I reported to Lt Col E.V. Binney, DSO, who was commanding 142 OCTU at Malta Barracks, Aldershot. Col Binney had been called back from retirement. He had retained a thin, upright figure and was a fine officer and gentleman and just the right man to be in charge of training cadets. He was quiet but firm and stood no nonsense.

My company commander was Captain Brett Cloutman, VC, MC, who had been recalled from the reserve. He had won his VC in the last week of the 1914-1918 war and was a QC and notable defence counsel. He was a short, chubby man with a round face under a bald head, and one would never have imagined that he was a VC winner. He usually dressed in service tunic, riding breeches, and rather fine pig skin leggings. He had a quiet, dry sense of humor, and I liked him enormously.

I was to be the class officer of No7 Class joining the following week. At that time the intake consisted of civil engineers and architects usually some ten years or more older than myself. The OCTU curriculum consisted of eight three-week courses, each with their own instructor. As they only had three weeks with a class of sixty odd, the only officer who got to know the class intimately was the class officer. So apart from looking after the discipline and administrative needs of the class, the opinion of the class officer, even though he was so young and inexperienced, counted a great deal when it came to deciding whether a cadet should continue or be returned to his unit as unsuitable for officer training. I think, in retrospect, that having only been exposed to the very high standard expected of regular officers, I might have been instrumental in returning to their units some I should not have returned.

Sometime in March, we all had to have our first TAB injection. I couldn't go on the morning that I was supposed to, being involved in something else, so I asked the MO at lunch if he could give me a jab in the afternoon. "You are a bloody nuisance; I shall be playing tennis." "Well, can't your medical orderly do it?," I asked. "Yes, he can, but he's not really supposed to. But I'll tell him to expect you."

So I went to the MI Room after lunch, had the jab, and immediately passed out on the floor. I came to feeling rather a fool but seemed to be okay. Later I went to a Bette Davis film with David Willison. In the cinema, I began shivering so badly and felt so awful that David had to take me back to my quarters.

Later, after repeatedly being violently ill, I was taken to the Cambridge Hospital, where at first it was thought that I had scarlet fever as my temperature was above 105°F. Eventually it was realized that the inoculation had given me typhoid, and I was moved into a room on my own where the MO sat with me saying that if I died, he was in for a court martial for allowing the orderly to inject me. So I was glad someone had a substantial interest in my recovery. I was injected with what I was told was a mercury compound, which brought my temperature down so quickly that I turned from scarlet to yellow overnight and I now had jaundice.

To cut a long story short, I spent three weeks in hospital, had two weeks sick leave, and, after three months regaining weight, recovered completely.

When the German attack began in the west, the media all warned of the threat to Paris. But David Willison insisted that they would go for the channel ports to cut off the BEF. He was nearly arrested for causing despondency and alarm, but he was dead right.

The instructor in demolitions was a Captain Hawkins, an extraordinary person. He invented the Hawkins grenade made out of a Johnson baby powder tin. All the top brass came down to see a demonstration of this. I remember he threw a grenade to the CIGS to catch, and he, too, was threatened with causing despondency and alarm. But his grenade was manufactured in vast quantities and was used throughout the war.

Hawkins also invented the hollow charge which was used for beehive charges for demolitions and in anti-tank shells. He invited me to share in his experiments for this.

Cloutman (we always called him Q) used to get his wife and daughter Jane down to stay at the Lismoyne Hotel in Fleet some five miles away for several weekends. They kindly used to invite me over for lunch on Sundays, and it became evident that they hoped I would become engaged to Jane, who was a lovely girl. But she was tiny, really tiny, and I was six foot three inches. Some would say she would have been quite a catch. Mrs. Cloutman was the heiress of a fortune from Mappin and Webb, the London jewellers.

Meantime Cloutman was badgering the war office to post him to a field unit, and eventually he announced that he was off to join 26th Field Company R.E in Scotland. Tim Juckes, who was the 8 Class officer, and I begged him to take us with him. He promised to do what he could.

He was as good as his word, and at the end of July I got orders to join the 26th in Kirkcudbright in southwest Scotland. I drove up in my Ford Popular and stopped for lunch on the way with my sister Joan at Oswestry in Shropshire. Her husband, Dick Stead, having been called up with the supplementary reserve of officers at the beginning of the war, was at the anti-aircraft gunnery school there. I stopped the night with my Aunt Ethel, my father's younger sister, and Uncle Willie Cowan in Shrewsbury. I never saw them again.

I found 26th Fd Coy in some warehouses and offices about a mile up the river from the town. Cloutman greeted me on arrival and took me to the officers' mess, which was accommodated in the Royal Hotel in the centre of Kirkcudbright. After unpacking my things and settling into my room, I came downstairs to meet the OC.

It has been my good fortune in life to serve under several absolutely brilliant men. Vivian Dykes was perhaps the most outstanding of them all. He was already a Brevet Lt Col and a CBE in 1938 although he was only forty. He had been Military Assistant Secretary of the Committee of Imperial Defence and Secretary of the Overseas Defence Committee. As such, he worked directly with Lord Hankey and came into contact with all the leading figures of the armed forces, the civil service, and members of the cabinet. For a short period he was an instructor at the Senior Staff College, Minley, and then was recalled on the outbreak of war to serve under General Ismay in the War Cabinet. He desperately wanted to see active service and so had got himself posted to 26th Fd Coy RE.

Very quickly, his efficiency, his dynamic energy, and his warm personality caused me not only to admire him but also to love him. He was absolutely straightforward and had no use for any sort of prevarication. He could be fierce but was always just. He is the only man I have ever seen bring cold sweat on a man's brow merely by giving him a dressing down. He could sum people up in an instant and could slice through red tape like a knife through butter. He had a pretty rich vocabulary and choice of swear words which were terribly blasphemous but never dirty. I have to confess with shame that I followed his example for many years, and added the dirty words as well.

26th Fd Coy consisted of about thirty original members who had escaped from St. Valerie after the debacle in France, together with about a hundred and fifty sappers who had been posted in from Line of Communication units which had been evacuated earlier. There were only about thirty rifles, a Boys anti-tank rifle with its sights shot away, and no tools or vehicles. The men, because they had been "Dunkirked," thought they knew all the answers, whereas we, who had not been out of England, knew nothing. Dykes very soon showed them how wrong they were.

The three platoon commanders were Andrew Leslie from the term below me at the Shop, and Dick Boase and Babe Taylor from two terms below. Tim Juckes joined us later, and Babe left us on transfer at his request to the Royal Fusiliers. Both Dick Boase and Tim Juckes were killed in the Battle of Normandy.

Dykes made me the training officer, and, as we had nothing to train with, we began with drill, PT, map reading, and knots and lashings.

Soon we got three requisitioned civvie lorries, and we used our private cars for the rest. We were sent crates of American Ross .300 rifles packed solid in grease with six rifles to a crate. It took the unit days to clear the grease off and out of the barrels.

Church parade was still compulsory, and we used to march into town each Sunday and clatter into the episcopal church with our rifles. Dykes was determined not to be caught unarmed by German parachutists in the same way as the troops had been caught in church in the Indian Mutiny. The service was as dull as ditch water, the hymns unknown, and the sermon unintelligible. It was a total disaster.

So one Sunday Dykes said we were not to be surprised if he did a right wheel in town as he was going to do a reconnaissance in the Church of Scotland, while we were to go straight on to the other church as usual. On first parade on the Monday morning, Dykes addressed the unit and reported what he had found in the C of S: hymns we could sing, a reasonable sermon, and so forth. If there were no objections, he suggested that the whole unit should do a right wheel the following Sunday. So next Sunday we did just that, and on the following Monday, Dykes asked for a show of hands. There was a unanimous vote in favor of the C of S. "Fall out the pay corporal," ordered Dykes, and after briefing him, the unit was told to report to the pay corporal with their service and pay books, called AB 64s. C of E was deleted and C of S was inserted and an enormous Part 2 Order was published changing the denomination of the unit to C of S. It was just as well we had no padre as there would then have been no end of a hoo-haa, but I think Dykes would have got his way anyway. I wonder if such a thing has ever been done before or since.

2/Lt Richard James Glynn Begbie, aged 19,
at the outbreak of the war.

Lt Col Vivian Dykes, CBE, RE.

After a few days, four 350cc BSA motor cycles arrived, and quite a lot of tools and equipment. So training could be made more interesting, and we also taught the local Home Guard how to dig slit trenches and camouflage them. I taught the subalterns to ride the motor cycles, including across country. Having one day demonstrated how to jump a ditch I told them to follow me over it. Having done so, I turned round to watch them come over it, and not looking where I was going, finished up upside down in a clump of blackberry bushes, much to the amusement of all concerned.

Then we got a message that Dumfries airport had been bombed and there were several unexploded bombs. As I was the senior subaltern, Dykes ordered me to go and deal with them. Well, that was okay but the problem was that I had never seen an RAF bomb, let alone a German one, and neither I nor anyone else had the least idea how they worked. So I took a corporal and four sappers with me and found on arrival that one unexploded bomb had dropped into a marsh and could safely be left where it was. The other was just outside the hangar and had to be removed.

All I could see was a hole about a foot across where the bomb had gone into the ground. I thought some water wouldn't do any harm, so we emptied several buckets down the hole. This was pretty stupid as we now had to dig it out. Only two could dig at a time, and we all took turns. After about four feet, we came upon the fins of the bomb. I scooped the earth carefully away round this with a borrowed trowel, only to discover that the bomb had detached itself from the fins and was further down. We learnt later that this always happened.

About six or seven feet down we got to the bomb, and again I cleared it myself to expose the fuse on the side of what turned out to be a 250lb bomb. I drew a sketch of the fuse head and made a copy for the corporal whom I sent about fifty yards away, and told him to lie down and write down what I said.

So I started on the screw I had labelled "A." "Turning screw A half a turn now," I called, and proceeded like that so that, if I blew myself up, someone else wouldn't do the same. I must say I was very frightened, but comforted myself by thinking that I wouldn't know much about it if the bomb did go off. When I got the fuse out, I saw that the detonator had gone off but had failed to detonate the primer (or the gain, as some call it). So I had in fact been perfectly safe all along.

Just as we were leaving, the bomb disposal staff officer from HQ Scottish Command in Edinburgh arrived with the Mayor of Dumfries, who took photographs. The staff officer demanded the bomb. He was a temporary and seemed a bit of a wet, so I told him I had orders to take the bomb back to my OC and that was that. So he took himself off with a bad grace.

For once Dykes's usual *sang froid* was disturbed when I dumped the bomb in front of him on his desk when I got back. I was proud of my bomb. Later I did drawings of it and lectured on how the thing worked before we sent it to Scottish Command, who were demanding its immediate return to them.

Later, Dykes took me with him to prepare a bridging camp for the unit on the River Tay. We called in at the District HQ in Perth to meet the staff and state our requirements. The speed with which Dykes summed up the staff was an education to me. As we left each office, he would say, "Don't waste your time with him, he's useless," or "Deal with him even if your problem isn't his immediate concern."

We then went to a small park beside the river below Stanley, about eight miles upstream from Perth. It was an ideal place for a company camp. "The Coy HQ will be in this boat house, officers' lines here on the river bank, troops' lines here, officers' mess tent here, and I want a nice fireplace in it...." Dykes had the whole layout of the place clear in his mind in an instant. Then we drove round to a stretch of river frontage on the estate of a retired general. This was where I was to set up the bridging camp. We called on the general, who readily gave permission for the use of his land, but Dykes warned me to keep on the right side of him.

We returned to Kirkcudbright where Dykes put Babe Taylor and his platoon under my command, and with some lorries which by now had arrived, we went to Stanley by road. I had a week to get everything ready. This included collecting all the tents and barrack stores from Perth, erecting all the tents, digging surface drains round them, erecting corrugated iron sheds for the cookhouse, ablutions, and latrines, and unloading all the bridging equipment at Stanley station and transporting it by road to the site. I tried to put two pontoons, one on top of the other, on one lorry to speed things up. But going up the slope from the station, the front wheels came off the ground, which somewhat perplexed the driver. So we had to transport the pontoons one at a time. In addition to the pontoon equipment, there was the old Mark 2 Folding Boat Equipment, assault boats, recce boats, and stores for erecting derricks, etc.

When Dykes arrived with the company a week later, he was quite surprised to find that everything was ready, including a fireplace and chimney in the mess tent which did not smoke!

The training Dykes organized there was excellent and getting used to navigating rafts on the fast current of the Tay has stood me in good stead ever since. Not least of our activities was to improvise with pontoon bridging equipment a T-head pier for use when we invaded Europe. In the light of what has been written about British reluctance to mount a cross channel invasion in 1944, it is worth noting that the army was already thinking about it in 1940!

In the middle of October, Dykes received orders to return to London to work under General Ismay. He was bitterly disappointed as he wanted active service.

We were inspected by the Chief Engineer, Scottish Command, who declared that we were now the best prepared fd coy in the army. Dykes told me that Cloutman would take over as OC. He told me that he was quite confident that I was capable of becoming second-in-command but far too young to take over as OC if anything happened to Cloutman. So someone would have to come in from outside. I was made temporary 2i/c and promoted temporary to captain at the age of twenty.

Before leaving us, Dykes asked us what we would like to do. I can't remember all the choices he offered us, but the one we all opted for was to be affiliated to the Brigade of Guards. After leaving, us Dykes was promoted to Brigadier. He was included in Mr. Churchill's staff for his second meeting with Mr. Roosevelt, the American President, in December 1941. Flying back with the results of the Casablanca conference in January 1943, Dykes' plane crashed into the Welsh hills and he was killed. It was a terrible and tragic loss to the whole army.

Dykes was as good as his word, and on 12th November we moved south to join 24th Guards Independent Brigade Group. Travelling through London, we saw for the first time all the damage caused by the Blitz and the people hurrying home before the nightly raid began.

On arrival, Coy HQ was established in a vacated girls school in Pampisford Road, South Croydon, and the rest of the unit was accommodated in houses in the same road. Just behind us was an open common, and beyond that was Croydon Airport, which was used by several squadrons of Hurricane fighters. There had been a terrible disaster a few weeks before we arrived when a brick surface shelter on the common had received a direct hit and some twenty children in it had been killed. By this time almost all our unit transport had arrived, but we were still short of a lot of tools and equipment.

The brigade was commanded by a Brigadier Fraser who was shortly replaced by Brigadier Browning (later Gen. Sir Frederick Browning). The Brigade Major was Gordon Lennox, and Captain Goosen, who had been one of my instructors at the Shop, was one of the staff. The other units in the group included the first battalions of the Scots, Irish, and Welsh Guards, the first Middlesex Machine Gun Battalion, and the 24th Field Regiment RA. We were the Imperial Reserve for the defence of London in the event of invasion, and were the first formation to be fully reequipped after Dunkirk.

One of my first jobs in the new location was to go with the CSM to choose the company beer. So we went together to a brewery in Croydon to taste every beer they had from X beer to XXXX beer. I forget which we chose, as well I might, because we were both pretty merry by the time we left.

There were air raids most nights, and often the sky was lit up by fires in London. Although bombs occasionally dropped around us, I only remember one night when Croydon for some reason seemed to be the main target. On this occasion, the bus station just below us on the main road was hit and set on fire. At considerable risk, most of the busses were driven out and parked along the main road. Then a stick of bombs came down on the length of the road and almost all the rescued buses were set on fire or otherwise destroyed, together with a number of fire engines and ambulances which had come to the rescue.

Another evening we were sitting in the lounge of our house when we heard a bomb coming down making a noise like a racing car accelerating fast through low gears. Cloutman and the others all dived under the table, but I was too slow and just lay down beside the sofa. Then there was silence. The thing had not gone off. We waited in case it was a delayed action bomb. Then we got up and went outside to look for the thing, but in the black-out, with only shielded torches allowed because there was a raid in progress, we could find nothing.

Next day we found where a large bomb had landed in the back garden of two deaf old ladies who had a house between us and the Coy HQ. A bomb disposal squad came to dig the thing out. They went down twenty-three feet through solid chalk and found a bomb some nine feet long and two foot six inches in diameter, tilted up in the opposite direction to which it had come in. It was a Hermann Goering bomb which was later emptied and placed outside St. Paul's, where it became a collecting box for contributions to repair the cathedral.

Early in January, Cloutman went off on a company commanders' course at the SME Ripon. While he was away, we had a most interesting job. At that time the only bomb shelter available was the Anderson Shelter which householders dug into a hole in their gardens. It consisted of curved, corrugated iron sheets which one covered over with earth dug from the hole. As can be imagined, more people were likely to die of pneumonia than from German bombs. So instead, many people were taking shelter under their dining room tables.

This gave someone the idea of making a shelter which could be used as a dining room table by day and as a shelter by night. We were now given two proto-type shelters to test by blowing up a house on top of them. For this purpose, we were given a semi-detached house in Hammersmith which had been damaged in an air raid. Its other half was down, but the houses on both sides of it and across the street were all still occupied.

So as much brickwork as possible was cut away, but still a total charge of some twenty pounds of guncotton was necessary to bring the house down. The outside walls of the house were also shored up to make as much fall on the shelters as possible and to restrict the number of bricks which would fly about. Two dummies were put in each shelter.

When the great day arrived, all the residents of nearby houses were evacuated by the police. But we first warned the housewives to put all ornaments down in a safe place. ARP Rescue squads were waiting round the corner. A whole crowd of VIPs came to watch the test. These included the Home Secretary, Mr. Herbert Morrison, the Lord Mayor of London, the Mayor of Hammersmith, the GOC London District, and fifty or more others. With British Movietone News buzzing by my ear, the exploder was activated, there was a considerable explosion, and all the VIPs were covered in a cloud of brick dust. We'd forgotten the direction of the wind. The residents were allowed back in their houses immediately, only to find that we had forgotten to tell them to get their chimneys swept! Next the ARP squads found the shelters collapsed and the dummies squashed flat. At which point we decided to make a hasty exit. But the Morrison Shelters which were issued eventually were far stronger than the ones we had tested, so perhaps we saved a few lives indirectly.

I had to take a returned deserter to the HQ of the Irish Guards for punishment as my powers, not being a field officer, were insufficient. Attending the CO's orders of the Guards was quite an experience.

All six company commanders and the adjutant stood to attention ranged round behind the colonel, who sat behind his desk. All of them were wearing their black service caps with the peaks pulled down so low over their noses that their eyes were almost hidden.

From outside the door we heard the RSM's shouted commands. "Escort, witnesses, an' accused, shun." "Quick march, left roight, left roight, left" (at a very quick pace). "Escort, witnesses, an' accused, halt, roight turn. Guardsman Duffy, Sir."

Then the colonel in a bored voice, "Adjutant, read the charge." This done, the colonel said to the accused, "Have you anything to say?" "No, Sir." "Right, seven days field punishment, march out." "Escort, witnesses, an' accused, roight turn, quick march, left roight, left roight, left," shouted the RSM at the same pace as before. So this went on till they got to my sapper.

Sapper Brown was quite the most slovenly soldier in my experience. He was a cabinet maker by trade and had gone absent without leave on several previous occasions. So from outside the door came, "Escort, witnesses, an' accused, shun. As ye were. Escort, witnesses, an' accused, shun. As ye were." This went on several times, until, with an even more bored voice, and with a disapproving look at me, the colonel called to the RSM to send them in. So in they came with the RSM calling the same rapid pace which nearly ended with Sapper Brown landing on his face. He got twenty-eight days field punishment with the Guards, and that is quite something.

The RSM then announced that the messing committee were assembled outside. This was a wartime innovation to cater to the needs of a conscripted citizen army. "All right, march them in," said the colonel. Again from outside the door, "Messing committee, shun. Quick march, left roight, left roight, left (at the same pace as before), halt, roight turn. Messing committee, Sir." The messing committee consisted of the cook sergeant and a guardsman from each company. The colonel, in the same bored voice, "Anything to say?" "No, sir" (in unison). "Well then." "Messing committee, roight turn, quick march, halt, dasmiss." This was the Guards conforming to an Army Council Instruction with which they did not agree.

When Sapper Brown came back from his punishment, he was a changed man. He became the talk of the unit. He had actually survived twenty-eight days field punishment with the Guards! This, for the first time, gave him some pride in himself, and he became something of a unit hero and one of the smarter men in the unit.

I, as 2i/c, opened all the incoming mail. Some time after Cloutman got back, his course report arrived, which I read. We shared the same office, and I said, "Here you are, the OC of the oldest and most famous fd coy in the whole of the Corps, and all you can get is an average report, just look at it!" I don't know how I had the nerve or the cheek to say such a thing. Cloutman's response was, "All right then, you will go on the next course, and see if you can do any better."

My parents came up from Cheltenham and took me out to lunch with Major and Mrs. Cloutman at the Selsdon Hotel for my twenty-first birthday on February 2nd. They gave me a wire-haired fox terrier for my birthday, and I called him Scotch. Scotch became a great friend of the unit, and Tim Juckes looked after him when I went off to Ripon on a bridging course a few weeks later. In view of Cloutman's challenge, I really had to work.

When my report arrived, it read, "Distinguished, recommended as an instructor at an OCTU." Having taken some trouble to get into a field unit, this was the worst thing I could have done.

Early in April the brigade moved out of town, and we moved to Rotherfield, a few miles south of Tunbridge Wells. Soon after we arrived there, John Thomas (later Gen. Sir Norman Thomas) joined us to take over as 2i/c and I became commander of 2 Platoon. Apart from my experience with the railway tunnels, this was my first command and I thoroughly enjoyed it. One of our first jobs was to prepare a camp for the field regiment in Eridge Park, the seat of some noble lord whose name I forget. Apart from erecting corrugated shelters for cookhouses, ablutions, and latrines for each battery, regimental HQ, and officers' and sergeants' messes, this also involved putting in a water supply.

The plans were given to me by the local garrison engineer who, being a "works type," was rather looked down upon by us "Field types." Anyway, his plan did not show a ring main, which the good Major Bennett had taught us at such length was absolutely necessary. So I decided to put this in. Its total length was over a mile. This involved digging a trench across the noble lord's polo field. This nearly gave the garrison engineer a fit, but I stuck to my guns, and in any case no one was in residence at the castle.

I had to get the water engineer out from Tunbridge Wells to indicate where we could tap into the main. We dug a trench at right angles to the line of the main he had indicated and struck virgin rock throughout its length. I called him out again, and he seemed a little surprised, but advised that we should extend the trench further to intersect the main. My suggestion that perhaps the main was in a tunnel under the rock was greeted with amusement by him. After he had gone, we ran a line of survey poles between the nearest manholes which were about half a mile away on either side. Our line ran right through the middle of our trench and exactly where the water engineer had originally said we would find it.

So I sent for our compressor truck, and the chaps got busy on the rock with pneumatic drills. Three feet through the rock, we broke through into a tunnel. At the bottom of the six foot high tunnel, we found the main some twelve feet underground! By this time I was somewhat acid as time was at a premium and I made some comment on water engineers who didn't know where their mains were when he and his chaps came out to tap the main for us.

Meantime I had every plumber, bench fitter, engine artificer, and anyone else who had some aptitude for cutting and putting screw threads on pipes, fitting at least seventy bib taps, making the joints and working like mad. In the general rush, a good deal more white lead and hemp was used on the joints than was necessary. Before connecting the two ends of the ring main together, I flushed it through with water, and an amazing amount of white lead emerged. Then we ran the taps to make sure everything was working. Next day when I handed the camp over to the gunners, I noticed that the water or white lead had turned the grass black under the taps. I never heard that my water supply had any ill effects on the stomachs of the gunners!

The brigade commander didn't consider that the driveway to his HQ was worthy of the Guards, so my platoon laid a nice driveway with bricks salvaged from bombed houses. So someone who owns that private house in Rotherfield today has a nice brick driveway laid by the Royal Engineers.

Early in May came the dreaded orders for me to return to 142 OCTU where I became, not the instructor in bridging, but the instructor in mines and demolitions. One very soon learns when one has to teach. This had a sequel after the war when I was selected to go to the Military Engineering Experimental Establishment at Christchurch to develop a new range of demolition equipment. But I didn't think that this was in my line, and turned it down at the interview.

At this time my brother Denys was going through a terrible time. He had been called up as a sapper to the training regiment at Clitheroe, where he had become very ill with pleurisy on top of his asthma. This led him to be medically down-graded, and he was posted to the military hospital at Winchester as a medical orderly. I obtained leave to go and see him and found him in a desperately depressed state, not unnaturally, as his chosen career was the army, like me.

I appealed to Col Binney on my return, and told him I was certain my brother's health would come right if he would accept him for training at the OCTU from which Denys was precluded by his present medical category. I suppose, knowing that we were an army family, Col Binney pulled the necessary strings, and almost within days Denys was at the OCTU and marvelously recovered. How thankful we are to Col Binney, who sadly was killed two years later in a road accident.

After six months as instructor in demolitions and mining, I became the bridging instructor at Wouldham Camp on the Medway between Rochester and Maidstone. The equipment when I arrived was still the old pontoon equipment which would only take loads up to twenty-four tons, the Mark 3 Folding Boat Equipment which took loads up to nine tons and the 50/60 ton raft, both of which remained in service till long after the war, and the incredibly cumbersome Inglis tubular bridge. But early in 1942, to replace the Inglis bridge and the pontoon bridge, came the first Bailey bridge to come from the factory.

Shortly after it arrived, a couple of chaps arrived who said they were from the Ministry of Information and had come to take photographs of the new bridging equipment. We had not been told to expect them, nor did they have in their possession any authority to enter the camp. They became so abusive when I told them they could not be allowed in the camp, that I had them locked up in the guard room for the night to cool their heels. Next morning we found out through the usual channels that they were not spies, but that the War Office had forbidden them to see the new equipment. This was just as well for me, and I let them go.

I thoroughly enjoyed my time as the instructor there, and in the course of my duties I became completely confident in my ability to build any equipment bridge and to navigate large, heavily laden rafts in strong currents. The Medway would reach seven knots in a spring tide.

Each class would spend three weeks with me. They came by MT training convoy on Saturday while the previous class departed the same evening by a night MT training convoy back to Aldershot. By now trainees were younger than the ones I had met as a class officer in 1940, and many consisted of undergraduates from the universities. From them I learned every bawdy song in the book as we would all meet for drinks in a pub after work two or three times during the course.

We did a night FBE bridge scheme at Westbury upstream on the Medway, and we did most of the pontoon bridging training at Heartlake Farm, popularly known as Heartbreak Farm, not far from Tonbridge. There we stayed in wooden hop pickers huts which were freezing cold in winter. I remember washing up was quite easy because all you had to do was to hold your tin porridge plate upside down and give it a sharp rap and the remaining porridge fell out in frozen lumps!

I used to visit the sergeants' mess from time to time where we used to play housy-housy, so much better named than the wretched Bingo of today. There was a Sergeant Gardner there who had been shot thought the palm of his right hand during the Great War. Because he couldn't straighten his hand, he was given special permission to salute with his left hand, or so he said. Anyway, when his luck at housy was out, he used to turn to the picture of King George VI and salute him with his right hand for luck.

My brother, and my future brother-in-law, Adrian Sandes, came through with one class. The first time my brother met me in the camp, he saluted me and said out of the side of his mouth, "Just for the sake of appearances, and don't forget it!"

Before twelve months with the OCTU was up, I applied to Col Binney to be posted to a field unit so that I could get some active service. I was very disappointed that all he could get me was second in command of 754 Army Fd Coy, which was at a place called Skegness which, I thought, must be somewhere in Scotland. I wanted to be in a division and not buried away somewhere in the L of C or the base. It was certainly "back again Mr. Begbie."

I found Skegness on the coast of Lincolnshire. It was cold and bleak when I arrived there in July 1942. The OC was Bruce Hubbard, a supplementary reserve officer who had won an MC at Dunkirk. He and I did not hit it off together, and I suppose a clash was inevitable from the word go.

He took me with him to meet Mr. West, who was not only the Mayor of and county councillor for Lindsey, he was also the regional defence commissioner in the event of invasion and that part of the country being cut off from the rest. Mr. West was also chairman of the bench, governor of the grammar school, and a staunch member of the Primitive Methodist Church.

At home with Mr. West was his daughter, to whom I was immediately attracted. I think it was her naturalness, lack of any sort of pretention, and nothing but the minimum of make-up which first attracted me to her. We hardly spoke a word to one another at that first meeting as our business was with her father. Yet somehow, instinctively if you like, I had a strong feeling that she was the girl for me.

Later we used to go to dances together at the RAF club, and we clicked again there. Win used to wear a long, black dress with a green coatee. She danced superbly, especially the old fashioned waltzes which we so enjoyed doing together. We also played golf together, Win wearing grey pin-striped slacks, and she used to beat me, which I think was not too difficult.

I used to walk two miles in the black-out most evenings to see her. We talked for hours about many things and found ourselves in agreement on most. Win was far better read than I, and she is a graduate of London University, having a diploma in domestic science. She was teaching in Grimsby at the time and later became an inspector of education for schools in Lindsey. She is a brilliant educationalist, as was proved later on in South Africa.

After a while the unit went up to the Yorkshire moors for training in minefield breaching and clearance. Hubbard put me in charge of this training and ordered me to put live charges down with the dummy mines to make the training realistic. I remonstrated with him and said the charges ought to be placed at least several yards away from where the men would be lying on their stomachs prodding for mines. But Hubbard insisted that a quarter pound carton of gelignite be placed with each dummy mine. I protested that this would blow someone's head off, but he replied that he would have me court martialled if I did not do as he said. I was furious with him for not accepting my advice. Had I not been a demolitions instructor? And did he think I did not know what I was talking about?, etc. In his mind he was certain there was no possibility of an accident.

So as I could not persuade him, I decided to try this out on myself. I went off alone to a secluded place with my batman and buried a carton of gelignite a foot in the ground and stood by it while my batman operated the exploder some yards away. Well, there was just a puff of dirt coming up almost at my feet, and I thought, surely Hubbard can't be right. So I put down another carton in a similar hole and covered it with a filled sandbag and sat on it. My batman pressed the plunger, and I was conscious of a tremendous kick in the bottom and up I went, some twelve feet I believe, seeing the sky one moment and the ground the next, and landed with a thud. I felt as if my limbs had been almost wrenched off my body, and the first thing I did was to feel if my matrimonial prospects were still in place, which they were. Most of the buttons had been torn off my uniform and I was feeling pretty groggy. Anyway, I had told my batman to bring along some brandy, and I felt better after that but could hardly walk as I'd cracked a bone in my leg. After that I gave various orders, which apparently were nonsense, and I was quietly told to go back to the lines. I think I had a bit of shock. I was given two or three weeks sick leave and went off to Cheltenham to recover.

When I returned, I had the satisfaction of knowing that Hubbard had decided not to place the live charges with the dummy mines. The unit was now to be mobilized for service in the Middle East, which involved me as second in command in a great deal of administrative arrangements and office work. But Hubbard had arranged for me to be posted as emotionally unstable for immediate active service, a feeling which I may say was entirely mutual so far as service with him was concerned.

Before leaving Skegness I proposed to Win, and we became engaged early in October 1942. Despite all the inevitable separations of war-time, our love for one another has never been in any way diminished.

Although I was sorry to have missed the opportunity of going overseas, I was delighted that my posting was to a field unit again, in fact to join the 15th Scottish Division RE at Morpeth in Northumberland.

When I reported in at HQRE, the CRE was away and I was interviewed by the adjutant, a territorial by the name of Peter Taylor. He sent me on as 2i/c to 278 Fd Coy at Felton House, about halfway to Alnwick. The Officer Commanding was Major P.F. White, a regular officer who was in his middle forties and a good deal older than most OCs at the time.

The unit was divided between two country houses, one of which was Felton House, located a few miles apart. The unit, in common with the rest of the division, was on lower establishment, which meant that it was at barely two thirds of its proper strength and lacking a lot of equipment and transport. It was supposed to be doing further individual training to prepare the men for service overseas, for which drafts had repeatedly to be supplied. The result was that there was a constant movement of men through the unit, and no one knew from one day to the next how long he would be there. Morale was therefore not good. This was not helped by the fact that Major White kept the unit fully employed on improving its accommodation instead of getting on with the business of training for war, which is what the men had been called up to do and what they wanted to do. The accommodation was adequate, just as it was.

The CRE was Lt Col R.K. Millar, who had played rugger for Scotland and who knew my father at least by reputation. He had been in the Norway campaign. On first meeting he did not make a remarkable impression. He was short, wirely built, clean shaven with a sallow complexion, and had an aquiline nose and heavy black eyebrows.

We moved down to Hurworth-on-Tees near Darlington soon after I arrived. But again, despite the excellent facilities of the Tees and the plentiful bridging equipment available to us, we did no training but were still kept fully occupied improving our accommodation. After a while Major White damaged his eye and had to go away for operations and subsequent sick leave. The consequence was that I became acting OC, and as quickly as possible we finished off the work which was in hand and began rigorous training. This was popular with the whole unit and morale improved quickly. Nevertheless, we still had a frequent movement of men and officers through the unit.

Win, who by now was serving with the St. John's ambulances, visited me twice and stayed once in the hotel down the road and another time with a kind lady living alone a few doors from the company HQ.

We were married in Cheltenham on 29th December 1942 in a snowstorm. The service was taken by old Rev. Mr. P. Unwin, who had taught both my father and myself at Cheltenham College. He seemed to be more nervous than either Win or I. I was in service dress and sword, and when Win joined me at the top of the aisle she asked, "Is it really necessary for you to wear that knife when you marry me?" Being a war-time wedding, only my parents, brother and all three sisters, and a few friends were present. After a three day honeymoon at Broadway at the foot of the Cotswolds, we travelled by train together as far as Derby, where Win had to change trains to rejoin her ambulances and I continued to Darlington. Unfortunately Win left her hat behind with me in the train. Early next morning, I walked in past the sentry at Hurworth with this hat, which was quite unpackable, dangling from my hand. I cannot remember exactly what the comment of the sentry was, but it was certainly not polite. Win got up to Hurworth once more, and we rented a couple of rooms in a bungalow outside the village where we spent a very happy ten days together. I remember I gave her an eternity ring there which cost me sixty pounds, about two months pay.

In June 1943, Major White who had just returned to duty, was promoted and posted as CRE of an airfield construction group, and was replaced by Major Cocks, a most excellent man. But he had no sooner arrived than Col

Win and myself at our wedding on 29th December 1942.

Millar wrote and asked me whether I would come and serve him as his adjutant. As there was no 2i/c of the divisional engineers in those days, the role of adjutant was an important and challenging one and I leapt at the opportunity.

So in July I joined Col Jock Millar in the Workhouse at Morpeth, where HQRE was accommodated. Jock was really rather a dour, Lowland Scot who took a lot of knowing. He was a very humble man, so was never anything of a figurehead such as for instance Field Marshal Montgomery, yet he knew his job inside out. He was an absolute stickler for obedience to orders, and more so than anyone else I have known. I admired him tremendously.

The Divisional Commander had decided that all units of the division should wear the balmoral. They all conformed except us. Jock told the general that he must first obtain the permission of the Colonel-in-Chief of the Corps of Royal Engineers. "And who might that be?," demanded the general. "His majesty King George VI," replied Jock, and that was the end of it. Jock was a devout member of the Church of Scotland, and I remember him telling me I ought to go to church, which, following his example, I then did. He was far better read than I was and could quote poetry from various authors, especially Robbie Burns. I think he rightly regarded me as something of an illiterate. He had a rather dry sense of humor. And he had some surprising accomplishments which included being a very proficient tap-dancer. Over the two years I served him as his adjutant, I came to love him, and he became almost a second father to me.

Jock told me that Taylor had been posted at his own request because he did not agree with the way Jock was running the divisional engineers. Taylor thought that Col Jock was not supervising the company commanders closely enough. Jock's response was that the companies had to operate independently in support of their respective brigades in action, and that therefore the company commanders had to get used to taking full responsibility now. I agreed with Col Jock.

We were soon out with Divisional and Brigade HQs on wireless exercises, and these later expanded into full scale divisional exercises. On lower establishment, the division had lost 45th Infantry Brigade. In September 1943 we were brought onto higher establishment, with all units being brought up to full strength in men, equipment, and transport. The division consisted of 44th Lowland Brigade, to which 278 Fd Coy were affiliated, and 46th Highland Brigade, to which 279th Fd Coy under Major P.T. Wood were affiliated. 624 Fd Pk Coy under Major Mike Wilkinson joined us as our field park. His 2i/c was Capt Archie Archibald. I remember Archie putting in for leave to get married and then rather sheepishly asking to change the date of his leave because he had miscalculated some vital dates concerning his bride.

6th Guards Tank Brigade joined us, so that we now became a mixed division with two infantry brigades and a tank brigade. But that policy didn't remain for long. 6th Guards Brigade became part of 8 Corps Troops, and 227th Highland Brigade joined us with 20th Fd Coy under Major John Gillington to complete the divisional engineers.

In September, Major General Gordon Macmillan took over command of the division. As a brigade commander in 51st Highland Division he had been wounded in Sicily and was now recovered. He immediately filled us with confidence. At the end of one of our exercises he assembled the whole division for an Assault-at-Arms on Rothbury race course. All the men not taking part watched the proceedings while sitting on a hill overlooking the race course.

The proceedings began with marching and counter-marching by the massed bands of the division. I counted no less than 196 pipes and drums. It was a thrilling sight. This was followed by a variety of competitions, including highland dancing, tossing the caber, tug-of-war, piping, and athletics. One of our sappers won the piping competition rather to the surprise of the pipers of the massed bands. Our sappers put on a display of building a sixty foot Bailey bridge in about forty minutes. The massed bands played again in the lunch interval and again as the sun went down over the rocks of the hill opposite. The effect on morale of this gathering was electric. This was the first time the men realized what a big formation a division is. There were over 18,000 of us sitting on the hill, and this massed band was *our band*! The division never looked back after this.

At the end of September the whole division moved south and HQRE became accommodated in three requisitioned houses just above Kirkstal Abbey in Leeds while Div HQ went into Rawdon, a small town a few miles further west.

There was a tremendous amount of individual training to be done of bulldozer operators, wireless operators, stretcher bearers, cooks, sanitary men, despatch riders, compressor operators, drivers, and so on. For all these, Col Jock would allot vacancies and I would have to see that these were taken up and joining instructions issued. It was quite a business keeping track of them all. Exercises were becoming more and more large scale, and, ambitious and for all these, I would help Jock to work out and order the stores and equipment required and compose the necessary orders.

Soon after arriving in Kirkstal, Jock and I alone of the divisional engineers were put on the Bigot list for invasion planning. The Bigot list was strictly limited to those officers who alone were privy to top secrets concerning the coming invasion of Europe in so far as it became necessary for them to be known.

From now on, Jock and I, who shared an office, worked behind locked doors with a sentry in the passage outside and with the windows blacked out in case someone higher up the hill with a telescope could see into our office. Actually, at this time we only worked on loading tables for the landing ships. In this we had to include provision for the engineer stores we thought we should need in the first few days of the invasion. All we knew at that time was that we were to be a follow-up division whose role would be to break out of the bridgehead to let the armour out, possibly in conjunction with a landing by an airborne division. But we did not know where or when. Apart from minefield gapping stores, it was difficult under the circumstances to foresee what we would need. I know we put in for Armco culverting, and I think for some mines and wire in case we were thrown onto the defensive, but I can't remember what else. Space of course was at a premium.

We also had what were called wireless days when we were not allowed to use the telephone. Everything had to be done over the air in Slidex code in every field formation in the UK. This was to simulate the vast increase of wireless traffic which would occur when the invasion began. If the Germans were made to get used to this, they would not become alerted when the real thing began. Also, during these wireless days, I personally was given certain coded messages to send of which I had not the least idea what they meant but which, as I learnt only after the war, formed part of the huge deception plan master-minded to confuse the Germans as to the time and place of our attack.

At this time Capt Macmannaway, our Medical Officer, became very inquisitive as to what I was doing behind locked doors. I never divulged anything to him. Sometimes he would say, "Oh, I know you are doing the same thing as they are in HQ RAMC," and he would try to infer that he really knew, hoping that this would draw me out. I thought he was just one of the many people in this world who just hate to be left out of a secret.

At about this time the CSM of 278 Fd Coy, Sergeant Major Dunsmuir, whom I knew well, of course, since a year before I had been his acting OC, tipped me off that Major P.....B..... was drinking heavily. I just said to Col Jock, "I think you had better go over to 278 for first parade one morning and see what goes on." I didn't have to say any more. Col Jock knew I wouldn't have said such a thing without good reason. That OC was posted immediately, and his place was taken by Jimmy Osler, a Canloan officer. (i.e. an officer on loan from the Canadian Army because we were becoming so short of suitably experienced officers).

Later in October Win was given leave to come up and stay with me for ten days in Kirkstal, and Jock gave me permission to live out. On the way up from the station, Win and I met Macmannaway in the road outside the house we used as our mess and I introduced her to him.

We stood chatting for a few minutes, and after we moved away Win said, "I wouldn't trust that man." The thought flashed through my mind that perhaps he was not just an idle questioner after all. So next morning I reported the whole matter to the security police and they said, "Thank you very much, we've been waiting to know where he was getting his information from. He writes to his mother who lives in Dublin, and she is passing his information on to the German embassy there." Macmannaway was arrested and taken away that day, and I never heard what happened to him, though I can guess. He was replaced by Capt Mackenzie.

Shortly after, Jock arranged for his wife to join him for ten days, and after enquiring from me whether Win and I had been quite comfortable in the digs I had found, he booked the same accommodation for his wife and himself. Some days after she had arrived, Jock enquired whether the bed we had had was only a three quarter bed. "Yes," I said, "we were alright." Mrs. Millar was a large woman, and I rather gathered that Jock spent most of the nights almost on the floor!

At the beginning of February, the division was visited by General Sir Bernard Mongomery, who, a few weeks before, had been appointed Commander-in-Chief of 21st Army Group, of which we were part. The visit was a most remarkable occasion. About 5000 of us were drawn up near the Headingly cricket ground in six ranks in a three sided hollow square. The senior officers were standing in a single line across the front of the square. These were introduced to Montgomery first. Our front three ranks were then ordered to turn about and break ranks so that Montgomery could pass down the middle like royalty at a garden party. He walked alone very slowly in front of our general and staff officers. His arms were thrust behind his back and his head forward. Not a word was spoken, and he glared at every one of us on either side as he walked. His bright blue eyes seemed to pierce right through to the back of my neck like a challenge.

After that, Montgomery climbed onto the bonnet of his jeep and beckoned us forward so that all 5000 of us were crowded closely round him. He said, "I've come so that I could take a look at you and you could have a look at me. I like very much what I have seen, and I hope you like what you've seen!" He then went on to say that he had observed some apprehension about the coming invasion. This was stupid as the invasion had already begun. "The Air Forces began it weeks ago, bombing the Germans and their defences. I like bombs!" This was said to our men from Glasgow, many of whose homes had been bombed. He went on to express his absolute confidence in the outcome of the projected operations, and he undoubtedly changed all our forebodings into confidence. It was the most effective and astounding morale raising performance I have ever witnessed. Neither General Eisenhower nor Lieutenant-General Sir Richard

O'Connor, our 8th Corps Commander, had anything like the same impact, and I don't remember anything that they said.

Only Colonel Jock seemed to remain somewhat doubtful, although he didn't disclose this to me till we received our final orders just before D-Day, when he said, "So they're really going to go ahead with it." I think all those who could remember the slaughter on the Western Front in the Great War were more aware of the dangers than us younger men.

The biggest exercise in which we took part was Exercise Eagle, held on the Yorkshire Wolds. This included vacating our accommodation and handing back all our furniture and utensils to the barrack officer just as we should have to do when we would leave permanently to take part in the invasion. The whole of 8 Corps, including, besides 15th Scottish Division, Guards Armoured Division, 11th Armoured Division, 6th Guards Tank Brigade, and the whole of Corps Troops which included the Corps artillery and engineers, took part. The "enemy" were to be elements from 9th Armoured Division and 38th and 47th Infantry Divisions, none of which were to take part in the forthcoming invasion. The exercise was to run for twelve days in February 1944, and although the weather was freezing cold and wet, we were all forbidden to take shelter in any kind of building. It was a very big show with at least 100,000 men taking part. It also introduced us to the thrill of armoured movement in mass and the sense of invincibility which it brings. We again did a major night breaching of a minefield exercise to let the armour through.

The CRE of 8 Corps Troops Engineers was Lt Col John Marsh, who was a wealthy man of the "huntin', fishin', and shootin' type" and who liked his personal comforts. He did an appreciation before the exercise began and worked out more or less where he would be. Against orders, he asked a farmer to give him a bed during the exercise, and the farmer's wife promised him a hot bath on arrival and roast chicken for dinner.

One wet and cold evening, one of the fd coys of 8 Corps Troops went into harbor at a farm whereupon the farmer invited the OC in, saying his hot bath was ready and dinner would be ready in an hour's time. After all the officers had bathed and consumed the chicken, John Marsh appeared, but history does not record what happened then!

All through those early months of 1944, the constant juggling with shipping tables went on behind locked doors and screened windows, and between a series of exercises to evolve policy to meet every conceivable situation. By now we knew some ships would leave from London, some from Newhaven, and others from Southampton. The picture and focus was narrowing.

In the middle of March, Jock went away on ten days leave and so I was now the only Bigot officer in the divisional engineers, even though John

Gillington now became acting CRE. So I had to keep the Bigot stuff away even from him. All Bigot officers were summoned to Div HQ in Rawdon, where we were told that the division was to move down to Sussex in early April. A dummy exercise on the Yorkshire Wolds was to be laid on as cover plan. I was to go down to Sussex a day or two later to plan the accommodation for the divisional engineers, but it was to be given out that I was going to do a recce in connection with the dummy exercise. All the usual papers for an exercise came to HQRE, and I had to help John Gillington with the planning for that, well knowing that it would not actually take place.

Early one morning, before there was any traffic about, I left HQRE in the CRE's car with a driver and my batman, Sapper Beveredge. Outside Leeds, I stopped the car and ordered them to cover the divisional signs on the car with materials I had brought along with me. We also removed the divisional signs from our battle dress, to the growing mystification of my two companions. Back in the car, I now ordered the driver to take the Great North Road to London and I'd give further orders there. I ordered them strictly to tell no one where we had come from nor to breath a word to a soul when we got back.

So we arrived at Parham House near Storrington, which is not far from Worthing. There were sufficient Nissan huts in the park, which I allotted to the four companies, together with hard standings for their vehicles. HQRE would be in the grooms' rooms above the stables which were across the courtyard from the house and the officers' mess, and all officers would be accommodated in the house itself. It was a strange coincidence that I should find myself in Parham House, as it had been the home of my great-great-great-grandmother Elizabeth Bishhopp, granddaughter of Lord Zouch of Storrington. Financial difficulties compelled the Bishhopp family to sell the house to Mr. Pearson of Pearson's magazine in 1932.

Mr. and Mrs. Pearson and their two daughters, one of whom had lost her husband at Dunkirk, lived in the other half of the house. They told me we could use the large swimming pool. I did all the usual things, arranging for supplies of rations and petrol, and taking over accommodation stores.

While in the south, I attended at Aldershot a demonstration of a new method of breaching minefields put on by Lt Col H.H.C. ("Boy") Withers, whom I had met as a boy when he played for Blackheath. He and his wife had stayed with us at Murvagh a few days before they went to India in about 1934. Tragically, his wife had been killed in a shooting accident soon after they arrived in India.

In the demonstration, an AVRE tank, that is a Churchill tank converted for engineer purposes, towing an armoured trailer containing three tons of liquid nitroglycerine advanced to a minefield. It then shot out a rocket which towed out a two inch fire hose for a distance of nearly 200 yards. The tank then backed a little to straighten the hose, which it then filled with nitroglycerine which was pumped from the trailer with compressed air. This was then detonated from the tank, and all mines within four yards of the hose on both sides were detonated sympathetically, thus clearing an eight yard gap in the minefield. Anyone familiar with the extreme sensitivity of liquid nitroglycerine will realize what an extremely hazardous operation this was. But the times were desperate and the minefields surrounding our likely bridgehead had to be breached.

We stopped the car again when we approached Leeds and uncovered the divisional signs and sewed the signs onto our battledress again before returning to HQRE.

One morning in the middle of April, having returned all our barrack stores and thoroughly cleaned our accommodation, we moved out in convoy for our exercise on the Wolds. Again outside Leeds, the whole division stopped, top secret orders were broken open, and the true destination was revealed to officers of the division. It was rather sad in a way because, of course, many of the men had acquired girl friends in Yorkshire and they didn't even have the opportunity to say goodbye. But the needs of security were paramount. So it was that we moved south with the divisional engineers accommodated in Parham.

Down in the south we found the whole country packed with troops. Many of the roads were even used as tank and armoured vehicle parks. We constructed dummy hards for loading landing craft on the beaches near Dover. We constructed dummy ships' sides so that the men encumbered with all their equipment could practice clambering down ships' sides on to landing craft. We bulldozed large holes in the ground and flooded them so that the waterproofing of vehicles and the ability of drivers to drive out of deep water could be tested. Everything was provided for and practiced. Our postal address had become "APO Expeditionary Force," and it was obvious that D-Day was not far away.

Early in May, all the officers of the division who were on the Bigot list were summoned to St. Paul's School in London to be briefed for the invasion. This included all officers down to Lt Col and their 2i/cs who were majors. As Jock had no 2i/c, I went and with Patrick Attlee, the GSOIII (Intelligence), who was the nephew of the deputy prime minister, we were the only two captains present. Security was terrific. Each of us was issued with a special pass for the occasion with our photos on it. On arrival at the school, we showed our identity card at the first check and our special pass at the second, where there were armed guards present ready to shoot at once if anything untoward occurred. Then, in the passage leading to the hall, we all had to be identified personally by Patrick before being allowed to proceed to the hall.

On arrival in the hall, we were all at first struck speechless by the enormity of the plan which was portrayed before us, and, after the initial surprise, if I remember correctly, we only spoke with hushed voices. At last we knew where we were going. On an inclined platform which covered the entire stage of the hall, there was a map of Northwest France bounded on the south by the River Loire and on the east by the Seine, and including both the Brittany and Cotentin Peninsulas and Normandy as far as Le Havre. On the map were the phase lines for the objectives for each day up to D+7 and for each week up to D+63, when the Loire and the Seine Rivers would be reached. The landing beaches, Utah, Omaha, Gold, Juno, and Sword, were shown together with the names of the formations which would assault across them, and also the landing zones for the three airborne divisions.

The entire wall at the back of the stage was taken up with a map of the Channel. This showed how all the invasion fleets from every harbor from Cornwall to London would converge in an area at sea off the Isle of Wight called "Piccadilly Circus" and then proceed along cleared channels through the German sea minefields and then diverge to the landing beaches. The positions of the ships of the bombarding fleets were also shown on this map. On either side of it were side drops showing on the one, the heavy bomber program, and on the other, the fighter bomber and fighter program. All round the hall at shoulder height were pinned air photographs, mostly obliques taken at such low altitude that you could see the German soldiers who had been working on the beach obstacles running for cover. Some of these had only been taken the day before.

General Macmillan then briefed us on the entire plan. It was an absolutely staggering revelation, huge in scope and planned in comprehensive and minute detail. The main purpose was to keep the main German forces in the Caen area and to defeat them there so that the Americans in the west, having taken Cherburg, could turn south and break out between St. Lo and Avranches. The whole front would then swing left, with the British 2nd Army holding the hinge about Caen. I do not remember any great emphasis being placed on getting the area south of Caen for the construction of airfields.

Thereafter, my work at Parham grew to prodigious proportions. I used to get to the office at 0900 hours and work through till 0200 hours next morning, seven days a week. In addition to all the normal administrative work of an adjutant, I had all the Bigot filing and typing to do. Having no Quartermaster in the divisional engineers, there seemed to be endless problems from the companies in making up last minute deficiencies. Then there was worry over getting enough materials to complete the waterproofing of all the vehicles. Then, because the Germans were erecting so many more obstacles on the beaches, there was a sudden demand for waterproof charges to demolish them. So thousands of "stooks" had to be made in a hurry. These were little sheet metal boxes with wire legs which could be bent to fix them to the obstacles. We put every available tinsmith and whitesmith onto making these.

I used to have my lunch sent over to me, partly to save time, but also because I was frightened to speak to anyone in the mess in case I let some secret out. I never wish to be privy to a secret again. I rather think the Pearsons guessed my position and were terribly kind to me, and I was welcome to walk in for afternoon tea any time, and sometimes for supper. They were awfully good at keeping the conversation off the war.

My parents came up to London one day, and to my very pleasant surprise, Jock allowed me to go up to meet them. He trusted me completely, and it was a trust I was not likely to abuse. My parents, youngest sister, and I had a picnic lunch in St. James's Park. My father asked, "When's this war going to be over, Dick?" I begged him to keep off the subject as I knew too much. As a soldier, he respected this at once, of course.

Monty came down to see us once more and was quite confident the European war would be over by Christmas and the Japanese war six months later. The division was called together again for an assault-at-arms in Brighton Greyhound Racing Stadium, and we were entertained by our glorious massed pipes and drums once again before going into action.

ENGLAND, SCOTLAND, AND WALES

Homes and Stations 1920-1945

MILES
0   50   100

Stanley 1940

nverary 1943

Glasgow 1945

Kirkcudbright 1940

Felton House 1942

Morpeth 1943

Hurworth 1942-43

Halifax 1945

Kirkstal 1943-44

Skegness 1942

Nottingham 1945

Mabws 1920-1923

Blackheath 1920-32

Woolwich 1938-39

Cheltenham 1932-38

Chatham 1939-40

Winterbourne Gunner 1939

Wouldham 1941-4

Aldershot 1940

Rotherfield 1941

Southampton 1944

Croydon 1940-41

Parham House 1944

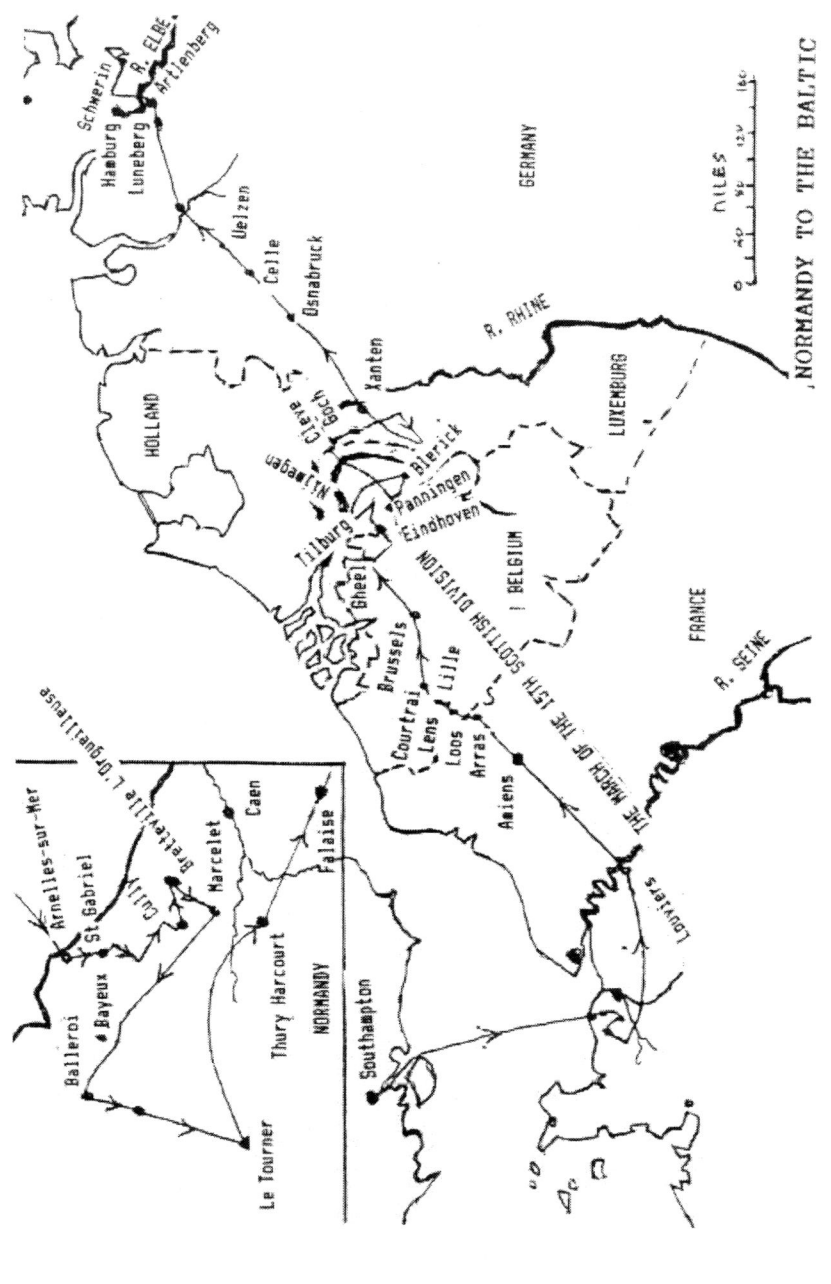

NORMANDY TO THE BALTIC

Chapter Five

Normandy To The Baltic

In the first few days of June, Win went down with appendicitis and had to have the operation. Jock, who must have obtained clearance from the general, since I was fully briefed on all the top secret invasion plans, gave me the exceptional privilege of going to see Win at Skegness. She was recovering well and was her usual cheerful self.

The day after I returned, we received the code word "Edinburgh," meaning invasion at twenty-four hours notice, followed the next day by "Castle," meaning invasion next day and putting us at twenty-four hours notice to move. It was June 5th. Late that night I could hear the roar of thousands of aircraft flying overhead and headed south. Next morning I burst into the subalterns' room saying, "Wake up, wake up, put on the news. You are going to hear the greatest news of your lives." But there was nothing on the 7 o'clock news, and I withdrew shamefacedly wondering what secrets I had let out. But the great news was on the BBC eight o'clock news and all was well.

On June 7th Jock Millar, with 2/Lt Philip Taylor, batman, and driver, left in his jeep as the HQRE advance party. Besides myself, HQRE consisted of 2/Lt Dick Lilley, who was our intelligence officer, 2/Lt Ewen Work, who was a field engineer assigned to assist me, 2/Lt Philip Bull of the Royal Signal Corps, Capt MacFarlane, the medical officer, R.S.M. Burton, who acted as platoon officer for HQRE personnel and organized our close defence, Sgt Bullock, the chief clerk, and about twenty other ranks and signalmen. For transport, besides Lt Col Jock's jeep, we had a lorried command vehicle (LCV), an office lorry, a stores lorry and water trailer, two armoured scout cars and two motor cycles for the despatch riders, and a 15cwt truck for the MO. On June 11th I led HQRE to join up with Main Divisional HQ for the drive to Southampton. It was a most memorable drive. We went with weapons loaded and with a round "up the spout" for the first time away from a shooting range because German parachutists were expected to try to disrupt the movement to the ports. But they didn't put in an appearance.

It was a glorious summer day, and Southern England never looked more beautiful. Somehow the grass never looked greener, hawthorn and honeysuckle were out in the hedges, and wild parsley was flowering in the verges. The scent of wild flowers lay heavy on the air. The gardens of the cottages we passed were ablaze with early summer flowers and a heat haze softened the landscape of hill and woodland in the distance. I think we saw the countryside with a new eye as few of us thought we had a better than one in three chance of seeing it again. Whenever the long column of vehicles, many miles long, checked or halted, the people came running out of their cottages to offer us beer, and ring our hands, and wish us good luck. I found this intensely moving. With the invasion under way, there was a real prospect at last of an end to five years of suffering and deprivation. We bore with us all their hopes — and a great deal of responsibility.

At Southampton, whole streets and the park had been barricaded off with double rows of barbed wire. Anyone attempting to cross between the fences would be shot on sight for security reasons. Within the wire, exact plans of the decks of the landing ships had been painted on the road and also the exact parking place for each vehicle. As we parked on the road so we would park on the ship. This is typical of how detailed and thorough all the planning was.

In the park, tents had been erected and there we spent two rather frustrating and very hot summer days. Desmond Tyler, the GSO 1 of the division, briefed all ranks of Main Div HQ including HQRA and HQRE. Here we also received our French francs and also printed post cards on which we could tell our next-of-kin that we were going overseas and no more.

On June 13th we drove down to Southampton docks, from which we backed our vehicles through the doors in the bows onto an LST and into the same spaces as they had occupied on the road in the marshalling camp. I found myself to be the senior combatant officer on board, and therefore OC Troops, although two lieutenant colonels, Syd Walker ADOS and Whitfield CRASC, were also on board.

In the afternoon we steamed down the Solent, both banks of which were absolutely packed with moored assault craft which had been used on D-Day. In the evening we anchored off Spithead, with the Isle of Wight to starboard and Portsmouth to port because, we were told, German U boats were active in the Channel and had to be cleared out of the way before we could go further. So there we spent the night. I was allotted a very small cabin to myself in the stern of the vessel, directly under an Oerlekon gun battery.

After the best and longest night's sleep I had had in months, I woke up and went up on deck next morning, June 14th, to find that we were now in mid-channel, and an amazing sight awaited me.

We were in a single line of LSTs which at quarter mile intervals stretched to the horizon both ahead and astern of us. Each LST was flying a barrage balloon fore and aft. Our Oerlekon gun batteries were manned both fore and aft. Half a mile away on our port side and at about one mile intervals was a parallel line of tugs with each one towing an enormous concrete section of Mulberry harbor. The sections towered over the tugs and had anti-aircraft guns on top of them. Each tug and section also flew a barrage balloon. Away to starboard, about half a dozen frigates and a destroyer were milling about, presumably on the look-out for German U boats. It was a beautiful, clear summer day with a cool breeze. High above us we saw at intervals allied fighter planes keeping a watch over us. All in all it was a most reassuring outlook.

The first we saw of France was the tip of the Cotentin Peninsula almost on the horizon off our starboard bow. We could see warships bombarding the coast there, or perhaps at Cherbourg.

In the early afternoon the whole expanse of the Normandy coast from the Cotentin to the mouth of the Orne came into view, or rather it should have done! For right across the front there was such a vast concourse of shipping that at no place was it possible to see the beaches!

As we steamed slowly across the channel, we played twenty questions over the ship's loud speakers to amuse the ship's company. I was asked to become a member of the brains trust for it. All the questions we were asked had to do with the war or the armed services and weren't difficult to answer.

As we approached the enormous armada, the nearest ship hailed our skipper to give him directions to reach our anchoring position. "Turn right past the third ship, then round the second on the left, then right round the second one, and so on." As we threaded our way through the armada, it was for all the world like a huge regatta. Our ship and all the others had their wirelesses tuned on to the BBC Forces Programme, and light music and the voice of Vera Lynn wafted here and there across the water. The usual service humor was exchanged as we passed other ships. Launches were carrying senior officers between ships, and, as we got nearer the beaches, we watched DUKWs and Rhino ferries going to and fro taking stores from the ships to the beaches.

Away on our left we could see *HMS Warspite* and other RN ships firing on targets inland. The sheet of flame and smoke as the battleship fired her broadside and the thunderous explosion which reached us over the sea seemed redolent of the power of the allied expedition. This and a few heavy German shells which exploded on the cliff to our right front were the only sights and sounds of the battle in progress.

But when we reached our anchoring position we were in the nearest line of shipping to the shore. The beach was a hive of activity as troops and equipment were marshalled and moved inland past numerous wrecks of landing craft, burnt out tanks and vehicles, and breached beach obstacles. The block ships for Mulberry harbor had already been sunk out to sea behind us, and work was beginning on the beach ends of the floating piers.

We stayed on board that night, either because the tide was too shallow or because it was not yet our turn. As darkness fell, smoke generators were let off by all ships, and soon the whole fleet was shrouded in choking smoke. We were all sent below as the army was not allowed on deck after dark.

Soon an air raid began. The Oerlekon gun battery above my cabin opened fire and my cabin acted like a resonance box for it, and my teeth were just about shaken out of my head. A few bombs dropped close to our ship, and one explosion was followed by sundry metallic bumps and clangs and oaths from above.

Next morning when we came up on deck, we discovered that one of the bombs had cut our anchor cable. Because of this, we had drifted and collided with two other LSTs, so that we were now lying in a triangle of three ships. I'm afraid we in the army rather ragged our skipper, remarking that while he had the whole sea to navigate in, we in the Sappers only had a narrow river, yet he had managed to collide with not one but two other ships. He couldn't disembark us quickly enough.

Meanwhile, we had been getting news by wireless from ashore, and I was concerned as the concentration area near Caen to which we had to go on landing was still in enemy hands. I knew from the planning that every possible space in the bridgehead had been allocated to some formation, installation, or other, and I wondered where I was to lead the troops and vehicles of our LST to.

About 11am on June 15th, our LST ran up onto the beach. I could have landed dry shod by remaining in my LCV but was too excited and waded ashore only knee deep. On the beach I asked the beachmaster, a naval lieutenant, where we were to go. He told me not to worry as our route was marked the whole way to our destination with our red lion divisional signs.

I led the convoy of vehicles off the beach through a gap in a minefield marked with German skull and cross-bones "achtung minen" signs. At the back of the beach was a group of two dozen sappers headed by a second lieutenant and an NCO who were our first reinforcements in the event of our suffering casualties. I thought that landing our first reinforcements before us was really carrying planning too far! Behind some low dunes we turned right along a sandy track, and after half a mile we entered the badly shattered village of Asnelles sur Mer, inevitably promptly renamed by the troops, "A-------s in the Sea."

Just up the hill from Asnelles we turned left into a field where we removed the waterproofing from our vehicles. We also "scrounged" some discarded steel extensions for the sides of the Bren gun carriers which had been used to stop the sea slopping into the guns. These would become extremely useful, as will be described later. We then carried on through narrow windy and dusty lanes and some little villages which had all been rather badly knocked about in the fighting. The French people appeared sullen, and none welcomed us. This might have been due to the damage done to their homes, or because there was fear that this might turn out to be another Dieppe type raid, in which case there would be fierce German reprisals for anyone who fraternized with us.

In the middle of the afternoon, we passed through the small hamlet of St. Gabriel and turned right into the drive of a farm just beyond it. There Jock Millar and Cliff Taylor were waiting for us. We parked under the trees on either side of the drive. We camouflaged the vehicles as best we could, but there was no way we could conceal ourselves from low flying aircraft. Slit trenches were dug immediately, both as defence posts and to sleep in, and I checked the local defence plan with the RSM. All were warned to wear steel helmets after dark because of the shell splinters which descended like hail from the nightly anti-aircraft barrage. The splinters were far more dangerous than the occasional bomb.

HQRA were parked either side of the drive between us and Main Div HQ, who were in an orchard alongside the farmhouse. In and about the farmhouse sundry items of German uniforms were lying about indicative of a hasty departure. There was a burnt out Churchill tank lying in the field on the other side of the lane from us. Otherwise there were few signs of war around us except the endless columns of infantry and vehicles making their way forward along the lane outside the gates. Occasionally we could hear the booming of guns in the distance.

For the next two weeks we were on twenty-four hour ration packs. Each pack consisted of a tin about six inches long, four and a half inches wide, and about two inches deep. The pack contained six boiled sweets, a small bar of highly concentrated chocolate, five Woodbine cigarettes, a folder of matches, and a miniature stove with three tablets of Meta fuel. There were a number of cubes which one flaked off with a clasp knife into water which one boiled in a mess tin on the stove. Three brown cubes the size of dice made tea, milk, and sugar. A cream cube made porridge, a yellow one scrambled eggs, a light brown one minced meat, and a white one mashed potatoes. There was also a pack of four army biscuits which were as hard as iron. After each meal one felt reasonably well satisfied, but soon there was an escape of wind and one felt hungry again. At the end of two weeks we were ravenous. Each day they also gave us a small orange pill in lieu of fresh vegetables. But these caused a very awkward male physiological effect which was most embarrassing, especially to the Highland staff officers who were still wearing kilts. So we did without our "vegetables" after a while. Some said they would save them up till they got to Paris!

Jock and I were soon immersed in planning our first battle which was to begin on Sunday, 26th June. 8th Corps were to attack west and southwest of Caen and its airfield at Carpiquet. 49th Div on our right were to attack in the evening of the 25th to take the Rauray feature from which the enemy would have observation over our battleground. 15th Scottish were to attack through the 3rd Canadian Div holding FDLs just north of a line through Le Mesnil Patrie (inevitably renamed "Mess in the Pantry") and Norrey en Besin on the left. The attack would be mounted with 46th Brigade on the right taking Le Haut du Bosq and Cheux (called "Chucks" by the Canadians and "Shoe" by the Jocks) and the high ground just beyond, and 44th Brigade on the left taking the ridge on which stood the villages of La Gaule and St. Mauvier. 227th Brigade were then to pass through the leading brigades to secure two crossings over the River Odon, which was just a small stream. Thereafter, 11th Armoured Div were to pass through and engage 21st Panzer Div on the high ground about Point 112 beyond the Odon. Simultaneously, 3rd Canadian Div were to begin widening the salient which our attack would create directed on Carpiquet airfield. A regiment of 31st Tank Brigade would support each of our brigades, and the attack would be supported by some 700 guns and the RAF.

The main sapper tasks would be to clear gaps in the minefields, clear the divisional axes, or roads, named "Oban" and "Moon," open cross-country tracks for tanks, and construct two crossings over the Odon for tanks and later for wheeled vehicles.

Jock and I worked for ten days on this and late into the nights. There were constant alterations as the plan firmed up. One of our main concerns was that 624 Fd Pk Coy were unlikely to disembark in time for the battle because of the delay caused by the storm in the Channel which had also badly damaged Mulberry harbor. So we improvised a field park with lorries borrowed from the Div RASC, a few wireless sets borrowed from the Div

R Sigs, and stores supplied by the CE 8th Corps. Cliff Taylor was put in charge of the stop-gap unit.

For their tasks, the fd coys would be in support of their respective brigades. The point arose as to what to do with their administrative personnel and lorries. Jock wanted to keep them out of unnecessary trouble and possible casualties by having them back with the Fd Pk and under our control. The coy commanders supported by their brigade commanders wanted them forward. Eventually the Div Commander decided in their favor and the dye was cast. I suppose we ought to have foreseen this dilemma during exercises and developed an agreed answer, but the problem never occurred to us. But then there is no danger on exercises.

Jock and I went to a number of conferences as plans took shape. He went to the ones with the GOC while I went to the ones chaired by the AAQMG (Lt Col Kingsford Lethbridge, "KL" for short) which were often held at Rear Div HQ. At these conferences, such things as traffic control, and ammunition, supply, petrol, and water points were discussed. Traffic control was important to us as this included which routes were to be developed and maintained by us, and what would be the one-way traffic plan as all the lanes were narrow and would have to carry a far greater weight of traffic than that for which they were designed. Jock and KL did not get on with one another and Jock always grumbled about anything which KL wanted. I had to be very careful not to commit us to any more than the bare minimum at these conferences. I had to resist repeated requests for more than two water points in the Div area so that no more sappers were taken away from operational tasks than was absolutely necessary.

Jock and I worked together on the engineer operation order for the battle. He always wrote the aim himself, and I had only to write down what he had already fixed at conferences with the company commanders at which I had taken down notes.

Nearly every night the Luftwaffe put in an appearance, but with only one or two planes. I disliked being bombed at night as, unlike shelling, one could never tell where the bombs were going to fall. The searchlights and tracers made a spectacular display, but splinters came down on us like hail and were quite lethal. This was where our Bren gun carrier side extensions came in so useful for those who had them. We would prop a pair of them up over our slit trenches with a groundsheet over them to keep out both splinters and rain. Cliff Taylor and Ewen Work got their drivers to drive their Morris scout cars over their slit trenches after they got into them each night. They were awakened each morning by the cars being driven off them. It always amused me to see their tousled heads popping up from the ground as soon as the cars were clear.

Main Div HQ moved up after lunch on June 24th to the small village of Cully about a mile south of the main Bayeux to Caen road and centrally located between Le Mesnil Patrie and Norrey. I led our little HQRE convoy sitting in the front of the LCV.

Owing to the congestion of traffic in the bridgehead, the orders were to keep moving even when attacked from the air. From St. Gabriel, we wound our way southwards through narrow lanes till we struck the main road to Caen, onto which we turned left. This was a Roman road and ran dead straight as it travelled up and down small undulations in the countryside. Behind me the convoy stretched as far as I could see for there were other units behind us.

After a while I could see the crossroads on the top of a rise where we would have to turn right for Cully. From a mile away, whenever we topped a rise, I could see that it was being shelled repeatedly. As we reached the top of each rise I looked hopefully to see whether the shelling had stopped. But it had not.

I wondered what to do if it was still being shelled when we got to it, because the orders did not say whether we should continue when being shelled as well as when being bombed. Looking back, I could see that if I stopped, everything behind me would have to stop, perhaps even as far back as the beaches. Such was the congestion in the bridgehead in those early days there. I decided to drive on and hope that a "stonk" would not arrive just as we were at the crossroads. I told my driver to get through the crossroads as fast as he could make the turn.

As we reached the crossroads, the MP on point duty dived into the ditch, but we couldn't hear the shells coming because of the noise of the engine. I'd left my tin hat in the back, so I shielded my face from glass with my map board. We hurtled right at the crossroads and then left round a small paddock into which a dozen or so shells exploded. Providentially we weren't touched. There was not even a mark on any of the HQRE vehicles.

After we had set up in an orchard at Cully, Jock came in, and I told him what had happened. I asked him if I had done the right thing. He gave me quite a ticking off for risking the entire communications of the Div RE.

I should explain that the LCV had two compartments at the back. The smaller one immediately behind the cab contained two wireless sets and two signalmen on duty. In those days the wireless sets were very bulky. The larger one was a Canadian No 9 set which had a range of a hundred miles or so depending on conditions and was our rear link to the CE at Corps. The smaller one was a No 9 set which was our command set with links to our fd coys, the fd pk coy, and any other Sapper units which were put under our command from time to time. I could also flick this set to listen in to the Div command net for short periods if I needed to.

The two signalmen sat facing me behind a glass screen which would slide open for me to speak to them when necessary. In the rear and much larger compartment, we had a desk which ran almost the whole length of the off side, but with a chair right at the back end of it. On the near side we had a safe at the front end and then a map board which covered the whole of the wall on the near side. Beneath the map board we had made a bunk out of the back seats of two wrecked cars. It was quite comfortable. The CRE and I sat on swivel chairs so that we could turn easily from the desk to consult the maps. Dick Lillie kept the larger map up-to-date with the enemy, and own troops' positions in the whole theatre. I kept the smaller and larger scale map up-to-date with our own Div positions. All the RE Manuals, the Manual of Military Law, and King's Regulations were on a shelf above the screen. Earphones and microphones hung from the ceiling above our two swivel chairs. I usually operated with the command set phones on my head and the rear link phones on my shoulders so that I could switch quickly from one to the other. We also had a phone to the Main Div exchange on a shelf above the desk and between the two windows. When stationary for any length of time, we could get through on the phone to the CE and his staff at Corps. Sometimes if the Div Sigs had a line to spare, they would give us a connection to the fd pk coy.

For the CRE's orders the OC of 624 Fd Pk Coy would sit on the chair at the end of the desk, the three fd coy commanders on the bunk and Jock and I on our swivel chairs.

When we parked, the office lorry with the HQRE clerks backed up to the rear of the LCV. We had a six foot platform to join the two vehicles together and from it steps down to the ground. Also, six foot rods between the two lorries and others parallel to the side of the LCV supported a canvas cover for the IORE's office and the entrance to HQRE.

On 25th June, to our great surprise, a consignment of whisky arrived. It turned out that some welfare organization in Scotland had decided to donate a bottle of whisky each month to every officer in the division. It is the only welfare organization I have ever heard of before or since devoted solely to the comfort of officers.

That sunny evening, the company commanders, Jimmy Osler of 278, P.T. Wood of 279, John Gillington of 20, and Mike Wilkinson of 624 Fd Pk, elements of which had only just landed, came in for a final briefing. Mike had an enormous waxed moustache which he had sworn not to cut till the war was over. Unfortunately, a few weeks later he got too close to a petrol cooker and burnt one half of it off. So he had to trim the other half to match.

After the briefing by Jock, we gave out the whisky and I opened mine and stood drinks all round. When we parted we didn't know quite what to say. "Good luck" seemed rather banal, certainly not "Goodbye," so we just shook hands with one another and left it at that. If I had been a Christian at the time I might have had something better to say.

Next morning, 26th June, our D-Day, we found, as was usually to be the case, that Main Div was slap in the middle of the gun area. The noise had been considerable when 49 Div attacked the Rauray feature and failed to get it the evening before. But it was deafening when all 700 guns fired precisely at 0730 hours to begin the 15th Scottish's barrage. The crack of the twenty-five-pounders firing was so sharp that it hurt ones ears.

It was overcast and raining. So, in addition to the right flank being open and under observation from the enemy on Rauray, the air support had to be cancelled. Nevertheless, the attack went well, supported by the tanks of 31st Army Tank Brigade. But delays were caused by German counter-attacks, particularly from the Rauray feature, and heavy rain was turning everything into a quagmire. A terrible traffic block built up in Cheux where Oban and Moon nearly converged, and both were blocked by fallen houses. Although our sappers were soon at work, the second phase of the attack was so hopelessly delayed that 227 Brigade did not get to the Odon that night.

Dick Lilley, our IORE, happened to be in Cheux when an enemy sniper in an upstairs room further delayed matters by firing on the confluence of the roads. Dick stalked this sniper and eventually silenced him, but not before setting the house on fire. The gunners were not amused by "the ass" who had ruined their observation with the smoke.

We had some sixty sapper casualties that day, many of them amongst administrative personnel of the fd coys. Jock blamed himself for this, but there was nothing more he could have done. I tried to console him, but he remained saddened for weeks. It was his birthday, too.

Next day, the 27th, 227 Brigade fought their way forward and captured one of the bridges over the Odon. The countryside beyond Cheux came to be known as "Bocage" country. It consisted of small fields and orchards barely 100 yards square enclosed by thick, high banks which were bound together by the ancient roots of the hedges which grew on top of them. The red soil made it very like South Devon. These hedgerows were effective anti-tank obstacles and made natural defensive positions for the German infantry. Every hedgerow had to be fought for, and the banks had to be bulldozed by our sappers before the tanks could advance.

Tragedy struck when Brigadier Mackintosh-Walker and his entire staff, who were mounted in a White scout car, received a direct hit from a Nebelwerfer and were all killed. Jimmy Osler missed his way and drove out into no man's land in his White scout car, which was set on fire by a hit

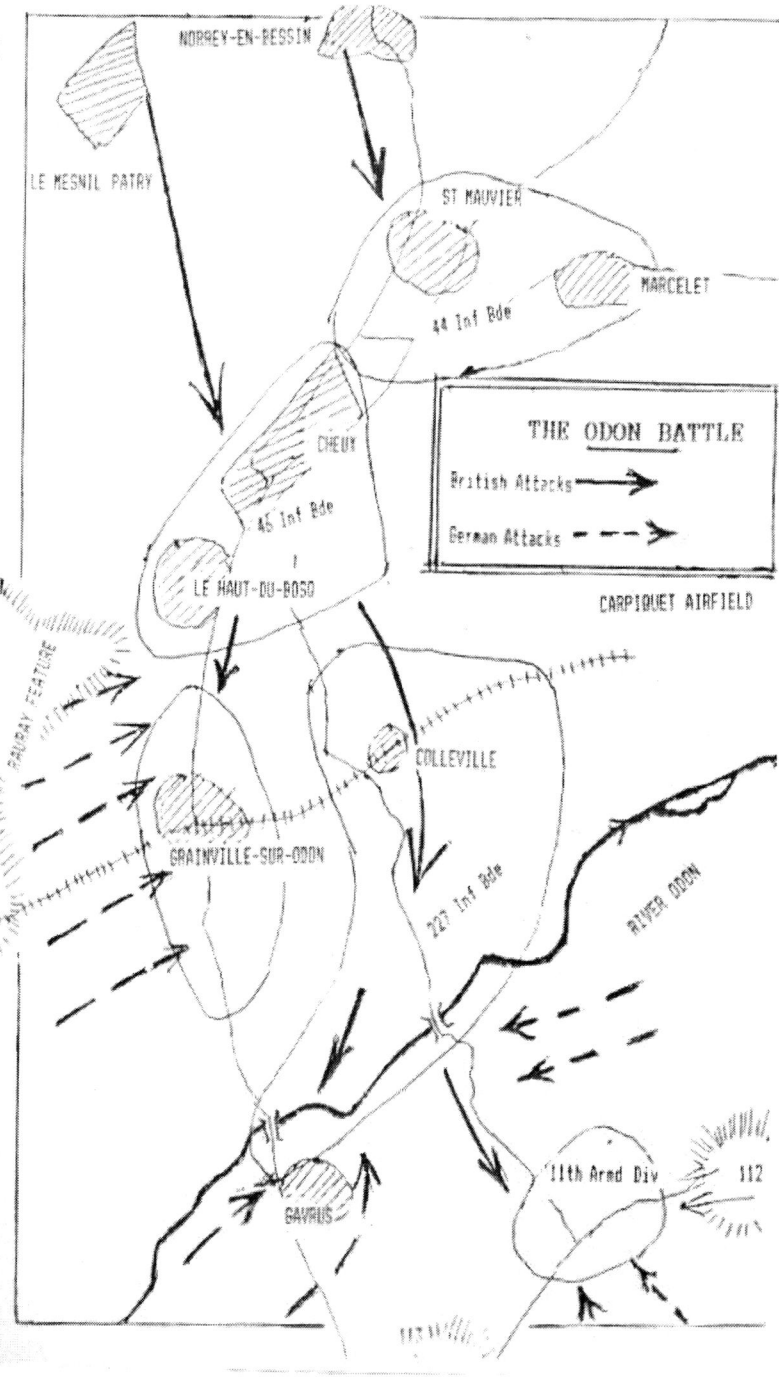

THE ODON BATTLE

British Attacks →

German Attacks ⇢

NORREY-EN-BESSIN

LE MESNIL PATRY

ST MAUVIEU

MARCELET

44 Inf Bde

CHEUX

46 Inf Bde

LE HAUT-DU-BOSQ

CARPIQUET AIRFIELD

FONTENAY FEATURE

COLLEVILLE

GRAINVILLE-SUR-ODON

227 Inf Bde

RIVER ODON

GAVRUS

11th Armd Div

112

from an 88mm gun. He, his batman, driver, and wireless operator were all killed, and their remains could not be retrieved for burial for some days.

The enemy were the 12th SS Hitler Jugend Panzer Div. They were young and fanatical fighters. The rate of fire of their Spandaus was as much as three times as fast as our Brens, so they could always let loose a far denser fire on our Jocks than we could on them. This largely accounts for the reason why quite small bodies of Germans could hold up much greater numbers of British troops.

As the SS soldiers were forced to retire, they left piles of human excreta on the carpets and booby trapped the houses they left. They also left snipers behind in the cornfields which were standing waist high. Some of these would tie themselves up in the trees and fire from there. A despatch rider whom I had sent to one of the fd coys came back with no less than thirteen bullet holes in his motor-bike and its panniers. None had hit him, none had pierced his petrol tank, and two had shattered the bakelite top of his battery without breaking the leads so that the bike was still a runner. The rider had been saved because when he fell off, the bike protected him from the sniper, who was killed when a Sherman tank arrived and opened up on the tree with its heavy Besa machine gun. On his return, the rider was in such a state, not surprisingly, that Col Jock sent him back to the rest camp on the beach for forty-eight hours to get over the shock.

Meanwhile, the 11th Armoured Div were passing through what came to be known as "The Scottish Corridor" and over the crossings we had captured or made over the Odon. They then climbed up Hill 112 on the far side of the river to take on the famous 21st Panzer Div. Very fierce fighting continued throughout the 28th and 29th, with 15th Scottish trying to widen the corridor against increasing enemy strength and pressure and with 11th Armoured battling it out with 21st Panzer.

In the evening of the 29th, both the opposing armoured divisions decided at the same moment that they had lost the battle and withdrew behind their respective infantry. That night the traffic congestion in the div area was indescribable, with our sappers struggling to clear the mines from the verges and to keep the country lanes passable as they collapsed under the weight of traffic. Hedges were also being bulldozed and cross-country tracks were being cleared and marked for tanks.

By the 30th the Germans had concentrated round the corridor the remains of 12th SS Panzer, 21st Panzer, 2nd SS Panzer, 9th SS Panzer, 1st SS Panzer, and elements of 10th SS Panzer, a total of no less than six panzer divisions! They also had two infantry divisions against us there. The situation was becoming very dangerous.

Each day, I collected over the wireless details of what the fd coys were doing, what roads and tracks had been cleared of mines, what stores had been used up and what needed replacing, where and on what the mechanical equipment and tipper trucks were being used, and what casualties to men, vehicles, and equipment had been suffered. So when Jock returned each evening I was able to give him a complete picture of his command. He would then brief the liaison officers who came in each evening from the fd coys on the tasks their coys were to perform the next day.

After dinner, Jock would come back from the GOC's mess with further information, which sometimes meant that I had to send more orders to the coys over the air. We seldom finished much before midnight. The Luftwaffe continued to come over most nights, and occasionally their bombs fell fairly close, but we were never hit. The tracer shells from the light anti-aircraft guns were always spectacular, and the guns made loud crack-crack-cracks as they went off, followed by dull thuds as the shells exploded in the sky above.

After breakfast each morning, Col Jock would give me the latest information from the GOC before setting off on his usual rounds of the fd coys, and I seldom saw him again till evening. He was often out of touch on the wireless, so I had to give decisions on his behalf and in accordance with his orders when necessary. Jock kept me so much in his confidence that I always knew his intentions, and this made it possible for me to act for him in his absence.

The Germans seemed to have as many guns as us, about 1000, but they never could put down a concentration of fire from all of them at once on a single target, as ours could, because of their inferior wireless communications and, I suppose, because of their Teutonic inflexibility. But their guns were supplemented by numbers of six barrelled mortars (Nebelwerfers) which were called "Moaning Minnies" because of the noise they made. They were most unpleasant but did not reach Div HQ. The Odon valley became known sarcastically as "Happy Valley" because of their sustained and very dangerous fire. The railway crossing was a notoriously dangerous spot.

We soon became quite expert at judging what shells would explode close to us. A loud whistle getting ever higher in pitch as it came closer was liable to be dangerous. If in addition you heard a distant plop as the enemy gun fired, it would certainly be close. If it was an 88mm and you heard the shell explode, then the incoming whistle, and then the gun fire, you were certainly safe because the thing had come faster than sound. If you heard a whistle getting softer and decreasing in pitch, it was one of ours going the other way. You could sometimes see the big shells from *HMS Warspite* going overhead, and they made a sort of woob-woob-woob noise. I don't know why it was, but whenever I went to the latrine, which was just a narrow trench over which you squatted, the Germans seemed to send over a stonk. This became such a regular event that the chaps used to warn, "Watch it lads, t'adj is going to the loo!" Suffice it to say that I never suffered from constipation throughout the battle.

On the evening of the 30th, because of the strength of the enemy now deployed against us, orders were given to go over to the defensive, to dig in, lay mines, and to prepare to withstand heavy attacks. There were immediate calls from the infantry for sheets of corrugated iron as the orchards and hedges turned so many of the shells and bombs into air-bursts. This was a need we had not foreseen in England. We had to pull down farm buildings for the iron and scavenge doors from wrecked houses to help the infantry until corrugated iron sheets arrived from England.

The Argyls were ordered to withdraw from their position at Gavrus beyond the Odon where they were practically surrounded, and the CO gave orders for every man to get out that night as best he could. As the CO and 2i/c were crawling through an orchard past German sentries, the CO's alarm clock went off in his haversack! You can imagine the 2i/c fumbling with the straps as he hastened to get the clock out and stop it. But the Germans took no notice. After all, who would expect the Tommies to announce their presence with an alarm clock?

On the 1st July there were repeated German attacks. At 0700 hours the 2nd SS and the 9th SS Panzer Divs came in on the right front north of the Odon, and more panzers came in on the left flank. 227 Brigade in the tip of the salient was almost cut off and 46 Brigade were largely overrun. Altogether, five panzer divs were engaged (1st, 2nd SS, 9th SS, 10th SS, and 12th SS).

A conference was called at Div HQ. I could not get hold of Jock, who was out, actually stopping a bit of a panic on the Div axis, as I found out later, so I had to go in his place. The conference was presided over by the Commander 8th Corps, Lt. Gen. Sir Richard O'Connor. Also present were the GOC 15th Div, Maj. Gen. G.H.A. MacMillan, the GOC 43rd Div, Maj. Gen. Thomas, the CCRA 8th Corps, Brigadier Hammar, the CRA 15 Div, Brigadier Hilton, the Commander 44th Brigade, Brigadier Money, the Commander 31st Tank Brigade, the GSO 1 15 Div, Lt Col Desmond Tyler, the BMRA 15 Div, Major "Flit" Edmeades, and myself, a lowly captain.

Col Tyler, Flit, and I had our remote control head sets with us tuned into our respective command nets. The purpose of the conference was to make a plan to drive the Germans out of the Div area. As each tentative plan was made, news came over our head sets that the Germans had now overrun the proposed start line for a counter-attack. The tension was terrific. It was an eye opener for me to witness the extreme strain endured by higher commanders in such a tense situation. If the Germans got through us, they would be through to the beaches. At one point General MacMillan lost control of himself and shouted, "For God's sake make a plan which will stick. In the meantime we are losing the finest division in Normandy!"

Eventually such a plan was made and 44th Brigade, having been relieved by a brigade of 43rd Div, and supported by the whole of 31st Tank Brigade and all artillery within range, counter-attacked. As they went forward, 46th Brigade, which had been overrun but not mopped up, arose from their slit trenches and joined the attack. At the end of the day the whole Div position was restored and a decisive defeat had been inflicted on the Germans. After this action the German high command knew that they could never drive us back into the sea and that the Battle of Normandy was lost to them. From then on, they tried but without avail to persuade Hitler to order a withdrawal to behind the Seine.

Very congratulatory messages now came in from Gen. O'Connor, Gen. Sir Miles Dempsey, and Gen. Montgomery. For this battle, Col Jock was awarded the DSO and I was mentioned in despatches. But the division had suffered 2720 casualties, mostly amongst our precious infantry battalions. It was after this battle that Rundstedt, in a phone conversation with Kietel, told him, "To make peace, you fools."

The Battle of Normandy was one big battle made up of a number of smaller battles, and it lasted some two and a half months. Gen. Montgomery launched attacks alternately east and west of Caen, forcing the Germans to rush their tanks to and fro to stem attacks by the British and Canadians and to keep them from getting at the Yanks. The break out of the latter seemed to us to be endlessly delayed, so that we had to go on putting in yet more attacks to hold the German army against us. As far as I was concerned, as soon as one battle lasting a week or so was over, Jock and I were busy planning the next, working day after day and late into the night. Once a battle began, there was hardly any sleep at all, just a matter of snatching a few hours when I could. There was really no one I could delegate to, though Ewen Work would man the sets while I took a snooze. I found I could keep going by sipping brandy and smoking a lot of cigarettes. I could not smoke my pipe while a battle was on as I needed both hands to do my work.

It would be tedious to chronicle my further experiences in Normandy in any detail as the work for me was much the same in each battle and in the preparation for it. But there now occurred an incident which was to have a decisive influence on my life.

After the first battle, the division was withdrawn to rest and recuperate, and we found ourselves parked alongside a hedgerow near Bretteville L'Orgueleuse. Jimmy Osler having been killed, a new OC was needed for 278 Fd Coy. As senior captain and as one who had previously been acting OC of that company, I rather naturally expected to be promoted to that post. Already several of my juniors were temporary majors in other divisions. But Col Jock decided to import Charles Nichols, who was SORE 2 at 8 Corps and far senior to me, to fill the vacancy. I was bitterly disappointed. I did what was very wrong and voiced my chagrin before my juniors in our semi-buried officers' mess tent. Coming out of the tent I came face to face with Col Jock, who was in his camp bath a few yards from the tent.

He just looked up at me from under his shaggy, dark eyebrows. For some reason it seemed as if God was looking at me. As I walked on, I was almost overcome by a deep sense of disloyalty for what I had done. Quite suddenly I was overborne with a conviction that if I made my own personal advancement my life's ambition, it would be wrong and selfish, and would inevitably involve climbing up over the backs of other people. Yet I had been taught that an ambitious officer was a good officer. I was very disturbed. Although I didn't realize it at the time, this was God bringing me under conviction of sin for the first time in my life.

I had in my kit my mother's Bible, which she had given me during a leave home in 1942. I nearly didn't take it with me, but then I thought that if I got killed, God wouldn't think so badly of me if a had a Bible with me. I am sorry to say that up till then I had been using it as no more than a good luck charm! But from that day early in July 1944, I began to read my Bible daily whenever battle conditions permitted. Being then still unconverted, it did not have the meaning for me that it should have done. I read it as a drill because I thought I ought to, not because I wanted to, nor because I particularly enjoyed reading it. But at least in retrospect I can see that it was a beginning.

So the Battle of Normandy continued. Jock and I were either up late at night preparing for the next action, or we were sleeping in short snatches while an action was on. I was getting very tired. We were ordered into attack again and again to keep the panzers against us while the American break-out on our right was endlessly delayed, or so it seemed to us. A feeling of unease began to develop, and I remember John and PT asking me if all was well. All they could see was a stalemate, with the countryside becoming more and more blasted and devastated, and with an unceasing toll of casualties. I tried to assure them that all was going according to plan, but I could not divulge to them that there never was any intention to break out at Caen. It was essential to keep the Germans thinking that the break-out would come down the Caen-Falaise road so that their armour would remain against us, and be defeated by us, to allow the Americans to break out on the right.

One day when we were parked in an orchard near St. Mauvier, I was shaving while standing in my slit trench with my mirror propped up against the trunk of an apple tree. My mirror was suddenly broken in half by a shell splinter. I cursed, then corrected myself. I thanked God it was my reflection and not I that had been hit.

The same morning, we saw first hundreds of American Flying Fortresses, and then the Lancasters of Bomber Command flying high overhead to lay the bomb carpet in front of the three armored divisions as they launched Operation Goodwood southeast of Caen. There were so many bombers in the sky that it seemed as if the heavens themselves were on the move. The explosions of the thousands of bombs sounded like a continuous roll of thunder. Whether such an enormous expenditure of effort achieved as much as expected is a moot point, but it certainly did things to our morale.

One was never out of the all pervading dust in Normandy, nor away from the smell of death. Often one would see wayside notices, "Dust brings shells, drive slowly," "Drive slowly, we live here, or hope to," "Caution, enemy can see you," and so on. There were dead animals everywhere, but the smell of dead men was worse. I remember seeing a wayside Calvary with an arm shot off the figure of Christ. This whole terrible battle seemed like a new crucifixion, and I think I did wonder what God might have thought of it.

Another day we had just moved into the grounds of a chateau near Balleroy, between Bayeux and Caumont, and had not yet had time to dig our slit trenches. Suddenly the air raid alarm rattles were sounded, and we all took cover behind the trunks of trees. The sapper cook was behind a tree four or five yards from me. He was a fat cook, and he'd got behind a rather thin tree. At the last second, he decided to join me behind my tree. As he ran across, a Messerschmidt fighter came over the chateau firing its machine guns, and I swear its bullets hit the ground under the cook's heels as he ran across to me. All he got from RSM Burton was, "The next time that happens you'll stay behind the first f---ing tree, otherwise you'll ruin my bloody dinner, won't you, you silly little man!" It's that sort of remark from our warrant officers and sergeants which is so characteristic of the indomitable spirit of the British Army.

One day Dick Lilley came in with an Italian "Regal" mine which had been recovered from a minefield full of them. It was a long, narrow mine with a charge at each end. He dismantled it and wrote a full description of it for our nightly Intrep to CE 8 Corps. A few days later, Dick was killed in a traffic accident whilst riding a motor cycle. He was replaced by a newcomer, Frank Green.

Eventually the massacre in the Falaise pocket occurred. A signal came out from 21st Army Group, calling on every gun and weapon within range to open rapid fire until further notice on an area defined by a series of six-figure map references. There was also continuous bombing by relays of planes. Every time a 10,000lb Blockbuster exploded, it looked exactly as if someone had thrown a pebble up into the sky, as the pressure waves rippled out in ever widening circles through the clouds and even the blue sky. I was sent forward with the divisional assistant provost marshal to find a route forward for the division. So I saw the carnage. Dead men and bits of dead men were everywhere as were dead horses and wrecked tanks and vehicles of every description. It was impossible to move without driving over dead bodies, and the stench was awful.

Next day, 24th August, the advance of 2nd Army to the Seine began. It was led by the Household Cavalry and the Royals in their armoured cars, and the Corps Maintenance Area so that the following divisions could replenish with fuel and rations as they leap-frogged forward. 15th Scottish with 4th Armoured Brigade under command led on the left while a division of 30 Corps led on the right. Because of the carnage on the main roads, tedious diversions had to be made along narrow earth roads winding through woods and forests as we worked our way round Vimoutiers. Even on these side roads, there was everywhere the slaughter, destruction, and stench of war. Overturned tanks, smashed armoured cars, and burnt out transport lined the roads, bearing silent witness to the effectiveness of allied air power.

But at last on the 25th we left behind the carnage, stink, and destruction of Normandy and began a triumphal drive in clean air for the first time since leaving England. We drove through glorious country and reached the Seine late on the 27th at Louviers. It was on this march that we had our first and unforgettable experience of the welcome which was awaiting us in the days ahead — a veritable crescendo of welcome which would reach its delirious peak in Belgium. In every village, even at every crossroads, crowds gathered to shout themselves hoarse in paroxysms of joy. Whenever the column checked the girls rushed forward to embrace and kiss us. We were having a good time through the windows of the LCV when Col Jock appeared, having come up to join us in his jeep. He said, "Now then, enough of that." But when he got back into his jeep, where he was more accessible, he became lost to view altogether under a dozen girls. So we had no more objections to what was going on in the LCV!

No sooner had we reached the Seine than the Corps Commander ordered the division to cross that evening. This meant that the storm boats, which were propelled by Evinrude outboard engines, had to be used immediately after an advance of over a hundred miles over dusty roads. There was no time to test the engines or to run them up, as is the proper procedure, despite Col Jock's vehement protests. The result was that our poor sappers spent fatal minutes feverishly pulling the strings trying to start the engines while the Germans shot them down from the far bank. Eventually enough storm boats were started and went across to enable our infantry to disperse the very light enemy opposition. I doubt whether the haste of the crossing justified the cost in sapper lives.

The following day, Div HQ moved across the river and took up residence in the chateau and grounds of M. Reynault, the car manufacturer, who had been shot by the Resistance a few days before. Madame and madamoiselle were both at home and were apparently quite unperturbed by the recent demise of the head of the house.

We were told that the division was now to rest and no task was foreseen for it in the immediate future. For the first time since the beginning of 1944, the pressure was suddenly lifted off me.

HQRE was parked in the garden and during the day I became terribly ill. I vomited repeatedly and suffered an acute diarrhoea. But worse, I completely lost my memory. I couldn't remember what had happened in the morning, and I couldn't even put a sentence together. I retired shivering to my bivouac shelter.

Jock, coming in from visiting the field companies, saw how I was, immediately vacated his room in the chateau, and had me carried in while he made do in a bivouac. This was so typical of him and his care for all under his command. He called the ADMS, Col Richardson, to see me. I must have been given a sleeping pill and something to hold my insides together, for I slept solidly for two days and nights. When the division moved, I was allotted an ambulance to myself and did the advance from the Seine lying in the back of it. After a day or so I was well enough to sit in front with the driver, and so witnessed the feverish welcome we received from the people who lined the road with hardly a break all the way across Northern France.

On 6th September we passed through all the battlefields of the Great War in the course of a single afternoon. Our route took us through Arras, past the damaged Canadian War Memorial on Vimy Ridge, past the slag heaps round Lens and Loos, through the industrial town of Lille, and then across the frontier to the southern suburbs of Courtrai. The crowds were even more rapturous as we crossed the frontier, as if the French, with their farewells, wanted to outdo the Belgians with their welcome. There were national flags everywhere. Not a house was without one, and some of the flags were huge. How the people had managed to keep this enormous quantity of flags hidden from the Germans remains a mystery to me.

The Germans still occupied the northern half of Courtrai. So next day we travelled northeast to head off the Germans who were trying to get back to Germany from the coast about Calais. For once we were on the higher ground, and our gunners had a fine time, whenever there was an opportunity to unlimber, shelling enemy convoys on the roads across the plain to the north of us. Eventually the division was strung out in a long line to make a cordon to block the way back to Germany. Even we, in Div HQ, came into line on the old battlefield of Oudenarde. Fortunately, whenever a German van bumped into the slightest resistance, it sheared off towards the northeast. But we didn't realize at the time that their main forces were escaping into Holland across the lower Scheldt.

We entered Brussels not far behind 11th Armoured Division, who had led the advance from the Seine to Antwerp in the fastest advance of military history, faster even than the Yanks under Patton. The population of Brussels was still absolutely delirious with joy. All day, street and cafe orchestras were playing the songs of 1939 and before, having been cut off from everything else since, and the girls were investigating what lay under the kilts. Altogether it was a hilarious time.

By contrast, we were parked in the northern outskirts of the city just a short distance from the now empty Breendonck concentration camp. This was an old semi-buried fort. There were tiny cells in semi-darkness in which a man could hardly lie down. There were no sanitary facilities, and the cells reeked with filth. Food was pushed in through a little trap in the bottom of the door onto the floor. In the centre of the fort there was a torture chamber equipped with a rack, thumb screws, and chains to secure prisoners to the walls while they were flogged. With typical Teutonic thoroughness, there were runnels in the concrete floor to flush away the blood. Outside in the yard, half-a-dozen twelve inch by twelve inch baulks erected upright had been almost shot through by the bullets of the executioners. There were bodies in a mass grave outside the fort.

A few days later, we moved up to the Dutch frontier, where we were again welcomed by crowds which even rivalled those on the French-Belgian frontier. It was intoxicating stuff. But almost immediately the division bumped into determined resistance just when we thought the war was over, bar the shouting.

Our leading infantry battalion had taken over a bridgehead south of Gheel over the Albert Canal. On 13th September the Div Commander decided to advance rapidly to rush a crossing over the next canal to the north, which was the Junction Canal, before German resistance could stiffen further.

But German resistance, provided by paratroops, was very determined indeed, supported as it was by guns of every calibre up to the heaviest from the German artillery school at Turnhout. Against this, we were restricted to only six rounds per field gun per day, and no medium artillery. This was due to Eisenhower having dispersed his forces over the whole front from the coast to Switzerland, so that all his armies ran out of ammunition and fuel at the same time, just when we had the Germans reeling and awaiting only a knock-out blow. But for this appalling generalship, the war would have been over before Christmas, as Montgomery had predicted before D-Day.

As it was, we got a small bridgehead over the Junction Canal but could not expand it despite heroic efforts by the Jocks, by 279 Fd Coy and P.T. Wood, who had to get weapons and supplies across to the bridgehead under unchallenged artillery fire and even machine gun fire. He had later to evacuate the Jocks and their weapons under the same fire when the bridge had to be abandoned. I remember P.T. coming into the LCV after this ordeal with his eyes sunk back into his head with exhaustion, saying, "I don't know why I'm still alive." He was recommended for a VC but was awarded a DSO and immediate promotion to Lt Col, a very near miss from the highest award. During this battle, Cliff Taylor was wounded with a shell splinter which penetrated a lung. He was evacuated to England and was replaced by John Hinton.

The loss of assault boats and bridging equipment from enemy fire during this operation was so serious as to cause the CE 12 Corps, Brigadier Parker, great concern. I remember him coming to our LCV and asking Col Jock what to do next! To add to our difficulties the Germans flooded the approaches to the canal to a depth of five or six feet, even drowning one of our bulldozers before it could be evacuated.

One morning the CE rang up Ewen Work, who was relieving me in the LCV, to enquire what the level of the water was. Ewen, wakened from sleep, replied that he couldn't tell because it was still dark. "Well, let down the black out shutters, you ass; it's eight o'clock in the morning!" was the opening salvo he received from the brigadier.

On 17th September, during the later stages of the fighting in the bridgehead over the Junction Canal, we witnessed the enormous aerial armada which transported the airborne army to Arnhem, Nijmegen, and other points to the south and nearer to us. There were just hundreds and hundreds of planes spread right across the sky.

Very soon we got orders to abandon the bridgehead and side step to our right. So we crossed the canal further east behind 30 Corps and advanced northwards past the Phillips Works and halted just north of Eindhoven. Still under command of 12 Corps, we were committed to widening the left flank of the corridor up to Arnhem. Our infantry were soon engaged in a fierce fight for the village of Best. The village was divided in half by a very large square. The Germans held the northern half while our Jocks had taken the southern half. At the left end of the square in no-man's-land was the railway station which contained large quantities of nylon stockings from Bata's factory. All of a sudden in the middle of the battle some American paratroops appeared in their jeeps and drove across the square to loot the stockings. Both the Germans and the Jocks opened up on them, both being determined that whoever got the stockings, it wasn't going to be the Yanks! In fact, it was the Jocks.

While this was going on, I was sent on a recce up the corridor to Moll near Nijmegen. It was quite a hazardous business because the situation was very fluid and the road was often being cut by German counter-attacks. In fact there was a German supply dump halfway up the corridor, and both the Germans and ourselves were drawing rations from it. The German quartermaster was still in charge of it, and all he was concerned with was to get a signature from whoever drew supplies, whether German or British, so that his books would be straight for whoever finally captured the dump. So British and German signatures alternated in his book!

Anyway, on the way back from my recce, I said to my jeep driver that I was sure that we were on the wrong road. He assured me that he recognized the windmills, but we were too recently in Holland to realize that there are windmills on every road. Soon we were on a road on which there were no unit signs, and later there were twigs on the road, a sure sign that no one had been along it recently and that it had probably not been checked for mines. I was sure now that we were on the wrong road and told the driver to stop at the next village for directions. We came to a crossroads with a few houses round it and were immediately welcomed by the inhabitants with hugs and kisses from the girls. It was an uncomfortable feeling to realize we were the first British there. When we managed to break free from their embraces, we enquired where we were. On checking with the map, we found we were miles behind the German FDL's!

So I told the driver to drive fast westwards and to stop for no one. We got back into the corridor without seeing either a German or a British soldier! That's how fluid the situation was.

"By now 15th Scottish was long overdue for relief. For a hundred days it had never been out of range of the enemy's guns. In that time it had had only one week's rest. From the Seine it had come 400 miles with no rest at all. It had had no time whatever to assimilate the countless small drafts that it had received. Exhausted, weak in numbers, and inadequately supported, the Division had found itself pitted against young and fanatical troops in extremely strong defensive positions. It had fought on devotedly. So long as it was called upon to do so, it would still fight on - but to ever lessening purpose. Soon its fighting would serve merely to lengthen its casualty lists still further.

"Such were the views on the state of the Division which the Divisional Commander had already put to the Corps Commander who had satisfied himself that these views were sound. The 15th Scottish was to be relieved at last." (Quoted from the History of the 15th Scottish Division by Lt Gen H.G. Martin, CB, DSO, OBE.).

Div HQ moved to Gemeert, not far from 2nd Army HQ at Helmond, and I managed to beat the general to the local gin shop, where we set up HQRE. The shop owners were very hospitable, and they had a lovely, warm lounge where they revitalized us with "Tiger's Breath," which was a mixture of Bols gin and Bols brandy. It was a real tonic after the cold outside. For the first time since leaving England, we slept indoors and on beds. It was marvellous, and we were so grateful to our Dutch hosts.

Soon Jock and I were involved in planning an advance from Best to Tilburg. It was going to involve the construction of a number of Bailey bridges. The advance began on 22nd October, and even more bridges had to be built than we had foreseen. On my initiative, we dumped the emergency Bailey equipment which we carried in 624 Fd Pk Coy and sent the Bridge Platoon lorries back to collect more Bailey equipment from the 21 Army Group dump near Brussels. That and our own emergency equipment saved the day, and the division took Tilburg with minimal damage to the town on 27th October.

I entered the town quite soon after it fell. The people were mad with joy. A bank manager accosted me in the street and said, "I have a beautiful wife and a beautiful daughter, which would you like to sleep with tonight?" I thanked him but said I thought it was rather early in the day to think of such things. That evening I shared a room with Robbie Ewbank (later Gen. Sir Robert Ewbank and president of the Officers Christian Union). Robbie was then 2i/c of 42 Assault Engineer Regiment, one of whose squadrons had been supporting us in the advance. I remember Robbie asking our hostess whether there was a curfew in the town. She replied in her broken English, "Oh yes, it's under the bed!"

Later that evening, the whole division was celebrating its liberation of a major Dutch town in fine style. Our particular party broke up singing "God save Lloyd George," and one can understand the Dutch being somewhat confused, especially on such an occasion.

Then about midnight we suddenly got orders to move immediately as a German counter-attack had broken through the American 7th Armoured Division and was threatening 2nd Army HQ at Helmond. It can be imagined what a problem it was to round up mostly inebriated Jocks from parties all over town, and the more amorous from even more inaccessible places.

The seventy-two guns of the divisional artillery were away well before dawn, followed closely by 227 Brigade and Div HQ. It was a fast career from the west flank of 21 Army Group to the east flank. I saw my first flying bomb on its way to Antwerp or England as we drove across. It turned out that the US 7th Armoured had panicked before the German attack and run away, leaving many of their Sherman tanks for the Germans to use against us. These were soon destroyed by our guns firing over open sights. As the Germans were driven back, we occupied the positions previously occupied by the Yanks. The mess was indescribable. The litter from their K ration packs and other rubbish was scattered everywhere. They must have been the most undisciplined mob that ever campaigned. We heard that their commander and several senior officers were sacked soon afterwards.

This reoccupation involved battling in bitterly cold, wet weather over the bleak and desolate flat Dutch landscape towards the Deurne Canal in the east to its junction with the Noorder Canal, which ran back to the southwest and constituted the right flank of our advance. The whole area before the Deurne Canal consisted of "De Groote Peel," a vast peat bog, over which the few tracks ran on raised embankments. The Germans from the far bank of the Deurne Canal had observation over the whole area, particularly over the limited tracks. They also had more artillery and mortars than we had experienced since Normandy, and movement along the tracks brought down heavy concentrations from the Germans, who apparently had unlimited ammunition.

In order to supplement the few tracks, and in order to produce a road which was not up on high banks exposed to enemy fire, an attempt was made by our sappers to build a road across the bog. Army track, laid with pre-bituminised sheets was laid as a base for corduroy track but everything just sank into the bog despite tons of hardcore being dumped on top of the corduroy. We were only saved in the end when the whole place froze solid, and then one could drive anywhere over the bog.

In November I was sent to do a recce in a US Armoured Div area. They were holding the line of the Noord Canal south of Weert. For this trip, I had to cover my British uniform with my trench coat and wear one of those Yank chamber pot helmets, which was not much to my liking. The possibility that 15 Div was to do an attack through their area was to be kept secret. My driver and I drove across in a jeep, and I reported to their Div HQ expecting to be told where their combat command HQ was on my way forward. But this they would not divulge. In the British Army, one first reports to the div HQ, then the brigade HQ, then to the battalion HQ, and finally to the company HQ, so that everyone knows who you are, and you know where you are so that you don't get lost. Instead, I was directed right to their leading troop, which was in a small village called Elst about 2000 yards from the canal.

I approached the village, which turned out to be only a few houses grouped round a crossroads, with caution, as I expected the village to have all round defence, with guns covering my approach. But not a bit of it. I came slowly up to a camouflaged tank parked in a garden beside the road and facing the direction from which I had come. I got out of the jeep and walked across to the tank, but there was no one in it. We then drove on a few yards to the crossroads and stopped. Then we could hear voices and singing coming from the estaminet across the road. Inside, I found the whole troop playing crap with their officer.

When I told him I wanted to go to the canal to do a recce for a bridge, he told me I couldn't do that as the "krauts" were in the woods on this side of the canal. I told him that my information was that they were all on the other side of the canal. He replied that he lived here and ought to know. So I conceded the point, and he said I could go as far as his leading tank. At my request, he came with me to it. It also was unmanned, and so there was no one looking out towards the enemy. Ahead of us there was some flat, open ground for about half a mile, and then there was a quarter mile band of pine trees along this side of the canal. There was absolute silence. No guns of any sort were being fired by either the Germans or the Yanks, and through glasses I couldn't see any signs of enemy occupation of the wood. I asked the Yank officer if he would give me an escort to try to get to the canal as I had only my driver with me. He declined, and so I asked him please to man the tank so that he could give me covering fire if I got into trouble. This he agreed to do, but with a bad grace.

So my driver and I squirmed our way forward in the only cover there was which was in the ditch, half filled with freezing mud and water, alongside the road. We saw no sign of the enemy, but when we got to the wood we could hear lots of German voices singing straight ahead. Through the trees, we could see the canal, which ran between high banks above the level of the ground. So we crawled forward and up the bank and under cover of the bushes which were growing there. Peering over the top, we could see a whole German company digging in on the opposite bank. They had their jackets off, many of them were smoking, and no one was looking our way. So with my compass I took the measurements I needed from two points on our bank, and then returned to the village. The tank had not been manned. I told the Yank officer what was going on opposite to him and suggested that he call on his artillery to put down a stonk on the Bosch. "Aw, if we fire on them, they'll fire on us!," he replied. "But isn't this what war is all about?," I asked, but to no avail.

I had to do a similar recce further along to the right. So I asked the Yank who was on his right and where they were. He didn't know the answer to either question. So I went along a track about 2000 yards from the canal but there was no other way down to it. On the way back, a Yank sergeant came out of a house I had passed previously on the arm of a Dutch girl. When I asked him what he was doing there, he replied that he belonged to the outfit in the orchard over there. As I had seen the tracks of tanks which had clearly vacated the orchard, I told him his unit had gone. I then noticed a track leading towards the canal alongside the house and proposed to explore down there. He warned me not to, as they had laid mines there the day before. Contrary to allied orders, these were not marked.

When I reported back to Col Jock, I told him that a whole Bosch army could be massing against those Yanks, who would not know what hit them before the Germans were on them. It was not surprising that this is precisely what happened in the Ardennes a few weeks later.

We fought our last battle that year on 3rd Dec. when we drove the last Germans over the Maas from Blerick. The capture of Blerick was a textbook operation carried out entirely from armoured vehicles. Blerick was protected by a minefield and an anti-tank ditch. Covered by our usual artillery fire, six troops of flail tanks, put under our command from 79th Armoured Div, flailed six gaps in the minefield, setting off the mines with their flails as they went. At the ditch, they parked themselves in parking places which they flailed clear for themselves. From their positions they also gave covering fire with their turret guns. Following the flail tanks came AVREs from the armoured fd sqn placed under our command for the operation. The AVREs now came up past the flail tanks and dumped the huge fascines they were carrying into the ditch, and then parked using their machine guns to keep the enemy's heads down. Following the AVREs came our sappers mounted in kangaroos, from which they banged in specially long pickets to mark the edges of the cleared lanes. Following them came the gun tanks of 3rd Tank Brigade and our Lowlanders mounted in more kangaroos, which took the infantry straight on to their objectives. Blerick was captured with the loss of only fifty lives. It was in my opinion our most successful battle of the war.

We then went into winter quarters with the division spread out along a twenty mile front on the Maas and Div HQ in Paningen, about four miles short of Blerick. HQRE was accommodated in the school, which was minus its windows, and the officers bedded down in the convent. We occupied the upstairs rooms while the nuns kept downstairs. There wasn't a pretty one amongst them, or she was kept hidden from us. We soon got glass substitute for the windows of the school and convent, but it was bitterly cold all that winter with the ground frozen hard.

On 16th December there was great excitement when something like twenty Luftwaffe fighters came screaming in low over the Div area. Our ack-ack guns shot down several, but the RAF were caught on their airfields and many of our fighters were destroyed on the ground. The cause of this excitement was the German Ardennes offensive which began that day. It never worried us unduly as we were quite sure that Monty would see the Huns off alright, which he did with US troops under his command.

On that day also, and of more immediate concern for us, there was a ballot for ten days leave in the UK. I drew one of the later dates, which was in April.

The Germans used to shell us every day. But they were so stupid that they invariably shelled us precisely at one o'clock. The shells, and they were big ones, never came a minute too soon nor a minute late. So one just went for lunch before or after one o'clock and took care never to be in the open at one o'clock.

At Christmas, the staff officers in Div HQ put on a pantomime which was called "Ginderella or Piss in Boots." It was quite hilarious, and Col Jock almost stole the show with an excellent exhibition of tap dancing on the top of a barrack table. I would never have expected this from my staid elder of the kirk and beloved colonel.

One morning in the middle of January, we woke up to find that there had been a sudden and very rapid thaw during the night. Before I knew what had happened, my phone was going incessantly with calls for sappers to come and clear mines. It turned out that the whole division had been sitting on a minefield all winter, and now that the ground had thawed, men and vehicles were blowing themselves up all over the place. Not a single path or track which had been used all winter, not even the track to the latrine, was now safe. Everywhere had to be checked. It was a most uncomfortable morning, and we suffered several casualties in the division.

In about mid-January, Col Jock went off on his ten day UK leave and on the 24th we moved to a monastery near Tilburg. There we began planning the battle to breach the Siegfried Line east of Nijmegen. P.T. Wood from 279 Fd Coy became acting CRE, but as he was busy with his brigade commander, most of the load fell on me, and in any case I knew all the Div staff intimately. All the officers of the division were addressed in a cinema in Tilburg by Gen. Sir Brian Horrocks, the Commander of 30 Corps, which we were to join for the battle. I remember him saying, "This is going to be the biggest battle of the war even though the Marshal won't admit it." (Monty would never concede that anything was bigger than Alamein). "No battle has ever been launched under more propitious circumstances. The 5th and 6th Sugar Sugar boys (i.e. the 5th and 6th SS Panzer Armies) after their fray in the Ardennes have gone back to the Russian front." The overall plan was for 1st Canadian Army to attack east and southeast from Nijmegen, with the Maas on its right and the Rhine on its left, while the 9th US Army were to attack across the Roer River some fifty miles further south and advance northeast to meet us coming down from Nijmegen. Practically all the divisions of 2nd British Army were put under command of the 1st Canadian Army, while the rump of the 2nd Army were to hold the line of the Maas in between the two wings while its HQ began planning the Rhine crossing.

The German defences in front of us were formidable. They began with a strong outpost line just beyond the Canadian FDLs east of Nijmegen, then nuisance mines, then a continuous minefield some 2000 yards deep, then an anti-tank ditch with, behind it, the huge concrete pill boxes of the Siegfried Line interspersed with houses whose cellars had been strengthened and converted into machine gun nests; these last fortifications stretched south from Kranenburg. Behind these fortifications were more scattered minefields, a fortified line running north and south through Cleve, and finally the Hochwald Forest lay-back position some twenty miles beyond our start line. In the centre of the German front, and stretching back to Cleve was the Reichwald Forest, which created a complete obstacle to tanks. The whole battlefield was covered with snow, and it was difficult to read the air photographs. It was assumed that the frost would continue throughout the battle.

Col Jock went down with a bad go of flu when he got back from leave, and so I was left very much on my own to coordinate the RE plan, and I wrote the operation order myself.

1st Canadian Army was to attack with five divisions abreast which reading from right to left, were, 51st Highland, 53rd Welsh, 15th Scottish, 2nd Canadian, and 3rd Canadian. So 15th Scottish were right in the centre and had the major role of opening the main road and capturing Cleve, and in particular the Materborn Feature which we must get before German reinforcements arrived. The feature lay between the northeast corner of the Reichwald Forest and the town of Cleve. It was approximately eight miles from our start line!

We moved up to Nijmegen during the night of the 5th-6th February, and I got our LCV in under the concrete canopy of a petrol filling station in the eastern suburb of the town. I felt nice and safe under there. Just behind us was a battery of medium artillery, and as usual we were in the middle of the gun area of a total of 1300 guns of all calibres up to 210mm. In front of us was a terrace of houses quite undamaged by the fighting of the previous autumn.

Then the thaw began, and the sky was overcast with a drizzle falling throughout the 7th. So as usual, the air support was somewhat curtailed as the weather continued bad on the 8th. Cleve and other towns ahead of us were bombed that night by Bomber Command, and we could see the eastern sky lit up by the fires in Cleve.

At 5am, all 1300 guns fired at exactly the same second. The concussion was so terrific that all the slates slid off the roofs of the terrace houses opposite, together with the glass from most of their windows, and we seemed momentarily to be lifted off our feet. The guns continued without cease for the next five hours. At 9am two machine gun battalions, each with seventy-two machine guns, and two light AA regiments, each with fifty-four Bofors guns, which had been moved right up into the FDLs, opened rapid fire over open sights at the enemy for one hour. At 9.40am a Canadian battalion equipped with lorry mounted rockets shot off their rockets and reloaded in time to get off another salvo precisely at 10am. Precisely at the same minute, H Hour, all guns fired simultaneously again, and the infantry began their attack under the cover of a creeping barrage which, together with concentrations of fire, lasted another five hours.

Under this bombardment, the German 84th Infantry Division virtually ceased to exist, and prisoners came in terribly shell-shocked. But with the thaw and the drizzle, the whole place became a quagmire: the flail tanks bogged down and the mines had to be cleared by hand. Nevertheless, the second phase of the attack, which involved breaching the main minefield and making crossings over the anti-tank ditch, went very well with a repeat of the successful Blerick operation.

We only had one road forward, and the congestion became appalling. The SORE 2 at Corps, Major Cave Brown, gave me a company of pioneers to fill in the railway so that we could use it as a second road. After Kranenburg, we also found a secondary road round the southern outskirts of Cleve. As information came in I marked on a mosaic of air photographs what roads had been cleared of mines, which also had their verges cleared, and which were suitable for forty ton and which for nine ton traffic. Apparently my reports on the roads were the only ones to reach 30 Corps HQ. A further worry was that the Germans had opened the Rhine flood gates, and all the land on our left, except the villages, where the Canadians were operating was under water. They had to assault each of these villages in turn, being transported from one to the other in amphibians.

We moved up to the outskirts of Nutterden on the 10th, and then the floods closed the road behind us. From then on the whole division was supplied by DUKWs. But at Nutterden we literally hung up our washing on the Siegfried Line! Col Jock rejoined us there.

15th Scottish continued to fight a series of messy and bloody engagements towards the Hochwald Forest while we moved up to Cleve, where we occupied a large house which clearly belonged to a colonel in the SS. There were lots of photographs of Nazi rallies and others indicating that the fellow was a homosexual. We also found a Nazi leaflet which revealed all the secrets of the Freemasons. One day we were visited by the CE 30 Corps, and Ewen Work stood with his feet at right angles to one another. To his horror, the brigadier responded. "For goodness sake don't leave me alone with the brigadier, he thinks I'm a mason, and I'm not!," Ewen later pleaded. When we left, we set fire to the house and burnt it down as we were revolted by the character of its owner.

Later the division's axis was turned south, and we moved to Bedburg just South of Cleve. From here we saw the first jet propelled ME 262s streaking across the sky. Our gunners were completely perplexed by their speed as the AA shells were exploding miles behind them. Then we moved to the gun area just north of Goch which was still held by the enemy. I was amazed to see elderly German men, and women and children, coming out to watch our guns firing on their army and even appearing to applaud our efforts. It seemed they would cheer any army as long as it was a good one!

A problem was where to build a bridge over the river which ran round the northern side of Goch. The air photographs indicated that the best access seemed to be blocked on the far side by some sort of building across the road. So I referred to the TIS dossier (Theatre Intelligence Summary) which I have not mentioned before in these pages. But months before D-Day, 21st Army Group had appealed to the general public to send in any holiday snaps and picture postcards they had of anywhere in Europe. These, together with an immense amount of information, had been reproduced in TIS dossiers. Sure enough, in the TIS dossier there was a holiday snap of an ancient archway over the road in Goch. A few measurements confirmed that it was wide enough and high enough to take all our vehicles and tanks. So that settled the bridge site.

For once, a few days later, Col Jock took me with him in his jeep to inspect a bridge which 278 Fd Coy had built across the river to the east of Goch. When we got to the bridge, we found no bridge guard had been posted, and tools and spare bits of Bailey equipment were lying about all over the place. This led to some critical remarks from us both. Just then a shell fell in the river a few yards downstream, followed by another a few yards upstream. It seemed pretty obvious that these were ranging shots. At last, to my considerable relief, Jock said, "I don't much care for this." To which I replied, "Nor do I, Sir." Jock started walking up the road away from the bridge; neither of us would run but we walked faster and faster. We just got round a building before about sixty shells landed on or about the bridge. There we found the sappers sensibly under cover till the shelling ceased. Jock never took me with him again as it wouldn't do for both of us to get knocked out together.

That night, RAF Bomber Command were to attack the next town south of us on the river. Unfortunately, one squadron bombed short and some 10,000 pound blockbusters landed amongst 51st Highland Div on our right, and their CRE, amongst others, was killed. Even where we were half a mile away the ground shook under our feet.

The US 9th Army, having failed to capture the Roer dams before the winter as they had been urged to do by Monty, were faced with an impenetrable flood when the Germans blew the dams, and so they never crossed their start line. So the right wing of our battle never even got started. The result was that all the German reserves were free to come up against us. These were destroyed principally by 15th Scottish, 51st Highland, and 43rd Wessex Divs as they arrived on the scene. When the flood eventually subsided, the US 9th Army were able to cross almost unopposed and drove up to meet us against no opposition, and once again we were accused of being slow!

The last action fought by 15th Scottish in this battle was to clear the high ground southeast of Goch so that 51st could advance next day down the valley to the south of the town. I attended the GOCs orders, in which he said, "15th Scottish will take hill UVW, and if any of them are left (!), they will exploit to hill XYZ." We had already suffered casualties on a scale which we had not endured since Normandy, and the total for the operation came to over 1500 killed, wounded, and missing. Many decorations were awarded, and I received the MBE at the personal instigation of the Corps Commander, Gen Sir Brian Horrocks. On 26th February we were withdrawn at last from the battle and went to refit at Tilburg.

Two weeks later we moved down to the Maas near Roermond to train for the Rhine crossing and to plan the battle. In order to build the three bridges and build and operate all the ferries which would be required, as many sappers were put under command of the division as there were infantry in it. In consequence, Lt Col Jock was as it were "huffed" by Col Ronnie Foster and his staff, who were put in command of the engineer operation. This was not a satisfactory arrangement as Foster and his staff lacked the mutual trust which had been built up over years between us and the Div staff. It was the consequence of the divisional CREs being under-ranked throughout the Second World War. Nevertheless, Foster was an outstanding officer, his staff were very efficient, and all went well. With someone lacking Jock's humility things might not have gone so well. Our sappers took no part in the crossing as they were made responsible for clearing mines and opening roads on the far bank. The battle began on 23rd March.

To build the ferries and bridges, 1200 three-ton lorry loads of equipment were required. Four hundred lorries were available, and these had to be reloaded twice during the operation. Each load had to arrive at the right ferry or bridge site in the right order at the right time. These lorries had to share the routes which would be used by the vehicles and guns crossing the river on the ferries as soon as they began operating. So every lorry and gun had to be given a serial number, and these were called up by wireless as the situation developed. Planning also had to be sufficiently flexible to allow lorries to replace any destroyed by enemy fire to be fed in easily into the system. In this organization, I acted as mediator between Foster's staff and the Div staff once vehicles for the far bank came into the system. It all worked out marvelously well.

HQRE was in a quarry on high ground overlooking the Rhine flood plain. So we had an excellent view, and, more importantly, excellent wireless communications. We saw 6th Airborne Div fly in low overhead. One minute the chaps were waving to us from the open doors of the Dakotas, and then a few minutes later some of them would go down in flames. It was a terrible sight.

A day or two after the crossing, we moved into the bridgehead. I remember seeing many prisoners being marched back. They were very young but still as truculent as Nazis always were.

On 4th April, 15th Scottish joined in the advance to the Elbe under command of 8th Corps on the axis Borkum, Osnabruck, Celle, Uelzen, and Luneburg. As we left the Rhine each house we passed had been burnt down by our flame throwers till they ran out of fuel. I think we all wanted some revenge for all the misery the Germans had brought on a world which would never be the same as it had been before. Thereafter, as far as we could see on either side of the road, white flags or bed sheets were hanging from every German window. It was a most satisfactory sight.

But unlike the advance across France and Belgium, there were no welcoming crowds. Instead there were thousands and thousands of released slave workers walking ever westwards towards their homes in Holland, Belgium, and France. They were in a pitiable condition, mostly in rags of clothing, and many with no shoes or boots. They were all haggard and thin, and not many managed a wave or even a smile. There were so many, mile after mile, that it almost seemed as if the road were moving towards us.

One evening we drew into the moated schloss of the von Moltke family. There was an enormous oil painting of the first general-field marshal in the hall with a kist beneath containing his full dress uniform, dress sword, and decorations. I was very tempted to loot the latter, but, being the adjutant, I had to set a good example. But in the kist was a box of German lead toy soldiers. These I did take, with the mental excuse that it would be better for the world if the next generation of Germans were not brought up as young militarists! I still have them, and I believe they are quite valuable now.

Shortly after this, I returned to England for my long awaited ten days leave. I had arranged to meet Win in Berner's Hotel in Oxford Street. I remember running up the steps from the underground and rather rudely pushing slower movers out of the way in my anxiety to see Win again. After greeting one another, the first thing necessary was a bath. It must have been weeks since I'd last had a proper wash. I was so filthy that I had to have a rinse in a second bath!

We spent a few days on our own at Berner's, then went to Cheltenham to see my parents; I think we drove to Symond's Yat on the Wye to have a day or two on our own, then to Skegness to see Win's parents, and then it was back to London. I stayed with Win an extra day, which technically made me a deserter, because I was confident I could hitch-hike my way up the L of C quicker than the leave party. This I did, and to everyone's surprise I rejoined HQRE outside Luneburg a day too early, which took a bit of explaining!

Eisenhower, for no valid reason, had stopped the armies on the Elbe, but we got orders to cross in order to head the Russians off from Denmark. So we were the only allied division to do an assault crossing over the Elbe, and it began on 29th April. For some reason the Luftwaffe put in a final appearance and came and straffed our sappers as they were building the bridge. In consequence, we suffered more casualties there than on either the Seine or Rhine crossing.

Suddenly on the 30th, the axis of our advance on the far side was changed, which would mean we would have another bridge to build that night over a small river which barred our way out of the bridgehead. I couldn't get hold of Col Jock, so on my own initiative I made arrangements with traffic control to get the Bridge Platoon of 624 Fd Pk Coy across the river immediately.

I went forward into the bridgehead myself to find a harbor area for the platoon. Just as I was crossing on our floating Bailey bridge, there was an enormous explosion, and a huge pillar of black smoke billowed up just where our advanced engineer dump had been established. I went forward to investigate and found that just as a small column of RASC lorries were going through a village, it had been hit by a stonk. Fuel and ammunition lorries were set on fire, and the flames came forward in waves every time another lot of jerricans of petrol exploded. In addition, ammunition was flying about in every direction. Seeing the smoke, the enemy were shelling the place as well. It was very dangerous. Suddenly I remembered that my uncle, after whom I am named, was killed in the last week of the South African war in February 1902. The thought went through my mind that this was where history was going to repeat itself, and for a few minutes I quite lost my nerve.

That passed in a few minutes. The platoon of 279 Fd Coy, who were there, managed to save all the mechanical equipment from the blaze, but otherwise everything was destroyed, and they had only the clothes they stood up in and their personal weapons left.

I told them to have a guide at a certain road junction in the bridgehead by 1600 hours and I would get survivor's kits to them there.

Meantime I got the bridge platoon settled in and told their officer to come to HQRE in the bridgehead at 1800 hours for orders. At HQRE, I phoned Ian Grant, the DAQMG at Rear Div HQ, and he sent up the survivor's kits immediately for the platoon of 279 Fd Coy.

Around 1700 hours Col Jock came in in quite a flap, having just heard from the GSO 1 that he had another bridge to build that night. "Can anyone tell me where the nearest bridging equipment is?," he demanded. "Yes Sir, the bridge platoon is at map reference so and so, and Stan Light is coming in for your orders at 1800 hours." "Who ordered it forward?," Jock demanded. He was always very jealous of his command and would have raised hell if any staff officer had intervened in his command. "I did, Sir," I replied. Silence. In fact, the sixty foot Bailey bridge was built that night under fire in the record time of one hour fifty minutes including unloading the equipment.

All the vehicles and equipment to reequip the platoon of 279 Fd Coy arrived in the bridgehead that morning. I asked Ian Grant how he had managed this so quickly. He explained that before every battle, the general had to estimate what the scale of casualties would be. On this occasion, the scale was such as to allow for a whole sapper platoon to be knocked out. So the replacement equipment, and indeed the men, were readily available.

Hamburg surrendered to 15th Scottish and was handed over to 7th Armoured. Our people rushed up the autobahn to Lubeck and headed off the Russians from Denmark in the nick of time. Meantime we ceased to use code on the wireless, and we listened in to the Div command net. There were some remarkable messages. One brigade would report, "We've got the Duke and Duchess of Brunswick," another would say, "That's nothing, we've got Keitel," and so on. Others included the German plenipotentiaries who were conducted through the lines of the 15th Scottish on their way to surrender to Field Marshal Montgomery on Luneberg Heath.

That was pretty well the end of the war for us. We moved into the village of Hammor just north of the Hamburg-Lubeck autobahn. I demanded accommodation for HQRE and was offered a loft over a barn. It gave me considerable satisfaction to instruct, "No, you and your family will go into the loft. My soldiers will occupy your house. Now move." We needed to leave these infernal Huns in no doubt that they had been thoroughly and completely defeated.

David (later Lt Gen. Sir David Willison, KCB, OBE, MC) and Logan (later Maj Gen L Scott-Bowden, CBE, DSO, MC*) came over to celebrate with me one day. David at that time was undecorated, having been wounded in the neck on D-Day, while Logan was already sporting a DSO which he was awarded for reconnoitring the beaches in the months before D-Day. David said, "Here you are, Logan, with a DSO which you got before the battle ever began, and here am I, who nearly got my block knocked off on D-Day, with nothing!" All three of us were convinced that we should go straight on to Moscow, and with the help of the German army could easily do so, as the Russian army had clearly shot its bolt. Their soldiery were in even worse condition than German POWs, and many did not even have boots. If we'd known at the time that we had the atomic bomb, we would have been even more certain. But of course the politicians had the bombs dropped on the wrong country.

Meantime tens of thousands of prisoners were coming in. Several came riding horses or with horses and carts, as some of the German army transport was still horse-drawn even at the end of the war. The prisoners were just being parked out in the fields opposite our house as there was no possibility or need to guard them all. But if one had an eye for a horse, one could pick oneself some magnificent mounts just by waiting at the gate where the Germans had to surrender their horses. I collected six. The general decided I had too many, and I had to give him two. I gave two to Mike Wilkinson and kept the two best ones for myself. I required the local farmer to supply me with stabling, straw, and oats.

VE Day came while we were there. We had a terrific party in our house, and we got horribly drunk. We had the wireless full on and heard all the singing and celebrations going on in London. When we went outside to attend to nature, we could see the thousands of prisoners sitting round their campfires singing their folk songs. The contrast between the bawdy singing going on in the house and the solemn and mournful singing going on outside made a lasting impression on my mind.

Further up the road, the gunners, having nothing else to burn, set a house on fire as a victory bonfire while some Bofors guns were firing tracer shells into the air in the shape of a vast victory "V." It was a heady and memorable night.

One day Col Jock took me to see a camp of Russian POWs. The stink was appalling and it hit us as soon as we got out of the jeep. There were thousands of Russians there camped out in the open. One field was piled with human excreta. It was in rows about a yard apart and a foot high. Some Russians were doing their business there when we arrived; their bare behinds looked filthy. The Russians were in a terrible state, grossly underfed and with their uniforms in tatters. Col Jock gave orders for the Germans to clean the mess up.

After a day or two we moved into Ahrensburg, a very wealthy suburb of Hamburg. I sent Ewen Work ahead to find us the most lush house he could find in Bismarck Alley. He was greeted in a very obsequious manner by the owner, but before the owner could say anything, Ewen demanded to know what the rubber truncheon and nine tailed whip were doing on his hat and coat stand just inside the front door. "Oh, they're to beat the Polish slaves with," the German said in such a tone as to imply that Ewen would accept this behavior. That was enough for Ewen. He tore the German's coat and shirt off and let him have it with the whip. Then he gave him ten minutes to get out of his house with his family. Going down to the cellar, Ewen found two Polish slaves and released them. They went bounding off after the German family, and whether they killed the family or not we neither knew nor cared.

Jock and I went one day to Kiel for an inaugural meeting of "The British South Baltic Yacht Club." It was held on one of Hitler's strength-through-joy ships which was later taken over as a troop ship and re-named *The Empire Windrush* officially but to the army she became known as *The Empire Belch*, and quite appropriately due to the vast clouds of black smoke which always poured from her funnels. At the meeting, every German yacht in the Baltic was acquired by the new club, and eventually some of these found their way into the ownership of the RE Yacht Club, notably *Overlord*.

At this time, some bomb disposal chaps were attached to us. They had been retrained in safe breaking, first by some lags from Dartmoor prison, and subsequently by the police at Scotland Yard. You may imagine the surprise of a police sergeant when he gave some of these chaps a lock to pick and they had it open before he could say "Jack Robinson!" The Dartmoor convicts had been good teachers. Anyway, these chaps were attached to us to break open German official safes. We got hold of the German Naval archives in this way.

Our numbers were further increased by a couple of RE Works officers who arrived to help in the enormous amount of reconstruction which was going to be necessary. To make them mobile, we were given authority to requisition a couple of German cars. I got an enormous Mercedes limousine with a glass screen behind the driver for Col Jock, while he handed over his jeep to one of the Works officers.

One day I went into Hamburg and saw the acres and acres of ruins caused by the fire storm lit by Bomber Command eighteen months previously. Down at the docks, there were parts of U boats which had obviously been pre-fabricated elsewhere lying like stranded whales all over the docks. Some were half submerged in the water, but others had been thrown up onto the quays by the violence of the bombing.

No fraternizing was allowed with the Germans. Officers were even supposed to force German civilians off the pavements as we walked because that is what these civilians were used to doing in deference to German officers. But this was so against our natures that we could not do it, much as we loathed the Germans at that time.

Many of the Germans deeply resented the non-fraternization ban. It deeply offended the racial pride of "the master race," as indeed it was intended to do. Some Germans went to some lengths to try to break it down. The buxom girl next door used to swing on a garden swing facing our house so that her short skirt was blown up her thighs in a very suggestive manner. This enticed our Dutch liaison officer and medical officer to go next door, one evening where they were reported to me by RSM Burton, to whom the guard had reported. As they would not come away voluntarily, I had to send for the guard and remove them under arrest. The Dutchman became violent and drew his revolver on me, but I got it away from him quite easily and eventually had to handcuff him to his iron bedstead.

Once the guard, who had called the RSM, were involved, there was no way to hush the matter up. Eventually I had to prosecute the two officers at a court martial, and I earned the displeasure of Col Jock for not getting them a big enough punishment. It was the only unpleasant incident I had in the 15th Scottish. Later, after I left, the medical officer got drunk again and killed himself in a traffic accident.

Col Jock was away having a tooth out in hospital, so I took his car to get myself and the witnesses to the court martial. Coming back along the autobahn, I put my foot down to see how fast the car would go, and got it up to 130 mph. Seeing a long wet muddy patch on the road some way ahead, I had allowed the car to slow down to about 70 mph, when a German lorry came straight out from a farm track in front of me. There was no way to avoid it, and even though I slammed on the brakes, we must have hit it at at least 45 mph. The next thing I knew was coming to in a field with my face covered in blood as I'd broken the rear view mirror with my forehead, and my knees had broken the dashboard across the full width of the car. The chap beside me was okay but one of the sappers behind me had come right through the glass screen and dug his teeth into the back of my head. I thought he had lost an eye as he had a cut right down his face beside his nose, but apart from a scar he was alright.

When we got out of the car, we saw that it had been bent upwards in the middle by the force of the collision. So the car was a write-off. Screams were coming from the German lorry. We had knocked the cab clean off the chassis, and one of the men inside had a broken femur. I don't remember much more, but it was a providential escape. I was exonerated at the court of enquiry, and I got an enormous Mercedes drop head coupe for Col Jock before he came out of hospital. He was quite pleased with the exchange, except that the bonnet was so long that you blocked the main road when turning in from a side road before you could see whether the road was clear.

After a few days, we got orders to move to Schwerin to the north of Berlin. Fortunately Cpl Maughan, our MT corporal, had been a groom at Newmarket and was a capable horseman. So he and I rode the horses across to our new location, taking two days over it and stopping the night in the 15th Scottish HQRA mess halfway along the route. We took the byways as the roads were cluttered with army traffic. We rode through the beautiful Mecklenburg countryside, which is mostly forested and interspersed with many lovely lakes. One day in a forest, we came upon a group of some thirty armed German soldiers who had not as yet surrendered. As soon as I saw them, I told Maughan to keep his hands away from his Sten gun and ignore them. They ignored us as much as we ignored them, and we were relieved when we got out of sight of them. They'd have been a nuisance if they had surrendered to us.

At Schwerin we found an opera house with a complete opera company and orchestra still in being. So the general renamed it "The 15th Scottish Division Opera Company." He made the Germans sit in the upper circles so that we all went free and occupied the stalls and dress circle while the general and his staff occupied the royal box. He quite enjoyed inviting the corps commander and other dignitaries to join him in the royal box of "his" opera house. So we had a different opera each week and an orchestral concert on Sunday afternoons.

It became known that we were going to have to withdraw almost to Hamburg as we were now in what was to be part of the Russian zone. At the same time, we learnt that numbers of the ATS were going to be sent out from England to relieve the men so that they could be demobilized. This meant that proper WCs would be needed. The CE 8th Corps, Brigadier HHC Sugden, used this as an excuse to remove every toilet from the zone the Russians would occupy. Lorry loads of WCs were seen moving westward to mark the disapproval of the army for this political arrangement.

We were called the BLA, the British Liberation Army, but for all of us regulars it meant Burma Looms Ahead. Sure enough, there were soon orders for me to proceed to Burma. It was a tremendous wrench for me to leave the division where I had been so happy. Jock had become like a second father to me, and it was hard to keep back the tears when I said goodbye.

I caught a troop train at Hamburg, and the train made its way back across Germany painfully slowly. Only a single track was functioning, and every permanent bridge was down and replaced by a railway equipment bridge constructed by railway construction companies of the RE. The devastation on every side was amazing. Every railway station was in ruins, and all the sidings were cratered and blocked with wrecked rolling stock.

Eventually the train got to Ostend, and as we left the harbor our ship set off an acoustic mine sufficiently far from the ship not to do us any harm. But it seemed an appropriate parting shot from a war-torn continent.

Officers of HQRE 15th Scottish Division on the day the war ended outside Hamburg - May 1945.
2/Lt Frank Green, Capt R.J.G. Begbie, Lt Col R.K. Millar, DSO, 2/Lt Ewen Work, Lt Phil Bull R. Sigs.
(2/Lt John Hinton had been wounded shortly before and was not replaced).

On the road between Harrar and Diredawa, Abyssinia. My foot is
still bandaged. Ali, Abdi, myself, and two Italian army drivers.

Chapter Six

East Africa

I reported to the RE Depot at Halifax in Yorkshire when my leave was over towards the end of July 1945, there to await drafting to Burma to take part in the closing campaigns of the war against Japan. Even after all the tedious documentation and inoculations had been done, there was still no news of a move. So I asked for permission to live out, was given it, and then looked for accommodation for Win and myself.

We soon found ourselves the paying guests of a typically kind and homely, middle-aged Yorkshire couple. Listening to the BBC one August morning, we heard the shattering news of the dropping of an atomic bomb on Hiroshima. The extent of the damage and the death toll were horrifying and sickening. I cannot remember what our joint reaction to the news was, but I do recall a feeling of relief that the war would be over before I could get there, that Win would not be left a widow, and my child without a father, and even perhaps that I would not have to leave her at all. I also had the sense to see at once that the bomb heralded a new age in which no one would ever feel secure from sudden, annihilating attack. My mind flew back to the chaos portrayed in the film version of H.G.Wells,' "The Shape of Things to Come." Our post-war world was clearly going to be dangerous and insecure. But I was somewhat comforted by the fact that, for the first time, the politicians would be as likely to get hurt as anyone else and might therefore be more efficient at preserving peace than at any time previously.

Within a day or two of the ending of the Japanese war, I was ordered to East Africa and was told to take a draft of REME soldiers with me. I was therefore posted to the REME Depot at Nottingham to take over the draft before proceeding overseas.

So Win returned to Skegness. It was awful having to say goodbye as we had had so little time together since we were married. I had no idea when we should see each other again, nor when I would first see our child. I hated not being able to be with Win during her pregnancy. But other men had been separated from their families for years already in the Middle and Far East. So we could not complain.

But again there was delay in Nottingham, and so I got permission for Win to join me in a hotel there, and we had a few more precious days together. My father came up one day by train from Cheltenham as I'm sure he realized how miserable I was at leaving Win at such a time. It was very understanding and kind of him to make the trip as train travel was still under war-time conditions and very slow and onerous. Once again, Win and I bid one another a sad farewell, I collected my twenty odd REME men, and took the train to Glasgow. Queen Street station, which was semi-underground, was full of smoke and smuts, filthy dirty, and did not give us a good impression of Glasgow.

There we boarded the *Capetown Castle*, which was still serving as a troop ship. I saw my soldiers accommodated on one of the troop decks and then went up to a first class cabin which I was to share with three other officers. I got to know a Mr Lillington who had twice been caught in the Western Desert and done two spells as a prisoner of war. He was going out to join the staff of Thomas Cook in Nairobi. During his captivities, he had learnt every detail of *Culbertson's Golden Book of Bridge*. Many at the time were familiar with his shorter *Official Book*, but few knew the much larger *Golden Book*. Lillington knew it backwards and forwards, and he taught it to me during the voyage. Thus equipped we consistently beat all challengers.

Soon we sailed down the Clyde past all the shipyards, passing Ailsa Craig to starboard as we entered the North Channel. The last we saw of the UK as the sun went down was the Isle of Man away on our port side.

Next morning we were well across a calm Bay of Biscay. We passed down the west coast of Portugal, and the captain pointed out over the loud speakers the site of the Battle of Trafalgar. It was thrilling to me to see all the places I had learnt about at college. Especially so was our entrance into the Mediterranean through "The Pillars of Hercules," with Tangier to starboard and the Rock of Gibraltar to port. I could see the harbor in the distance looking quite grey with a multitude of ships of the Royal Navy.

I thoroughly enjoyed the voyage. I soon made several friends, and we played chess in the mornings on the sun deck and made up a four for bridge in the afternoons and evenings. As the weather got warmer, we interspersed this with sun bathing, deck quoits, swimming in the pool, and much discussion on the likely shape of the post-war world. It never dawned on us at that time that Russia could ever be a threat, because the Western Powers had the bomb and the Russians did not. There was also a lot of religious discussion largely provoked by me. I used to ask people, "Are you a Christian?" If the answer was "Yes," I would then ask, "Well then, how do you get to know God?" I never got a satisfactory answer to my question, or perhaps I was too dead in trespasses and sin to understand. But I never doubted that there was a personal God, and my desire to know Him was deep and sincere. I knew I was supposed to love God, and that with all my heart, but how could I love Him if I did not know Him? My quest to know God continued unabated, and I think I rather disturbed some people by my questions, and, not unnaturally, some got rather fed up with me.

I remember one morning the captain pointing out Cape Bon, the scene of the final Nazi surrender in Africa, and Pantellaria, where the Italians had surrendered to the Commandos. After passing the narrows south of Italy, the captain diverted the ship northeastwards so that he could point out to us the site of the British naval victory over the Italian fleet off Cape Matapan.

All the time the weather was getting warmer, and after a few more days the flat coast of Egypt came up over the horizon through the heat haze. An upright needle in the haze soon revealed itself to be the De Lessops monument on the mole at the entrance to Port Said and the Suez Canal. The ship came drifting slowly in until we came alongside a little short of the Suez Canal Company head office. The distinctive, pungent smell of Africa wafted in over the ship together with the cries from traders and coolies on the wharf. On the other side of the ship we were entertained by naked boys diving for the coins we threw down to them, and by the traders in their bum boats. Furious shouted arguments passed between potential customers on deck and the sellers drifting below. There didn't seem to be anything worth buying, and a great deal of bargaining had to be done before any deal was concluded with the price at a reasonable level.

Lillington, a few others, and I took a short stroll in Port Said, where we were immediately accosted by those wishing to sell us "feelthy pictures," and by pimps who were quite difficult to shake off. So we didn't go far and were happy to return to the cleaner atmosphere of the ship.

One morning we got under way down the canal. I was fascinated to watch the water rushing past the ship's sides to replace the space the ship had just left. There wasn't very much clearance on either side. From the deck one had a good view over the sweet water canal and the cultivation on the west side. By sweet water was meant the relatively fresh water, as opposed to the salt water of the canal, which was used for irrigation. There were several pumps to get the water up from the canal operated by blindfolded buffaloes walking round and round. Such trees as there were were palm trees. But on the east side of the canal there was no irrigated strip and the desert came right up to the canal bank.

We were awakened next morning to hear the captain announcing that the ship was stopped in the Bitter Lake, the gangway was down, and anyone who wanted could have a swim. The sea was so salt that one almost floated on top of the water, but the dip was most welcome as the days were now pretty hot and humid.

When we proceeded further across the Bitter Lakes, the SME Middle East came into view with a Bailey suspension bridge erected on the training ground. I had not seen one before.

That night we waited in the Bitter Lakes for a northbound convoy to come up from the south. When we awoke next morning we were on our way south, with desert on both sides of the canal. We reached Port Said that evening and anchored amongst a company of ships off Port Tufiq.

We remained stopped off Port Tufiq next day, and an enormous shark took to coasting around more or less under our stern. We borrowed a line from the boatswain and a hook and two large pieces of meat from the ship's butcher. Having baited the hook with a hunk of meat, we lowered it to the shark hoping to catch him. The shark swam right up to the meat but sheared away just before taking it. He did this so repeatedly that eventually we lost patience and withdrew our line and then threw the meat to the shark. He took both pieces immediately. That old shark was no fool.

Next morning we proceeded down the Gulf of Suez with the Sinai Peninsula on our port side. I have never seen such a desolate piece of country. There is not a spot of green anywhere to relieve the red sandstone and the sand beneath the incredibly wild and craggy mountains. How Moses managed to lead all those hundreds of thousands of people through such terrain for forty years without them dying by thousands of hunger and starvation must remain one of the most astounding administrative achievements of world history. They could only have survived by the miraculous provision of manna, quails, and water by Almighty God. One has only to look at that country to believe in miracles.

It got terrifically hot as we carried on down the Red Sea. One evening the captain actually steamed the ship back the way we had come to try and get some cooler air into the ship, which was not equipped for the East Coast run. Although we had scoops fitted to our portholes, it didn't seem to make much difference. I was quite surprised to find that one can sail down the Red Sea without seeing either shore. It all looked so narrow on the school atlas, but it is about a hundred miles wide throughout almost its entire length. I was also intrigued to find some locusts landing on our decks on their way from Arabia to Africa. It hadn't occurred to me that they could fly so far across water or that they would know that there was a land to go to beyond it.

We didn't call in at Aden, but in the Gulf of Aden we came across a school of whales cavorting in the water and blowing a spray of water up through their blow holes. Then we rounded Cape Guardafui, better known as "The Horn of Africa," which just consists of pretty high sand dunes and nothing else. I little knew at the time that this desolate spot was to become part of my "parish" before the year was out.

We were out of sight of the coast for most of our voyage in the Indian Ocean, but as we approached Mombasa we came in sight of the endless sandy beach backed by palm trees and forest which constitutes the coast of Kenya.

At last we came to a gap in this vista and headed towards it. Clearly we were approaching an almost land-locked lagoon. Straight ahead of us in the lagoon was a grassy mound with bushes of many colored bougainvillia framing it. It looked rather like part of a golf course. We veered a little left and were soon in a spacious lagoon with the little port of Mombasa on the landward side of the island.

Here we disembarked amidst much shouting and excitement as old friends were reunited. Two trains were drawn up alongside. One was the mail train for civilians and officers down to Lt Cols and the other was the troop train for the rest of us. The mail train would leave first and get to Nairobi five hours before us.

Our train, drawn by two enormous Garret steam locomotives, trundled out of Mombasa and across the viaduct to the mainland in the late afternoon. Soon we were climbing. At one point we were climbing so steeply that the line looped over itself and the locomotives were on a bridge directly above those of us at the rear of the train.

We reached Voi before darkness descended. From there we could see Mount Kilimanjaro, the highest mountain in Africa, looking exactly like an enormous plum pudding with the snow looking like sugar on the top. In my opinion it is not a particularly impressive mountain.

Next morning we were winding through pleasant, hilly country which seemed to support a fairly adequate subsistence agriculture and with native grass huts scattered over the hillsides.

We entered Nairobi about lunch-time, and I was given quarters in the transit camp in the afternoon.

Next morning I reported to the Chief Engineer at East Africa Command Headquarters. He was Brigadier R.L. Withington, who, it turned out, had been instructed by my father when he was a cadet at the Shop in 1912. The Brigadier said, "I've got an excellent job for you as adjutant to the CRE Northern Brigade Area at Nanyuki about 130 miles north of here." "Oh,

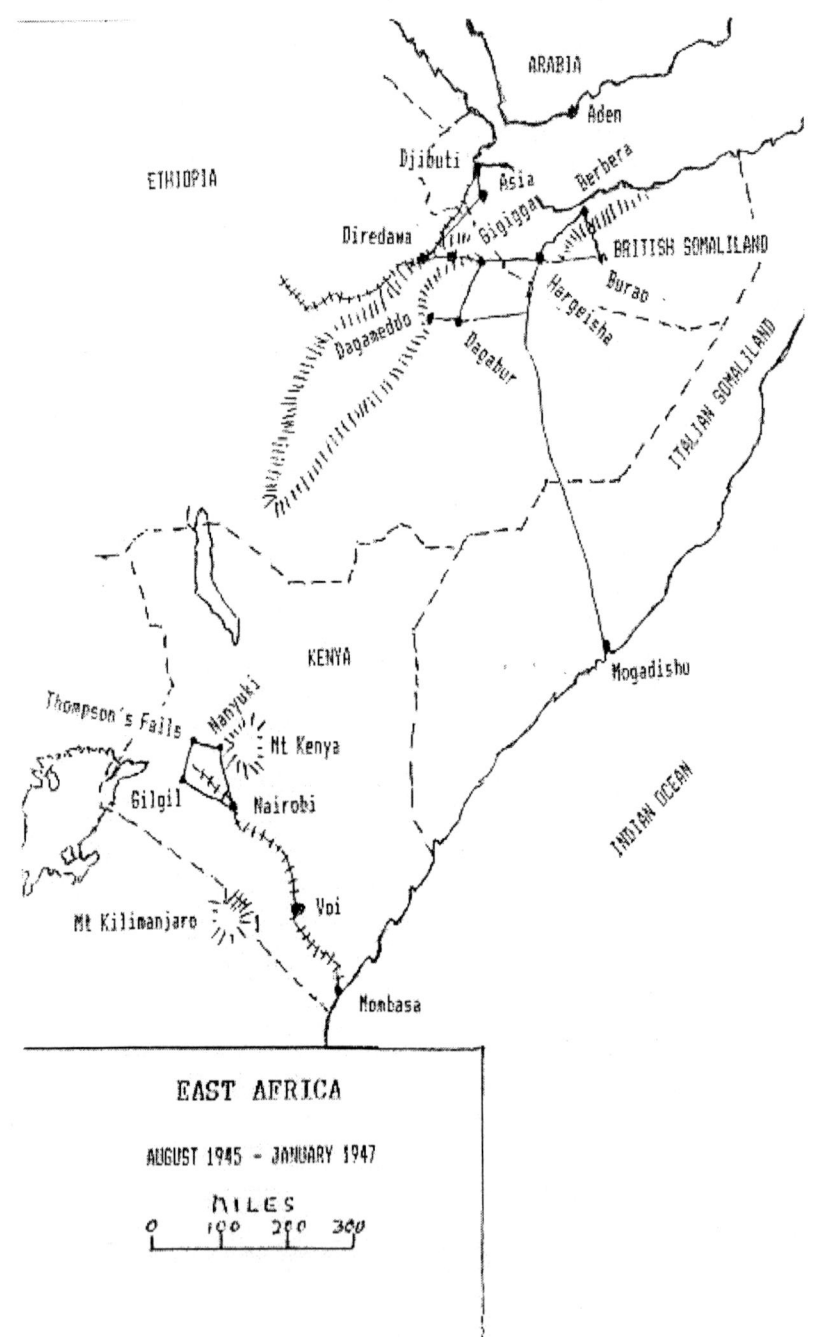

ARABIA

Aden

ETHIOPIA

Djibouti

Asia

Berbera

Diredawa

Gigjiggag

BRITISH SOMALILAND

Burao

Dagameddo

Hargeisha

Dagabur

ITALIAN SOMALILAND

KENYA

Mogadishu

Thompson's Falls

Nanyuki

Mt Kenya

INDIAN OCEAN

Gilgil

Nairobi

Mt Kilimanjaro

Voi

Mombasa

EAST AFRICA

AUGUST 1945 — JANUARY 1947

MILES

0   100   200   300

no, please," I said, "I've just completed two years as adjutant of 15th Scottish Division and I need a change." The brigadier was immediately understanding and said he would get me something else as quickly as he could. So I went by road up through the beautiful highlands of Kenya. I saw the lovely gardens and falls at the Blue Posts Hotel at Thika, and then travelled on up through Nyeri, from where there were magnificent views of the 17,000 foot Mount Kenya. Mount Kenya remains the most beautiful mountain I have ever seen. I saw it rising to a perfect cone and framed between the sides of an afforested valley. Although it is right on the equator, the top 3000 feet have snow on them all the year round. Quite large glaciers slide slowly between massive cliffs. Below that are 2000 feet of moorland, then 2000 feet of bamboo, and then 3000 feet of tropical forest reaching down to the 7000 foot altitude of the Kenyan highlands.

On either side of the earth road were prosperous white owned and managed farms, all with beautiful homesteads with gardens ablaze with flowers. Then, like round Fort Hall, we drove through native reserves where again subsistence agriculture was being carried on. But everywhere the soil was red and looked so good and fertile and the grass nice and green.

Eventually we approached Nanyuki across a fairly flat plain over which wild game roamed freely. There were just thousands of them, all sorts of buck, zebras, giraffes, and buffalo.

Nanyuki seemed to consist of a single street with dukas (shops) on either side. At the end of the street we turned left down a slope into the CRE's yard and offices. I was greeted by Lt Col Rinaldi, who took me up to "C" Mess, which was up a road which took off from the opposite side of the street. The road climbed up slowly towards the mountain past the askari lines, the club with its race course, and brigade headquarters. "C" Mess was the wooden structure nearest to the mountain of all, and set in beautiful parkland which a mile or two further on became the tropical forest of the mountain. Here we were at nearly 8000 feet.

Next day I set to work getting to grips with the entirely different paper work of an RE Works set up. A Capt Cubitt took me in hand and explained about financial votes, construction accounts, and so on. I must say I was very much at sea at first.

The climate was ideal with cold, sometimes frosty, mornings followed by cloudless sunny days which were never too hot. Mount Kenya itself was often hidden in clouds or appearing in breaks between them, which made it all the more intriguing.

After a few weeks, Rinaldi called me in to say that it had been discovered that my war substantive rank as captain was senior not only to every other engineer captain in the command, but also to all the majors, and not least to himself! I was therefore to be promoted to temporary major and would be posted to Hargeisha as DCRE Somaliland Sub Area. I was to go to Gilgil a few days later, from whence I would be taken by air to Hargeisha.

So early in November 1945 I went by road to Gilgil via Thompsons Falls. Leaving Nanyuki, I crossed a plain which abounded with wild game; I remember particularly the giraffes and zebra. I stopped to admire the very beautiful falls which drop several hundred feet into a narrow gorge. From there the road winds steeply down 3000 feet to the great rift valley. From the top one can look down almost into the craters of the volcanoes on the valley floor and across to the cliffs some fifty miles away on the other side of the rift.

It is a great deal hotter down there, and the night before I flew from Gilgil, I proudly fixed my major's crowns to my epaulettes, my promotion dating from the following day, the 12th of November 1945.

So on the 13th I flew for the first time ever and it was in a Dakota. In those days one flew quite low, and it was quite a bumpy ride in the clouds. At first I was rather alarmed as the wings seemed to waggle up and down an awful lot when we hit the bumps. We had a wonderful view of Mount Kenya, and then we crossed the escarpment where the ground falls steeply down to the desert of the Northern Frontier District and Italian Somaliland. We landed at Mogadishu to refuel and for some passengers to disembark. Then again over desert and great black lava streams northwestwards to British Somaliland.

We landed on a bleak, gravel landing strip and taxied across to the primitive huts which served as a terminal building. At the bottom of the steps as I disembarked stood a short, rather dumpy sapper captain. "Captain Good, Sir, your adjutant, welcome to Hargeisha," he said with a pleasant, welcoming smile. He was clean shaven with a chubby round face, wore horn rim spectacles permanently, and had thick, dark brown hair turning grey at the sides. He gave an immediate impression of friendliness, cheerfulness, and willingness. So now I had an adjutant, which was a pleasant surprise as I thought only colonels had them.

Norman Good drove me the five miles down to Hargeisha. The country round the airfield was just sand that was fairly thickly covered with stunted thorn bushes, which I discovered later was typical of the whole of Somaliland. The hillside down which we drove was just bare rock and stones without a vestige of soil, as was also the hillside the other side of the shallow valley.

In the floor of the valley, which was mostly bare sand, was the magalla, the Somali township, on the right, and on the left was the military cantonment quite well sprinkled with gnarled evergreen trees. All the buildings of both the magalla and the cantonment were white-washed. Along the valley from left to right was a dried up river course, called a tug, pronounced "toog," lined with the same parched and gnarled evergreen trees. Rising from the valley some miles away on the right were two rounded hills which Norman told me were together called Sheba's Breasts.

At the bottom of the steep hill from the airfield, the ground sloped gently down for some 300 yards to the tug. Near the top of this slope, beneath the rocky hillside, was the DCRE's yard. The officers' mess was a small bungalow with an anteroom and dining room with a kitchen at the back and a veranda in front. In front of the mess, a few tomatoes and aster flowers were growing watered with an overflow from the mess. There was not enough water to grow a lawn.

Most of the officers were accommodated in bell tents with concrete floors and low, plastered, mud brick walls under the flies. Norman and I were accommodated in two captured Italian general's caravans. Mine was divided into a tiny bedroom and a study with a desk, chair, and easy chair. I had my folding camp basin and bath with me. I had two Somali servants, Abdi and Ali Mohammed.

The office was below the mess "garden," and there Norman introduced me to my staff. These included the Garrison Engineer, Hargeisha, the Electrical and Mechanical Engineering Officer, the Mechanical Transport Officer, the Roads and Airfields Officer, three Military Foremen of Works (staff sergeants), a sergeant chief clerk, and three or four corporal clerks. Outside Hargeisha there was a Garrison Engineer and MFW at Gigigga, which was on the frontier with Ethiopia.

There was another yard with a Clerk of Works (Warrant officer Class 2) in Diredawa nearly, one hundred miles beyond Gigigga in Abyssinia. To the east about fifty miles away, was another Clerk of Works, Sergeant Major Siddons, an Australian, at Mandera, where there was a hospital and other installations. Halfway there there was a KAR battalion at Darbarruck. fifty miles beyond Mandera the road led to Berbera, where I was responsible for the maintenance of the harbor installations and the operation of an ice factory.

All in all there were about thirty-six British ranks, but in addition I had under my command some 1100 captured Italian Army engineers with their officers, led by a colonel to whom Norman introduced me. The Italians were divided into stores, electrical and mechanical, and works units. Most of them were accommodated in a camp near my offices in Hargeisa with detachments at Mandera and Gigigga. Their morale was not good as they had been in Ethiopia and Somaliland ever since the Italian conquest of Ethiopia in 1936. All this time they had been separated from their wives and girl friends. In consequence, we had trouble with Somali prostitutes, and several suicides. Finally I found that I was the employer of some 3000 directly employed Somali laborers.

In addition to the KAR battalion at Darbarruck, there was another at Gigigga with a company detached to Asia on the border with French Somaliland. There was a battalion of Somali Scouts at Dagabur, some 200 miles by track southwest of Hargeisha. This had detached companies at Farso and Dagamedu on the Mahda mountains which divided the Ogaden in the east from the rest of Abyssinia. The northern boundary of the Ogaden was the frontier with British Somaliland and its eastern boundary was the frontier with Italian Somaliland. Neither of these boundaries were marked or controlled in any way, and the Somalis with their herds of goats and camels crossed them at will in search of water and grazing for their animals.

Since the Public Works Department had not yet been set up after the war, I, as the DCRE, was responsible for all engineer services, both military and civil, for the whole of Somaliland Sub-Area. This included not only the whole of British Somaliland, but also the reserved area of the Ogaden which was peopled by Somalis, although part of Ethiopia, and the road to Diredawa where there was another battalion of KAR, with a foot on the railway between Djibouti and Addis Ababa pending a decision on the railway's inclusion in the peace treaty.

The intention of the British Government at the time was to combine British and Italian Somalilands, the Ogaden, and the NFD of Kenya into a single territory to be called Greater Somalia, and to lead the united Somali nation to independence. (The inhabitants of French Somaliland are of an entirely different race to the Somalis).

The British plan was, however, thwarted by the combined efforts of the USA and Russia at the United Nations, and all the warfare and suffering in the region thereafter are a direct result of this conniving by the United States with Russian intrigue in the area.

I found that I was responsible for the maintenance of some 1300 miles of dirt road, the water supplies, the electric power stations in Hargeisa, Mandera, Berbera and Gigigga, the maintenance of Hargeisha airport at Mile 5, and of five emergency landing strips scattered throughout the territory, and the maintenance of all public buildings in the territory both military and civil. I was also responsible for any new engineer works which might be necessary. When I arrived, we were completing the construction of an officers' club in Hargeisha, a control tower at the airport, and a pathological lab at the hospital in Mandera. All construction in the territory was with sun baked bricks rendered with cement plaster and white-washed inside and out, and corrugated iron roofs.

The Public Works Department was just beginning to get itself organized and had so far taken over responsibility only for the Hargeisha Magalla and the civilian hospital located in it.

The day after I arrived, I introduced myself to the brigadier and staff of the sub-area and a day or two later to the governor, Sir Philip Mitchell. But I rather think Ruth Mitchell was the governor behind the scenes! The Sub-Area Commander, who took over a few days after my arrival, was Brigadier "Crasher" Nichols, who had commanded 50th Division but been fired by Monty after the Battle of the Mareth Line at the end of 1942. "Crasher," it almost seemed, was determined at all costs to regain general officer status even if this meant provoking a scrap between his sub-area and Ethiopia in order to get more troops under his command.

When I arrived there was bad feeling between the DCRE and his staff and the DPW and his staff. This was largely due to the personality of my unpleasant and ineffectual predecessor. Although this feeling improved after my arrival, I can't say that relations became as cordial as they ought to have been. I think the PWD chaps were rather jealous of us as they were guests in what was our mess and not theirs.

As I have described above, the whole of Somaliland is near-desert. The climate is hot all the year round, and humid as well down at the coast. The rain, when it comes, all falls in a period of six weeks in April and May, but in any one year the whole lot comes down in one week in that period, all thirty-seven inches of it! It rained in Berbera for the first time in three years while I was there. Within days of the rainfall the whole place turns green, as grass, seemingly miraculously, springs up through the sand. The Somalis, who in the latter half of the dry season have gathered with their camels and goats round the few wells, begin moving out into the wilderness before the rains come in order to squat on what will become the best grazing land. But if they go too early and the rains are late, they risk dying from thirst, and each year some do.

Then at various times during the year we would get plagues of beetles, of ants, and of locusts. There would be so many beetles crawling up the walls of the mess that it appeared as if the wall were on the move. One night I was driven from my caravan by millions of ants. But the locust plague was the worst, when in the course of a few minutes all our carefully watered tomatoes and asters were devastated.

Of course Somaliland was a very lonely place with little contact with the outside world. There was just one flight a week from Nairobi and Mogadishu, an occasional flight across to Aden, and an occasional road convoy from Kenya with rations and stores. It was not considered a suitable place for women, so there were only one or two wives there, and five, very gallant, Irish nursing sisters in Mandera hospital. I don't know what it was, whether it was the loneliness, or the heat, or the wretched condition of the local inhabitants, or the successive plagues, but the place did have a strange effect on the mind. In consequence, army postings there were limited to nine months, and not more than a further three months if the medical officer would certify that one was still perfectly sane!

The Somali people are not negroid, although they are so black that they are almost blue black. They are small boned, and their features are finely chiseled, lacking the thick lips and wide noses of the negroid peoples. Their women have excellent posture through carrying water pots on their heads. The people dress in long, flowing, white, or near white, robes. The young women are very good looking, but they age very quickly and become toothless old hags by the time they are forty. Besides child bearing, they do all the work as the men do nothing except talk and fight.

The Somalis have adopted a religion which is primarily Islamic but with ancestor worship overtones. Each Somali can have up to four wives. If he dies, his four wives go to his brother, who may then have eight wives. But if he has no brother, the four widows are regarded as defiled and are cast out of the tribe. To keep alive in that barren country they become prostitutes, and so one can see outside most towns and villages a brothel encampment where one imagines hygiene and sanitation are nonexistent. Somalis are also free to divorce their wives at will, and these, too, join the brothels out of necessity.

Each Somali girl is circumcised when she is little. The clitoris is cut out and her privates are skinned and then grow together so that she is left only with a small aperture through which to pass water. When I gave my servant Abdi fourteen days leave to go and get married, he came back after a week to ask for an extension. It transpired that his bride-to-be had run off into the desert because she was terrified of being cut open. Abdi needed extra leave to find her and do the deed. It is terrible to think that this is the fate of every Somali girl. It is worse to realize that, under pressure from America, the British government had to give these people independence before the people had been weaned from such barbaric practices.

By contrast, I had a wonderful time in Somaliland. To begin with, my next superior engineer officer was in Nairobi, some 1000 miles away, so I had complete freedom of action within the limits of my votes, or budgets. I had separate votes for building maintenance, roads and airfields maintenance, water supply, electricity supply, and minor works, and separate votes for each capital project. I cannot remember the total for the year, but to the best of my memory it totalled about two million pounds.

My predecessor took me on a tour of the whole area. One had to be a bit careful near the western border of the Ogaden as one might meet a band of Shifta in the area, although the Somaliland Scouts would do their best to stop their incursions. The Shifta were brigands who would raid into the Ogaden to steal cattle, women, and boys, and murder the old women and men. Not long before I arrived, they captured two British officers and held them for ransom. Red tape prevented the rapid payment of the ransom, and the two officers were sent in tied to camels with their testicles sewn into their mouths. They were dead on arrival. From then on the orders were that the ransom would be paid immediately if one was caught, but that one would be court martialled for negligence for allowing oneself to be captured.

On this trip we came across several places as we approached Dagabur where the wrecks of Italian army lorries had been pulled across the track. In each instance we had been able to drive round the obstruction without stopping. But on the track between Dagabur and Gigigga, we came to a place where there was an obstacle in a defile for which we had to dismount to remove it. We had just got back into the vehicle when half a dozen Shifta bobbed up and surrounded us with their rifles pointed menacingly in our direction. I had the Sten gun but couldn't find the magazine. So I poked it out of the window while my predecessor accelerated the car as fast as he could. The sight of an automatic was enough to cause the Shifta to hesitate, and we got away with it.

I used to do two safaris a month, one to the west and one to the east from Hargeisha, and each lasting about a week. I travelled in a large Chevrolet saloon car followed by a 15cwt truck with a forty-four gallon drum of water and a forty-four gallon drum of petrol and rations for my party in the back. In my party I had two Italian drivers and Abdi and Ali Mohammed, my two Somali servants. Abdi was my personal servant.

I used to shoot a buck on the way out in the morning. Abdi and Ali would run across to "hallel" it whether I had shot it dead or not, as their religion would not allow them to eat it if I knew I had killed it first. They would then clean the buck, and it would hang in the back of the truck for the rest of the day.

In the evening, after inspecting works in progress and maintenance that needed to be done, I would choose a camp site before dark. I would always find a stunted tree which would give at least a little shade next morning. The servants would put out my camp chair, and there I would sit smoking a pipe and sipping a brandy while they prepared dinner and erected my stretcher bed. Dinner would consist of roast venison, potatoes, and warmed up tinned vegetables, followed by fruit salad and condensed milk, and coffee. I used to love sleeping under the stars and sometimes hearing the roar of a lion. The Somalis and Italians took it in turn to keep the fire going all night and chase away any hyenas that might pitch up. They had been known to chew a sleeping man's face!

Next morning we would have for breakfast the liver and kidneys of the buck shot the previous day. Before leaving, the local tribal headmen would come to pay respects to me, and often these were ex-service men who would show me their medals with great pride. It was generally known that I was "the bara sahib" and by far the biggest employer of labor in the country. To assert my dignity, I had a Sapper nine flame grenade emblem mounted on the radiator of the car and the words "Deputy Commander Royal Engineers" painted on the door panels.

I soon found that the road gangs, being isolated all over the territory, and not under constant supervision, were doing precious little work. What they were doing was to shovel the fines back onto the centre of the road. It didn't take a great deal of thought to realize that this could be done more efficiently and more cheaply with drags towed by bullocks. After some experiment, I found that if I kept a film of sand an inch or two deep and ran a drag over it at frequent intervals I could rub out corrugations as they formed and before they reached the hardcore underneath.

So I applied to HQ East Africa Command in Nairobi for funds to buy bullocks and feed them. I was rather sharply informed that no public money was available for such a purpose. So there was only one thing to do. None of the Somalis could write, so they used to make a cross after their names when they were paid. So I purchased a number of bullocks who appeared on the pay roles as Mohammed Ali, Aftab Mohammed, etc. and made the crosses on their behalf. With their wages I was able not only to feed them but also to pay for them!

This meant that I could reduce the size of the road gangs considerably, and so on balance costs were reduced substantially. There is a great advantage in being a thousand miles from bureaucracy!

There remained the problem of getting some discipline and a bit more productivity into the reduced road gangs. On my arrival, the gangs consisted of men from different tribes all mixed up. So I did a general post and put all the men of one tribe into one gang, and did this throughout the territory. I found out from the local chief who was the senior man in each gang, and put him in charge if he showed reasonable signs of leadership. I had the men paid individually but had the rations put into the custody of the headman. I told the local chief that if his gang didn't work properly, I would recruit a gang from another tribe. That did the trick because I think the local chief took a small levy from the wages. Not long afterwards, I was congratulated by the district commissioners for calling the gangs to order, because previously they had been the most troublesome members of the community. Certainly in this instance separate development worked much better than integration.

Driving out to Dagabur one day to have lunch with the Somaliland Scouts and to inspect their camp, I asked Abdi what Dagabur meant, and he told me it meant "place of stones." Beyond Dagabur we drove up what was called the Farso Steps. This was a mountain road over bare rock. The trouble was that the strata was slightly tilted upwards so that the road climbed up over a flight of rock steps. If you tried to shave off the steps with hammer drills operated by our mobile air compressor, the rocks just broke back again and the steps stayed the same as before. So the steps remained and one had a slow and uncomfortable drive. After fifty miles we came to the top and the small village of Dagamedo. On enquiry, Abdi told me this meant "place of more stones," a pretty accurate description I thought. There was a company of Somaliland Scouts at Dagamedo and another at Farso, some fifty miles north along the top of the Mahda Mountains. Each of these had a lieutenant in command, and there were no other white people anywhere near them. Not long before I took over, the two subalterns preceding the present incumbents had shot each other in a mutual suicide pact. It was incredibly lonely for them up there and precious little for them to do. Their role was to stop the Shifta incursions, at which they and their detached platoons were fairly effective. My main concern was the maintenance of the water supply in each camp.

For recreation I bought a polo pony from my predecessor. It was an Isobella roan, so called, I was told, because it matched the color of the old queen's bed sheets! Norman and I used to knock a polo ball about on the old airfield just opposite my offices, which was as far as I ever got towards playing polo. Norman was not a very good rider, and one day his pony ran off with him and he disappeared in a cloud of dust at the far end of the airfield. When I caught up with him, I discovered that his pony had crashed broadside into a string of camels tied nose to tail. The front and back of the string had closed in behind Norman, and there he was, still mounted on his cavorting pony, in the middle of this milling crowd of camels whose noisy objections to this intrusion were matched by the shouts and curses of their Somali owner. It was a hilarious sight, and Norman eventually emerged none the worse for his adventure.

One day Norman Good informed me that, while searching through some old files, he had discovered that there was a rest house for the sole use of the DCRE. It was off the road which ran south from Berbera and up the escarpment to Burao, a distance of about seventy-five miles. This information came to light just before the arrival of Colonel F.E. Buller, who was the East African representative of the War Graves Commission. Frank Buller was a friend of my parents, and we used to meet with him and his family during our summer holidays at Sidmouth before the war. Frank was a sapper and had been heavy weight boxing champion of the army. So I asked him if he would like to come with me to explore this mysterious rest house. He readily agreed.

We drove to Berbera, where he checked if there were any isolated graves of soldiers killed during the Italian invasion of the territory in 1940 while I checked the ice factory, power station, and the maintenance of buildings.

We had a skinny dip in a delightful lagoon just along the coast from Berbera. When I came out, I had a small scratch on the inside of the ankle of my right foot of which I took no notice.

Driving south from Berbera we drove across a level sandy plain for about ten miles and then through a wilderness of strange hills in the late afternoon. I say strange because the hills were all bare rock but of every conceivable shape, rounded, sharp-pointed, some with vertical cliffs, and all scattered haphazard on the almost level sandy floor. It was difficult to find the track as obviously no one had been that way for months, perhaps for years. We found that if we kept headed south we would pick up signs of the track at sufficiently close intervals to reassure us we were on the right way.

After some miles, we began to climb more steeply, with a dry river bed on our left. The climb became steeper and steeper until we were on a narrow track with a precipitous cliff on our right and a sheer drop to the tug bed hundreds of feet below on our left. The light was beginning to go and the headlights would illuminate a rock wall ahead, but as the road wound round there would be a sheer drop between us and the illuminated bit of wall.

After a while we found that we were on the floor of a higher part of the gorge. Through the twilight we could see an island in the river bed and beyond it, on the far bank, the rest house.

We had to dig a way down to the river bed for the car, and when we got across to the island we thought we saw an ape inside the house. I nearly took a shot at it. Thankfully I did not, for the ape turned out to be the faithful old servant who had been keeping the place spotlessly clean all the years since he had last seen a white man in 1940! He even had some vegetables growing in the garden at the back, which he watered from a well at the end of the garden.

We gave him what money we could, and I promised that I would bring him the balance of the four years wages due to him on my next trip. The faith of this humble man in the word of some British officer who had promised years before that he would be paid eventually, was to me most moving. But I think it was typical of the faith the inhabitants of the Empire had the world over in the integrity of British officers.

We continued up the precipitous pass next morning and called on the District Commissioner in Burao on our way back to Hargeisha.

Frank Buller flew back to Nairobi soon after our return. Within a day or two, my foot became very inflamed and painful, and I got our Italian Army doctor to attend to it. He put some black ointment on to it and told me to keep it up for a day or two and it would get right. Well, it seemed to be alright after a few days, and so I left on my next safari to the Somaliland Scouts, but when I got to Dagabur my foot became terribly painful again, and I decided to drive the 250 miles across to Mandera hospital immediately.

By the time I got there I was in a fever of over 105 F° and in excruciating pain. My foot was turning black and my leg was inflamed up to my knee. They gave me morphia on arrival and put me to bed. I came to on the operating table to hear the surgeon saying, "He's left it too late, we'll have to have his foot off!" This brought me round pretty quick, and I shot up and announced I would get right in one piece or not at all. "Well, you might then lose your leg." "One piece or not at all, is that understood?," I ordered and passed out again.

Thank God, they took me at my word and I came to in one piece in the ward. As I came out of the anesthetic, I was struggling like mad with four sisters holding me down and was singing my head off with every bawdy song in the book. I shut up as soon as I realized what was happening, but apparently I had been creating this hub-bub for about half an hour. All they could say of me was that it appeared that at least I had remained faithful to my wife. It turned out that the anesthetic used at that time was Pentethol, which had the effect of making some men drunk. Eventually I was let out of hospital with my leg in plaster up to my knee. But I had to return for two more operations, and each time I determined not to make a fool of myself again, but each time, to my chagrin, I created as bad a scene as before. But I learned the hard way just how poisonous is coral.

Penicillin was in its infancy in those days, and there was a poor chap in the ward who was on a course of thirty Penicillin injections in his behind. When the sister appeared with the needle, we used to sing, "Roll me over in the clover, lay me down and do it again." To which the sister in her Irish voice rejoined, "Ah, I think I'll score a bull tonight," accompanied by the groans of her patient. There was a chaplain in the next bed to me who read Evening Prayer to himself every evening, and then offered me a whisky, but never the Gospel! In between operations I was allowed out of hospital with my leg in plaster and walking with crutches so that I could carry on with my duties. It got right eventually, and I still have a perfectly good foot.

It turned out that Norman Good was giving his servant Bible lessons in the evenings in his caravan. This had to be done secretly, for when Somaliland had become a British Protectorate, not a colony, in the last century, the government had undertaken not allow the spread of the Christian religion in return for the right to station troops in the territory. The purpose was, with Aden, to safeguard the southern approaches to the Suez Canal. Further, any Somali who was discovered to be a believer was liable to be executed. I asked Norman whether he was justified in putting his servant at such risk. Norman explained how much more precious was eternal life than mortal life, which was something I had not thought of before. But it sounded logical, and so I let Norman carry on.

Norman and I had several religious discussions after that, but I think I was too proud to articulate my need to my subordinate. However, Norman began to leave "Practical Christianity" the magazine of the Officers Christian Union, on the mess table for me to read. I found that it contained articles by Christian officers written to help other officers to find the Lord. I very soon realized that these officers had the answers to my big question, which was still how to know God so that I could love Him as I should. I resolved to join the OCU so that wherever I was sent I would get this magazine. With the magazine came *Scripture Union Daily Notes* and at last I began to understand the Bible.

Norman also obtained permission to hold services in the military chapel, there being no chaplain or clergyman in Hargeisha. The chapel could only be used by Europeans in terms of the agreement with the sheiks which I have already described. Although Norman was a Baptist, he kept to the Prayer Book and asked me to read the service for him while he preached. I did this as there was no one else. We only ever had a congregation of six or so, which included the brigadier and his ADC.

On 23rd December I received a telegram from my father-in-law to say that Win had given birth to a son and both were well. I remember throwing my crutches across the office with joy and thankfulness and then sharing my joy with my staff. Within minutes, a second telegram arrived from my father congratulating me on the birth of a grandson! That was pretty quick work.

An interesting job I had was to rebuild the bridge over the Tug Errer, about halfway between Gigigga and Harrar in Ethiopia. In both the two preceding rainy seasons the bridge had been washed away when the tug came down in flood. A large sum of money had been approved before my arrival to build a bridge more than twice as long as before. A few calculations indicated that this was quite unnecessary. What was needed was to eliminate turbulence from the water as it flowed through the bridge, and to provide protection for the rebuilt abutments. Fortunately I always indexed my RE Journals as I received them. So I was able to look up an article by a sapper who had had a similar problem in India. From this I learnt about river training works and how to slow up the current near the banks with barbed wire fences. So I bulldozed out a new course for the river so that it had a straight flow through the bridge and put in river training works to train the river to keep to its new course. Then I rebuilt the bridge on its original foundations. The total cost was substantially less than the approved budget, and I had the satisfaction later of seeing the bridge stand up to the flood in the next rainy season.

The Italian cook for the mess of the Garrison Engineer at Gigigga also ran a cafe in the Magalla there. He attracted custom by having a troop of dancing girls performing each evening. Unfortunately, as he was a member of my staff, the place became known as "Begbie's Bright Spot," which was rather embarrassing.

When my CRE, Desmond Fitzgerald, came up to visit me from Nairobi he insisted on a visit to "Begbie's Bright Spot" as apparently it had become known all over East Africa! The dancing girls performed various dances of the belly dancing variety while we had dinner and drinks. The CRE was suitably impressed. Desmond, who had won a well deserved DSO in Holland whilst with 7th Armoured Div, retired early as a Lt Col and became a consulting engineer based on Nairobi.

One day I received a signal from Addis Ababa to say that General Foulkes, the GOC East Africa Command, was going to fly to Dagabur to visit the Somaliland Scouts. At Dagabur was one of the emergency landing strips which I was supposed to keep in good order. But my resources were so limited that I had not touched it since my arrival. I ordered my roads and airfields officer with a party of Italian sappers to go there post haste and I would follow as soon as I could. "Fluffy" Foulkes had a terrifying reputation as being the most bad tempered general in the British Army. When my chaps arrived at the air strip, they found that the Somali camels had worn a furrowed path right across it. When I arrived they were still hard at work filling and trampling it in. But there was no time to finish it before Fluffy's plane arrived. As soon as it hit what was left of the furrow, it did the mother and father of all bumps, and I thought, there goes my commission. When the plane stopped, the pilot got out first and said, "I'm sorry, that was a nasty air pocket just as we landed, Sir." There was just a deep "Humph" from the general and all was well. I stood the pilot several drinks that night in the mess, and no one let on to Fluffy what had really happened. It was a lucky escape for me.

Towards the end of the dry season in March 1946 the water supply situation was becoming desperate. At the best of times we could only manage a ration of three gallons a head per day. This ration was for all purposes, including water for the vehicles. It wasn't much in a hot climate. But towards the end of the dry season in March, I had to reduce the ration progressively to two gallons and was only maintaining that by trucking water in from Darbarruck. In the end I appealed to the Chief Engineer in Nairobi for help as I was at my wits end.

He flew up on the next plane, full of confidence that he would solve my problem. It turned out he was a water diviner. He used a watch spring. He held the two ends in his hands with a loop in between. He told me to drive him slowly over the ground and when the loop dipped we would stop the car and get out. He would then walk slowly over the ground where he had got the reading in the car. He would then find three spots several yards apart where the loop bobbed up or down. The water would be under the second spot and its depth would be half the distance between the first and third spots. Sure enough, we found water in good quantity at exactly the depth he had said. He encouraged me to try divining, and to my surprise I found that I could, though not as accurately as he could. The water was only about thirty feet down there, and I've no idea whether I would be effective at finding water at greater depths. Anyway, he returned to Nairobi well satisfied with his efforts.

But my problems were not over. A week or two later the governor sent for me and told me I would have to shut down at least some of my new wells. It turned out that we, following the practice of the PWD before the war, had employed a local to indicate to us the best places to find water. But this man was in the employ of the local sheiks, who had instructed him to show the white men only the poorer sources of water. I was now drawing water from the best sources upstream from the Somali wells which not only supplied water for the population, but also for all the camels and goats which were in Hargeisha for the dry season. So, said Sir Philip, he would have a riot on his hands if we didn't reduce our consumption from the new wells. So I had to reduce the ration again and revert to trucking water in the forty miles from the Darbarruck wells. Fortunately, a week or two later the rains came.

There was a series of violent thunder storms with pelting rain. As soon as it started, the servants rushed around lifting everything off the floor. Almost before we knew what was happening, the water was pouring off the bare mountain behind us, running a foot deep through the back door and out through the front door of the mess. Then I noticed a number of Somalis standing in the rain outside my yard gates. "What on earth are they doing there?," I asked. "Oh, they're waiting for your timber to float out through the gates," was the casual reply from one of the PWD members. "That'll be the day," I said, "Come on, we're all going out there to chain down the timber." This we did, but the rain was so heavy that it became trapped in our clothes so that we could hardly move. So we had to do the job stripped to our underpants.

During the rainy season a man was stationed a quarter mile above the tug crossing to give warning by ringing a bell when the tug came down. I was at the crossing one day when the warning was sounded. Within fifteen minutes, the water reached the crossing perhaps an inch deep. Within a few more minutes it was three feet deep, and then anything up to twenty feet deep with standing waves six feet high. It carried everything before it, gouging out a new course for itself some ten feet deep into which the governor's tennis court disappeared. I made him a nice new one with the soil from ant heaps.

Immediately after the rain, we had no water at all because the tug had filled all the wells up with sand. But we had some wells going within twenty four hours, and thereafter our water troubles were over.

I used to fly over to Aden by RAF transport to arrange for engineer stores to be supplied by dhow from the Air Ministry Works Department in Aden. I very much regret that I never had the time to come back in a dhow myself. I flew back on one occasion in a converted Beaufort torpedo bomber. It took the vegetables and six passengers across to Hargeisha. We entered through a door in the floor at the back of the plane. I was last man in and had to squeeze up against everyone else while the door was shut. Then a seat folded down from the side of the plane, and I sat on that with my feet on the door.

At about a thousand feet, I was looking through my feet and through the door, which was made of perspex, at some ships below when the door flew open. I just had time to jam my feet against the floor opposite and to grab my brief case. There I was with a great hole underneath me and a gale which either was blowing in or trying to suck me out. The door had blown up on runners to the top of the plane. I eventually pulled it down, and the only way I could keep it down was to sit on it for the rest of the flight feeling anything but safe or comfortable. When we landed, I went round to the front of the plane and demanded to know of the pilot if he knew what had been going on in the back of his plane. "Oh, did the door come open? You shouldn't worry about that. It often happens!" I've always found RAF transport command disconcertingly casual.

At Diredawa I had a substantial workshop and yard full of captured Italian Army engineer stores and machinery. My orders were that these could only be used for works in Abyssinia and that what was left over would be handed over to the custodian of enemy property for eventual hand over to the Abyssinians. As all this had been captured at the cost of British and South African blood, and as the Abyssinians were letting everything the Italians had built up go to wrack and ruin, I determined to take as much of this stuff out to Somaliland as I could. I therefore built a new track from the Abyssinian side of the frontier into my yard at Gigigga and smuggled out convoys of lorries into the yard and out on the Somaliland side, thus bypassing the customs post on the main road. What I wanted most was a steam roller which I had to dismantle to transport. But while we were doing this the Abyssinian police woke up to what was happening, and we had to drop the steam roller like a hot cake. But I took out about sixty thousand pounds worth of stores and machinery and took it all on ledger charge in the Hargeisha yard. It amuses me to think that I have also been a smuggler amongst my other accomplishments.

On the first anniversary of VE Day we threw a party in our mess for everyone in Hargeisha. For some reason the local BOAC representative hated my guts. I think it was jealousy, really, as I was by far the youngest major on the station. After a while he said to me, "Yours is a lousy party, I'm going out to hang myself." "Okay," I said, "You'll find a suitable tree outside," and off he went. I never for a moment thought he was serious, and we had an awful shock next morning when, suffering from a hang-over, we found him hanging from the tree.

Later on we heard that the Countessa Bioncola was coming up from Mogadishu on her way to Addis. Brigadier Nichols determined to throw a party for her and to accommodate her in the transit camp, where a special tent was put at her disposal. He required me to erect a dance floor for the occasion. I made this a sprung floor by mounting it on old lorry tyres. The Countessa, known as the "Redoubtable Pussy," had been the Duke of Aosta's secretary during the Italian occupation. The party was really a farce with only three or four women present and a crowd of sex starved men. After a while I persuaded a young Highlander subaltern to dress up as a girl. So with Pussy's assistance we got him looking quite attractive and introduced him to "Crasher," who danced with him looking down his dress front as assiduously as he had Pussy's.

After the party I brought the stores for the floor back into the yard to keep my books straight as there was no public vote to cover such expenditure.

Dust in Hargeisha was a great problem, and so we obtained a vote to black top the main road through the cantonment. I had a stone crusher to make our own chips. My RE volume on roads showing the cut-back required for the bitumen at various temperatures did not go up as far as the temperature we were experiencing, so I had to interpolate figures. I quarried chalk for the road surface which I consolidated and rolled at optimum moisture content, and it baked hard in the sun. The bitumen and chips then sealed the chalk, and I had a magnificent road surface. This was the first black top road anywhere north of the equator in East Africa. It was a source of great satisfaction for me nine years later to meet and learn from a member of the Somalian government on the ship going out to Pakistan that my road was still in good condition.

During May and June, Italians were gradually being repatriated to their homes, and the Public Works Department became ready to take over all engineer services. So at the end of June I handed over and flew home for my end-of-war leave. I flew in a converted Wellington bomber to Aden. From there I flew in a Dakota to Cairo, coming down at Asmara, Khartoum, and Wadi Halfa to take on passengers and fuel. We stopped a night at Khartoum, and I had time to see the statue of General Gordon on his camel, a replica of which stands outside the SME at Chatham.

In Cairo I was accommodated in the barracks at Heliopolis for a few days and had time to visit the Gezira Club, where I met "Crasher" Nichols' sister for lunch. I then travelled by troop train to Alexandria, where I took ship to Toulon. From there I was driven to the transit camp at Hyeres. Each day a bus went from the camp to the beach at Le Lavandu where several of us bathed and chatted up the French girls. Seeing them in their bikinis was quite a sight for sore eyes after our monastic existence in Somaliland. After a day or two we took a train which took us non-stop and very fast to Calais.

On arrival in Dover, I could hardly wait to meet Win and Christopher, who were staying with her parents in Skegness. They were both very well, and Win and I had a joyful reunion somewhat saddened by the fact that we both knew it would be short. So I met Christopher at last when he was six months old. He was a fine, strong, and good looking baby, and I was very proud of him.

After a few days we went down by train to Cheltenham for a family reunion. Besides my parents and two younger sisters, Denys, now also a major, and my brother-in-law Dick Stead, were both there back from Italy. My eldest sister Joan and daughter Valerie were also there. Leave passed all too quickly, and arrangements were made for Win and Chris to follow me out to Kenya as soon as he was old enough to have the necessary inoculations. I was given permission to take my military chest of drawers, which packed into two crates, each weighing about a hundredweight, and I sent them ahead to Dover, where I collected them as I boarded ship for Calais.

On board, I made friends with some REME officers who were taking a draft out to the Middle East. Not only did I then enjoy a bridge four with them on the train to Toulon, but their men humped my military chest at each change of conveyance.

This time one didn't feel inclined to hurry through the transit camp at Hyeres for "the birds" at Le Lavendu called! Anyway, after a few days we boarded the Durban Castle for the trip across "the Med." On the way, one of the crew developed acute appendicitis, and he had to be landed at Naples for treatment. So we enjoyed that superb view of Naples and Vesuvius as one approaches Naples Bay. At night we saw Stromboli, which duly erupted precisely every twenty minutes. Not for nothing is it called the lighthouse of the Mediterranean. At dawn next day we passed through the Straits of Messina and had a magnificent view of Mount Etna with a long streak of smoke across the sky from its summit.

On arrival at Port Said, we were taken to a transit camp in the desert on the east side of the canal. It was a most depressing place, hot as blazes with nothing whatever to do. The officer in charge was a guards captain, so I asked him how he proposed to get me on to Kenya. "Oh, by steamer up the Nile valley route," he said. I would have none of that as it was now the hot weather season. "Alright," he said, "I will get you on by plane." "That's no good," I expostulated, "What about my military chest which I've been authorized to take with me. I'll have to go by ship to Mombasa." He said there were no ships, but after some investigation I found out that there was a ship, called the *Maloja*, even now approaching Port Said which was going on to Mombasa. So when I confronted him with this information he said this ship was not stopping at Port Said. Whereupon I ordered him to send a signal to the ship to call in at Port Said to pick up a field officer and his baggage.

By the time the *Maloja* arrived there were some six others to board her, including a South African officer who was being conducted under close arrest back to the Union. When the embarkation staff officer arrived to take the party out in a launch to the ship, my name was not on his list. I had to argue with him to take me, and he said he would have to ask if there was room for me on the ship. I must say I was very annoyed as I explained that the ship had been stopped specifically for me and on my initiative.

When we reached the *Maloja* he went aboard while we waited in the lighter from which the baggage was being taken on board by the ship's derrick. I had the satisfaction of seeing my two crates containing my military chest safely hoisted aboard before the embarkation staff officer returned to say there was no room for me. He gave up when I informed him my baggage had already been stowed. The OC Troops on board found me a bunk in a six bunk cabin with four Mauritian officers down in the bowels of the ship. As soon as we were under way, I did a recce of the ship and discovered that there were two Marine lieutenants in a cabin on the boat deck. It didn't take me long to persuade the OC Troops to arrange a swop, and so I had a very nice cabin to myself for the rest of the voyage.

As we approached Mombasa, I began to see what I could do about travelling on the mail train to Nairobi instead of the much slower troop train on which I had travelled before. The OC Troops assured me that there was only room for Lt Cols and up on the mail train. I saw he had a "General List - 1" on his list for the mail train. So I said that if by any chance General List failed to turn up, would he kindly let me have his berth. To this he agreed. He was a rather simple war-time officer. Anyway, there was some general list captain who was easily shifted into the troop train, and I had the comparative luxury of the mail train, much to the envy of the other majors who had to travel on the troop train.

On arrival in Nairobi in July 1946 I was interviewed by the Chief Engineer, who appointed me to be the DCRE Northern Brigade Area, which previously had been a Lt Col's appointment. So I now travelled up to Nanyuki to occupy the offices which had previously been occupied by Rinaldi, who had by now been demobbed.

The brigade commander was a Brigadier Fryer, and the brigade major was "Lucy" Fields, of the Royal Sussex, with whom I became great friends. Quite soon after my arrival we had a visit from General Sir Kenneth

Anderson, the GOC East Africa Command, who inspected my staff and yard. He had commanded First Army for the invasion of North Africa and been dubbed by Monty, "a good plain cook." My impression was that was about right.

The four main jobs I was given to do were to construct the road from Nanyuki to Thompsons Falls as a good dirt road, to convert twenty go-downs into temporary married quarters, to build a nursing sisters' mess, and to plan a permanent cantonment for an infantry brigade group which would cost some £3 million. In addition, there were the usual maintenance tasks.

I couldn't understand why the road to Thompsons Falls was being given such priority until I learnt that several of the top brass in Nairobi had bought farms along the road to retire to! It was quite a simple job, just a matter of putting in one or two culverts, excavating ditches, grading, and providing a surface of murram which I could quarry locally.

The go-downs were just thatched roof sheds with grass walls. I removed these walls and replaced them with one inch mesh chicken wire, over which I stretched hessian which I plastered inside and out. Internal walls and ceilings were done in the same way. We manufactured the doors, windows, and frames in the workshops. The floor was a screeded concrete slab. Hot and cold water was laid on with cess pits for sewage. I took particular interest in the house I was building for Win, Chris, and myself which had a lovely view towards Mount Kenya.

The problem about permanent buildings in Nanyuki was that there was no building stone within a hundred miles and no brickfields. So we went to work baking our own bricks and after some trial and error managed to produce a reasonable stock brick. But we had not the facilities to produce these in large quantities. I had read in the RE Journal of attempts at stabilizing earth which had been carried out successfully in West Africa. So I decided to try to produce our own building blocks. I found a deposit of what I took to be volcanic ash just outside Nanyuki which contained fines as well as hard, rough clinkers. I mixed this with cement in the ratio of one part of cement to twenty parts of ash and poured it into boxes eighteen inches by nine inches by six inches deep. I then spread a slurry of neat cement over the filled boxes. This produced a nice building block, and the cement slurry on the outside gave the appearance of Portland stone. I sent these blocks down to the government laboratory in Nairobi to test them in compression. They were amply strong enough for single storey work, including the gable ends. Given generous eaves and coating the plinth with bitumen, there would be sufficient protection against the weather. The bricks would be used for the chimneys, and stone would have to be brought in for the fire places.

There remained the problem of roofing material. Thatch was not a suitable material for a barracks, so I decided to see if we could make tiles. The easiest one to make was a Spanish tile, which is a half round tile with one radius a little shorter than the other. So we put the clay into a trapesium former and then, while the clay was still soft, slid it off the table over a half round rolling pin. We then placed the tile on the floor to dry and slid the rolling pin out from under it. When the tile was dry, we stood it up on end to dry more thoroughly before it was baked. At first the tiles cracked while they were drying, then they crumbled to dust in the kiln, but eventually we had it right and we were in production.

So we built the sisters' mess with these materials, and it looked very well with a red tile roof, white walls, and black plinth. The only thing was that the anteroom chimney smoked, and the matron was a terrifying battle axe of a woman. Whatever I did with that chimney the darn thing smoked, and I only escaped from the matron when I finally left Nanyuki!

But the great thing was that the successful sisters' mess pointed the way for the construction of the cantonment. The first thing was to get the site properly surveyed. Two staff sergeant surveyors were sent up to me from Nairobi, and we located the place using Mount Kenya, Mount Elgin, and Mount Kilimanjaro as base points.

Just a little South of Nanyuki was the Silverbeck Hotel. It had been built and was owned by a retired Naval officer. On the bar in his pub was a brass strip which marked the equator. This doubled his sales as everyone always had one for the Southern Hemisphere and one for the Northern. I told him privately that our survey showed that he was about 200 yards out but that he had done remarkably well to get so close with only a sextant. I assured him I would not divulge this information, and he often stood me free drinks thereafter.

I checked that the water supply would be adequate for the cantonment by building a V notch weir in the stream and having the flow read weekly starting very soon after my arrival. I then laid out the cantonment, allotting areas for each unit which in turn decided the road layout. The Chief Engineer's office in Nairobi sent me up the designs for the married quarters. There were four types: one for senior officers, one for all other officers, one for warrant officers and sergeants, and one for junior NCOs and privates. I made little templates to scale of all these houses and laid them out with their gardens in a very desirable area to one side of the cantonment.

I obtained records of rain in Nanyuki and worked out what the run-off would be from all the parade grounds, roofs, and roads, and designed the storm water drainage accordingly. This could have presented a major problem if not foreseen early. Brigadier Fryer and his staff were delighted with my plans when I showed them to them. In turn, the CRE and CE, and the GOC, Major General W.A. Dimoline, who had taken over from General Anderson, all waxed enthusiastic over the plan. General Dimoline took a tremendous interest in all I was doing and was quite fascinated by my brick, tile, and building block manufacturing.

All this time I was getting letters from Win, who was being absolutely frustrated in all her efforts to join me in Kenya. The problem was that no one was prepared to give a baby under two years old the inoculations which were required for Kenya, nor would they allow Win to travel without the inoculations. We appealed to higher authority for help in England and in Kenya but to no avail.

Lucy Fields always used to refer to me as "the mayor." He would ring me up and say, for instance, "Is that the mayor." "Yes," I would reply. "Well this is the town clerk. The brigadier's water supply has gone wrong and he's waiting to shave, please fix it." So when the Christmas dance at the club was announced, he and I decided to go as the mayoress and mayor, respectively. I had my drawing office make me a black tricorn hat out of drawing paper trimmed with ostrich feathers. They made up a scarlet mayoral gown out of some linen trimmed with cotton wool facings splodged with black ink to represent ermine. My mace was a drain cleaning rod and brush decorated with four brass bib taps strung round the top. My mayoral chain was a toilet chain from which was suspended the ball of a ball tap and two bib cocks. This gave rise to sundry ribald comments as to the unusual ratio between ball and cocks. Lucy was a magnificent sight in a long ball gown, prominent bosom, wig, and highly made-up face. He and I did a ceremonial entrance to the dance, and while he danced with the brigadier I danced with Mrs. Fryer, tripped over my robes, and brought her down on the floor!

I had become a regular churchgoer by now. Only a handful of us attended in the garrison chapel, and I can't remember anything about the sermons except the one for the Christmas Day service which was packed out. I remember that the padre began his sermon by asking everyone why they had come to church. They had never come before. Why now? He then gave them a tremendous ticking off. I admired his courage, but church attendance didn't get any better.

Just before Christmas I received a War Office Memo to the effect that, owing to the tremendous back-log from the war, it would not be possible to send me to Cambridge as had been promised when I was commissioned. Instead, arrangements had been made for me and other pre-war young officers to go to the Military College of Science to get an external degree in engineering from London University. This was the last thing I wanted. I had already proved my competence in works services and hoped to make my career in field units and on the staff. I was gaining invaluable experience and learning all the time. I was using RE Manuals and Journals to solve problems as they came along, and had no desire to go back to "X chasing" at school. So I replied to the War Office memo to this effect. This drew a pretty preemptory order from the Engineer-in-Chief at the War Office. Then my CRE, the Chief Engineer, and General Dimoline all appealed on my behalf. But no amount of string pulling could prevent this most unwelcome move.

So Win never came to Kenya and we never occupied the lovely house and garden I had made. Nevertheless, I had been very fortunate while I was only twenty-five to twenty-seven years old to have had two such responsible jobs. To go back to school again was back again Mr. Begbie with a vengeance.

The "Mayor" of Nanyuki, Kenya
Christmas 1946.

Chapter Seven

Shrivenham To Camberley

My father met me at the RAF Station, Hendon, on my arrival in England. I had landed into the worst winter that had been experienced in my life time. It was freezing cold, and snow was to lie about till Easter. We drove to my parents' new home in Fleet, Hampshire. It was quite nice but not to be compared with Murvagh, which sadly would have been impossible to run without servants. So there was less work for my mother, and my two younger sisters were still at home to help her. The garden, which included a tennis court, large vegetable garden, and orchard, promised little let up for my father, who was now nearly sixty-two.

After a day or two with the family I hastened up to Skegness to rejoin Win and Chris, who was now two years old. Having seen him last as a chubby little baby six months old, he at first seemed to me by comparison to be thin, though he was not. His earlier pneumonia had left him liable to attacks of asthma, but otherwise he was a fine, very good looking little boy with fair hair and skin. Win was fine, and it was such a joy to be with her again. I was very fond of her parents, who were fine Christians, and I used to go with father to his Primitive Methodist Church.

I soon got down to studying for the Staff College entrance exam which I had been flown home especially to take. My studies were not helped by a heavy chest cold which I soon contracted after the heat of Kenya. Father's remedy was bed with a hot rum toddy which was so strong that it either killed you or the bug. Fortunately in my case the bug got the worst of it, and I was soon on my feet again. There was more and more snow outside, and Skegness became cut off by road and rail. Coal became rationed to one shilling worth, and one had to collect it oneself from the station yard. One either carried the bag back two miles to home or wheeled it back in the pram, as there was little or no petrol. Win and I augmented the coal ration by collecting coal off the beach, where it had been washed ashore from ships sunk during the war. It was fascinating to see the sea frozen into great chunks of ice where the waves had broken it up.

I travelled up by a wearisome train journey to Catterick to take the exam. It was freezing cold in Catterick camp, but I took the exam and passed it, only to be told a few weeks later that I should not have taken the exam, as I was disqualified from entering the Staff College till I reached the age of twenty-nine!

Meantime my father had bought a bungalow in Fleet for us to rent from him. It had previously been occupied by Queen Victoria's coachman. Early in March 1947 Win and I set up home there together for the first time since we were married in December 1942. We bought a Wolsley 10HP car from a cousin of hers for £300.

But almost immediately I had to leave her to go to the Military College of Science at Shrivenham to study for an external Bachelor of Science (B.Sc.) Engineering from London University. I loathed having to do this. I knew I could cope with any engineering I might have to do with the RE manuals and a Molesworth pocket book. To go back to "x chasing" after the responsibilities I had carried was frustrating in the extreme. Such an exercise could only be of use as a qualification if I decided to leave the army and get a job in civvy street. This, at that time, I had no intention of doing. Besides, the staff college year was a far easier and quicker way of earning the five shillings a day qualification pay than a B.Sc., and far more useful for the career I wanted in the army.

But many friends from 43 Batch were there with me, including John Cowtan, who went on to be a major general, Stanley Peploe, who finished up as administrative manager of a leading firm of engineering consultants in Hong Kong, Ian McNaughton, who became chief inspector of railways in the UK, and many others. Logan Scott Bowden, who also became a much decorated major general, with a far more distinguished war record than I had, had more cheek than I and informed the Engineer-in-Chief that he would not go to the Military College of Science or any other kindergarten that the Chief might dream up. He got away with even that! I was fortunate in that I was one of the few there to retain my temporary rank of major, otherwise Win and I would have been even more strapped for cash than we were.

A day or two after I arrived, I was approached by Bill Lucas, with whom I had shared a room at Chatham just before the war, and Bill Ewbank, younger brother of Robbie Ewbank, with whom I had shared a room in

Major Arthur William (Bill) Tyndale Lucas, MBE, RE,
shortly before his death, aged 28.

Tilburg when we liberated the town, to invite me to a meeting the following Monday evening. "What meeting?," I enquired. "The OCU meeting for Bible study and prayer. OCU HQ have told us that you have joined and we thought you would like to come." They had evidently spotted some hesitation on my face. It was true, there was, for I had never heard of such a thing and I wasn't sure what associating with such a thing would do to my career, as it all sounded a bit cranky. But I had joined the OCU and committed myself, so I thought I had better go at least once to see what it was like. These thoughts passed through my mind quite quickly, so after only a slight hesitation I said, "Oh yes, I'll come, thank you for asking me."

I duly turned up to the meeting in Lucas's room where, besides the two Bilis and myself, Stanley Peploe and Ian Usher were also present. Bill Ewbank led the study using "100 Days Bible Study," written by General Sir Arthur Smith when he was captain and adjutant at the RMC Sandhurst many years before. Within a very few weeks of these sessions I was really beginning to understand my Bible at last. As we were led in *ex-temporare* prayer by the two Bills, I was also learning how to pray myself. I began to look forward to these sessions with the keenest anticipation. I began pretty quickly to get an intellectual understanding of the Gospel. I acknowledged that I was a sinner needing the salvation which a merciful God had provided in the Lord Jesus Christ, but I still remained my own master. I remained pretty much in this condition throughout 1947, but I was learning many memory texts. "100 Days" notes were based on the Arminian position, dispensationalism, and pre-millennialism, all of which I now know to be false. Yet I think I have not been alone in travelling this route to the Reformed and truly Biblical faith.

I used to get back home to Fleet most weekends, and in the summer we used to go up to my parent's house on Sunday afternoons for tennis and tea. My father had talked to his friends about my joining the OCU. Their opinion was that it was a fanatical organization which could only do harm to my career. My father urged me to leave it alone. I hated the Military College of Science and was told the only way to get out was to fail the Inter B.Sc. exams. Well, I'd never failed an exam in my life, and I wasn't going to start doing so now. I would pass the exam and then get out. I was determined to get to the Staff College at the earliest opportunity. So I resumed studies for the entrance exam as soon as I was through the Inter B.Sc.

Our second son, John, was born on 2nd January 1948. Win had had a dreadful pregnancy, as she had twins each of which weighed over six pounds, but the doctor strangled one with the cord of the other partly because the twin had not shown up on the X-ray for some unexplained reason. That evening, when I returned home from visiting her in the maternity home in Hartney Witley, I wept for Win and the little boy we had lost. My sister Lorna came to me, guessing how distressed I would be, and she brought me comfort when I most needed it.

We had a very anxious time with John in the first few weeks of his life which only came right after calling in a specialist. The solution was to give John such enormous quantities of food as would have killed any other baby! He has never looked back since.

Early in 1948, although Brian McKenzie and one other whose name I forget had joined us, the two Bills decided we ought to make a special effort to try to increase the number in our fellowship. After prayer, we were guided to hire the first two Fact and Faith films, which were called "God of the Atom" and "God of Creation." We also thought that those who came should be given a leaflet when they left to remind them of the message they had heard and also to invite them to join us at our meetings. So we all undertook to draft such a leaflet and to select the best draft at our next meeting.

At the next meeting, none of the drafts seemed satisfactory, and they were all given, to my surprise, to me to use to produce a final draft for consideration at the following meeting. I had never been asked to do anything for the Lord before, and, although I had never failed to do anything I had put my hand to, I could not even begin this one. I don't think I ever really prayed before relying totally on the Lord to enable me to do what He, not I, wanted. I said to Him, "Lord, I know I can do nothing without Thee, please help me now to do Thy will in this." I got up from my knees and I wrote so fast that I had to read through afterwards to comprehend what I had written. This is what I wrote. As can be seen, it consists of a string of texts, which I really hardly knew at the time; put together, they made a clear and challenging message:

SOMETHING UNUSUAL

GOOD NEWS!

Almost every day we hear of bad news of the worsening economic situation, of starvation, of evidence of the collapse of moral standards, and of the increasing threat of another war with weapons such as you have seen in the film "God of the Atom." In the film "God of Creation" we have seen how all things have been wonderfully created in accordance with a supreme purpose which most of us acknowledge to be Divine. Why should man be the exception? The answer is that man is no exception, that there is a plan for him as well, God's plan, and it is because we neglect that plan that all worldly things are going so terrifyingly wrong.

God's plan is disclosed in the Bible, and the plan starts with you, the individual. "All we like sheep have gone astray; we have turned everyone to his own way." We have concentrated on our own plans and selfishly neglected God's plan with the result that "all have sinned and come short of the glory of God." This includes you, and although you can deceive others, and even yourself, you cannot deceive God. Furthermore "your iniquities have separated between you and your God, and your sins have hid his face from you," so that "destruction and misery are in your ways." You have become blind to God's plan. That blindness can only be cured by God but you have got to acknowledge that God has the only cure first. Surely you have seen enough of the way the world is going to convince you that there is no other cure (not even the United Nations). This acknowledgment by you involves repentance by you. Repentance is a genuine sorrow for sin accompanied by a change of heart. "Repent ye therefore, and be converted, that your sins may be blotted out." Blotted out? Yes, blotted out by the "blood of Jesus Christ His Son which cleanseth us from all sin." Then comes the GOOD NEWS, "he that believeth on the Son HATH everlasting life." Notice the tense; just as soon as we repent, believe, and surrender ourselves to God, then are we given eternal life. "Therefore if any man be in Christ, he is a new creature; old things are passed away; behold, all things are become new." Those of us who have claimed in faith these promises given by God in the Bible have actually experienced, and do experience, the reality of new life under the Lord Jesus Christ. So it is that God is building up, day by day, a great new body (called the church in the Bible) of men and women, who, in due time, will live for ever, on this earth at first, in absolute peace and righteousness under the direct sovereignty of Jesus Christ.

If you want to hear more of this, come to a special meeting of the College Christian Fellowship at 8.15pm on Wednesday, 5th May, or at 5.45pm on any Monday in the

SACA READING ROOM

BORGARD INSTITUTE (NAAFI)

References	Isaiah 53:6	1 John 1:7
	Romans 3:23	John 3:36
	Isaiah 59:2	2 Corinthians 5:17
	Romans 3:16	Acts 2:47
	Acts 3:19	Isaiah 9:6

I knew when I had finished, in a wonderful way which I cannot explain, that the Lord had made Himself known to me at last. I knew it with a certainty that has never left me. I believe He gave me this gracious visitation because at last I had confessed my total reliance on Him. I ran down the passage, hardly containing tears of joy, and burst into Bill Lucas's room. He took one look at my face and said, "Praise the Lord, Dick, this is what we have been waiting on the Lord for for months." I handed Bill the paper, and he recognized at once that this was from the Lord. We both knelt down to praise God and to thank Him for showing us in this way that we were in His will by having this cinema show.

In the weeks that followed, we prayed that the Lord would over-rule in every detail and particularly that He would ensure a good attendance. In answer to that the army projector broke down two weeks before our show, so for a fortnight there were no shows to go to except ours, as the Fact and Faith Films people brought their own projector. The result was that so many came that we had to have two showings and I suppose most of the college saw the films. Only one or two extra came to our meetings as a result, but who knows that there may not have been other long term results?

In the spring of 1948, the MCS Shrivenham boat club was formed. We used an old discarded boat house of Radley College on the Thames, and they kindly rented out to us a spare eight. Our stroke was a gunner who was a Leander oar, and I was the youngest member of the crew and usually rowed at six. We raced against Radley and various schools which had boat clubs on the Thames. We never won a race and spent rather an uncomfortable time in the wash of the boat in front. Finally, rowing against Beaumont College, we were surprised that one boy detached himself from the crowd cheering on the school boat ahead and ran along the bank abreast of us cheering us on like mad. When afterwards we discovered that the boy was our stroke's son, we realized that it was really time for us to retire gracefully from this energetic sport. Anyway, I was awarded a half blue, which was not surprising since there were only twelve oarsmen in the club competing for the eight seats available.

In March that year, I sat the Staff College entrance exam in the Prince Consort Library in Aldershot and passed it again.

In April the annual general meeting of the OCU was held in a hall in Westminster. At the meeting, each OCU group gave a report of its activities and plans for the ensuing year so that the prayer associates, consisting of retired officers and their wives and officers' widows, who also attend might know how to pray for the active groups.

The two Bills bullied me into giving the report for our group. So on the great day we drove up to London in Ewbank's car. On arrival I found myself sitting near the end of the platform without even a bank of flowers to hide behind. The hall was filled with retired people, and just below and right in front of me was the forbidding figure of General Sir William Dobbie, the heroic governor of Malta during the siege, and Lady Dobbie. As fate would have it, I was the last to speak, so I had a long apprehensive wait till my turn came.

All I could think of to say was how the Lord had at last made Himself known to me in the manner I have already related. I sat down feeling even more embarrassed than when I began. On the way back in the car I said to the two Bills, "It's a funny thing that when we went up to town this morning I still wasn't sure that I had been saved. But now I am absolutely sure that I have been born again and have spiritual life. I am absolutely committed to Christ as my Saviour and my Lord." To this Bill Lucas replied, "That's why we asked you to speak for our group, for it is written, 'Whosoever therefore shall confess me before men, him will I confess also before my Father which is in heaven.'" That verse came true in my life even before I knew of its existence.

The first weekend that I got home to Fleet after this, I went to see the vicar to offer my services in any capacity in the church. I described to him the circumstances of my conversion, but he had nothing to offer and no words of encouragement. Instead he just sat there puffing away on cigarettes, and although I was a new convert, he seemed to me to be totally lacking in any spirituality. In fact, during previous weekends since my conversion, I had noticed that his sermons seemed to consist of his own speculations on such subjects as what heaven might be like instead of being clear cut expositions of Scripture.

So whenever I was home, I began to go to the Baptist Church, where the Rev. Richard Drake became a wonderful support in my early months and years as a child of God. This departure from the Church of England did not have the approval of my parents, but then they had ceased to be regular church-goers themselves. I cannot blame them, for they were being starved of any spiritual food in the parish church, and their Victorian ideas of class inhibited them from going to a Baptist Church which was mostly patronized by the working classes.

By and by the Deputy Engineer-in-Chief at the War Office came to visit us at Shrivenham and gave me an interview at which I persuaded him to get me out of the place, especially as I had by now been selected for the Staff College the following year. So in June 1948 I left the Military College of Science without a B.Sc but with a B.A, born again, which I am convinced is why the Lord had sent me there, whatever the intentions of the War Office might have been.

To fill in the six months before the Staff College assembled in January 1949, I was posted to Aldershot, only five miles from our home, to command A Squadron in 4th Training Regiment RE at Gibraltar Barracks. This was a driver training regiment.

As a keen new Christian I was anxious to witness for my Lord in the only way I knew, and that was by holding meetings for Bible study and prayer. I prayed that the Lord would give me some sign by which I would know when to start. I was anxious not to go ahead in the power of the flesh, against which I had often been warned by the two Bills.

After some weeks of this, the Commanding Officer called me in one morning to tell me how pleased he was with the way A Squadron was performing since I had taken it over. When I got back to my office my Squadron Sergeant Major suddenly volunteered much the same opinion. A little later the same morning, I was accosted by a lance corporal who said what a difference it made to be serving under a gentleman again. I knew at once that these three complimentary remarks coming so close together were the sign I was waiting for. Clearly one cannot be an effective witness for Christ until one has demonstrated that one can do one's job properly. "Whether therefore ye eat, or drink, or whatsoever ye do, do all to the glory of God."

I put up notices that evening to say that weekly meetings for Bible study and prayer would begin in the Officers' Mess Library starting the following Monday evening. So I prepared myself with the help of "100 Days." To my horror, on the Monday the only ones to come were the C of E chaplain, the Methodist chaplain, and the Romish chaplain! You may imagine my embarrassment. Suffice it to say, they never came again, nor did they offer to help. But slowly the meetings built up, and we eventually moved them to Miss Daniel's Soldiers' Home in Aldershot, where they continue to this day.

The talk I had given at the OCU General Meeting in London was published in the OCU magazine, which at that time was called *Practical Christianity*. Following its publication I received this letter dated 4th December 1948 from Mr. Norman Good, my erstwhile adjutant in Somaliland:

Dear Dick,

I was very delighted to read the extracts from your address which were published in the October issue of the OCU newsletter. Ever since we met and had conversations on religious subjects in Hargeisha, I and others have been praying that you may be led to know Christ as your personal Saviour. From the newsletter, it certainly looks as though prayer has at last been answered. The tremendous zeal which you always bring to bear on any project which you undertake, turned into

Christian channels, under the guidance of the Holy Spirit, will accomplish great things to the glory of our Lord and Saviour.

Norman, who had resumed his civilian occupation as a builder, was now the organist and choir leader at Eric Hutchins' Lansdowne Baptist Church in Bournemouth. I hastened to write to him to share the good news of my salvation and to thank him and his friends for persisting in prayer for two whole years before the heart of this hardened sinner was broken down in repentance.

One morning my SSM showed a Mrs. Dickinson into my office. She was in great distress. After I had comforted and calmed her, she said that her husband, one of my NCOs, had tried to strangle her in bed the previous night, and would I please speak to him. Later I sent for L/Cpl. Dickinson. After he saluted I told him to sit down. Before I could say anything he said, "I suppose the old woman has been in to see you?" I said, "Yes, indeed she has. What have you to say for yourself?" "It's like this," he said, "Sometimes I wake from sleep in the middle of the night with such a terrible 'ead ache that I don't know what I am doing, and I find meself assaulting me wife." "You know, no one on earth can help you unless you tell them the truth," I said, looking him very straight in the eye. "Well yes, you're right," he said, "It's really like this. I 'ad a mistress when we was in Berlin, you see, and I 'ave the most terrible nightmares and I feel awful about what I did with 'er. Then I think it's 'er in bed with me and I try to strangle 'er, but it isn't 'er, it's me wife!" "Look," I said, "the Lord Jesus Christ came to this earth especially to help chaps like you. You are terribly unhappy because of your guilt over what you did with this woman. But Jesus came to lift the guilt off sinners and took it all upon himself and then suffered the punishment for whatever we have done wrong so that we could be forgiven by our Heavenly Father, and have peace and joy by trusting in Jesus as our own personal Saviour and Lord."

I used to have Dickinson to the office after work in the evenings to show him the way of salvation in more detail. Eventually he asked one evening what certainty there would be that he would not fail the Lord in some way again. It so happened (by God's providence, no doubt) that the previous evening we had been studying the opening verses of 1 Peter 1 at my OCU Bible study. So I said to Cpl. Dickinson, "Sadly we all sin from time to time, but not wilfully, and the Lord will not let us go beyond a certain point. He will always bring us back who are 'kept by the power of God through faith unto salvation ready to be revealed in the last time.'" With that he said that nothing now kept him back, and so we both got down on our knees while Dickinson confessed his way through to Jesus, and I prayed for the strength of the Holy Spirit for him and praised God for His mercy in enabling me to witness effectively. At this moment the sergeant major came in to find his OC and a L/Cpl. on their knees, both with tears of joy streaming down their faces.

Before Mrs. Dickinson had come to me with her troubles, it turned out that they had both been to the Woking Congregational Church for help. I now received a letter dated 7th November 1948 from the Rev. Frank Shield, the minister there. He wrote:

> Dear Major Begbie,
>
> I have heard from Lance Corporal Dickinson. He tells me the good news that he has given his life to Christ. You will not want me to congratulate you on this personal work, but you will permit me to rejoice with you in the working of the Holy Spirit through you. It is grand that this young couple are now able to make a new start in their married life and that they may be dependent, not upon their own strength, but upon Christ Himself.
>
> Harry Dickinson has asked that they may meet Mrs. Herbert (with whom Mrs. Dickinson first got in touch) and myself again. You may rest assured that we shall build upon this great fact of conversion. We have been praying for this couple since they first came to us, as you have been too, no doubt.

My wife and I kept in touch with the Dickinsons for years after that by mutual exchange of Christmas cards but eventually our many wanderings caused us to lose touch. No doubt we shall meet again in glory.

A chaplain used to come several times a week to conduct "padre's hours" for my troops. I told him that as I was their OC and therefore responsible for their welfare, which included their spiritual welfare, I hoped he would not mind if I dropped in from time to time to his padre's hours. After I had heard him once or twice, I found that he really had nothing to offer and, he was boring my chaps to tears. So I had him into the office and enquired of him what message he was trying to put across to the chaps. The poor fellow broke down and confessed that he had lost his faith. I hope I prayed with him, but I said he ought to resign and go to a retreat or wherever it was ministers went to for help in such circumstances. Well, he took my advice, and I never saw him again.

During this time I was sent on a commanding officers' refresher course to the army chaplains' centre at Bagshot Park. Bagshot Park had been the home of the Duke and Duchess of Connaught, and I slept in what had been Princess Alice's bedroom. We listened to lectures and took part in various discussions during the three-day course and on the last day we were asked to give our impressions, the Chaplain General being present. I stood and said my impression was that the place was spiritually as dead as a dodo and gave my reasons. This rather brought the discussion to an end. After it was over, the warden drew me aside and thanked me for my comments and said it did them good to be so challenged. Indeed, I hoped so. The Chaplain

General said he guessed I must be a member of the OCU. He said he regarded the OCU as his spiritual commandos, to which I replied that it would help if he were to say so publicly.

I left A Squadron at Christmas and was given a great send-off. In the New year I joined with eleven other sappers for a three week pre-Staff College course at the SME Ripon taken by Bill Jackson (later General Sir William Jackson) and Cecil Eking, later to be my commander at the SME Chatham. We were told that as far as the army was concerned, the gloves were now off and Russia was the likely enemy.

I joined the Minley Manor Division of the Staff College early in February. This was most convenient as it was just up the road from our bungalow in Fleet. At that time there were four divisions at the Staff College, each of sixty students; two were based in Camberley, one in Farnborough, and one at Minley Manor. All four divisions would gather together in the Rawlinson Hall in Camberley for major presentations and lectures. At the opening lecture the Commandant, Maj Gen Dudley Ward, began with the words, "Gentlemen, welcome to the Imperial General Staff," and I must say I really felt that I had set my foot on the first rung of a ladder which, if it would not take me to the top, would at least take me a good way up it. At twenty-nine I was, I think, the youngest on the course. In retrospect I don't think this was an advantage, as I did not have as much war experience, as many of the others. But the course was a marvellous experience and we had lots of interesting speakers down from London. These included the CIGS, Field Marshall Sir William Slim, the First Sea Lord, and the Chief of the Air Force, Field Marshall Lord Montgomery, Lt. Gen. Lawton Collins of the US Army, Sir Vincent Tewson, General Secretary of the Trade Union Council, Mr. Emmanuel Shinwell, the Secretary of State for war, Lord Alexander, the Minister of Defence, Sir Arthur Bryant, to give us a historian's view of the war, Mr. Alan Morehead to give a war correspondent's view, and many others.

We tried to trap Tewson in question time, but he was as slippery as an eel, never answered the question he was asked, and gave us more socialist doctrine. We tried the same with Lord Alexander, and a guardsman asked him whether it would be a good thing for Spain to be invited to join the NATO alliance. The question clearly annoyed Alexander, and so he was asked, political considerations aside, wouldn't it be good for strategic reasons to have Spain in the alliance. He refused to answer the question and was quite rude. So no more questions were asked, and the general escorted him out of the hall in complete silence. Emmanuel Shinwell was quite another matter. He had taken the responsibility for the coal crisis a year or two before and had been forced to resign from the ministry of fuel. When he came to the War Office he expected to have some opposition, knowing that officers were conservative to a man. But instead he had been given loyalty such as he had never known before. He just stood at the front of the stage with his hands stuck into his jacket pockets and spoke to us, without a note, more sense than one can usually expect from a politician. We put away our trick questions and gave him a friendly ovation when he left.

By far the most memorable of the lecturers was Field Marshal Lord Alanbrooke. He began his lecture by saying that despite what he was going to tell us, he was certain that England would have been defeated in 1940 had it not been for the leadership of Mr. Churchill in rallying the country. But as a future CIGS was in this room, he was going to tell us of the problems of a CIGS in wartime. Any politician who became prime minister in wartime was likely to be a genius who, like Churchill, would have many idiosyncrasies which would be as difficult to deal with as were the Churchillian ones. For the next hour, he then gave us one anecdote after another about Churchill's idiosyncrasies and the time and trouble it had taken to deal with them. Only some of these have subsequently appeared in Sir Arthur Bryant's biography of Lord Alanbrooke. It was an absolutely fascinating lecture.

Several times during the course we had discussions in the Rawlinson Hall in the main Staff College building in Camberley. We would be told the day before what the discussion was to be about, but we were not told who would be called upon to speak. So on the day all four divisions assembled in the Rawlinson Hall and one tried to hide behind one's neighbor in the hope that the general's eye would not fall on you. The subject was, How would you maintain morale in conditions of nuclear war?

As fate would have it, the general's eye fell on me! So I said, "We've been taught that a nuclear war would begin with an exchange of long range nuclear missiles aimed at the home bases of the two sides. At that stage the army on the Continent would not know what had survived in the UK. No one would know whether their homes still existed, whether the king was still alive, and the army would be left to fight with what ammunition and supplies it had with it when the war began. In these circumstances the army's morale could only be maintained if it had been convinced before the war that the only way by which conditions for the spread of the Gospel could continue would be by force of arms. And the Gospel is this..." And I then gave a clear and challenging Gospel message whose details I forget, and then sat down feeling rather apprehensive as to how this would be received. For a time there was complete silence, and then the general cleared his throat and said, "Well, I think we'll have the next speaker."

I played rugger for the Staff College. Our first match was against the Royal Military College, Sandhurst. They were as fit as fleas, all of them being about nineteen years old, whereas all our team, except myself, were into their thirties. We held Sandhurst until half-time more or less, but after that their fitness told and they beat us by a large margin. So we then did what, as budding staff officers, we should have done before, and that was to make an appreciation of the situation. Since our average age would be greater than that of every team we would meet, we would have to make the ball move where we couldn't, and we would have to conserve our energy. So we decided that when the opponents got the ball, our forwards would remain in the middle two thirds of the field. There was to be no exhausting charging to the corner flag in defence. When we got the ball we would pass it out quickly to the wings to draw the opponents to one flank or the other, and then the wing would cross kick the ball to the forwards, who would be waiting for it in the middle of the field. Then with short passing between the forwards, we would run straight down the middle of the field and score between the posts.

Thereafter we never lost a match and beat home and away all the London-A fifteens of clubs, such as Blackheath, Harlequins, Richmond, London Scottish, etc., and Guildford, the strongest local side. If we couldn't move, the ball did, and to good effect.

In June the College went over to Holland and Germany for its battlefield tour. We studied the action of 6th Airborne Division at Arnhem, and the Siegfried Line battle and Rhine crossing by 15th Scottish Division, which, of course, were of nostalgic interest to me.

We had a four week break in July, and Win and I went off in our Wolseley with a two man bivvy tent to tour France while Win's mother came down from Skegness to look after Chris and John. We spent the first night at Louviers, where we had crossed the Seine in 1944, and then went on to see the Normandy battlefields. It was amazing to see how quickly the ravages of war had been repaired, and I found it quite difficult to recognize where I had been. We visited the 15th Scottish war memorial at Cheux and saw the graves of Jimmy Osler and my little command crew, all buried together. I could so easily have been in Jimmy's place. The hotel we stayed in at Vire was still unrepaired, and one end of the hotel was closed only by a huge tarpaulin which was draped down from the roof.

We drove down the west coast of France, and I was disturbed and annoyed by the number of cars which shot out from side roads on the right onto the main road. I hooted at them while their drivers shook their fists at me. It was only when we got to Paris that I learnt that the rule in France is to give way to everything which comes in at you from the right, even if it is only from a lane!

We got lodgings at St. Jean de Luz near Biarritz where we stayed a few nights and then drove along the foothills of the Pyrenees to Lourdes, where we visited the shrine. We were appalled by the idolatry and Romish superstitions of the place. One approaches the shrine via the Boulevard de Grotte, in which the shops on both sides sell "holy" water from the spring and various presumed relics and images of the so-called lady of Lourdes. At the end of the street there are lodgings for cripples, and a number of them were sitting out in the sun on invalid chairs hoping for a cure. They were a pathetic sight. Beyond that there was a garden for which Win had to cover her head before she was allowed admittance. In the garden there was a statue of the lady at which several people were practicing idolatry, and finally there was the grotto, which was bedecked with crutches of those whom one was supposed to believe had been cured. We couldn't get out of Lourdes quickly enough.

We continued along the lovely foothills of the Pyrenees and in the late afternoon came out onto a plain across which we could see a mound with the town of Beziers perched on the top of it. Somehow, in the orange light of the evening it had a most sinister appearance. We drove up through its narrow and mysterious Moorish streets till we found a hotel, where Win was very insistent that I should lock the bedroom door.

But we spent an uneventful night, and next day we drove on to Sete only to find that the banks were shut that Saturday and we could not change our traveller's cheques. We just had enough money to buy some bread and cheese and *vin ordinaire* to supplement our rations for the weekend, and then camped on the beach near the mouth of the River Hepault.

Win was most concerned that the tide would come up during the night and soak us and our things. She wouldn't believe me when I assured her that the rise and fall of the tide in the Mediterranean is hardly more than a foot. So in my halting French I had to ask a fisherman for confirmation. He looked at me as if I was quite mad and said with some vehemence, "La mer reste ici," indicating the spot with his foot.

There were swarms of mosquitoes on the beach. Fortunately I had brought a double bed mosquito net with us which completely covered our two man bivvy. Along the beach from us were two girls and a young man. The girls retired into their bivvy tent, leaving the young man to doss down in the open. But he didn't survive the mosquitoes for long, and the girls had mercy on him and allowed him into the tent for the night. In those days, before the permissive society had arrived, this was such a remarkable concession that there were several anxious glances in our direction before any of the three would emerge from their tent next morning.

Having visited the bank in Sete on Monday morning and replenished supplies, we drove up the Rhone valley and camped in a disused quarry which had a lovely lawn grass bottom. We were awakened at dawn by a party of strawberry pickers on their way up to a field above us. They returned while we were having breakfast, and we bought an enormous basket of lush strawberries from them for the equivalent of two and sixpence.

Eventually we got to Chalons, where we stopped at a wayside restaurant and sat down. We were by now running short of cash, and when we read the menu we saw that there was nothing on it which we could afford. Sheepishly, we had to make our exit under the interested glances of the other customers. So we arrived hungry in Paris and stayed in a cheap but reputable hotel which had been recommended to us.

We went to the Follies Bergere, where the show was so spectacular that the scantily clothed girls didn't really seem at all unseemly. We visited the Louvres and were quite unimpressed by the Mona Lisa and thought the meaning of her smile was quite inconsequential, if indeed it meant anything at all. We visited Notre Dame and thought the interior terribly dark and gloomy, but the view over Paris from the tower was magnificent. We shrank from ascending the Eifel Tower, and then headed for Calais and home.

The remainder of the staff college year included a night visit to the *Daily Telegraph* in Fleet Street, where we watched an issue of the paper being put together from start to finish. We were amazed to see men being kept on doing utterly useless work because of the power of the unions. Then there was a visit to an aircraft carrier off Portsmouth. The noise on the flight deck was deafening, particularly as aircraft took off with the assistance of a hydraulic catapult. I thought the pilots should earn a medal every time they landed in that restricted space. They seemed to be stopped from going overboard by the arrester wires only at the last moment.

We flew across to Northern Ireland to visit RAF Coastal Command in a couple of Ansons whose pilots were intent on scaring the life out of us by flying so that the wing of one Anson was between the wing and tail plane of the other and then circling over our plane and down the other side in the same position. It wasn't difficult to imagine what would have happened if we had hit an air pocket. Fortunately we had a wing commander as a passenger, and, his nerve having failed first, he ordered the pilots to stop it.

On arrival at Castle Archdale we boarded an RAF Sunderland flying boat. It was enormous inside, with three decks, one above the other, and a huge cargo hold. I got myself into the bomb aimer's position in the nose, where I had a marvellous view as we skimmed across the water on take off and again on landing. Apparently no one was supposed to be in that position on landing; the captain was furious, and couldn't think why the machine was so nose heavy. But I wouldn't have missed the experience for worlds.

At the end of the course we were summoned individually to the Minley Division commander to be given our results. I was told I had got a high grading "despite my peculiar religious views and neglect of college social activities," which meant I hadn't gone to the endless drinking parties. An

"A" grading is reserved for a future CIGS, and I got a "B" and retained my rank as temporary major. So I had reassurance that if we are prepared to stand up for Jesus, He will also look after us. "Seek ye first the kingdom of God, and His righteousness, and all these things shall be added unto you."

Chapter Eight

The War Office

The most sought after appointment on leaving the Staff College is brigade major of an infantry or armoured brigade. The next is to be GSO 2 of a division. After that, any other grade 2 staff appointment, and after that a grade 3 staff appointment for the "also-rans." The latter were captains' postings.

My appointment was to be Deputy Assistant Adjutant General in the officer's policy section of the Adjutant General's Department in the War Office, called AG 1 (Officers). It was a top grade 2 "A Staff" appointment. Before taking up our appointments, all of us who had been given "A Staff" jobs were sent on a three week course to study matters within the purview of "A Staff" officers. I remember very little of this course except a visit to the military prison at Colchester, which also enabled me to go to Frinton-on-Sea to visit for the last time my Uncle Colin, my ex-prep school headmaster, and Aunt Muriel, and a trip to the army in Germany which enabled me to visit Lorna, who had married Adrian Sandes, a sapper serving in Bad Oynhausen.

Early in February 1950 I reported to the War Office at Lansdowne House, Berkeley Square. At that time the policy branches of the Adjutant General's Department were housed in Lansdowne House while the branches looking after the individual arms and services, such as AG 7 for the Royal Engineers, were housed with the Military Secretary's Department out at Stanmoor. There were three policy directorates in Lansdowne House answering to the Adjutant General. They were the Directorate of Personal Services, the Directorate of Manpower Planning, and the Directorate of Personal Administration. Each Directorate was headed by a major general, and the DPA had two Deputy Directors under him who were brigadiers. They were the DDPA (Other Ranks) and the DDPA (Officers). Answering to the latter was the Assistant Adjutant General AG 1(Officers), to whom answered the DAAG AG 1 (Officers) P and the DAAG (Officers) C. I was to fill the latter post.

AG 1 was on the fifth floor, which we shared with the Army Chaplains Department. For this reason the old soldier lift attendant, when we asked for the fifth floor, used to say, "Holy City, going up."

The AG was General Sir James Steel, who was known as "Daddy Steel" because he called every one "sonny" whether one was a general or a lieutenant. A few months before my time was up, he retired to become the first chairman of the nationalized coal board, and, as this was a socialist appointment, he was generally considered a traitor to his class. I only met him once when I was suddenly called up to his office on the top floor wondering what I had done wrong. It turned out he only wanted to know how his daughter could get a commission in the WRAC. He was succeeded by General Sir John Crocker.

The VAG was Lt. Gen. John Woodward, a brilliant man who had qualified as a barrister in the same year as he took the Staff College course. He left to become the GOC Northern Ireland.

The DPA was Maj. Gen. C.S. Sugden, a Sapper, and a brilliant man. He interviewed me on arrival and told me that, like any good regimental officer, I had probably come to the War Office with reforming zeal. He told me that I should imagine that my job was to move a big ball of chewed-up chewing gum from one corner of the office to the other. If I took a flying kick at it my foot would merely stick in it. But if I tapped it gently along it would arrive there in the end. I have found this extremely good advice for the rest of my life, though I regret that my natural impatience to get things done has not always caused me to heed it.

"Cuthbert," as we called him, though his real name was Cecil, did not suffer fools gladly, but once he had confidence in one he was a wonderful man to work for. "A Staff" work always involves a tremendous amount of detail, and Cuthbert had an amazing capacity to absorb detail whilst at the same time grasping the essentials and the solution of any problem with lightning speed.

The day-to-day business of the War Office was handled by the weekly triangular meeting of the DSD, the DMP, and the DPA, who took the chairmanship in turn and called such staff officers as they needed to attend to solve the variety of problems which came before them. These might involve the army anywhere in the world, and some of the problems were baffling in their complexity. I was called to attend once, and I heard the other two generals giving their opinions, which were anything but clear. Then Sugden would put his pencil down neatly, chuck his glasses on the pad before him, and say, "I suggest we do A, B, and C," clear as crystal every time. Then the others would say that was what they really meant, but I don't think it was that at all!

I came to know Cuthbert quite intimately, and whenever I came up to London by car for a change from the monotony of the train, I used to give him a lift back to his home in Farnborough while I continued on to Fleet.

I often wondered how the civilians who spent their lives commuting to London stuck it out. I left home in Fleet soon after 7.30 each morning to catch the 8.09 to Waterloo. The train arrived there an hour later, and then I had to dive into the tube, change at Piccadily Circus, and emerge at Green Park and walk to the office, arriving there at about 9.40. The journey home in the evenings took the same time, so that in winter I only saw home in daylight on the weekends. I hardly saw the children at all during the week because they weren't up when I left and were already in bed by the time I got home.

Cuthbert told me that after nine years in senior staff appointments, the only way he kept sane was to put on his hat and walk out of his office at 5.30 whatever the crisis situation might be. He had been Brigadier General Staff under Eisenhower for the invasion of North Africa, then Director of Military Operations at the War Office, then Chief of Staff, Middle East, and now DPA. He went on to be Chief of Staff BAOR, Commander in Chief NATO Northern Europe, with headquarters in Oslo, then two tours on the Army Council, which is almost unique, as QMG and then MGO. Sadly, he died of cancer when still quite young. His successor as DPA never had the same grasp of the problems as Sugden did.

The DDPA(Officers) was Brigadier Eric Sixsmith, who also became a major general. He was a delightful man to work for, with an incisive mind and a rather dry sense of humor. More importantly, he was also a Christian.

The AAG AG1(Officers) was Hugo Chesshyre, also a sapper, who understood my side of the work perfectly, and when I was under pressure he would take some of the files off my desk and deal with them himself. I was very grateful for that as mine was a very busy section. He left quite soon and was replaced by Dick Fyffe of the Rifle Brigade, who became a Lt. Gen. and was knighted. He was an extremely nice chap to work for but never understood my side of the work as Hugo had done. The calculations I was involved in remained a mystery to him, which is perhaps why I received such a good confidential report from him!

My section, AG1(Officers)C, was responsible for all commissioning regulations for regular, short service, and emergency commissioned officers for all arms and services of the British army and colonial forces. My section was also responsible for the processing of individual emergency commissions and, with my opposite number in the Military Secretary's Department, the processing of all British regular army commissions. I was secretary of the War Office Commissions Board and of the War Office Commissions Appeals Board.

To help me, I had a staff captain and a Grade 3 Civil Service Executive Officer who did all the processing of emergency commissions, and I seldom had to get myself involved in their work in any way. I also had a staff captain, John Rogers, who sat in my office, under-studied me, and dealt with a lot of the day to day correspondence. The chief clerk, Mr. Styles, who'd been in the section since the year dot, was an enormous help and a mine of information.

Part of my job was to work out how many officers should be commissioned each year in each arm and service in order to provide the right number of officers in the corps as a whole and the right number of majors from whom to select the lieutenant colonels in due course. The policy was that two thirds of officers should have the prospect of making Lt Col, and that half the Lt Cols should make Brigadier. This meant forecasting the average wastage rate per year of officers due to deaths, sickness, early retirement, and cashiering. This worked out at 2% per annum per age group. From this, we constructed a pyramid for officers of each arm and service showing how many had to be put in at the base each year to arrive at the right number for promotion to Lt Col at the average age of forty-two some twenty-three years later. The figures were based on a 320,000 man army with a regular content of 185,000, which it was thought in 1950 was the figure below which the peace-time army was unlikely to fall. Incidentally, the casualties amongst regular officers in World War II were much the heaviest in the infantry, as one would expect, a good deal less amongst the Sappers and Gunners, and very much less in the Royal Armoured Corps.

Unfortunately, a large number of war-time officers had been given regular commissions very soon after the end of the war and before any sort of pyramid structure had been worked out. The result was that in the early fifties there was a bulging excess of officers in the age groups twenty-five to thirty in every arm and service.

To broaden the base of the pyramid without lowering the chances of the regulars to go on to senior rank, it was clear that it would be desirable to retain short service commissions in the peace-time army. It was decided to give them the prospect of five year's service with the option, if vacancies permitted, of going on for eight years altogether. It wasn't too difficult to calculate how many of these would be needed in each arm and service. Although this scheme was approved by the Army Council, we had the devil of a job getting it through the Treasury. In the end, I and my opposite number in the Finance Department, a grade 2 civil servant, had to go over to the Treasury in Whitehall to see the official there. He turned out to be a grade 3 civil servant who apparently was the one responsible for recommending or refusing all votes for the Army Council. In appearance he reminded me of a science laboratory assistant. It was quite amazing to me that such a junior official could hold up schemes which had been approved by such an august body as the Army Council. There were similar junior officials for the Royal Navy and the Royal Air Force. Anyway, I and my finance colleague succeeded where the Army Council had failed!

I revised all the various schemes for obtaining regular commissions and published them in a single booklet of Army Council Instructions. One of these described how candidates from the British Commonwealth could obtain regular commissions in the British Army.

All of a sudden the British Military Adviser in Ceylon, who was a belted earl as well as being a brigadier, advised us that the nephew of the prime minister of Ceylon wished to come to Sandhurst with a view to obtaining a commission in the Devonshire Regiment. Well, the Devons are one of the most sought after regiments in the Army, and unless you come near the top of the Sandhurst order of merit, you have no chance of getting in, unless, you live there and have half a dozen kinsmen who have served in the regiment.

So I drafted a reply to the noble earl telling him all this and advising him to recommend the candidate come to Sandhurst for training for a commission in the Ceylon Army. Brigadier Sixsmith said I could not tell the brigadier what to do in such a preemptory manner and rewrote the letter in somewhat less unambiguous terms.

The result was that the earl misunderstood Sixsmith's letter and recommended this candidate for a commission in the Devons! So now Sixsmith had to write to Maj. Gen. Festing, who was president of the regular commissions board at Warminster, advising him to pass this man for a commission in the Ceylon Army but not for the British Army. At this stage the *Daily Mirror* somehow got hold of the story and splashed War Office racialism all over its front page! There was a terrible row, with the prime minister of Ceylon threatening to take his country out of the Commonwealth. So Festing had to pass this chap as suitable for a commission in the British Army, especially as he did well before the RCB. At Sandhurst he passed too low in the order to get any of the infantry regiments. So he got his commission in the Ceylon Army in the end and all was well.

I visited the RCB at Warminster and General Festing showed me around. He was an enormous man with a ruddy complexion, looking for all the world like a Somerset farmer. He had on a battle dress top over riding boots and gaiters, and hardly set a suitable standard of smartness for future regular officers. Although no doubt a distinguished member of the Rifle Brigade, I was surprised to learn that he later became a CIGS and a field marshal.

Two highlights each year were the commissioning of officer cadets from Sandhurst. I knew from my career pyramids how many officers should be commissioned into each regiment, arm and service. I also knew exactly what vacancies existed. Sandhurst would send up enormous sheets on which cadets were shown in their pass-out order of merit together with their first, second, and third choices of regiment and arm, and their family and territorial claims for joining the regiments of their choices. Those with strong family and territorial claims to a particular regiment could be advanced up to fifty places in the order of merit to get their choice. A strong claim would be at least three forebears or kinsmen in the regiment. The claims usually had to be validated by the colonel of the regiment concerned, and the MS captain used to come to the Board with a file of letters from colonels of regiments expressing, usually in pretty forthright terms, who they were prepared to have in their regiments and who they were not.

I used to take this list home with me the night before the War Office Commissions Board met, and Win and I would pencil in the destinations of most of the cadets that evening. Most of it was pretty straightforward, with only a relatively few problems for the Board to make a decision on.

The DGMT, who was also the Director of Infantry, presided. He was Lt. Gen. Sir Richard Gale, known as "Windy" Gale, who had commanded 6th Airborne Div for the D-Day landings in Normandy. He was an extraordinarily rude general. He had the habit of making a rude noise with his lips at any other general with whom he did not agree at the meeting.

The members of the Board were the six arms directors and the two services directors, all of them major generals, the DPA, the DDPA (Officers), and the DMS(B). The AAGs (full colonels) of each arm and service were present in attendance. I was the secretary and was assisted by the captain from MS(B). The competition for the Guards, Cavalry Regiments, Scottish and Southern County Regiments, Green Jackets, and Light Infantry Regiments was always pretty keen. Few wanted to go into the Lancastrian Regiments, and many who failed to get their first or second choices were commissioned into those Regiments. Even so, there was always a surplus of cadets who wanted to get into one or other of the six arms but who found themselves shunted willy-nilly into the RASC or the RAOC.

This led the DST one year to protest that filling his Corps with cadets who didn't really want to go there was becoming very bad for morale, and so he declined to take more than the minimum needed. So General Gale suggested the Armoured Corps should take some of them. This caused the DRAC to hit the roof, which in turn was followed by a rude noise from Gale. So Gale tried the DRA, to which the gunner expostulated that in that event he would not be responsible for shells falling short on the infantry. This brought a hurrumph from Gale and a climb down. The E-in-C, Maj. Gen Pat Campbell, to my surprise because his short temper was quite well known in the Corps, was not so strong and accepted one or two sub-educational standard cadets for the Sappers. In the end, the DRAC had to take some and bundled them into the Royal Tank Corps, flatly refusing to have them in any of the cavalry regiments.

In December 1950 our third son, David, was born. In the first few weeks of his life he yelled so much that we hardly had a wink of sleep. In the end, I just had to flee the house and spend a week in the Nuffield Officers' Club in Eaton Square to catch up on sleep! I've never really lived this flight down with Win since, and I don't blame her. But I had to do it for my work's sake, it being impossible to take leave at this time.

At this period of our marriage we were extremely hard up. The remuneration of married officers was now less than before the war because the Socialist Government had decided to tax allowances, including the marriage allowance. I used to ask Win to collect the monthly bank statement from the bank because it was often in the red and I didn't want to be accosted by the manager. Eventually this became too much for Win, and so we decided one Saturday morning to go together. We were delighted to find that we were fifty pounds in the black following a refund of income tax, and we both, without telling the other, bought badly needed new suits. So we were in the red again! It infuriated me that I, who was doing so well in my profession, being a major eight years before the normal time, should be constantly financially embarrassed. But then it was the stated socialist policy, as delineated by Sir Stafford Cripps, the socialist Chancellor of the Exchequer, to destroy the British officer class as an essential pre-condition to creating a Socialist Britain.

The War Office Commissions Board used to meet about once a fortnight to deal with candidates for regular commissions from university entrants and from emergency and short service commissioned officers who had applied to convert to regular commissions. Gen. Sugden presided over these meetings. The members were the DMS(B), the Directors of the arms or services for which the candidates were applying, or their deputies, and their respective AAGs. I would read out the report of the President of the Regular Commissions Board and reports from the candidate's commanding officer and any other senior officers who knew him. I would also inform the Board from my pyramid charts what vacancies there were, as many of these candidates belonged to later age groups. Often Sugden would say, "Oh, we don't need to hear what Brig XYZ has to say, let's hear Lt Col so and so." Sugden, and often the DMS(B), would know the reporting officers personally, and I soon learnt how often the report told as much, if not more, about the reporting officer than the candidate.

An interesting individual case which came before the WOCB just before my time was that of a certain Major Apps, who wanted a regular commission in the Gunners. He had served with distinction in Italy during the War, winning a good MC. After a lengthy period in action, it was decided that he should be rested, and he was sent to Cyprus as the permanent president of a court martial. One day he had too much to drink during lunch and became unfit to preside in the afternoon. He refused all suggestions by the members of the court that he adjourn the court till the following morning, saying that he had dealt with the Huns in this condition and was certainly capable of dealing with the accused. So the members had to arrest the president, who in due course was court martialled himself. He was severely reprimanded and sentenced to two years loss of seniority. He was sent back to the front in Italy, which is where he wanted to be anyway.

After the war he signed on for a short service commission and found that he enjoyed the Army in peace-time as well. So he applied for a regular commission, for which he was highly recommended, and passed the RCB in Italy with flying colors. When his case came before the WOCB his application was turned down as the Gunners were over-subscribed in his age group and in any case, because of his loss of seniority he would have no chance of promotion beyond major, which was his present rank.

So he now appealed to the War Office Commissions Appeals Board, of which I was the secretary. The WOCAB only met three or four times during my two years and consisted of the DPA, the Arms Director concerned, the DMS(B), and an outside major general to see fair play. So I had to prepare a shorter brief for them. I felt that Apps was clearly an above average officer, and if he was made aware of his limited prospects for higher rank he might well be accepted. So I loaded the brief in his favor, but the WOCAB turned him down because of his loss of seniority.

Apps then appealed to the King for His Majesty's pardon in respect of his one lapse and sentence for drunkenness on duty. His file was now getting enormous, and I made a brief of it again for the Army Council, who recommended to His Majesty that the appeal not be granted. It was signed by every member of the Council from the Secretary of State downwards. They realized that if the pardon was granted, Apps would get his commission.

I then produced an even shorter brief for the King and attached to it a couple of reports which had been written on Apps and the recommendation signed by all the members of the Army Council.

Meanwhile Mr. Styles had obtained a lovely ivory card file which some old man buried in the bowels of the War Office in Whitehall had inscribed in beautiful copper plate writing, "Appeal to His Majesty King George VI by...." I then inserted the papers and attached them with a piece of blue ribbon and sent the file over to Buckingham Palace. A few days later it came back signed on the top cover, "Appeal granted. George R."

I love to tell this story as I am a convinced monarchist. No president, who is only a promoted politician, can defy his entire council as a king can, and did. Apps duly received his commission but retired as a major in due course.

Occasionally I would be asked to draft a reply to a letter to the Sovereign. These requests would come in a note from an equerry of the King, or later from a lady in waiting of the Queen. They never presented any problem, and it was a privilege to write letters for the Sovereign, for which I am grateful.

From time to time I had to deal with parliamentary questions. These would arrive in a pink folder, and one had to drop whatever one was doing to deal with these immediately. Inside the folder was a sheet of paper with the question, together with three or four written supplementary questions on it, and also a note from the permanent under-secretary at the War Office. These were usually quite easy to deal with. One provided the answer to each question and added a few background notes to help the minister field any oral questions on the subject which might be directed at him in the House of Commons. That was almost always the end of the matter, but if the subject was a bit tricky, one might be required to attend at the House.

This happened to me once in my two years at the War Office. There is a narrow and very uncomfortable bench directly behind the speaker's chair in the House of Commons. So one sits on this back to back with the speaker, where one cannot be seen but can hear everything. In due course one hears one's question being asked and one's minister reading out the replies which one has provided for him. Then one hears him dealing with the oral supplementaries using the background notes if necessary. But if he gets a question for which the answer lies outside the notes one has given him, one begins writing very fast. In the meantime, one hears one's minister saying something to this effect, "I must congratulate the honorable member opposite for having such a deep understanding of the very difficult problem facing the War Office. I am happy to state that this matter is receiving very urgent attention at this moment." Meantime one is scribbling like mad, and one then passes one's scribble round the corner to the first occupant of the Treasury bench, who passes it along to one's minister at the despatch box, who then says, "And I'm happy to state that the very latest thinking on this subject is (one's scribble)."

Once a quarter or so one had to act as weekend duty officer for the Adjutant General's Department. One took over at mid-day on a Saturday and stayed in a suite on the top floor till Monday morning. During that period, one answered phone calls from all over the world. With nearly half a million men in the army, there must have been several million close relatives, including wives, children, parents, brothers, and sisters. It is not surprising therefore that one had to handle anything up to twenty death notifications each weekend in addition to serious illnesses and other emergencies. On one occasion I was rung up soon after midnight from Austria only to hear that they had a soldier there who would die unless he received some obscure drug within the next few hours. I had no idea where to get this from, but I did have the home phone numbers of all War Office officers. Eventually I managed to ring and wake up an RAMC colonel who knew the answer. It was to phone the army medical stores at Weybridge. This I did and all was well. There was a night duty officer there and a Dakota standing by for this sort of emergency.

About this time John Rogers left and was replaced by Captain Mark Lemon. Eric Sixsmith and I were going regularly every Wednesday lunch-time to the OCU meeting in Catherine Place, not far from Buckingham Palace. The meeting was called "Jolly Boys," and there we met up with Christian officers from other War Office departments as well as officers from the Admiralty and Air Ministry. Several of us were called on to lead the Bible studies there, and I did from time to time. We used to take Mark along with us too. He had been dabbling in Muhammadanism, and so I used to do Bible studies for him in our office as well. He seemed to profess conversion, but when I met him years later in South Africa, he had slipped right back and was disinclined to listen to me again.

Lt. Gen. Sir Arthur Smith used to attend, and occasionally I had the privilege of walking back with him to the War Office in Whitehall when I had business over there. Sir Arthur had been Chief of Staff to Lord Wavell in the Middle East and was a great Christian. He used to say that the fellow walking along the street with his Bible in a little attache case with "Are you going to hell?" written on one side and "Repent and believe on Jesus Christ" on the other, which he would show alternately to you, was not his cup of tea. But he'd add, "Who knows how the Lord may use such a witness?"

I also used to attend the lunch hour meeting of the War Office Christian Fellowship in Whitehall whenever I was over there on a Thursday, and once or twice I was asked to do a Bible Study for them. Sometimes when I was over in Whitehall I would look up Jock Millar, who was now a brigadier and Chief Engineer of London District. His office was alongside the old Duke of Wellington's office above the Horse Guard's Arch. He and all other sappers serving in London at the time had a miserable morning when the Sappers dropped the Bailey Bridge, which they were constructing for the Festival of Britain, into the Thames. We were only let off the hook when the Gunners dropped their gun down the inside of the Shot Tower.

A new problem which faced the country in the early 50s was the increased demand for brain power as we moved into a new technological age. This caused Sir Godfrey Ince, who was the permanent head of the Ministry of Manpower and National Service, to inform the War Office that we were taking too big a slice of the national brain power. In the discussions which followed, the Sappers, Signals, and REME particularly were forced, reluctantly, to reduce the minimum educational requirements for their respective corps. I had to amend the commissioning regulations accordingly.

In the middle of my time in the War Office the Korean War began, and it was necessary to call up some 2500 officers from the reserves. Each arm and service let me know what officers of what ranks and of what qualifications they needed, and these requirements were fed through the punch card machines at Stanmoor, and from there the calling up notices were sent out.

One day I was rung up by the permanent under secretary, who enquired whether I was the officer responsible for calling up the reservists. When I said that I was, he asked me whether I was aware that we had called up six Socialist MPs and no Conservatives. I said that I had no idea, as the political persuasions of officers were no concern of the Army and were not recorded on the cards. He said he thought this was the case and rang off. The next thing I had the Parliamentary Under Secretary on the phone. He asked if the officers could be posted within reach of London as the Government majority in the House was only five. I replied that these officers were liable to be posted anywhere in the world and no such undertaking could be given. "Oh!," he said, "If it was your party you would make some arrangement," and was quite rude. To which I replied with tongue in cheek, "My party is the fascist party and would ask for no such thing," and put the phone down. Shortly after, the Socialist Government fell and Churchill was back. I always think I had something to do with it!

An important project we were working on was to see if, instead of compulsory retirement for majors at the age of forty-five and of Lt Cols at forty-eight, we could guarantee a career to the age of fifty-five. To do this, the idea was to re-employ majors in uniform and Lt Cols as retired officers in captains' appointments. These soon became known as "red faced majors" and "retreads!" So I had to obtain from all commands at home and overseas the number of such appointments which were available for such a scheme. I knew from my pyramids how many officers passed over for further promotion would become available each year, but a problem was to estimate how many of them would opt for such a scheme. We did make certain discreet enquiries from serving officers but couldn't do anything like a gallup poll because we couldn't possibly divulge who were the officers likely to be passed over for promotion. In the end we worked on a figure of 50% and found that there were ample appointments available for such a supply in all arms of the service. Of course, all this required a mass of actuarial calculations which were rather beyond my two seniors. But anyway, I got the scheme passed at Director level, and it then went to the Army Council. The latter got cold feet and wouldn't go so far as to guarantee the career to fifty-five but would only offer it. This defeated the main object of the scheme, which was of course to assist in the recruitment of good material by offering a reasonable career to all.

However, it was also my job to write the officers part of the Secretary of State for War's speech when the Army estimates were debated in the House. I put our scheme in his speech as a guaranteed career to fifty-five and so it was duly announced. Strangely, I was never criticized for that.

In due course I got a very helpful retired Gunner Lt Col added to my staff as I was getting heavily overloaded. He took over most of the calculations from me.

Amongst other things, I wrote the commissioning regulations for the Brigade of Ghurkas and for several of the African Colonial Forces as they moved towards independence. I also wrote the commissioning regulations for the Womens Royal Army Corps.

The two senior women officers were a formidable pair, and neither the DPA nor the DDPA would have anything to do with them. So the whole business fell on me. The Director was Brigadier Coulshed and the AAG was Colonel Cowper, who used to slap me on the back with a sort of "how are you, old boy" attitude. I used to call them "Cowshed" and "Cowpat." A problem was to work out the WRAC career pyramid. The unknown was what the marriage wastage would be. I went to Somerset House (The Public Record Office) and found out from there what was the incidence of marriage per age group of British women. The figures were roughly that half were married before they were twenty-five, another quarter before they were thirty, and just a few thereafter. So I worked out the pyramid on the Somerset House figures and thus determined how many cadets should be commissioned each year from Mons Officer Cadet School.

The Princess Royal, sister of King George VI, took a very active interest in the WRAC and presided over many of their meetings in the War Office and personally approved their very smart bottle green dress uniform. She was at the first passing out parade at Mons, which Win and I also attended. The following year Gen. Sugden said I'd better be careful about what girls we accepted for training at Mons as we only had one set of bottle green uniforms. So I had better make sure we chose girls of the same size as before!

We also attended one of the Sandhurst passing out parades at which Princess Elizabeth took the salute. We sat quite near her. Maj. Gen. Hugh Stockwell (later to command the corps for the Suez operation), the Commandant, stood at the base of one corner of the dias while Gen. Sir Frederick Browning, Treasurer of her household, stood at the other. For some reason Gen. Browning was leaning ever so slightly against the upright of the dias. Princess Elizabeth had a very carrying voice and said, "Are you feeling quite well, General Browning?" "Yes, Ma'am." "Well, stand up straight then," in a very commanding tone of voice. General Browning stood up straight at once. It was a very public Royal rocket.

I was in Lansdowne House the morning the King died. We could see the Union Jacks coming down to half mast all over London. There was a sort of shocked silence even though those of us who had seen him recently knew how ill he was. I had seen him a few weeks previously being driven down Birdcage Walk to the Abbey for the Bath ceremony. He was so obviously painted up, poor man.

Later I witnessed the funeral procession from an upstairs window of the War Office in Whitehall, just opposite where it turned left under the Horse Guard's Arch. The coffin was preceded by the colonels of all the regiments, and the gold from the peaks of their caps gave the impression that the coffin was riding along on a sea of gold. After the coffin came the Royal Dukes on foot, followed also on foot by all the Admirals of the Fleet, all the Field Marshals, and all the Marshalls of the Royal Air Force. Some of them were by now very old, and I wondered how they would manage the long slow March all the way to Paddington station on this cold morning. London was silent except for the sad music of the funeral marches.

Not long after, John Thomas (later General Sir Norman Thomas), who was the DAAG in AG 7, said he had an excellent job lined up for me. It was to be the OC of 38 Fd Sqn., which was affiliated to the 4th Guards Brigade at Dortmund in Germany. This was the only Sapper unit attached to the Guards, and it was quite an honor to have been selected to command it.

So in February 1951, two very interesting years at the War Office came to an end. Several years later I called in at my old office where my retired gunner was still working. He said my only mistake had been a very wrong estimate of marriage wastage of WRAC officers. In practice, hardly any got married before twenty-five, and in the higher ages the wastage was less than the average for British women as a whole. The result was the pyramid was developing an ominous bulge!

Chapter Nine

Germany

In the first weeks of 1952, we packed up the bungalow in Fleet, put the furniture in store, sold the car for £300, and took the train to Harwich, where we arrived fairly late one February evening with three little boys aged six, four, and one up long after their bedtime.

The arrangements for travel for service families in those early years after the war were crude in the extreme. At Harwich we stood around in a large shed while mugs of hot cocoa were served. There was nowhere to sit, which didn't make it any easier to care for fractious children.

When we embarked, we found that wives and children were to be separated from their husbands. As an officer I was allotted quite a comfortable cabin on an upper deck where I could do nothing to help Win. Meantime Win and the children were herded down into the bowels of the ship to a cabin that accommodated eight. Her cabin mates included an unaccompanied whimpering little girl who needed comforting. Win is not a good traveller and the oily smells below did nothing to help her.

Next morning we boarded the troop train at The Hook for Dortmund and began our long, slow journey across Holland and into Germany. I remembered Holland as a spotlessly clean country from the war, and now one could tell when one crossed the border into Germany by the change in the windows, which in Holland positively shined. By mid-day the children were getting difficult to entertain. I took Chris and David to the back of the train where there was an observation platform from which one could see the level crossing barriers going up after the train had passed and the signals returning to their warning positions.

Eventually we stopped at a station for some time, and a steam locomotive came and attached itself to the rear of our train. Soon it started to pull us off in the direction from which we had come. This was a great excitement for Chris, and so I told him to go and fetch John. After a while he came back saying John had gone. I told him to go and have another look, and this time he came back in tears saying, "Mummy and John have both gone!"

I decided I'd better have a look myself, and true enough the back half of the train had been separated from the rest and Win and John and the luggage were off on their own! Fortunately at this juncture my part of the train stopped at a signal, and I jumped down onto the track with Chris and David. We then had about a mile walk along the track to the station where the separation had occurred, which turned out to be Oberhausen. The Germans on the platforms were rather surprised to see a British army major, in battledress, hatless and beltless, with a baby crying in his arms and a worried little boy holding his hand, walking back along the tracks.

With some difficulty, because I could speak no German, I discovered that I had been off to Mulheim and Win's part of the train was going on to Dortmund. There was another train going on to Dortmund in a few minutes, and I phoned through to the British RTO at Dortmund to expect a lonely wife and little boy and that I was on my way.

In the meantime, Win arrived at Dortmund to find the orderly officer, sergeant major, and an honor guard from 38 Fd Sqn. drawn up to greet their new OC. Win approached them with my hat, belt, and swagger cane, and enquired whether this was what they were looking for! After the position was explained they were most helpful in putting our luggage into a 15cwt truck and Win and John into the squadron Volkswagen. I soon rejoined the party, but it wasn't a very auspicious beginning. It took some time to live it down, and we became known as Major Mulheim and Mrs. Oberhausen.

38 Fd Sqn. was part of 23 Fd Engr Regt, which occupied the barracks of the erstwhile Hermann Goering Regt of the Luftwaffe. The barracks were splendid and the runway made an excellent parade ground. The quarter allotted to us was one of four double storey houses with cellars recently built. Ours was the one nearest the troops lines, and we were the first occupants. All the quarters were furnished exactly the same, and we could only break up uniformity by a different arrangement from our neighbors and by the few knick-knacks we had brought with us.

The garden was completely undeveloped and the soil a heavy clay. In the garage was a huge, grey painted Auto-union six seater saloon car which I bought from my predecessor for £60. It lacked a front side window.

I broke open all our crates on arrival and left, Win to unpack next day while I went off to take over the squadron. My predecessor had already left and it was immediately apparent that he had exercised very little authority and that the unit had been run by the sergeant major and the three troop sergeants. They were all excellent chaps who knew their jobs pretty well, and it was going to take time and tact to bring them into line.

Like all other units of BAOR, the squadron was very much under strength. Instead of a complement of almost 270, all ranks there were only about 150 in all. This meant an even more disproportionate shortage of working numbers as all essential posts had to be filled. The squadron consisted of one third regulars and two thirds national service men who were in at that time for a total of eighteen months. This meant that the latter were only with the unit for a year, having done their basic training in England, which meant that the unit virtually had to be retrained from scratch every year. Not surprisingly, the morale of the sergeants was beginning to suffer as they had to bring up their troop to standard each year only to see the troop vanish again at the end of the year. It was all the more necessary for me to train them on to even better things. They didn't know everything, and I had to demonstrate that they didn't before they would learn from me. They had been left too long doing things on their own, and doing it their way.

The CO of the regiment was Lt Col Jim Carr, a Canadian who had won the sword of honor at Kingston when he was a cadet. Unfortunately he had been in L of C units during the war and seen no action.

The introduction of the regimental system into infantry and armoured divisions was a post-war innovation. It was disliked by those of us who had served in the war at the sharp end because in war the fd coys work almost exclusively in support of the brigades to which they are affiliated. This also meant that a sapper major had considerably better status than majors of other arms since they would attend brigade orders on a par with the Lt Cols commanding the infantry battalions and field artillery regiment. The sappers had no regimental headquarters and no quartermaster, which meant that we always used to receive special consideration from the Royal Army Ordinance Corps as I related in Chapter 5.

I told Carr that I was utterly opposed to the regimental system, which seemed rather to upset him. I said that if he had three good squadrons, what more could he want, and I would certainly provide him with one. I think he was rather jealous of me because I had an MBE and a mention in despatches.

Carr's predecessor had been a most distinguished sapper, Col Arthur Morris, who had a DSO, an MC, and a GM. The troops called him "February Morris" because he always gave them twenty-eight days detention whatever the misdemeanor. He took the view that if a squadron commander had referred a case to him for punishment, it meant that the soldier needed punishing. But one day my SSM was standing in for the RSM at the CO's orders. The usual punishments were dished out, reduction of rank for NCOs and twenty-eight days for sappers. When it was all over Morris told the SSM to send the men in one at a time in the same order as before. "What did I do to you, corporal?," asked Morris. "You reduced me to L/Cpl, Sir." "Well, put your stripe back. Dismiss. Next." "What did I do to you," Morris asked the next. "You gave me twenty-eight days, Sir." "Cancel that; admonished, march out." And so it went on. All the punishments were cancelled. When they were alone, Morris said to the dumbfounded SSM, "Funny isn't it? It's my birthday." But that's the sort of man Morris was, and the troops loved him.

At the annual administrative inspection the year before I arrived, Morris had come on parade shortly before the inspecting general arrived. All the transport, bulldozers, and cranes of the regiment were drawn up on the left of the parade ground ready to do a drive past at the end of the parade. Morris noticed that two of the lorries were a slightly different shade of khaki paint from the rest. Immediately he called on the adjutant to fall out four painters to repaint the offending lorries. "But sir, the general will be here in a few minutes." "Do as I say, and don't argue." So the painters were fallen out, doubled to the paint store, and began painting the lorries, still in their best battledress.

When the drive past occurred at the end of the parade, the regiment was amazed to see the painters still clinging to their side of the lorries as they passed before the general! I do believe a good leader has the strength of character to display his idiosyncrasies, and the troops love it. Montgomery's black beret with two cap badges was another typical example.

I was shocked the second morning after my arrival to find that my captain second-in-command was not only not on parade but was also sitting unshaven in his office reeking with alcohol and wearing tackies on his feet. So with no ado, I had him in my office and told him in no uncertain terms that if this ever happened again he would go before a court martial. To my further amazement, he was in exactly the same state the next morning. This time I sat him down to find out his story. It turned out he was drinking with the padre in his quarter each evening. So my 2i/c was posted to another regiment where he came right, and the padre was sacked.

Meantime I was setting a pretty high standard of smartness to be worthy of our affiliation with the Guards. This meant tightening up on discipline, which had been slack before, and this apparently did not suit my new 2i/c an ex-ranker and quite notable athlete. I rather think he became a sort of spy on me on Carr's behalf. So I got rid of him too. His successor only lasted a few weeks as he wanted to become a railway engineer, and he was succeeded by Hugh Roland Price, who did me proud.

I was surprised to find that all 38 Fd Sqn. knew of its history was typed on one side of a sheet of foolscap, although it had the longest history as a field unit in the entire Corps of Royal Engineers. By writing to my predecessors and those before them, I was able to obtain first-hand accounts of the unit's history back to 1888, and rather sketchy snippets from the Corps history back to the unit's founding in April 1861. The history was published as "38 Field Squadron Royal Engineers 1861-1957," and a copy is in the Corps library at Chatham. I also had a board put up in my office giving the names of all the OCs since the unit's founding.

There was a sad amount of unhappiness amongst the men. Out of my 150 or so, I always had about twenty with home problems of one sort or another. So most evenings I had sessions in my office for welfare cases, which gave me the opportunity to present the Gospel to these troubled chaps. I cannot now remember with what effect, but I can certainly remember one marriage which was put right on a Christian basis. But the fact that I was spending time with anyone who had a problem became known throughout the unit and I soon knew that the chaps would do anything I asked of them. I would punish chaps who needed it but made it a rule to have them in as soon as their punishment was done to find out what was their trouble. When it comes to rehabilitating offenders, one cannot do much until guilt has been assuaged by punishment, and then one can build on a clean start. (For this reason I loathe imprisonment, because it is ungodly, long drawn out, and a breeding place for more crime). Years later, I met my sergeant major, who was now in his scarlet coat as a pensioner of the Royal Hospital, Chelsea. I said that I expected he was surprised that I had become a minister. "Not a bit of it," he said, "in fact I should have been surprised if you had not."

I interviewed everyone in the squadron and also newcomers as they arrived. I found out as much about their homes as I could, their interests, and, in particular, their sports and the standard they had reached. I entered all this information on a card for each member, and with a knitting needle and a system of slots cut in the cards, I could pull out, for instance, all the soccer players in the unit. From this I made an appreciation and decided what events we would go for in the year. I then addressed the squadron and told them that this year we would win the inter-squadron athletics, cross country, and soccer competitions. We would win the watermanship competition as the best sapper squadron just had to do that, and the drill competition as it was inconceivable that anyone should beat the squadron supporting the Guards at drill. If they won anything else it would not be in accordance with my plan, which only made them the more determined to win something else as well, which is what I intended.

I had the forty-odd HQ personnel together and asked them what they thought their role in the unit was. After various suggestions, I told them that their role was to look after me and my comfort. The efficiency of the unit largely depended on my brain working properly, and it could only do so if a lot of the detail was taken off my shoulders, which is what they did, and if I could stay alert for long hours. For this reason I should need to be fortified with brandy, and so a bottle was to be kept at all times in my jeep, in the office lorry, and in the mess.

From the new intake I had to send off individuals for training as wireless operators, despatch riders, compressor operators, medical orderlies, sanitary orderlies, and so on.

In the program in Germany in those days, there was a continuous series of exercises working up from regimental and brigade level to the large scale NATO exercises in the autumn. As a result one was out from barracks almost continuously from April to October. As soon as most of the individual training was over, one would, if one was wise, take one's unit on some preliminary exercises on one's own. So I took the squadron out on three night exercises, map reading, convoy driving, and harboring, which I called after my three boys Exercises Christopher, John, and David. Harboring was very important, particularly in conditions of nuclear war, as the last thing one wants is to be photographed from the air as one is pulling off the road into one's unit hide. Subsequently, the CE 1 Corps said he'd never seen a unit get into harbor and camouflaged up as quickly as mine.

SSM Skentelbery, an excellent and loyal supporter, was worried that he would be on leave when the drill competition came up. I wouldn't alter his leave and quite enjoyed training the squadron for it myself. I told the chaps to look upon it as a game and I was just the skipper of the team. I had to get ninety-one words of command off in the right sequence, and we won the shield easily.

All the families watched the competition, and as I was marching off proudly at the head of my squadron, John ran out and marched beside me. The comment from the file behind me was, "I wonder which little night exercise this one was!"

The first bridge we built as an exercise was a floating Bailey built at night over the Weser. In the middle of the night the SSM asked me what I wanted to call the bridge, it being the sapper custom always to name their bridges. I was preoccupied with the job on hand and told the SSM to call it what he liked. At dawn next morning the boards were up bearing the inscription, "DIXFURST BRIDGE."

Quite soon after I got to Germany, we began rehearsing for the coronation parade which every garrison town in Germany had to stage. 23

Fd Engr Regt paraded with a Field Ambulance, a REME Workshops, and an RASC Supply Company, totalling about 2000 all ranks. Hugh Hamilton took over the rehearsals as Carr commanded the sapper contingent in the coronation procession in London.

At each garrison parade a general had to be provided to represent royalty, and Maj. Gen. HHC Sugden, the CE BAOR came to ours. He was a first class sapper who had been CE 8 Corps during the Northwest Europe campaign. But he was not at his best on parade, nor had he taken an active part in any parade for donkey's years. The drill and the words of command had changed since his day, and so he was given an ADC to be near him to coax him through the parade. But even so his voice had become a bit quavery and lacked the punch as of old.

At the dress rehearsal he gave this sequence of commands: "Parade will unfix bayonets, bayonets!" The parade duly held their rifles between their knees with the bayonets held in their left hands just clear of the muzzles of their rifles. "Parade, remove head-dress." The parade took off their berets and held them in their right hands while still gripping their rifles with their knees and holding their bayonets with their left hands. "Three cheers for her majesty Queen Elizabeth. Hip, hip, hip, hurray," croaked the general. Indescribable comments came from the ranks behind me!

On coronation day, all the local Germans were required to attend, and the parade went off better, even if the Feu de Joi was somewhat erratic. But we did better than Iserlohn, where the tanks fired a twenty-one gun salute facing their barrack blocks and in succession blew out all their windows, much to the astonishment of the local German dignitaries.

The Divisional Commander had, I knew from my time in the War Office, been passed over for promotion to major general. But then he had commanded with distinction a Brigade in Korea, and so the powers that be had relented and here he was commanding 2nd Division. But I don't think he ever really understood anything beyond infantry tactics; certainly not sappers. He used to reprimand me because my sappers hadn't saluted him while carrying a 600 pound Bailey panel, for instance. One day some of my bulldozer operators, who admittedly are seldom the smartest of sappers, were unloading a dozer from a low loader trailer, a fairly tricky operation at the best of times. The general came by in his black Mercedes replete with the GOC's pennant. Naturally my sappers didn't salute, so the general stopped the car and sent his ADC over the road to fetch my chaps. "Why didn't you salute?," demanded the irate general. My sapper, who was from Somerset, replied, "Well, seeing as 'ow you were in this 'ere black car I thought you were one o' them square 'eads." The general gave up after that, and I had no more trouble from him. Throughout the British Army, of course, all Germans have square heads.

I was on the best of terms with the Guards who were based outside Dusseldorf with 4th Guards Brigade HQ at Hubelrath. The Brigade Commander was Brig Claud Dunbar, whom I had met during the war when he was commanding the 4th Battalion Scots Guards in 6th Guards Tank Brigade. He remembered me as Jock Millar's adjutant. I became great friends with Peter Leuchars, the Brigade Major, and we often used to go out together when I had to spend a night or two at Brigade HQ. Peter finished up a general, as did Basil Eugster of the Irish Guards and Digby Raeburn of the Scots.

Jim Carr received several very complimentary chits from Brigadier Dunbar for the performance of 38 Fd Sqn. In addition, the squadron won all the competitions I had forecast but none of the others. Nevertheless, Carr only gave me an average report. When I initialled it I told him I was only doing so because it was so out of line with everything else that had been written about me that no one would take the slightest notice of it. Next year he gave me an outstanding report. On 3rd July 1952, after thirteen years service, I became a substantive major, and that was after nearly seven continuous years as a temporary major.

All the Rhine bridges had been rebuilt by the Germans, but with instructions from HQ BAOR to include in them demolition chambers and conduit pipes for electrical circuits so that they could be demolished quickly in the event of a Russian offensive. For this purpose I had three tons of high explosive at Dortmund, and another three tons in reserve in a bunker near Hubelrath, with which to blow up the three Rhine bridges at Dusseldorf if the balloon went up. The communists knew about this and used to fill the demolition chambers with sand and remove the recovery wires from the conduits. I had to inspect the bridges every three months to check that they had not been tampered with.

I had a rail bridge which was a suspension bridge, and a roadbridge which was a single arch bridge rather like the Sydney Harbour bridge. It wasn't much fun clambering about on the icy girders of these bridges on a frosty morning anything up to 100 feet above the Rhine below. I remember, when a train came over and I was high up, the bridge swaying quite a lot and I got the feeling I was being shaken off it! The Dusseldorf-Neuss roadbridge was a most impressive and interesting bridge. It consisted of three arches which from the outside looked like typical reinforced concrete arches. But in fact they were made of steel, and there were two parallel arches with the roads running on top and tram lines running on decking covering the space between them. Cycle tracks and footpaths were cantilevered out from the outside of the arches. One could walk inside the arches, which were like huge hollow boxes from one end of the bridge to the other, up and down over the arches. The noise inside was terrific from the traffic on top. Access to the arches was from locked doors at the ends of the bridge so the communists couldn't get at the charge boxes on the inside of the bridge.

In the first year, 1952, the NATO exercise took the form of a simulated Russian army crossing of the Rhine. In this, separate brigade group crossings were to take place over a very wide front with the hope that at least one would be successful, which could then be reinforced in strength. In preparation for this, Brig Dunbar gave me the pioneer platoons of all three battalions to make up the squadron to full war strength. I took them with the squadron to do six weeks, training on the Rhine, for which we erected a tented camp for our accommodation near Rheinburg.

The Rhine is about 1300 feet wide and has a current of about seven knots. But on both banks it has a line of breakwaters about 300 feet apart. Between the breakwaters there is a reverse current of four or five knots. The division between the currents flowing in opposite directions is remarkably short, not more than a foot at the most.

The close support rafts we were operating took loads of twelve tons on a deck about thirty feet long. The deck was carried on two pontoons sixty feet long. At the bow and stern of each of these pontoons were 9HP engines driving propellers which could be turned through 360 degrees.

So the difficulty of ferrying with these rafts can well be imagined. As the raft passed over between the two currents, two propellers would be operating in a current running one way while the other two would be operating in a current running in the opposite direction. The danger of the raft going into a pirouette and drifting out of control downstream and possibly into one of the breakwaters was very real.

Sure enough, my most experienced sergeant lost control of his raft on his first trip and drifted off downstream a quarter of a mile, but fortunately without coming to grief on a breakwater. When he eventually clawed his way back against the current to the starting point, he came ashore very annoyed and telling me that no one could ferry here.

So I took over and set a BAOR ferrying record of ten trips per hour over a two hour period. My sergeant shook my hand after this, and from then on I had no more trouble from the sergeants taking instructions from me. Subsequently, one of the other troop sergeants did thirty-two trips in four hours, which for a sustained effort was really a better feat than mine. Part of the secret was to make the drivers drive on and off quickly the moment they got the order to go. I had the brigade send all their F Echelon drivers and vehicles down to Rheinburg and practised them all on driving on and off rafts. I had a bulldozer on the bank to tow off anyone I might drop in the water. Actually none had a dip, but the threat that I'd take away the raft from under them caused drivers to put their foot down the moment I gave the word!

We also practised some of the guardsmen in trips on storm boats. We had a problem with one Guards sergeant who, despite the protests of my corporal boat captain, insisted on marching his section, left, right, left, into the storm boat. No one was drowned, but some equipment was lost. I gave evidence at the subsequent court of enquiry but discreetly did not divulge to the court that the equipment alleged to have been in the boat would have sunk it anyway. That's one way to get the losses of a battalion for a year written off!

When the NATO exercise came off later, we took the Guards Brigade across so well that theirs was the only brigade crossing ruled successful. We were supposed to have failed so that we could take part in the later divisional crossing, but Brig Dunbar insisted that it would be bad for morale to rule a failure where there had been such an obvious success. The result was that my squadron didn't have to do it all again, much to Carr's annoyance, but merely had to keep a ferry service going to keep the brigade supplied across the river. After the exercise, Carr received this message from Brig Dunbar: "I am so grateful for the tremendous assistance we have received from Dick Begbie and 38 Field Squadron in our river crossing training. They have worked absolutely flat out and as a result we have learnt an enormous amount. I only hope that they haven't been overworked as a result. Thank you very much for them; we would have got nowhere without them."

Another interesting job I was given was to conduct a battlefield tour for the Danish Army Staff College. I was assured that I need not worry about the language because there are so few Danes in the world that they all speak English. So I took them over our old 15th Scottish battles in which we breached the Siegfried Line and the Rhine crossing. There were about forty students on the tour, and at the end of it they gave me a very nice glass dish engraved with the royal arms of Denmark.

I also acted as engineer umpire for a Belgian Corps doing a minefield exercise. There was a language difficulty, but I didn't think they were very efficient.

Early in 1953 there were terrible floods in eastern England, and Canvey Island was particularly badly affected. The Lord Mayor of London launched a flood relief appeal, and I waited a week for Carr to respond. But he did nothing, so I addressed the squadron on parade and suggested that 38 do something about it. I said we should either give the same amount each, say 2/6d, or a day's pay. The only snag about the second idea was that I should have to give more than anyone else, so which did they want to do? The reply was immediate and unanimous, as I expected and hoped it would be, a day's pay. I said I was sure that with such an amount we would receive a personal acknowledgment from the Lord Mayor. Of course, Carr eventually heard what we were doing and demanded that the 38 contribution be included with the regiment's contribution, which he was now calling for. This of course I refused to do, and he knew as well as I did that he could not force me to.

Soon I received a nice letter signed personally by the Lord Mayor which I put on the notice board. It read:

> Dear Major Begbie,
>
> May I express my sincere gratitude for the very generous gift of 55 pounds 13 shillings which you have kindly sent me on behalf of all ranks of 38 Field Squadron R.E. as a contribution to my fund.
>
> This prompt response to my appeal is deeply appreciated and I shall be grateful if you will offer my heartfelt thanks to all concerned.
>
> Such practical sympathy is an encouragement to me and an inspiration to all who have suffered.
>
> I have pleasure in enclosing my official receipt.
>
> Yours Sincerely,
>
> Rupert de la Bier
> Lord Mayor

The letter is of interest in that it shows how little a day's pay of an entire squadron was in those days. Carr, who failed to raise more than half of what we did from the rest of the regiment, received a roneod chit in acknowledgment, much to the glee of my chaps. Carr was furious.

He went to all sorts of lengths to try to catch me out, including encouraging sappers to speak to him behind my back, but to no avail as far as I was concerned. There was an occasion when I had to demolish a Siegfried line pillbox which was blocking the extension of the runway at the RAF base at Wildenrath. I detailed Capt. Sandy Busk and his troop for the job. Sandy met with an accident when a splinter of reinforcing steel penetrated his chest. Carr wasted no time in getting round to my office to see what safety precautions I had instituted. I showed him a copy of the written orders I had given Sandy, which included all the proper safety precautions, and that again was the end of the matter.

We returned to barracks at last in late October, and there was opportunity at last to do something about holding Bible studies. The Chaplain was doing nothing in that direction. I prayed for guidance, and the time seemed right. So I announced the beginning of OCU meetings, which we held in our quarter. One of those who came was Ken Neaves, one of my subalterns. Years later as a lieutenant colonel he became the chairman of the OCU General Committee.

About the same time in 1953, we were told that my next posting would be to the Middle East. This suited me very well as I hoped to be given home postings later when the boys were going through their schooling.

Therefore, during our annual leave, Win and I bought a modest house in Cheltenham to enable the boys to go to College there as their father and grandfather had done before them. It would mean a two or three year separation of course, but this was one of the penalties of service life which one had to accept.

In November we had the annual administrative inspection where the general with a team of staff officers goes through a unit with a fine tooth comb. In preparation for this, the SSM and I connived together to send as many of our less well groomed sappers away as possible. Leave programs were adjusted accordingly. Others were sent away on courses. Just before the day, the SSM told me that we really couldn't have Sapper Jones present, so he would put him on some cooked up charge and would I kindly put him away for seven days? I duly obliged.

All the tools and equipment after the long summer maneuvers had to be cleaned up and sharpened. All the mens' kit had to be checked over and over again to make sure it was alright. By fair means or foul, deficiencies in the SQMS's store had to be made up. One day we were driving in convoy behind an RASC convoy when the SSM drew alongside my Jeep and said he was taking over the lead in a three ton lorry. The next thing that happened was that some tyres on the back of the last RASC lorry were transferred to the SSM's three tonner while both were on the move. I of course saw nothing.

Contrariwise, some things which we ought not to have had to be spirited away. There was a disused German pillbox on the far side of the airfield which served the purpose well. We also did some swopping between squadron commanders. I remember Mike Andrews, OC of 5th Fd Sqn, was short of socks and I was able to oblige him.

My batman, Dick Marriot, was a married man and older than most of the other national servicemen because his call-up had been deferred. He slept in the servant's room of our quarter and often baby sat when we were out. But he had to go back to the barracks for the inspection. With Win's permission, he left his wireless set and other belongings hidden in the cellar for the inspection. When Win went down there to fetch some coal on the day of the inspection she couldn't get in. It was full to the ceiling with the personal belongings of the squadron, the OC's house obviously being a safe hiding place.

I warned all my chaps not to be afraid of the general when he came round the barrack rooms. He was really after me and not at all after them. So when he asked them a question, I told them just to give him a sensible answer. The general wouldn't know whether it was true or not. But on no account were they to say that they didn't know.

After the formal drill and inspection on the parade ground, my chaps were ordered to fall in beside their beds with their kit laid out and each troop in different orders of dress.

When the general came to the first barrack room he approached a sapper and said, "Now, my man, tell me how your unit has done at sports this year." My sapper then reeled off a whole lot of results showing that the unit had done pretty well. "Very good, very good, shows your chaps are alert, Begbie." Meantime the SSM and I were winking at each other behind the general's back because by good fortune he had picked on the one sapper in the room who had represented the unit in almost every sport.

In the next room the chaps had been ordered to wear their great coats. To my horror, there was a chap who had come back from somewhere early and had missed all our rigorous inspections. There he was, standing with a coat reaching only half way down his thighs! The general made a bee-line for him immediately. "How long have you had that coat, my man?" "A year, Sir." "Well it's a bit short for you, isn't it?," enquired the general. "Well I growed, Sir," replied my sapper in a somewhat indignant tone of voice, and there wasn't very much the general could say to that.

In the last room there was a sapper with no tea mug. Of course, after years of inspecting kits, a thing like that is spotted immediately. The general did just that. "I see you have no tea mug, how do you go on for tea?," demanded the general, this time sure he had a winner. "Never touch it, Sir," came the instant reply. As he left to go on to the next squadron the general said to me, "Well there's nothing wrong here, the men are right behind you, you can fall them out now, thank you."

Hugh was captain of the regimental rugger team, and he prevailed on me to turn out for the regiment. We won the 2nd Division Cup, and Hugh had the cheek to write in the divisional newspaper that "Major Begbie, brought out of moth balls, stood the pace very well!"

Win and I had two pleasant holidays in Germany. We went to Winterberg once in the summer and enjoyed lovely walks in the woods and mountains, and once in the winter for skiing. I could just about manage a Christie turn before we left. Gen. and Mrs. Cuthbert Sugden were there the second time, and it was nice to renew the acquaintance.

At the end of 1953 my future posting was suddenly changed. I was no longer to go to the Middle East but to go to the SME at Chatham as the DAA&QMG. Hugh Hamilton had the job before and told me I should welcome the posting as it was a very important one and very much in the public eye. There was a quarter in Gillingham for the job. Now Win and I had to decide whether to occupy it or not. I was determined that my sons should have the same education as I had and that Rochester Grammar School was not in that class. We decided that the family should go to

Cheltenham and that I should accept a room in Brompton Barracks. It was not a good prospect.

SSM Skentelbery said the squadron wished to make a presentation. Much as I appreciated the gesture, I said I was forbidden to accept. However, they decided that no one could stop them giving something to Win, and they gave her a very fine mantle clock which gave us some thirty years service despite all our many moves. Even so, they managed to slip a very nice desk set into my baggage when I wasn't looking. So with a rather heavy heart, I bade farewell to my chaps, quite a few of whom were in tears. A number had lost their fathers in the war, and I had, so it seemed, become quite a father figure to them. This was not withstanding my being called "Tiger Begbie" behind my back!

Chapter Ten

Chatham

We went back to England in late January 1954 by travel arrangements which were still no better than in 1952. We had one moment of alarm when the new mantle clock chimed as we went through customs, but the officials were kind to us.

Leave was spent settling the family into our house at Cheltenham, which included turning the kitchen into a dining room and the pantry into a kitchen. We were so short of funds that we couldn't afford curtains for the sitting room at the back, but we put up curtains in the drawing room at the front to hide from bypassers the fact that we couldn't afford to furnish it.

We kitted out Chris for the Junior School of Cheltenham College and John for a kindergarten school. We couldn't afford a car, so Win, Chris, and I rode bicycles, with David in Win's carrier and with John in mine. The Begbie family wobbling into town became quite a well known spectacle. After I left for Chatham, Win had an onerous time fetching and depositing the boys at school, looking after David, and doing all the housework.

In February I reported to the SME at Chatham, where the Commandant was Brigadier "Bags of Dash" Browning. He was due to retire soon to Devon, where he hoped to become a magistrate. He was succeeded after a few months by Brigadier Cecil Eking. In my time the Deputy Commandant did practically nothing except review various courts of enquiry and audit boards. The second encumbent in my time was Col. Peter Bickford, who also involved himself with the R.E. Drag and Point-to-Point meeting. He amused me by his solution to the Christmas Card problem. One year he sent them all back endorsed with, "A happy

Christmas to you too." Since then he has never received nor had to send another Christmas Card!

I found that, in addition to the normal duties of a Deputy Assistant Adjutant and Quartermaster General, I had the following extra duties:

Treasurer RE Corps Accounts
Treasurer of the RE Headquarters Mess Fund
Secretary and Treasurer of the RE Sports and Games Fund
Secretary and Treasurer of the RE Band and Orchestra Fund
Serving Officer representative on the Board of the RE Officers' Widows Fund
RE representative on the Committee of the United Services Sports Club, Chatham
Secretary and Treasurer of the RE Wine Fund

To help me, I had Capt. John Notley as a staff captain. He took all the "A Staff" work off me except officer postings in and out of the SME. Then there was a Mr. Pearce who did the bookkeeping for all the funds for which I was responsible. Finally there was a Mr. Risborough who did all the administrative work for the considerable civilian staff of the SME.

Every regular officer had to make a contribution each year to the HQ Mess Fund so that it could be maintained to a fitting standard and could be used by any officer as a club whenever he was in England. I found the mess to be in a disgraceful state of neglect, and no use had been made of the fund for years. The proportions of the superb Regency dining room had been ruined by blocking off the end window with hardboard. In consequence of my urging, the Commandant empowered me to go ahead with improvements. I instructed the CRE Works Chatham Garrison to put the structure into a good state of repair. He should have examined the wiring system, and perhaps I ought to have thought of it, which would have avoided a fire which occurred some years later. I also persuaded him to lay a nice oak strip floor in the entrance hall, which I enhanced with two Persian carpets and a chandelier for which the fund paid.

The dining room needed re-decorating, but there was disagreement as to the color scheme. The Commandant ordered me to convene a board of officers to decide the matter and I was to be its president. I solved that one by finding two color-blind officers to serve on the board with me.

There is a vast amount of Corps silver in the cellars under the HQ Mess. We used to loan some of the pieces to officers' messes at home and in Germany. It was part of my job to keep track of all the Corps silver and to arrange for its insurance. Two particularly interesting pieces are the Russian Punch Bowl and the silver statuette, "Winged Victory." The punch bowl, an outstanding example of Fauberge's work, was presented by the Empress Catherine to a Sapper, Colonel Scott Moncrief, who had constructed the Russian railways at the end of the last century. It is, of course, quite priceless and consists of a bowl about a foot in diameter decorated on the outside with the six arms of the royal families of Russia. The bowl stands on a pedestal on a tray in which are recesses to hold the cups. Each cup bears the arms of a Russian Duke.

"Winged Victory" was originally made by the Italian Government for presentation to President Wilson for his part in founding the League of Nations. The angel has a ring in her back to enable her to be hung from the ceiling of the oval office in the White House. When the American Government reneged on Wilson's work the presentation was withheld, and "Winged Victory" lay forgotten in some silversmith's workshop until discovered by another intrepid sapper who bought it for the HQ Mess. It is always placed before the mess president on guest nights.

As far as the RE Sports and Games Fund was concerned, this was a matter of receiving bids from the secretaries of all the RE sports clubs and allocating grants to them. I remember becoming quite involved in financing hulls for the yacht club, and deciding whether it was right to heavily finance the flying club, bearing in mind the relatively few officers involved on the one hand, and the desirability of encouraging this activity amongst serving officers on the other.

The RE Band is paid for out of public funds, but every musician is also capable of playing an orchestral instrument. The orchestra accepts a number of public engagements from which the net proceeds go into the fund. The fund is also subsidized by the officers by an annual subscription. With this fund, I persuaded the Commandant to allow me to restore the busbies for the band and also gold cord aigulettes. Scarlet tunics were authorized after I left but I had taken the first steps in the right direction.

I used to go up to Lloyds Bank in Pall Mall, London, for the board meetings of the RE Officers' Widows Fund. It was presided over by General Sir Eustace Tickell, who really gave us all the advice we needed. As far as I remember, the total assets in 1954 were about a quarter million pounds. Factors in the equation were the life expectancy of Sapper officers, the number of years their widows would survive them, and planning investments to mature in step with forecast needs. It was interesting for me to get some insight into the problems of long term insurance.

The Wine Fund was a fascinating affair. Every regular officer throughout his service contributes one pound a year to the fund. In addition, various public spirited officers have remembered the fund in their wills. In 1954 the fund was worth about eight thousand pounds, of which six thousand pounds was represented by wines in the cellars under the HQ Mess and the remainder in investments awaiting a good vintage year. The fund is non-profit making, so, for instance, in 1954 we were drinking a 1926 claret at 1926 prices. A retired Brigadier van Cutsem was our expert on the committee and advised us when and what to buy. I remember we bought a port during my term of office. The mess steward, who had been in the Mess for about thirty years, had throughout those years kept a single bottle of port in a niche in the cellar with a candle and a thermometer beside it. He used to inspect it every morning and move the candle nearer or further from the bottle to keep it at a constant temperature throughout the year for the sovereign to drink whenever there should be a royal visit. The Queen came in 1956 and partook of it, but history does not record with what result!

All these funds and the causes they supported came before the Corps Committee, which consisted of the Chief Royal Engineer, General Sir Edwin Morris, the Representative Colonel Commandant, General Sir Philip Neame, the Engineer-in-Chief, Major General Chris Walkey, and the Commandant SME. I had to brief the latter for their quarterly meetings in the E-in-C's office in the War Office.

I had suggested to Brigadier Browning that he take up with the Corps Committee the idea of inviting the Queen to Chatham for the Corps centenary in 1956. But he tartly refused even to discuss the matter. When Brigadier Eking took over I raised the matter with him, and he immediately undertook it. One morning he called me into the office to tell me I had got him a hefty kick on the shin from the E-in-C! It turned out that General Morris was a divorced person and therefore, in those days, as a *persona non-grata* at court would not be able to attend. Cecil undertook to raise the matter again when General Crawford, who would stand for no such nonsense, took over as Representative Colonel Commandant. I'm glad that it was I who took the initiative to invite the Queen to Chatham on a visit that did not occur until long after I had gone.

The SME consisted of four schools, the Field Engineering School, Construction School, Electrical and Mechanical School, and Roads and Airfields School, and three holding regiments in Brompton, Kitchener, and Gordon Barracks. I used to do all officer postings to and from the staff personally with the Commandant. We used to be offered a choice of officers by AG7, and Cecil Eking took the view that if neither he nor I knew them, they were unlikely to be any good. Sometimes we would ask for a particular officer by name. One such that I had known and brought forward finished up as a major general. He was not popular in the Corps, but he knew his stuff.

Soon after my arrival I joined the OCU group which met weekly in Gordon Barracks. The OCU local secretary was a captain in the Education Corps, and about twenty officers and wives attended. When the local secretary was posted away, I took over and remained the local secretary till the end of my time. Several of us did a cold canvas of civilian houses, leaving literature to encourage people to go to the Billy Graham meetings. I took a bus load of OCU members and young officers up to Harringay in 1954 to hear him. Mass evangelism of this sort was entirely new, and the crowd and the massed choir had a considerable effect. The sermon seemed excellent to me at the time, and several of our party went forward to be counselled. However, none joined our meetings at Chatham.

I took another bus load up to the meetings in Wembley stadium in 1955. Seeing the crowds coming in coaches from all over England was quite thrilling, but I do not recall that there was any lasting effect.

I arranged a showing of Fact and Faith Films in Gordon Barracks, and both the Commandant and Deputy Commandant came, but I received little support. In retrospect, I think I should have done more to motivate the chaplain, as his sermons were painfully lacking in Scriptural exposition.

One day Eking called me in and demanded to know what he was to do with the Archbishop of Canterbury for five minutes! After I confessed I had not the least idea, he showed me a signal he had received from that worthy to the effect that he was accompanying the Queen Mother to the opening of a new wing of Rochester Grammar School. He would take the opportunity to visit the Navy at the Nore and us as well for five minutes each. The problem was there were 6000 of us altogether. Eking said, "I'll tell you what we'll do. We'll have a parade in front of the Memorial Arch. On parade will be the Deputy Commandant, the Brigade Major, yourself, the Garrison Adjutant, and the Garrison Sergeant Major. I'll take the parade, Number 1 Dress, medals and swords."

On the day, we were lined up before the arch and Eking said, "There will be no words of command, but do everything I do." So there we were, looking like a row of prunes, while all the sappers went about their duties in their denim uniforms.

I was curious to know in what sort of car an archbishop might ride. In due course a chauffeur driven black Humber limousine rolled up with the pennant of Canterbury flying on its radiator, just like a general. As the car drew up in front of us, Eking came to the salute and we all followed suit. In the back of the car was a sea of white consisting of the Archbishop, the Bishop of Rochester, and their respective chaplains all in their robes. The archbishop waved to us from inside the car, and it was difficult to restrain oneself from waving one's fingers while still at the salute. The first man out on the far side of the car was Rochester's chaplain, who speedily assembled the two halves of the Bishop's crook, which had a bayonet coupling. As soon as that was done the Bishop dismounted. Meantime the Archbishop continued to smile and wave at us from inside the car, and it was really impossible not to make some welcoming gesture with one's fingers as we remained at the salute. Next out was the Archbishop's chaplain, who took some time to assemble Canterbury's crook, which, being no doubt more ancient, had to be screwed together. Only when this was done did the Archbishop dismount, and then we could drop salute. Eking then brought the Archbishop round for us to be introduced one after the other to him. He asked me what I did, and I gave him my appointment in full, "Deputy Assistant Adjutant and Quartermaster General, Sir." He said that was too much for him, and I voiced my agreement.

He then returned into his car. We all saluted, and the same pantomime with crooks then ensued in reverse order.

During my time, the City of Rochester resolved to grant the freedom of the city to the Corps and John Notley, and I had to see to all the arrangements. In particular, I had to compose the acceptance speech for the Chief Royal Engineer, General Sir Edwin Morris. I researched the historical connections between the Corps and the City. These included the fact that the first Chief Engineer of England, Bishop Gundulf, who had come over with the Conqueror, had built Rochester Castle, that the Mayor of Rochester had the courtesy title of Admiral of the Medway, on which sappers had always done their watermanship training, and there was something else which I now forget. Morris was pleased with my speech and accepted it.

The ceremony took place on the lawn of the castle. When the mayor made his presentation speech, he made all the same points that I had dug out. I saw poor Morris looking at his notes in some desperation. When he accepted the casket containing the freedom scroll, he had to keep saying, "And as you've just said Mister Mayor..." After it was all over Morris gave me such a wigging and said, "Next time compare notes with your opposite number."

At the conclusion of the ceremony, the mayor and corporation, accompanied by General Morris and General Sir Charles King, followed the band in procession to the mayor's parlor. Win and I had to conduct Lady Morris and Lady King to the parlor, but it was difficult because of the crowds. I knew a little side alley which would bring us out on the high street not far from the parlor. I took them down there at a fast walk, and we emerged into the narrow high street right into the middle of the procession before I realized quite where we were. So I whispered quickly to the ladies to pretend they were meant to be there. They played their parts magnificently, waving to the crowds as if they were royalty. Altogether it was quite an eventful day.

There were various formal occasions in the HQ Mess at which I had to arrange the seating plan. This was not always easy, and a copy of Debrett took its place beside the Manual of Military Law and Queen's Regulations in my office. With General Sir Edwin Morris as host, a typical guest list might include the C-in-C at the Nore, the Admiral Superintendent of the dockyard, the Lord Lieutenant of the County, the High Sheriff, the Bishop of Rochester, and the Mayors of Rochester, Gillingham, and Chatham.

What made it especially tricky was to know which wives took the precedence of their husbands and which did not. The wives of bishops, for instance, did not, and whilst a mayor was the sovereign's representative in his own borough, he had no precedence at all outside it.

The latter point gave us a great deal of trouble when it was decided to thank Rochester for its freedom by presenting a pair of silver candelabria to the Mayor of Rochester at a function in the HQ Mess which was in Gillingham. The Mayor of Gillingham refused to allow the Mayor of Rochester to come robed into Gillingham. The Deputy Commandant had the three mayors together over drinks to work out a solution, and it was agreed that Rochester should put on his robes only after he arrived in the Mess while the other two mayors just put on their chains. This idea was thrown out by the Town Clerk of Gillingham, who was anxious to preserve the status of his town. It was a proper mayors' nest!

I forget the final answer, but it took hours of discussion to hammer out a solution. We couldn't afford to offend anyone, and certainly not Gillingham, in whose borough we were situated.

It was my job to go up to the silver vaults in Chancery Lane to buy the candelabria and one or two other pieces for other presentations made during my term of office. I became quite well known to Mr. Wallace there, and he would always give me a good price to keep the silver in England as the Americans were shipping so much of the old family silver over to the USA.

It was also decided to give a silver kukri to the King of Nepal to mark the association between the Ghurka Engineers with the Corps of Royal Engineers. I commissioned Garrards to make this piece, and the Nepalese Ambassador and Military Attache were invited to dinner in the HQ Mess for the presentation. I had to find a score of the Nepalese National Anthem. After enquiry, I discovered that the only copy in England was in the possession of the Ghurka Liaison Officer in London. At first he refused to allow it out of his sight but eventually agreed to let an officer come and collect it. So I detailed some unfortunate subaltern for the chore, and then asked Major Arthur Young to come to my office to get it. When I gave him the card, he said this was no good to him as it all had to be orchestrated. When I told him that was his job, he replied that the card didn't tell him the tempo. So I told him, "Well, swing it." He said, "You can't mean that." Now one thing which annoyed me was to have any order I gave queried. So I said rather sharply, "Yes, I do, and let's have a good performance on Friday night." So off he went to do his best.

At drinks before dinner with the military attache, who was Major General Bahadur Rana Shah Bahadur Rana Khan, I discovered that he was a member of the Nepalese Royal Family. I hastily had to change the seating plan and advise General Morris to make the presentation to the right person. After dinner, General Bahadur said that he had never heard his national anthem played better, a remark which brought a look of rank disbelief on the face of Arthur Young.

Living a few doors up our road in Cheltenham was Lt. Comd. John Frederick, who was serving in Nore Command. He had a Morris Mini and went home alternate weekends. He arrived in Cheltenham about 10pm on Friday evenings and started back for Chatham at 3am on Monday mornings. John and I had been at Cheltenham College before the war and, sharing the petrol, I accompanied him on most of his weekend visits.

Another major event each year was the E-in-Cs conference, which was attended by all the CEs and CREs world-wide. The Brigade Major of the SME was the secretary of the meeting and John Notley and I did the rest. This included issuing joining instructions, arranging transport from and to the station, accommodation, installation of telephones at the conference centre, and so on. One of those attending, Lt. Gen. Sir Charles Jones, wrote and thanked me for the excellence of the arrangements. He had been CRE and then GSO1 of the Guards Armoured Division during the war and had come to know me quite well as Jock Millar's adjutant.

By early 1955 my financial situation was becoming quite desperate. I was having to dig into my limited capital to pay school fees, and I could see bankruptcy staring me in the face within the next six months. It infuriated me to know that a public school education was still being considered desirable for entry into Sandhurst while at the same time I, as a regular officer doing a good deal better than average, could not afford to give my sons that same education. I prayed earnestly to my Lord to help me, claiming His promise as recorded in Matthew 6:33, "Seek ye first the Kingdom of God and His righteousness and all these things shall be added unto you."

One day John Notley, who sat in the same office with me, said, "You ought to apply for this." "Apply for what?," I asked. "Well," said John, "You've just passed this out of your out tray to me. It asks for a volunteer to go to Pakistan to become a chief instructor at the School of Military Engineering at Risalpur in the Northwest Frontier Province, and I've heard that the pay there is very good and I know that you have money worries." On checking through the detail again, I thought this could well be the answer to my prayers. I worked out that I could spend two years in Pakistan without damaging my career. To stay longer than that probably would. I spoke to Cecil Eking about it, and he put my name forward even though it meant promotion to Lt Col when I was really five years too young for that.

I also wrote to Jock Millar, who was now a major general and the E-in-C of the Pakistan Army, explaining my situation. I asked if he would consider asking for me. He replied that he would be very glad to have me down at Risalpur and that he would write to the E-in-C at the War Office to ask for me. So in June 1955, I received orders to proceed to Pakistan, and so by some five years I became the youngest Lt Col in the Corps.

Chapter Eleven

Pakistan

In June 1955 began the very sad business of preparing the family for our change of circumstances. Christopher and John, who would be ten and eight years old respectively at the end of the year, would have to stay at school in Cheltenham. The headmaster of the Junior School kindly accepted Chris as a boarder immediately, but John would have to wait until January. In the meantime John would stay on at his kindergarten school, and the parents of a friend of his kindly agreed to accept him as a paying guest. David, aged four, would come with us. It was very distressing having to break up the family and leave Chris and John when they were so young. But we could only get the very substantial Pakistan marriage allowance if Win came with me and this alone would make it possible to give the boys the education to which, in my opinion, they were entitled. My parents agreed to have the boys for the summer holiday that year, but free air travel would enable them to come out to us for the Christmas holidays, for us to come back for the 1956 summer holidays, and for them to come out to us for the 1957 summer holidays. For the other holidays they would stay with their grandparents, my sister Lorna, or a close friend who had a farm in Cornwall.

A brother officer who had served in the Pakistani School of Military Engineering at Risalpur in the Northwest Frontier Province, told me about conditions there and what we should need. So one day Win and I took the train to London and bought two large steel lined boxes which were damp and vermin proof, white summer mess kit, khaki shirts, shorts, stockings, light summer weight clothes for Win and David, a refrigerator which would work off 100 volt DC current or paraffin, and three years supplies from a chemist. These necessities were unobtainable in Pakistan, and we had to take them with us to take advantage of the free baggage allowance. It was quite a problem to work out three years requirements of toilet and washing soap, toilet paper, shaving soap and razors, medicines and first aid supplies, etc. The latter included an enormous quantity of sulphaguanadine as we were warned to expect attacks of dysentery every three months or so. The recommended dosage was five tablets immediately followed by three tablets every four hours till one recovered. This was about four times as much as our doctor in England had ever heard prescribed! One piece of luggage which simply would not pack in anywhere was a very strong blue plastic two gallon bucket of a quality not made nowadays. As each crate was packed and the bucket was still left out, Win became all the more determined that she was not going to Pakistan unless her bucket came with us.

As a Lt Col I was allowed a huge baggage allowance which I think amounted to twenty tons. There seemed to be no end to the packing as we had to take all our own cutlery, crockery, cooking utensils and implements, curtains and mats for the floors, bedding and mosquito nets, as well as clothing and the things bought in London. I also had to take all my military manuals, and of course Win and David needed things to keep them busy and amused for three years.

We let the house furnished to the War Office for fifty pounds a month, if I remember correctly. The War Office sub-let it to an officer who we hoped would look after it properly. Then we had to bid an agonizing farewell to Chris and John, who were very brave, though they probably cried after we were gone. I am sure the parting, bad as it was for me, was far worse for Win. I at least was somewhat prepared as I was well aware that this was the common lot of service families.

We took the train to Liverpool, where we embarked on the SS Caledonia, a 11,000 ton single class cargo-passenger liner of the Scottish Anchor Line. The Caledonia was a very comfortable ship with a most obliging Goanese crew. Win was rather alarmed that the ship was so small, and, as she is a bad sailor, I booked a table near the door of the restaurant, where we had our dinner that evening.

Next morning the steward conducted us to the captain's table, where we remained for the rest of the voyage. Practically the only time the sea was calm enough for Win to appear was when we were going through the Suez Canal!

We stopped at Aden, and several of us made our way to the extinct crater in which is the main shopping centre of the town. We bought a few oddments to add yet more to our numerous pieces of hand luggage which included the blue bucket.

We arrived in Karachi early in July and were met by the British RSM of the Movements Staff, who conducted us through the bustling streets of Karachi. I was amazed to see camels with their coats apparently burnt off as their naked skins were quite black. We were accommodated in the transit camp which was located alongside the race course and polo ground. It was a very hot day, and we were quite unused to the heat. The first thing we needed was a drink of water, but there didn't seem to be any receptacles available. Her persistence rewarded Win, with a laugh, produced the blue bucket, in which she had packed some mugs, the very first piece of luggage we needed on landing!

Win was much bitten during the night and was certain there were bed bugs, which, I said, was nonsense. Next morning after breakfast we found the servants flicking bed bugs out of the wooden bed frames with pieces of straw! We spent a day in the camp, watching a game of polo some of the time, while the RSM extracted our baggage from the ship and loaded it on the train. The following evening he took us with our hand luggage to the station, where a squad of coolies, dressed in flowing pink shirts and baggy white trousers, under the control of a blue jerseyed head man were engaged to carry our things. I have a vision of twenty coolies with our hand luggage on their heads going ahead of us along the platform.

To take us to Lahore in the Punjab, a journey of some 600 miles, we boarded the Chenab Express, which, we were assured, was air-conditioned, and in which we had a compartment with adjoining toilet facilities to ourselves, there being no corridor on the train. The RSM told me how much to tip the coolies but told me to give it all to "blue jersey," who would keep his cut for doing nothing and distribute the rest to the porters. We thanked the RSM for all his help, and the train pulled off about 7.30pm that evening. Soon the three of us bedded down for the night.

Next morning we were well across the Sind Desert and travelling through flat country with sparse vegetation and a few mud walled villages in which the only shade was from a few palm trees. Amongst our hand luggage we had packed our food for the journey, there being no restaurant car on the train. We breakfasted off hard boiled eggs, bread, butter, and marmalade, and tea and milk from our thermos flasks. For our other meals we did very well on cold chicken, salads, tinned fruit, and bread, butter, and jam.

During the morning, Win remarked that she was sure the compartment was getting hotter, but I told her she was talking nonsense as we were hermetically sealed and air-conditioned. Eventually we reached Multan, which in the days of the Raj had been used as a punishment station since it

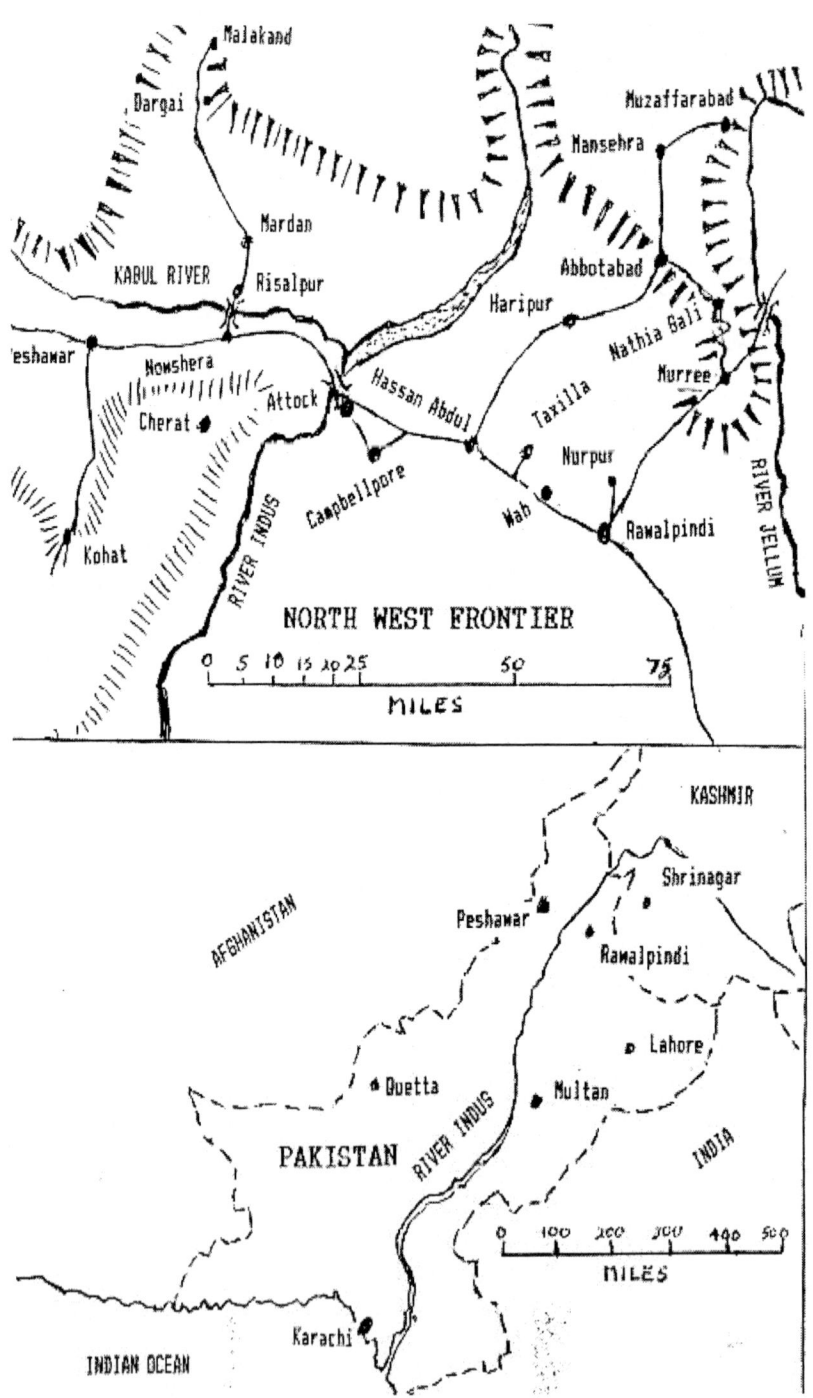

NORTH WEST FRONTIER

Malakand

Dargai

Muzaffarabad

Mansehra

KABUL RIVER

Mardan

Risalpur

Abbotabad

Haripur

Nathia Gali

eshawar

Nowshera

Attock

Hassan Abdul

Taxila

Murree

Cherat

Nurpur

RIVER INDUS

Wah

RIVER JELLUM

Campbellpore

Kohat

Rawalpindi

0 5 10 15 20 25   50   75

MILES

KASHMIR

AFGHANISTAN

Peshawar

Shrinagar

Rawalpindi

Lahore

Quetta

Multan

PAKISTAN

RIVER INDUS

INDIA

0   100   200   300   400   500

MILES

INDIAN OCEAN

Karachi

was the hottest place in India, the temperature reaching anything up to 125 degrees Fahrenheit in the shade. At the station it was so hot that electric punkahs were working in the open air on the unroofed platform just to make some movement in the dead still hot air. Eventually a squad of coolies appeared and shoved a block of ice some three feet long eighteen inches wide and a foot deep onto a tray under our compartment. This was our air-conditioning, and so Win had been right as the previous block had melted.

Late that evening we arrived at Lahore Station, where we had to change trains onto the Khyber Mail. The platform was packed with a milling crowd of Pakistanis, and no Europeans were amongst them. Almost miraculously, so it seemed, all our luggage was transferred onto the train without losing a single piece to pilferers. We were no sooner esconced in our carriage than a block of ice of the same size as before was pushed *into* the compartment on a tray and an electric fan in the corner of the ceiling was directed onto it. This was what one might call Mark 1 air-conditioning, but it was quite effective until the water from the melting ice began to slosh about on the floor. The best thing to do was to leave the door open so that the excess water could run out, retire to bed, and keep our feet off the floor.

We arrived at Nowshera Station early next morning, and we were met by Colonel Gordon Rogers, the Commandant of the SME, who had come in his car, with a lorry for our baggage which we checked off the train. He drove us over the Kabul River on a bridge of boats and took us the five miles or so to Risalpur. There was a range of rocky hills between Nowshera and Risalpur, otherwise the country was flat with little vegetation. The road, however, was tree lined to provide shade throughout its length.

Risalpur cantonment was about a mile square with roads running straight and at right angles to one another. Gordon Rogers took us to our quarter, which was number 21 Flagstaff Road and next door to his. The quarter stood in about two acres of ground with a semi-circular drive surrounding a large lawn at the front. There were several shady trees in the garden, including a peopel tree. The peopel tree has rather thick, large, round leaves which rustle in the slightest breath of wind and give the impression of falling water. This gives an impression of coolness, and for this reason the peopel tree is regarded as a holy tree. The house was single storied with a flat roof. There was a veranda on all four sides to keep the sun off the walls and a row of smaller windows around the house above the veranda. Inside, the floor was bare concrete with no other covering. All the rooms were very high, reaching up to the barrel vaulting of the roof. There was a hall and on the right a large sitting room with a fireplace and bow windows under the front and side verandas. A door beside the fireplace led to the main bedroom at the back. Leading off the bedroom were two bathrooms, neither of which had a bath, although the blanked off water pipes were in evidence. But there was a commode in one of them. Leading off the bedroom was a small veranda with a mesh wire screen across its front to keep out the jackals which roamed the cantonment at night. Another door led to a smaller bedroom which was directly behind the hall. It also had a bathroom with no bath. This would become David's bedroom.

To the left of the hall was the dining room, which also had a door at the back leading to a bedroom as large as the first. This also had two bathrooms with no baths and a communicating door to the small centre bedroom. Off the dining room was the kitchen, which contained only a charcoal fireplace with a hole in the top over which to place whatever cooking utensil was in use. It was crude in the extreme.

About seventy yards away at the back of the plot were the servants' quarters and stables. The whole of the back of the plot was a paddock with a coarse, rather sparse grass.

Gordon Rogers told us that the drill was to hire furniture from a contractor, and he had hired a few essential pieces to meet our immediate needs. As soon as we had had breakfast, he would take us up to a hill station called Nathia Gali (pronounced Nuttier Gully) as it was too hot for Win and David to stay in Risalpur till the end of the hot weather in September. We stored all our belongings in the spare bedroom and locked it and then left by road with Rogers driving.

It was terribly hot, with the shade temperature at 115° F and of course much hotter in the car. We had to keep the windows shut, otherwise the heat dried our eyes completely. We drove back over the boat bridge at Nowshera and then turned east, with the Kabul river on our left beyond fields of tobacco. Beyond them in the distance was the mighty wall of the Himalayas. On our right was a ridge of low, almost barren hills, and beyond them the mountains of Kohat and Sherat. We were driving through an eastward extension of the Vale of Peshawar. The vale is a fertile shallow valley producing fruit and mealies as well as tobacco. After a few miles we went past Akora Kattock, where there was a tobacco factory run by some British people. Some twenty miles from Nowshera we came to the Indus at Attock. Here the muddy brown Kabul River runs into the bright blue Indus running between white sand banks and fed from the snows of the Himalayas. Just below the confluence of the rivers, the Indus runs through a gorge guarded by the huge Attock Fort. This was the point at which all invaders of India, including Alexander the Great, had crossed the Indus. The piers of ruined bridges still stand in the river. The present bridge carries the road, and the railway on a deck above. It is guarded at both ends by small forts which are still manned, and the great gates are closed and locked every night. The Indus is the boundary between the Northwest Frontier Province inhabited by Pathans, of whom all others have a healthy fear, and the Punjab. Attock Fort must have a circumference of at least two miles and held several prominent politicians as political prisoners when we were there.

The road runs in a defile round Attock Fort and just below the defile is an old British cemetery fast falling into decay. Most of the graves are of children, and there is hardly anyone there who died older than the age of thirty. It is a sad place indicating the hardships endured in the last century, before medical knowledge had advanced so far as today. One grave is marked by a boulder on which is inscribed, "Beneath this stone which killed him lie the remains of Bombardier Moss." A rolling stone in the defile must have struck him.

Twenty-nine miles beyond Attock we came to Hassan Abdal, where a road forks northwards to Abbottabad and Gilgit. A few miles off the road to the left is the ancient Indo-Greek city of Taxila, which we visited in due course. It is a fascinating place because it is so well preserved, that much can be deduced of the lifestyle of its former inhabitants. A further nineteen miles brought us to War, where the Pakistan arms factories are situated. Ten miles further on we came to Rawalpindi, with the extensive cantonment on the right and the old town on the left. We turned left through the town, and, fifteen miles on, we began the long climb up the Himalayan foothills.

A thousand miles from the sea, the elevation in Pakistan is only 1000 feet. The consequence is that on approaching the massive barrier of the Himalayas, one sees some 19,000 feet of the 20,000 feet of the mountains.

The road climbed the mountains in a seemingly endless succession of bends until we reached Companybagh at 3000 feet. Here we stopped at a wayside cafe for a drink of tea while two little boys drained the boiling water out of the radiator of the car at the same time as they poured in cold water at the top. At 6000 feet the same process for us and the car was repeated. At 8000 feet and twenty-nine miles from Rawalpindi, we reached Murree, from which the road continued down into the disputed territory of Kashmir. At this altitude the weather was quite cool, and neither we nor the car needed any further liquid refreshment. Incidentally, the name of the tailor in Murree was "Suffering Moses." I wondered if he'd had a hard time from the Pukka Sahibs of days gone by.

Here we turned left onto a narrow dirt road. Soon we were winding through pine forests with, in many places, dizzy precipitous drops on one side of the road or the other. In the valleys we could see villages of mud walled, flat roofed cottages and numerous cultivated terraces on which vegetables were growing or goats grazing. We climbed to 9000 feet and then wound down to Nathia Gali at 8500 feet.

At Nathia, Gordon Rogers parked the car in a small, level area beneath a steep slope at the top of which stood the Pines Hotel. A number of coolies took our luggage, and at the top of the slope we found ourselves on a pleasant little lawn with the single story, wooden, green painted hotel at the back of it. A veranda ran the length of the hotel, and the bedrooms opened onto it. At the right end was the dining room, and there were several free-standing cottages across the lawn to the left. We were allotted one of the bedrooms opening onto the veranda. It had a bathroom with a commode at the back. We were greeted by Jean Gordon Rogers, who introduced us to several other wives and children who were there taking refuge from the heat of the plain.

Nathia Gali stands on a col between two mountains. The col is hardly wider than the length of a tennis court where the hotel stands, but widens out to a hundred yards or so further to the left where tennis courts, the village, and a ruined wooden church stand. To the right of the hotel the ground slopes up steeply through pine trees to the summit of Mokspuri at 9500 feet. To the left beyond the village the col slopes down a few hundred feet to the summer residence of the Governor General of Pakistan (which had been built by a cousin of mine when he was governor of the Northwest Frontier Province) and then up to the summit of the 10,000 foot Mount Maranjani.

Behind the hotel, the col slopes precipitously down to the valley of the River Jellum, 3000 feet below. Beyond the Jellum we looked across range after range of snow covered mountains until seventy miles away, we could see clearly the 26,660 foot summit of Nanga Parbat. Nanga Parbat has on its eastern face the highest vertical precipice in the world. It is a shear drop of 13,000 feet, and even then one is only halfway down the mountain! The hotel also had an outside privy at the edge of the col. It had no door, and it faced this magnificent view to give one whatever inspiration was necessary!

The air at Nathia was invigorating after the heat below, and wood fires were needed in the rooms at night. There was so much inflammable oil in the centre of the pine trees that the centre bit made an excellent fire lighter. The food at the hotel was excellent, and I especially remember the gorgeous eclairs often served as sweets. The manager was a very likeable individual by the name of Khan Zirman.

After the weekend I had to leave Win and David at Nathia Gali, and Gordon and I went back to Rawalpindi for me to be interviewed by my old chief, Jock Millar, now a major general and Engineer-in-Chief of the Pakistan Army. He gave me a great welcome and said, "There are certain things you must know before you go down to Risalpur. You must understand that the name of Mountbatten is a dirty word out here. On partition, the agreement reached between India and Pakistan was that princely states with a Muslim ruler but with a Hindu population should go to India, whereas a state with a Hindu ruler and a Muslim population should go to Pakistan. The boundary between the two new nations was drawn by the same judge who did the partition of Cyprus. The boundary which he drew, which remained undisputed up to twenty-four hours before independence, ran some twenty miles east of the border between India and Kashmir. Kashmir had a Muslim population with a Hindu ruler. Nehru knew that Mountbatten, the Viceroy, was mad keen to become the first Governor General of independent India. Nehru, himself born in Kashmir, so it is understood in Pakistan, promised Mountbatten he could have that post if he would arrange the incorporation of Kashmir into India. Mountbatten became the first Governor General and, only hours before independence, the Indian boundary was advanced to coincide with the Kashmir border. Indian troops then marched into Kashmir in response to an appeal from its Hindu ruler. Meanwhile Pakistan, in fulfillment of the treaty, renounced all claim to Hyderabad, which having a Muslim ruler with a Hindu population, became part of India. Worse from the Pakistan point of view is the fact that all the headwaters of Pakistan's rivers are in Kashmir, and can be interfered with by India." I asked General Millar, "How is it then that the British Government have not put right this blatant injustice?" "The sad answer to that is the fact that India is one of the biggest importers of British steel, and in the present state of affairs at home we cannot afford to lose that market."

Whether the general's answer was correct or not, there is no reason to forget that the Kashmir issue has been at the root of the subsequent fighting between India and Pakistan. Nor should it be forgotten that Muslim troops were some of the most loyal members of the old Indian Army before 1947.

Back in Risalpur I hired the furniture we should need, and I was fortunate to hire the last available bath. However, there was no plumbing and the water just ran out onto the floor and through a hole in the wall to water the garden. I unpacked and stowed our belongings, and the spare bedroom became our storeroom for all the supplies we had brought with us. The bearer, whose name was Bostan, was very concerned that there was no silver teapot but mollified when I assured him that we had left one in England. In those parts servants draw their status, or "izzart," from their employers. It was therefore good to be the bearer of a Lt Col, but a Lt Col without a teapot was apparently unheard of!

I also found that I had inherited an enormous staff. Since our object in coming to Pakistan was to save money, I began at once to pay off unnecessary bodies. When I got down to five, I was told that anything less would be inconsistent with the dignity of a Lt Col, so I finished up with Bostan, the bearer, who was the general factotum who did no work but expected to dress and undress me. I restricted him as far as I was concerned to the more normal duties of a personal servant. Then there was the cook, Nohr Zaman, who had previously been in the employ of the High Commissioner. He produced culinary miracles despite his primitive charcoal stove. Mir Zaman did all the housework, and the gardener, or mali, was Bahadur Khan, a very loyal and efficient young man. The sanitary man was a Christian boy called David. Later, I got rid of Bostan, who was idle and even more dishonest than is common in Pakistan. Mir Zaman became my bearer, and we took on Ali Zaman to do the house work.

In the Risalpur cantonment there were also the Engineer Depot, commanded by a bachelor, Colonel Dick O'Connor, and the Air Force College, the Pakistan equivalent of Cranwell, commanded by Group Captain Das, who had been a fighter pilot in the Battle of Britain.

Since the cantonment was quite level, a push bike was the accepted mode of travel, and I used to pedal daily to the SME. At the SME, besides Gordon Rogers and I, were Major Bill Mason, a bachelor who was the administrative officer, Lt Col Ahmed Tufael, who was the chief instructor of the Construction School, Lt Col Zingravi Khan, who was the chief instructor of the Electrical and Mechanical School, and a Pakistani professor who headed the School for Academic Studies.

My staff at the Field Engineering School consisted of Major Duff Cooper, the senior instructor of field works and Major Mohammed Shah, who had won an MC in Burma and who was the senior instructor of bridging. I also had five Pakistani captains, about a dozen junior commissioned officers, who in the old British-Indian Army would have been called Viceroy commissioned officers, and about a hundred other ranks which included a demonstration platoon.

My senior junior commissioned officer was Subadar Major Shah Wali Khan, a first rate old soldier with two rows of medal ribbons. He acted as company commander for the staff of the FE School. I relied on him very heavily for advice when dealing with disciplinary and welfare matters.

At any one time the FE School would have up to six courses running, which would make me responsible for anything up to five hundred men altogether. One of these courses was for civilian forestry officers whom we would teach track making, culverts, knots and lashings, sheers, gyns, and derricks, surface drainage, and so on.

Within days of arrival, I had to give a welcoming address in Urdu to an NCOs' course. So I had what I wanted to say typed out in black in double spacing with the Urdu equivalent typed out in red in between. Fortunately Urdu is pronounced as spelt, so I had no difficulty in reading it. On the day, when I referred to the blackboard no one seemed to take much notice, while a phrase later everyone looked at the board with rapt if somewhat puzzled attention. Equally, when I made a pun nobody laughed, but a little later they were all falling about on the chairs with laughter. The trouble was that the word order in Urdu is not the same as in English! As I left the room I could here the jemadar explaining what the colonel sahib had actually been trying to say. At least I had tried.

Down the road at Nowshera was the School of Artillery commanded by Colonel Pat Keane. Mrs. Keane had been awarded an MBE for her bravery during rescue operations following the dreadful Quetta earthquake in 1936. Later on I concocted a simulated atomic bomb explosion for Pat, which he needed for some exercise. It worked rather well, with a sixty foot diameter fireball and subsequent mushroom cloud.

We also became friends with John Wilson and Doris, his wife-to-be, whose wedding we attended some months later. He was a construction engineer and they lived in Mardan, a few miles north of Risalpur, not far from the entrance to the Malakand Valley which figures in Sir Winston Churchill's memoirs. We used to play bridge in the evenings with the Wilsons and often heard shots being fired in Mardan while we played.

I managed to visit Win and David several times at weekends while the hot weather lasted through being given lifts in other peoples' cars. On one occasion I travelled in a really old car. It was so worn out that I, being the heaviest, had to get out and walk up the steep climb as one leaves Murree on the dirt road to Nathia Gali. Leaving the car party to cool off, I set out alone. I hadn't gone very far when I came upon two snow leopards with three cubs. Providentially I was down wind of them and I froze. They crossed the road about seventy yards ahead of me and disappeared in the pine trees as they climbed up the mountain. It is one of my treasured memories as they are the most magnificent animals and not many people have seen them in the wild.

Win and David had to move to the hotel in Abbotabad after six weeks as the Pines Hotel at Nathia Gali was fully booked. They came down by bus in the middle of a monsoon storm. It was a terrifying journey. To begin with, they were the only Europeans on the bus, the remaining passengers being Pathans, of whom the men, as is normal, were all armed with ancient rifles and bandoliers of ammunition. The latter thought nothing of spitting the length of the centre aisle of the bus in a vain attempt to reach a spittoon. The pass down to Abbotabad is so narrow and precipitous that traffic is restricted to one direction only at different times of the day. There are no parapet walls, and one can see nothing at all out of the side windows of the bus except the valley floor thousands of feet below. Incidentally, a bus going up to Nathia Gali from Abbotabad has a boy sitting astride the bonnet with a watering can replenishing the radiator as the bus climbs the pass!

On arrival in Abbotabad, the bus stopped in the town centre and everyone debussed except Win and David, who were restrained from moving. As Win did not understand the language she thought, for an awful

My simulated atomic bomb explosion.

Colorel Pat Keane, RA, Commandant of the School of Artillery, Nowshera, Pakistan, myself and the Senior Instructor of Gunnery.

moment, that she and David were being kidnapped. But the bus driver was only delivering them safely to the hotel. Abbotabad is at an elevation of only about 3000 feet and, although much cooler than the plain, lacks the freshness of Nathia Gali. I managed to visit them once or twice there but could only do so by cadging a lift or by bus, as we still could not afford a car.

At the end of September it was cool enough for Win and David to join me in Risalpur. We found that in Pakistan one could either have a car licence or a drink licence but not both. One could not buy alcoholic drinks without a licence, so there was no drunken driving. I obtained a car licence ready for the day when we could afford a car and Win had the drink licence. Most of the drinks which were allowed on her licence went to the officers' mess. The only way a Pakistan Army officers' mess could obtain drinks was by retaining at least one or two British officers! We also retained one elderly Hindu sapper in the cantonment so that we could have Hindu holidays as well as Christian and Islamic ones!

One evening, soon after Win and David had arrived, we were sitting on the veranda when it seemed that all the Europeans within reach decided to make a welcoming call. These included the Keanes, the Gordon Rogerses, the Wilsons, some acquittances from Akora Kattok, and several others. It soon became apparent that they all intended to stay for dinner. This was somewhat disturbing because Win knew that we only had four pigeons in the fridge, one for David, two for me, and one for herself. There was nothing to be done other than to entertain our guests as if all was well whilst wondering what on earth would happen.

After a while Bostan appeared in clean uniform and pugaree, which normally he never achieved, and announced, "Memsahib, dinner is served." With the four pigeons all too clearly in mind, Win invited our guests into the dining room. We were puzzled, although not a little relieved, to see far more tableware laid out than we possessed and also more chairs than we had hired. Soon we were served with soup, followed by ample helpings of roast chicken, roast potatoes, and greens. I thought I had heard some squawks in the back yard while we were having drinks, so now there wouldn't be so many eggs for breakfast. This course was followed by a meringue sweet packed with fruit salad, with an enormous display of spun sugar on top. It being seemingly impossible to cut up this magnificent concoction, Win wisely passed the buck and invited the company to help themselves!

Afterwards we congratulated the staff on their ingenuity but learned that such resource was quite the normal form when the sahibs entertained. Later we would find ourselves rather short of tableware as someone else in the cantonment was having a party!

I found the standards of all ranks up to naik, havildar, and havildar major, (the equivalents of corporal, sergeant, and sergeant major in the British Army) and jemadar, subadar, and subadar major (for which there are no equivalents elsewhere) were quite superb and as good as any troops anywhere. But the standard of commissioned ranks right up to the highest was generally quite deplorable. All these ranks except the naiks and young subalterns had seen active service in the Second World War, most of them in Burma.

On my arrival, there was no course being offered in engineer organization and tactics. As no one knew anything about it, I had to do this myself. This included building a hall with a large sand model and with raised seats all round on which to discuss the engineer role in the various operations of war. The sand model could be covered over to convert the hall into a lecture or examination room, and I built a stage for playlets to demonstrate the sort of unforeseen problems which arise in war. We made the sand model to represent the actual ground over which we studied the various phases of war in situ. I designed two separate courses, one for junior officers and the other for majors and up. The standard of all these officers was really very disappointing.

I found that the young officers, all of whom were engineer graduates from Lahore University, were quite helpless when it came to the solution of practical problems. They would make mistakes that no young British officer would ever make because they seemed to have a different way of thinking. Yet they could reproduce in the examination room whole pages of a textbook word perfect. Few white men can do that.

We had a scandal with one young officer class when we discovered that several of them were indulging in sodomy. It turned out that one of the class was acting as the "madam" for the rest, and he'd arranged the same officer for two of the others. The whole disgusting thing came to light in the subsequent quarrel. But unlike in the British Army, they were not cashiered, "because we look upon these things differently in our country." Is the tendency amongst churches affiliated to the World Council of Churches to condone such behavior preparing the way for the inclusion of Mohammadanism in a syncretistic world religion?

It fell to me to set and correct the Pakistan Engineer Corps promotion examinations from lieutenant to captain, and from captain to major. The candidates didn't know that a British officer was setting and correcting the papers. Amongst those sitting the captain to major examination were six lieutenant colonels who had not passed previously. When I came to correct their papers there was nothing written on them, but inside each of them was a 500 rupee note! At this time General Millar had retired and been succeeded by a Pakistani general who was a graduate of Cambridge University, to whom I handed both the blank papers and the money, the equivalent in total of over two hundred pounds. I do not know what happened to the last, but the six lieutenant colonels duly passed the exam and retained their ranks, so presumably their investment had been a good one.

One of the Pakistani majors at Risalpur had married an American correspondent of *Time Magazine* when he was attending an army college in America. When she came back to Pakistan with him, she discovered that he already had another wife. She persuaded the major to divorce the first wife which, in Islamic countries, is easily done by merely repeating three times to the unfortunate wife, "I divorce thee," and sending her packing.

I used to have the officers round for a party periodically. In terms of the tenets of Islam, they were all tee-total and drank fruit juice. But this same major made an arrangement with us whereby a small glass jug was always filled with gin which was given out as being water. At one such party we forgot it, but our bearer came in with the jug and announced, "The major sahib's water, Memsahib!"

Like so many in India and Pakistan, this major had a land dispute with his neighbor. So I went along with him to Rawalpindi one day to see what went on in a Pakistani court of law. In the morning, evidence was led and summed up by the attorneys acting for each party. After lunch the court reconvened to hear judgement. The judge, in the course of a long rigmarole, said that he did not feel that all the deductions which might have been made from the evidence had been made by either side, and therefore he was adjourning the case for retrial! When we left the court I asked the major for an explanation for this extraordinary outcome. "Oh, I must have paid the judge the same amount as my opponent and that is why he could not make up his mind." "So what will you do?," I asked. He replied, "I shall have my spies out and make sure I pay the judge more than my opponent next time!"

One of my officers was Captain M. A. K. Wazir, the son and heir of the Wazir of Waziristan, which meant he was the crown prince of Waziristan in all but name. Wazir was a short, thick set young man with a cheerful, round face and dark, lively eyes. Waziristan, which is nominally part of Pakistan, is a huge tract of mountainous country sandwiched in between Pakistan and Afghanistan. Wazir was always armed, even when we invited him round for a chat. He told us that he always had to have no less than a platoon to escort him whenever he went home on leave. I asked him one evening to tell me frankly how he thought conditions now compared with conditions under the British Raj. "Well," he said, "I venture to suggest that the Northwest Frontier was the best training ground the British Army ever had." To this I agreed. "But for us, shooting up your convoys gave us our recreation! Now you people have gone, we have nothing but inter-tribal and even inter-family feuds. They go on and on. I shoot your cousin, and then you shoot mine, and then I retaliate again, and so it never stops. So in this respect things are not as good as they were. And another thing, these Pakistanis (Wazir would never identify himself as a Pakistani) don't give us nearly as big a subsidy as the old Delhi government used to send us." I interrupted to say that I knew this subsidy was given to keep the peace on the Frontier, but as they were all now Muslims together I was surprised that there was any subsidy, at all. He nearly spat as he said that if these Pakistanis didn't give them a subsidy they'd give them hell. He went on, "Also these Afghans have now got these modern bureaucratic ideas. All our men of military age have to go down to the Frontier as the Afghan subsidy is now given on a per capita basis." I interrupted to ask, "But how can you get a subsidy from both sides of the Frontier at the same time?" "Oh," said Wazir, "We've always had two subsidies. We keep the peace for six months of the year to keep the Pakistanis happy, and then we give the Pakistanis a hard time for the rest of the year to keep the Afghans happy. But you can imagine the problems we have in organizing guards for our camels and goats when the men go down in relays to the frontier for the head count, bearing in mind the inter-family feuds which go on all the time. But to some extent it is compensated by the fact that we now get a third subsidy." "How can that possibly be?," I interjected. "Mr. Nehru sends us a subsidy to give the Pakistanis a hard time." "Do you mean to say that Mr. Nehru, who is held up to the world to be a great and peaceloving world statesman, actually bribes his next door neighbor but one to cause trouble against his neighbor?" "Oh, yes," replied Wazir matter of factly, "But the trouble is it comes in via Iran and Afghanistan, and we only receive about half of what Mr. Nehru sends!" Wazir gave me a pair of beautifully engraved daggers before I left.

Another Engineer Major whom I knew quite well was a fabulously wealthy young man and owner of huge estates in the Vale of Peshawar. In the course of a single year he bought out of his own pocket for cash a large sugar mill, a canning factory, and a sweet factory. After this he asked me for my advice as to what he should do with the rest of his money. I suggested he should build an old age home, a hospital, and a school for all the people who lived on his vast estates. "Oh no, Allah provides for them. That is nothing to do with me." There was nothing I could say which would persuade him to spend a rupee on his own people.

One of my NCOs, L/Naik Aurangzeb, was caught by the Rawalpindi police with some detonators and explosives he had stolen from my magazine and was taken into custody. As is customary, I extracted him from the civil power and had him tried by court martial. He was reduced to the ranks and given three months in the military prison. Shortly after this, Win and I were sitting one evening having a sundowner on the verandah. Up the drive came an elderly Pathan with a flowing white beard and carrying a bundle under his arm. It turned out that he had come some two hundred miles on foot, by donkey and by bus out of the mountains, to thank me for safeguarding the family honor by having his son dealt with by court martial instead of by a civilian court. The latter would have involved a deplorable loss of izzart! In token of his gratitude, he presented me with the bundle under his arm. It turned out to be an eleven foot by five foot length of black silk embroidered in silk with all manner of beautiful and highly colored ten inch diameter medallions and a two foot wide border at each end embroidered with silk of every color of the rainbow.

It transpired that the Pathan was not as old as he looked, but that he had been in the occupying army in Japan at the end of the Second World War.

When I returned to England I took the silk to the British Museum where the silk was identified as a mandarin's cloak length. As the patterns included five clawed dragons, the cloak length could only have been made for a member of the old Chinese imperial family and was now some one hundred years old. It followed that a Japanese soldier must in turn have looted the cloak length during the Japanese occupation of China! It is now an exhibit in the Royal Engineers museum in Brompton Barracks, Chatham.

Win and I used to worship in the garrison church each Sunday. Including ourselves, there was only a congregation of six. The minister was from the Norwegian Lutheran Church mission. He would prepare his sermons in Urdu and then translate them into English especially for us, and we were very grateful to him. His name was Christisen, and he and his wife had been serving in the mission at Mardan, a few miles north of Risalpur, since the middle twenties. Earlier in his ministry, a Pathan girl had been converted but subsequently had been promised in marriage to a Pathan who remained a Muslim. Christisen had explained the Gospel to this young man who steadfastly refused to repent and believe. Christisen had then done what he could to prevent the marriage. The young man had left Christisen's study one day in a rage and had stabbed to death Christisen's only son, a boy six years old. Despite this tragedy, the Christisens had remained for thirty years at their post passing their son's little grave every time they entered the church.

We also came to know Jonathan and Molly Shaw, who were running the mission hospital in Peshawar. This devoted Christian couple ran the hospital without any other European assistance and with facilities which were crude in the extreme. They had no air conditioning despite the heat and were very short of all medical supplies. Molly was matron, anesthetist, and secretary. Jonathan did a lot of kidney and gall stone operations and showed us some of the enormous stones he had removed. He also had to treat a lot of gunshot and knife wounds as there was constant feuding between the tribes on the Frontier. When a patient was admitted to hospital for treatment, the family came as well, so there was a crowd of ruffianly looking characters with their children routinely camped in the hospital compound. When we left Pakistan the Shaws gratefully received what remained of our chemist's supplies. The balance of our soap was particularly appreciated, which gives an idea of how short of everything they were.

Early in December 1955 I took the train down to Karachi to meet Christopher and John, who, at the tender ages of ten and eight, were flying out unaccompanied from England. Chris, despite his youth, was quite confident that they could have made the journey up country without my having troubled to come to meet them, as they had already come halfway round the world on their own!

We spent the night in the transit camp, and John was astounded and much amused at where we should eat our breakfast. "In a mess!"

They thoroughly enjoyed the train journey to Nowshera, particularly travelling and sitting with the compartment door open and throwing the chicken bones through it onto the track as we ate our lunch. We hired a tonga to take us out to Risalpur, where the boys had a great and emotional reunion with their mother. A tonga is a pony cart with a sunshade cover in which the driver faces forward but the two passengers sit facing backwards. The poor pony is usually just skin and bone.

We arranged lessons in pony riding for the boys, and for David, while they were with us. Friends of ours took them for a trip up the Khyber Pass, and we all went to Peshawar one day, where we strolled through the bazaar. All the shops in each narrow street sold the same merchandise. So there was the street of the silversmiths, another of the coppersmiths, another full of shops selling brasswork, and so on. All the Pathans were armed with rifles, and knives stuck in their belts, and one or two bandoliers of ammunition slung over their shoulders. They are a fierce lot, and their appearance has been well described as having "eyes like two loaded revolvers and a narrow smile." Strings of camels loaded sometimes with very valuable carpets brought over the Khyber from Afghanistan and Iran trudged through the streets already crowded with jostling humanity. Pervading it all was that aroma characteristic of every town on the Indian subcontinent, consisting of a mixture of spices, excreta both animal and human, and sundry body odors.

Winters in the Northwest Frontier are freezing cold, and the sun does not appear for days on end. A freezing wind howls down from the Hindu Kush, and the chill factor is such that in the early mornings I found that I was still cold wearing woollen vests and "long toms," shirt, khaki waistcoat buttoned up to the neck, pullover, thick British battledress, British warm, scarf and gloves. Wood fires in the lounge were the order of the day.

Christopher, John and David aged 10,8 and 5
at Risalpur, Pakistan, Christmas 1955.

On Christmas Day we all went to church, where we increased the congregation by 50% and returned home to find a string of applicants for Christmas baksheesh. These included two chaps playing bagpipes at opposite ends of the garden, apparently competing with one another to make the most noise! Although we had given presents to our servants, we were totally unprepared for this invasion and did not have enough money to go round. We lost izzart over this but were better prepared the following year. With a sad heart, a few weeks after Christmas I took the boys in the train to Karachi to catch the Super Constellation back to England.

As the weather warmed in March, our first parade was put forward to 5.30am, and we did one and a half hours work before breakfast. We started again at 8.00am after an hour's break and continued till 1.00pm when we stopped for lunch. In the meantime, Win shut all the windows to keep the house cool from the early morning air. When I came home after lunch it felt like coming into a cold storage room after the heat outside. Everyone had a rest after lunch, and the bearer used to wake us with a cup of tea at 4.00pm. After that, Win and I used to play tennis with the officers. The temperature was still well over 100° F and we had to keep a piece of towelling stuck into our belts on which to wipe our hands after each rally. Win and Jean were the only women to play as all the Pakistani wives were in purdah. All women in Pakistan were kept isolated from the men and generally confined to their houses and high walled gardens. When they appeared outside, they were covered from head to foot in a burkah, with only a small opening covered with gauze to see through. This made conditions for Win even more lonely as she could only meet wives on their own with no men present. Only three wives were permitted to socialize with her even under these conditions.

On other afternoons I used to play basketball with the troops.

As Easter approached, Jean told us to expect a paradise flycatcher to appear in our garden. It came to our garden and no one else's, and it came each year in Easter week. It was always alone, and it stopped for a week in Risalpur as it migrated from the mountains round Kohat to the Himalayas each year. Sure enough, it arrived on time. It was about the size of a pheasant but slimmer, with a long, wavy tail. It had a blue-black crest, head, and neck, and the rest of its plumage was mother-of-pearl grey. It kept high in the trees and was a pleasure to see.

It didn't seem long before we were making plans for our holiday in England. By this time I could afford to buy a Ford Anglia which I had to have specially modified to cope with the heat. So the four blade fan was replaced with a five blade one, a steel and asbestos shield was placed between the exhaust manifold and the carburetor to prevent vaporizing of the fuel, and a sun visor was fitted over the front windscreen. Win and

David were to collect it in London as they were flying to England a few weeks before me.

For the second time when I flew home, I found that my parents had moved, this time to a large house closer to the shopping centre of Fleet Hampshire. Win and David had already driven down from her parents' home in Skegness and were staying with my parents by the time I arrived. My father was now seventy-one, showing his age, and dragging an arthritic leg, which he did for the last ten years of his life. My mother was still in reasonable health.

After a few days, my parents, my brother and sister-in-law and their two little girls, my youngest sister and her little daughter, and Win and I and our three boys drove in three cars to Newcastle-Emlyn, where my parents had taken over the entire accommodation at the Inn. It was a glorious reunion, with a variety of sandy Welsh beaches within easy reach.

I was following my brother's car in ours one day when a Welsh policeman came across the road and accused my brother of not having stopped at a halt sign. When we both expostulated to the contrary the policeman said, "Ah, but you didn't stop on all four wheels, man!" My brother was let off with a caution not to move off with the front wheels before the rear wheels had stopped in future!

During this holiday we visited Mabws, the old family home and estate which my father still owned when I was a small boy. The estate, which had been in the family for at least 1000 years, originally included not only the mansion but also the village and thirty six farms. My parents, and their forbears before them, recognized their responsibility for the care of the whole community and for providing work for all. The sick and the aged were regularly visited and cared for. No one was lonely. If anyone was without work, as occurs seasonally in a farming community, then that tenant would live rent free till work became available, and agricultural produce was always freely available if necessary. There was always a garden party for everyone on my father's birthday, and the children used to come up to the house for shiny new pennies on New Year's Day. By an unwise distribution of income under my great grandfather's will and by three successive impositions of death duties in close succession, the state in effect stole the estate from the family. Rather than let the misfortune which had struck his family extend to his tenants, whose families had been in their farms and cottages as long our family had been in the big house, my father sold the farms and cottages to the tenants for what they could give him. In consequence, the estate was sold off for a fraction of its true value.

My father could not face a visit to the place he had loved till thirty years later when, that year, we all went to attend Morning Prayer in Llanrystydd church and sat in the old family pews. To our complete surprise, when we came out of church the village street was lined by the tenants, their children, and their grandchildren, to shake the hand of the man who had saved their homes for them. The loving relationship had endured through a thirty year gap, and for once in his life I saw my father deeply moved. He deserved it.

The holiday was soon over, and again we had to leave Chris and John while Win, David, and I flew back to Pakistan. During this holiday, Nasser unilaterally expropriated the Suez Canal. When we arrived back in Risalpur, the Pakistanis were amazed that we had not immediately kicked Nasser out. "We knew those Egyptians during the war. How can you possibly let people like that get away with it?" Soon after that the British and French sided with the Jews to eject the Egyptians. Now the Pakistanis were furious with us for siding with the infidel Jews against Allah's people. We spent a rather uncomfortable week when we were confined to the cantonment and all the Queen Victoria statues were toppled off their plinths. But soon after, the Egyptians refused to have a Pakistani contingent in the UN peace force, and we were all friends again. However, Queen Victoria was never restored to her plinths!

It was still very hot in Risalpur when we returned in August. The mid-day temperature was around 115 degrees Fahrenheit, and it was still over 100 degrees at midnight. It was no use even trying to sleep before that, particularly as the bed would be even hotter than we were. We used to sleep without a mattress but with a sheet spread on the webbing of the bed to get some air from beneath. We had nothing on top and a punkah turning above us. One night I woke in the small hours to discover that Win was missing. "Where are you and what are you doing?," I called out. "I'm lying in the bath; it's cooler here." "Well, get out and let me get in." Thereafter we'd take turns in the cool water, not drying ourselves but letting the punkah do it as we tried to get to sleep again.

Perhaps surprisingly, we used to welcome an occasional duststorm. The cool air in such a storm would bring the temperature down 10 to 15 degrees within minutes, and it was a tremendous relief. Some of these storms reached enormous heights, and they came billowing and swirling across the plain often lit up golden by the sun. I've always thought Ezekiel's vision of the chariot and wheels must have appeared in such a storm. I can just imagine it.

In April 1957 I was moved up to GHQ Rawalpindi to become the Senior Officer Engineer Training. I worked directly under the Deputy Engineer-In-Chief, who was Brigadier Aga Shariff. He was about the same age as myself and learned very quickly. With his encouragement, I wrote two training manuals for the Engineer Corps and set and directed a river crossing exercise under nuclear conditions for the senior officers of the rank of lieutenant colonel and up. This was done with syndicates ranged

My last command: The Field Engineering School of the SME, Risalpur. The Officers, Junior Commissioned Officers, Warrant Officers and Sergeants (Havildars).
Front Row: Jem Ghazanfar Ali, Capt Riaz Muhammed, Capt Nawab Ali, Major Muhammed Shah, MC, Sub Lal Shah, Lt Col R.J.G. Begbie, MBE,RE, Sub Shah Wali
Khan, Major D.F.G. Cooper, RE, Capt Mirza Noor Muhammed, Capt G.S. Butt, Capt Arshad Muhammed.
(N.B. Jem =Jemadar, Sub = Subadar).

round a sand model. The syndicate solutions were so poor that at one moment Shariff interrupted to say, "Gentlemen, if our standard is really as bad as this, the sooner we ask the British to come back and run our country the better!"

I was present with a group of generals one day, and one of them remarked to me, "What towers of men you British sent out to administer India in the old days," and he mentioned Sir John Nicholson and General Havelock amongst others, and he added, "but they were always known of as men of the Book." How sad it is to realize that none in public office today can be known as men of the Bible, and that by a Moslem! The monument to Sir John Nicholson, who used to say that the only way to rule India was to keep one eye on the Frontier and one on Delhi, stands beside the road halfway between Delhi and Peshawar. It consists of a high obelisk with two round holes at the top, one facing towards Peshawar and the other towards Delhi.

In Rawalpindi, Win and I had a very comfortable quarter in a private hotel set in nice grounds. The catering was excellent.

Since being transferred to GHQ, I had been allotted a magnificent government charger. I named him "Cheno" because he had the number six burnt onto his hoof. I used to go for a ride most evenings, often with the Adjutant General of the Pakistan army, General Habib Khan. He used to dress in a very loud riding jacket and cap and tried to imitate an English country gentleman, "Great thing a slow canter, what, what?"

Another of my riding companions was a Canadian colonel who was in charge of the United Nations truce supervisory team in Kashmir. From him I learned that there was just as much bribery, corruption, and nepotism in India as there was in Pakistan.

I used to hunt with the Peshawar Vale Hounds each Saturday. My zeis, (groom) whose name was Feisal Mohammed, used to ride Cheno out to the meet in the small hours of the morning. I followed in my large American staff car, arriving at the meet at about 5.30am, and I immediately mounted. A bearer then brought round a stirrup cup which one sipped while chatting to other members of the hunt which included my Canadian friend and General Zia Khan, who was then commanding the armoured division and later became the president of Pakistan. At 6.00am the master blew off just as the sun was rising and illuminating the hazy blue and white capped Himalayas in the distance and yellow mustard in the foreground. Then we began to hunt either a drag or a jackal.

On the first occasion it was drag hunting, and the hounds were soon off in full cry. Those who had laid "the smell" had neglected to include any checks, and so we continued at full gallop without a pause. This was quite exhausting as we were hunting over terraced ground, so that we had a downward leap of four or five feet every seventy yards or so and a similar upward leap in the second half of the circuit. Cheno was such a splendid animal that I had a job to keep him behind the huntsman, but he easily outpaced the rest of the field.

On other occasions we would hunt a jackal, and we would then find ourselves tearing through crops with a feudal disregard for the rights of the owners. I remember on one occasion crashing through sugar cane some six or seven feet high and leaping a completely hidden irrigation canal some ten feet across. But Cheno and I had such an excellent rapport that we were over almost before I knew it. Subconsciously, I must have felt his muscles flexing for the leap.

Hunting had to stop about 9.30am because by then the sun's heat destroyed the scent. Someone always seemed to know where the hunt would stop because we would dismount at a place where a huge marquee had been pitched. Here Feisal took over Cheno and walked him home while I went into the tent. Inside, the ground and tent walls had been covered with magnificent Persian carpets. A large mahogany table had been laid with silver cutlery and trophies, and a bearer was standing behind each chair to wait on each officer. We then sat down to a full breakfast of cereals, fried eggs on toast, and toast and marmalade washed down with steaming hot coffee. After breakfast we drove back to our quarters in our sleek staff cars to shower and resume operations in the Rawalpindi club. It was a wonderful day and a nostalgic reminder of how things must have been in the days of British India.

Early in 1957 a new American military attache by the name of Colonel Rothwell J. Brown arrived. He was anti-British and sought to ingratiate himself with the Pakistanis by saying, "You are no different from us Americans except that we managed to throw the British out sooner than you people did," at each of the army schools he addressed. Eventually the Commander-in-Chief, General Mohammed Ayub Khan, had to tell him to restrain himself as "The British are our very good friends."

I was present one day when several of the generals were discussing the seating plan for a forthcoming mess night. "We'd better put Rothwell next to you, Habibullah, as you are well able to handle him." Lieutenant General Habibullah Khan was the Director General of Military Training. Nobody thought much of Rothwell.

Pakistan having become a signatory of the Baghdad Pact, American military equipment began to pour in based on the number of divisions fielded by the Pakistan Army. The same soldiers were sent ahead in front of Rothwell for him to count again so that there appeared to be more divisions than there actually were. I remember the American bridging equipment arriving on long railway trucks covered with black tarpaulins.

On each tarpaulin the Stars and Stripes was painted with "BY THE GENEROSITY OF THE AMERICAN PEOPLE" in large letters. But in one corner in small letters was written, "This equipment went obsolete in 1946." Not unnaturally, the Pakistanis found this combination tactless and humiliating.

I drove Win up to Nathia Gali at the beginning of May. At this time I was writing training manuals for the Engineer Corps and did my writing in long hand in the cool of the hill station and took work down for typing every few days.

In consequence, I spent most of that summer with Win and David in Nathia. It was so beautiful up there that I determined to try to capture some of it in watercolor as we could not afford color photographs. Two missionary ladies who were on holiday helped me, and I learned quickly from them.

With them, we also decided to start up services in the semi-ruined beautiful wooden church. I led the services, which were of a family service character, and one or other of the ladies gave the message at each service. They taught the children several choruses, and everyone on the mountain attended the services, including some Muslim families.

At the end of three months we had collected enough money to replace the main support of the tower, which had been eaten by termites, to replace broken windows, to repair the fences, and to pay the chokidar, or watchman, the three years wages which were due to him. Just as we were leaving, a Presbyterian minister arrived for a holiday, and I said to him, "Here is your church, here is the balance of the money, over to you, brother!" Nathia Gali is snowed up and inaccessible from October to April each year. Despite this, and to my amazement, when a family joined our church in Blairgowrie, South Africa, in 1970, they said they had customarily worshipped in the Nathia Gali Church. So despite the annual interruption, the formerly disused church was still functioning fourteen years later, no small cause for real thanksgiving to God. Because congregations are so small, the back third of the church has now been converted into a holiday chalet for ministers and other church workers.

In about August 1957, there was an outbreak of Asian flu which was spreading across India towards Pakistan. The authorities panicked about this and restricted travel to stop the virus spreading, although it caused little more than a feverish cold at a time when all sorts of tropical diseases were rife. Leaving Rawalpindi one day to go up to Nathia, I came across a road block where swabs were being taken of peoples' mouths to see whether they had got the bug. Pakistan being Pakistan, there was no guarantee that one wouldn't get someone else's swab in one's mouth. So I sent Mir Zaman ahead to sort the nonsense out. After much gesticulation at the barrier, Mir

Zaman came back saying, "Tika Sahib, drive on." Up went the barrier and all was well.

A few days later I needed to go up to Nathia again. "Put out my uniform," I ordered Mir Zaman. "Oh no, Sahib, that would be quite the wrong thing." "Mir Zaman, you know perfectly well that no one will stop a colonel sahib at the barrier, so put out my uniform and polish the buttons and stop arguing." Arriving at the barrier, it was raised immediately the moment I was seen. "There you are," I said to Mir Zaman, "What were you worrying about?" "Oh Sahib, last week I told them you were the doctor!"

Towards the end of July, Chris and John flew out again and I went down to Karachi to meet them as before. We all had a lovely six weeks holiday together at Nathia, where there were a number of other children for the boys to play with, even a fancy dress party. I spent as much of the six weeks as possible at Nathia and climbed both Mokspuri and Miranjani with them. There were magnificent views from the peaks. I took the boys back again a few weeks later.

That August, Pakistan celebrated ten years of independence by declaring itself a republic. The Governor General became the President and I was awarded the Pakistan Republic Medal for being there at the time.

That October we had to return to Risalpur for four weeks so that I could resume duty as Chief Instructor and run a course for senior engineer officers. Feisal rode Cheno over from Rawalpindi, and I found that supervising training from horseback gave me a very good view of what was going on, and riding between the courses doing practical work was pleasant and saved time. During that month we lived in a very uncomfortable house as most of the windows had been painted over with black paint to keep the wife in purdah!

While there, we took the opportunity to drive up the Khyber Pass and peered into Afghanistan from the top of the pass at Landi Kotal. In South Africa, only the Swartberg Pass even begins to compare with the ruggedness and grandeur of the Khyber.

To go there one has to obtain a permit which guarantees one the protection of the Pakistan Government so long as one keeps on the tarmac.

Every yard of the pass is kept under observation by armed Pathan tribesmen perched high up behind sangars in the mountains. One therefore tends to attend to nature only in dire emergency, and then at some speed!

We also visited a Pathan arms factory on the road between Peshawar and Kohat. It was housed in a ramshackle old shed in which boys were pedaling furiously on bicycle pedals to drive a lathe which drilled out concrete reinforcing bars to make barrels for rifles. .303 Lee Enfield rifles and revolvers were being turned out entirely by hand. The owner pointed out the inscriptions "Made in Birmingham" and the War Office "WD" sign with great pride. It was impossible to distinguish the finished articles from the real things until one looked inside to see the crude rifling. But the accuracy of the rifles didn't last long.

At the end of that time in Risalpur, it was known that I would not be coming back again. I was given a terrific send-off by the staff at an open-air banquet at which I was garlanded by each staff member until I had a huge ruff of flowers round my neck. I made my farewell speech in Urdu. Several wept as they knew they would never again have a British officer with all the standards that implied. In traditional manner, they pushed me in my garlanded car all the way out of the cantonment.

Win and I felt we could not ask the family to look after the boys again for the Christmas holidays, so we decided that Win and David should go back to Cheltenham in November in time to open up the house for the holidays. My tour of duty in Pakistan was to terminate in March, so it would not be long before I would join them in England. After their departure I moved into the GHQ Officers' Mess.

Before doing so, I sold everything we would not be taking back to England, such as the refrigerator, the gramophone and records, the wireless, and sundry games and books. I also sold the car, on the understanding that it would not be handed over till I left. I lived on the proceeds of these sales during my last months in Pakistan while my pay and allowances accumulated in England. We had been warned that it would be very difficult to take money out of the country at the end. As it was, I only had a small balance of less than fifty pounds at the end, and it took over a year to get this small balance out.

Sometime in November, I had the opportunity of attending the annual mela, or carnival, at Nurpur, a little village tucked close in under the foothills of the Himalayas. I have told the story of it in the next chapter.

Later the same month a letter came from the War Office to say that the size of the Army was being reduced and that some 2500 regular officers would become redundant. The letter added, that before any decisions were made, the War Office wished to know whether there were any officers who wished to take voluntary early retirement, in which case the terms were as set out in the letter.

I was aware of 1 Corinthians 7:20, which says, "Let every man abide in the same calling wherein he was called," and I had been called in the army. I was still the youngest lieutenant colonel in the Royal Engineers and was riding the crest of the wave as far as my career was concerned. A glittering career seemed to stretch before me in the Army. Moreover, the Lord had looked after me in a remarkable way in the service and had proved for me the truth of Matthew 6:33, "Seek ye first the kingdom of God, and his righteousness; and all these things shall be added unto you."

Farewell to the School of Military Engineering, Risalpur.

Our residence, 21 Flagstaff Road, Risalpur with David in my
father's camp bath, which served us in two world wars.

On the other hand there was still no certainty that I would be able to make ends meet in Cheltenham, with two and eventually three boys at public school. Further, continual separation from Win for the next eleven years would be inevitable as the boys would have to attend Cheltenham College as day boys, as my brother and I had done, since I would never be able to afford boarding fees. If I abandoned the idea of Cheltenham for the boys we could probably stay together as a family, but their education would be bound to suffer as we moved them from school to school as we were posted from one station to the next. If I left the Army I had no business qualifications or experience to help me make a new start.

It was an agonizing dilemma, and I did not know what to do. I came to the conclusion that the best thing to do would be to send in my papers, and pray, and leave my future in the Lord's hands. I was actually rather surprised to receive notification a few weeks later that I was to be granted early retirement. The way in which that decision was reached was even more surprising, as I was to find out upon my return to England.

I had no idea what I would do after I retired, nor whether to look for a job in England or to emigrate to South Africa where my eldest sister Joan and her husband Dick Stead, along with their two children, had been living since 1948. At my request Joan sent me cuttings from the Johannesburg Star giving details of appointments vacant. One of these was from a personnel consultant by the name of C.C. Askew, who was looking for executive trainees to work with an international company. As I would have to be retrained, I decided to apply to him. He replied that, at thirty-eight I was three years too old, but I replied that I would call on him the day I arrived in Cape Town.

One of my last duties was to visit the Staff College at Quetta in Baluchistan to brief the engineer directing staff on the changes to engineer organization and tactics which I had introduced so that they could be included in the Staff College teaching. I went there by train from Risalpur, changing in the middle of the night at Jacobabad onto the Bolan Express. Early in the morning we wound our way up the Bolan Pass with two steam locomotives pulling at the front and another pushing from behind, and heavy work they made of it too.

At Quetta, apart from the Staff College, I visited the mission hospital which had been founded by Sir Henry Holland, who had addressed us at an OCU meeting in London some years before. The hospital was now being run by his son Josh Holland, who was superintendent and surgeon, and his wife, who was anesthetist, matron, and secretary. Mrs. Holland had been stricken with infantile paralysis some years before and was confined to a wheelchair, although she could walk a little with Josh holding her hands and walking backwards in front of her. Despite her condition she had born a son, as they were determined that the Holland tradition should continue at Quetta. What a dedicated Christian couple they were, and what a privilege it was to be in their company!

When I arrived in Karachi for the last time, I met my cousin Kenneth Cowan and his wife Jenny, who took me out for the best Chinese supper I have ever had. Kenneth had been in the term below me at "the Shop." He used to play the organ for the daily chapel services there. One morning he played the "March of the Seven Dwarfs" as a voluntary and was given six hoxters for his pains by the chaplain, Victor Pyke, who later became the chaplain general and, later still, Bishop of Sherbourne. Kenneth had been commissioned into the Gunners and made a dramatic escape from Calais in 1940 by hiding under the pier while German soldiers were walking about on top of it. He had resigned his commission soon after the war and was now working for Vickers, selling tractors and other heavy equipment.

I boarded the Anchor Line *Celicia* the next morning. Unfortunately a dock crane had toppled over and killed two dockers. All the dockers were now on strike, so that we sailed without our cargo. The result was that the ship was showing an enormous amount of red bottom and was like a cork floating on top of the water.

On board was a woman and her teenage daughter. The latter introduced me to a new dance called "Rock and Roll" and told me — because I had never heard of it before — that I had never lived!

At Aden we were told that as there was a political rumpus going on in Port Sudan, we would not be able to call in for a cargo of cotton which the captain had hoped to pick up. So we continued all the way to England still much too high out of the water. We met our first storm in the Mediterranean, but as it was head on it was not too bad. We encountered our second while steaming up the Portuguese coast. It came in on our port beam, and I've never known such a night. Although the furniture in the lounge was chained down, there was plenty of movement, and things and china were crashing down all over the place. One had to strap oneself into one's bunk to stay in. Eventually the captain turned the ship into the wind.

Next morning I asked him how much the roll had been. He replied, "It was twenty-six degrees either side of the vertical. At thirty degrees we would have turned turtle so I turned the ship into the wind.

One sunny morning we steamed up the Mersey to Liverpool, and my first class travelling days at the Monarch's expense were over at last. From now on it would be third class or steerage!

In the New Year Honours 1959, I was made an OBE for my services in Pakistan.

Chapter Twelve

Carnival Night In Nurpur

The cantonment and town of Rawalpindi is dominated by the gigantic wall of the Himalayas, whose foothills rise some 5000 or 6000 feet above the plain only ten miles outside the town. Tucked right in under these hills in a bowl of the lower ridges is the village of Nurpur.

Like so many other villages and towns in this part of Pakistan, Nurpur has a saint all of its own. Some towns even have two, like Hassan Abdul. There, the tomb of one is in the town and the other is by a well at the top of the 500 foot cliff which almost overhangs the town.

Legend has it that in a time of drought, the saint in the town was having some difficulty with his followers because of the failure of his prayers to produce water. So he appealed to the saint at the top of the cliff for a supply of water from his well. But the hill saint shouted down, "If you were a proper saint, Allah would answer your prayers, so don't trouble me." To which the town saint replied that the hill saint was no proper saint to talk like that. Whereupon the hill saint hurled a boulder down the cliff onto the town saint, who attempted to shield himself with his hand but was nevertheless struck dead.

I have seen the tombs of the two saints, and interestingly enough there is a boulder at the bottom of the cliff with the clear imprint of a man's hand upon it!

I am glad to say, however, that not all saints are of such an irascible temper as these two. The Nurpur saint seems to have been more genial altogether for, in his memory, he has decreed that a carnival take place in

229

November every year, with the sole condition that no dancing take place within four hundred yards of his grave.

In 1957 I had an opportunity to go to the carnival, or mela in the Urdu language, and I suppose I must be one of only a small number of white men ever to have seen it. Accompanied by a young Pakistan Army officer and a police officer all in civilian clothes, I left Rawalpindi an hour or two after dark one evening.

The road was thronged with men, but no women, of all classes of society making their way in cars, buses, lorries, tongas, on bicycles, and on foot. The majority were wearing the familiar Indian baggy white trousers caught in at the ankles, and shirts with long tails hanging down outside. All these were in varying degrees of shabbiness and whiteness. Many were armed with pistols or rifles, with bandoliers of ammunition slung over their shoulders.

When we left the main road, we all moved forward in a cloud of dust forming an opaque blanket in front of the headlights. As we approached the village, car parks came into view on either side, all charging exorbitant prices. But my policeman friend spurned them all. With his influence, we were allowed past the barrier where no cars were supposed to pass. Here we parked the car under police guard.

We now walked in a throng of men of all types along an avenue lined on both sides with a succession of brightly lit booths and sideshows. There were cocoanut shies, swings, stalls selling sweets and refreshments, fortune tellers, magicians, snake charmers, and the fattest man in Pakistan. Except for additional cries for baksheesh from beggars and cripples, I received no special attention.

Entering the village, we made our way through narrow streets and alleys past evil smelling corners to the PWD bungalow on an eminence overlooking the village. From here we could see a park in the bottom of the bowl in the hills in which the village was set. At the centre of the park was a mass of hundreds of bright little flickering lights set on and about the saint's tomb, with others set, but not so thickly, on the branches of all the trees in the park.

Examining these later, I saw that they were made of earthenware, dish shaped, and with a lip to hold a wick, exactly like the widow's cruze we read about in the Bible.

The village itself extended almost all the way round the park. In the gaps between the houses of sun-baked bricks were pitched tents and awnings of all manner of gay colors. From chinks in these and from the windows of the houses came the comparatively yellow light of electricity and hurricane buttees.

Above all was the blue light of the moon and stars, against which the dark sinister craggy ridges of the mountains were silhouetted. In a gap I could see the lights of Rawalpindi twinkling in the distance. From the side shows on our right came the cries of those calling for custom, the shouts of those on the swings, and the buzz and rumble of a great throng.

From the awnings and tents round the park, first from here and then from there, as the light breeze shifted, came to our ears the drumming and lilt of the music of the dancing girls, and occasionally the high pitched note of a girl singing in the Indian fashion. The whole complex of light and shadow, and smell and sound, has made an indelible impression on my memory.

My friends explained that if I went to any one of the dancing places, we should see all the girls that evening as each troupe gave a show at each place and moved on round the circle to the next. So we made our way down through the alleys by which we had come up, and, after passing several awnings, each with its own show in progress, we came to one hired by a wealthy khan, the acquaintance of one of my companions.

The owner had rigged up an awning over the courtyard of his house, and the area beneath, say ten yards by ten yards was absolutely packed, except for a small central space, with men, mostly Pathans, sitting and squatting on the floor. With some difficulty but with every assistance and goodwill from the audience, we picked our way to the centre part of the court immediately in front of the door of the house.

Here the khan was sitting on a pile of brightly colored cushions smoking a hookah with his friends. We were introduced and instantly made welcome. A place at the front of the cushions was made for us, with the dancing space, only a few feet square, beginning at our feet. In fact I had difficulty tucking my legs out of the way.

Looking about me, I saw that every space, every available vantage point, all the room on the floor, on the walls, and on the boughs of the tree overhanging the court, was occupied. There were even half a dozen dark faces poked through between the flat roof and the edge of the awning.

There were two rather stout and ill-pleasing girls dancing on the floor. They were clothed in long chemises and long trousers. Behind them the orchestra consisted of three ruffians, one playing a finger drum, one a pipe whistle, and the other a sort of miniature piano the size of an accordion. I learned later that each girl, or troupe of girls, owned her own orchestra together with her cash collector, all of whom accompanied her round the mela. Every now and then one girl or the other broke into the high pitched, whining song typical of the East which has, after all, a certain appeal once one gets used to it.

The dancing was done with the whole body. There was little movement of the feet but a great deal of graceful and evocative movement of the arms, head, and eyes, and a certain swaying about of the hips.

After a time the dancing stopped and did not begin again until one of the audience produced a rupee. But it stopped again after a minute or two and could only be kept going with a more or less constant flow of rupees.

As these two girls were not in the least attractive, even to a young Pathan who would seldom if ever have seen a woman out of her burkah (a robe which covers her from head to foot including her face), the flow of rupees soon stopped. But when a girl wearing almost transparent trousers and top with her belly exposed, and with a lovely figure, arrived, the rupees flowed thick and fast. There was nearly a riot when this particular girl took a rupee from my teeth with her teeth.

And so the mela continued late into the night with a new troupe of girls complete with orchestra arriving every few minutes as they made their way round the village. Sometimes the rupees flowed thin and slow but at other times thick and fast.

At last the three of us took our leave and made our way back through the dark, narrow, and twisting alleys, found our car still safe and the driver asleep. But we learned afterwards that there had been six murders in the village while we were there.

Chapter Thirteen

In Business In South Africa

On arrival in London, I collected a green Ford Zephyr Mark 2 and drove to Cheltenham, where I was welcomed home by our reunited family. We had for so long been saving every possible penny that Win was quite shocked that I had spent so much money on such a large car. But we needed it with our growing boys.

I began applying for jobs in England because I still could not make up my mind whether to stay in the country or emigrate to South Africa. My long-suffering Win preferred to stay in England but, as ever, loyally agreed to go if that appeared right to me.

While waiting replies to my applications, I went up to London to visit the War Office AG7, which is the personnel branch looking after Sapper officers. As soon as I walked into his office, the Deputy Assistant Adjutant General, Hank Hart, exclaimed, "You've no idea of the trouble you've caused us." "What am I supposed to have done?," I asked. "When your application to retire came in, it was sent round the house and both the Military Secretary (for the general staff of which I was a member) and the Engineer-in-Chief ruled that under no circumstances were you to be allowed out. But the Director of Finance ruled that when the compensation terms were worked out, it was not envisaged that anyone as young as you would be eligible to go out on a lieutenant colonel's terms. He accordingly ruled that if you were allowed to retire you should first be reduced to the rank of major and serve as such for six months and then go out with a major's terms. At this, you became a 'cause celebre', and the MS and the E-in-C decided that if the finance people were allowed to get away with this,

233

there was no knowing to what extent they might renege on the agreed terms. So they now joined forces and insisted that you be allowed to retire as a lieutenant colonel and on a lieutenant colonel's terms. In the result, there was no end of a battle, which was won by the military side of the house, and so out you go, and jolly good luck to you."

I came away convinced that this extraordinary outcome was the Lord's doing, over-ruling in the affairs of men to achieve His purposes. The problem now was to try to discover what He had in mind for me.

Back in Cheltenham, one or two answers to my applications for a job had come in. The opportunities were all awful, including selling carpet sweepers from door to door. I attended a reorientation course at Bristol Technical College, driving over there each day. I did not find the course in business helpful, and the other officers on the course seemed to be the types whom I imagine the army was quite pleased to be rid of. The whole situation was terribly depressing. I was driving poor Win mad. In the morning I would say, "Let's go to South Africa," and by the evening I would have second thoughts and say, "No, I think we had better not." I didn't seem to get any leading one way or the other from my prayers. Eventually Win said, "Why don't you go up to London and make enquiries at South Africa House, and perhaps that will help you to make up your mind." I went and saw the 1820 Settlers' Association as well, and I just began to feel that the way was open. I can't really explain how it was that after weeks of shilly-shallying my mind was quite made up. I booked passages for the family in the steerage of the Capetown Castle and returned to Cheltenham to tell the family we were leaving in six weeks time.

We sold the house at a small loss and all the furniture except a few treasured pieces, and then went to Fleet to spend the last few days with my parents. My father was now seventy-three, and it was hard to part, yet all his life he had said the place to live was South Africa, and so he could not have been altogether surprised. Our car having been loaded in advance, we drove to Southampton in my parents' and my sister's cars and embarked on 26th June 1958. As we left the port we had an excellent view of both the *Queen Mary* and the *Queen Elizabeth*, neither of which I had seen before. They were colossal and the largest passenger liners in the world.

We ran into a storm in the Bay of Biscay, and the whole family was sick except myself. Otherwise the voyage was uneventful, and between us, we won five prizes, including the one for fancy dress by the boys. We steamed into Cape Town Harbour before dawn on 10th July. As soon as we were alongside, I was called to the lounge to meet someone who had come to welcome the brother of Dennis Begbie, the Springbok cricketer. I had to explain that my brother Denys was an oarsman and we were not related, as far as we knew, to Dennis.

Disembarked, we had a long wait on Cape Town docks as we were waiting for our car to be unloaded and cleared through customs. Eventually we drove to Sea Point, where my sister Joan had booked us into a hotel. Leaving the family there, I then called on Mr. C.C. Askew. On arrival in his office I found him packing his briefcase, and, introduced myself as Colonel Begbie. "Oh you," he said, "I'm far too busy to see you now." Nobody had ever dared to talk to me like that before and I was somewhat taken aback. "In any case, I'm leaving now for Johannesburg," added Mr. Askew. "Well, I'm going there too," I said. "Alright, you win, give me a ring at the Carlton Hotel when you arrive, and I will interview you there." Thanking Mr. Askew, I left him to his packing and returned to the hotel.

On Sunday we all went to church in St. George's Cathedral. It wasn't long before I began to feel very uncomfortable, for it seemed as if we were in a Romish church! We nearly walked out and I wish we had. I have never entered the portals of a Church of the Province of South Africa since. Judging from that one occasion and broadcast services I've heard since, that church propagates every sort of error except the truth. It appears to have no doctrinal discipline, having abandoned the Thirty-Nine Articles of Religion and the Bible as the final authority in all matters of faith and conduct. The harm it has done to human souls is immeasurable.

On Monday we began the long drive to Johannesburg, a distance of some 900 miles. From Cape Town to Worcester the country was fertile and the mountain scenery magnificent. But after that we found the enormous empty spaces of the near desert Karoo rather depressing. We had a picnic lunch by the roadside and drove on to Colesburg, where we spent the night in a comfortable hotel. The night was cold, and we were grateful for the hot water bottles provided for each of us.

On Tuesday we crossed the Orange River into the Orange Free State. As we drove northwards the country became a little greener but was still very bleak and bare after England. Much of the main road was still only surfaced with gravel, and where it was black topped the road was quite narrow by present day standards.

When we crossed the Vaal River the country became much greener and with many more trees. Our morale improved accordingly. But the approach to Johannesburg from the south was marred by the heavy industry factories, the shanty towns of the blacks, and the litter which desecrates the country all round them.

My sister Joan had given me directions to find my way through Johannesburg. "Go straight up Sauer Street, turn right into Empire Road until you come to Clarendon Circle, then left into Louis Botha Avenue, come down the hill and turn left at the first traffic light, and then right into Walter Street." At Clarendon Circle, I spotted Christ Church, Hillbrow, of

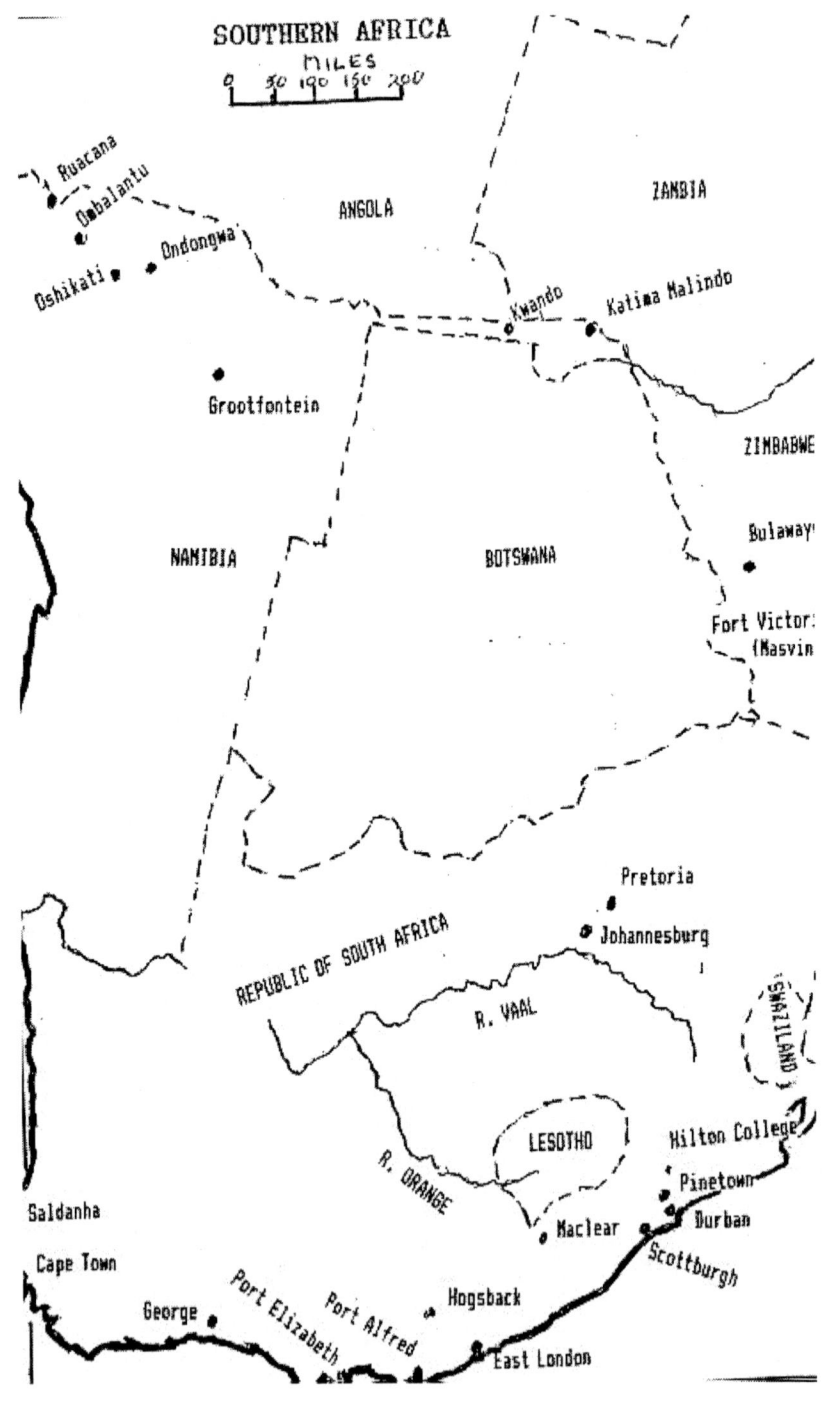

SOUTHERN AFRICA

MILES
0   50 100 150 200

Ruacana
Oshalantu
Ondongwa
Oshikati

ANGOLA

ZAMBIA

Kwando   Katima Malindo

Grootfontein

NAMIBIA

BOTSWANA

ZIMBABWE

Bulaway'

Fort Victor:
(Masvin

Pretoria

Johannesburg

REPUBLIC OF SOUTH AFRICA

SWAZILAND

R. VAAL

LESOTHO

Hilton College

Pinetown

R. ORANGE

Durban

Maclear

Scottburgh

Saldanha

Cape Town

George   Port Elizabeth   Port Alfred   Hogsback   East London the Church of England in South Africa, and I told the family, "That's our church."

When he heard that I was going to South Africa, Bill Ewbank (the same who had led the OCU meetings at Shrivenham in 1947-48) wrote to me and said that when he had stopped at the Cape on his way to the Middle East during the war, he had been made very welcome by a Mr. D.G Mills. Mr. Mills had led Bible studies for servicemen in a room above his garage and Bill had attended. Mr. Mills belonged to the Church of England in South Africa, and Bill had advised me to go to that church. So I was glad to find it so easily on my way to my sister's.

Arriving at Joan's house, we had a great reunion. We had not seen Dick and Joan Stead since they emigrated to South Africa in 1948. My niece Valerie was now eighteen and my nephew Richard was now fifteen. When Joan had last seen our children, Christopher was two and John only a few weeks old. David she had never seen before. They were now twelve, ten, and seven respectively. As Joan was having alterations done to her house, she had arranged to have Chris and John and had booked Win, David, and myself to stay in the Orange Grove Hotel just round the corner in Louis Botha Avenue. Dick Stead was now Vice-Principal of Athlone High School and prominent in South African hockey, while Joan was playing tennis for Western Transvaal and was the current ladies champion at Old Johannians Sports Club.

With Dick's help, the boys were entered into King Edward's Prep School. We rented an undistinguished flat just opposite the school in Louis Botha Avenue. Win and I busied ourselves immediately in buying essential furniture, and I applied for one or two positions as a reinsurance on Mr. Askew.

Mr. Askew interviewed me a few days after we arrived in Johannesburg. I think he at first thought a retired soldier wouldn't be much use to anyone, but he mellowed as he learned more about me. At the same time I warmed to him. Having been in personnel selection myself, I soon realized that Askew was asking all the right questions and conducting the interview very efficiently. He gave me an IQ test, which was rather a shock as, although I had often given other people an IQ test, I had never sat one myself. Anyway, I completed it and was revising one of my answers well within the permitted time when Askew stopped me as I was not supposed to have time to do that sort of thing. Having checked my answers, he said he would recommend me to the company despite the fact I was three years over the age they had asked for. "Who are they?," I enquired "The Vacuum Oil Company," he replied. "Who are they and what do they sell?," I asked. "You'd better find out before your interview. They sell Mobil oil," replied Askew with some surprise at my ignorance, and with that I took my leave of him.

From the first Sunday in Johannesburg, we worshipped at Christ Church, Hillbrow. The Rector was Bishop Fred Morris, who had been called out of retirement in England after years as a missionary bishop in North Africa to become the first Presiding Bishop of the Church of England in South Africa. Bishop Morris was now an old man and rather struggled with his sermons. But he was such a saint that his tall figure standing in the pulpit was a sermon in itself. He never failed to express his firm conviction that Our Lord was soon coming again. Despite all his heavy responsibilities, he visited us in our flat that very Tuesday! What a wonderful ornament of the Church of the Lord Jesus Christ he was, and no doubt is.

Shortly after that I was called for an interview with the Vacuum Oil branch manager. I was playing the "Colonel card" rather heavily, and everyone I saw there, including the branch manager, called me, sir. Most of them had served in the desert or in Italy during the war. Colonels were still a rarity in South Africa as the Defence Force was very small in those days before the Marxist offensive against Southern Africa began some ten years later. The branch manager recommended me to the Head Office in Cape Town, and soon I was flown down for an interview there.

The clerk responsible booked the colonel into the number one suite of the Grand Hotel, Cape Town, which was second only to the Mount Nelson in those days, not realizing that the said officer was only an applicant to join the company as a humble trainee!

The Operations Director spent the entire interview explaining why he had not been able to go to war as he was in a position vital to the war effort, etc. The Marketing Director appeared to be a sinister individual whose eyes were permanently hidden behind dark glasses. The Financial Director only showed passing interest in me. Anyway, they took me on as an operations executive trainee and ruled that, in view of my previous experience, my training period would be reduced from a year to six months. They started me on a salary of about a hundred pounds a month, which, with my retired pay of forty seven pounds a month and income from a few investments, brought me up to about a hundred and seventy five pounds. That was enough to keep the wolf from the door in those days. So we moved into a slightly larger flat in the same building. I began on 1st August 1958, the very day my paid retirement leave expired. Again the Lord had looked after me, but sometimes, thinking back, I wonder how I ever dared to come to South Africa, with no job to go to and a family to house, feed, and educate.

The training course was very interesting, and, apart from product knowledge, it included mostly practical work. The very first job I did in South Africa was to serve petrol on the driveway. My first customer asked for ten shillings of petrol, which had me flummoxed as I'd always bought petrol by the gallon, and for a moment I couldn't think how to stop the pump on the right price. I overran by sixpence and offered to pay that myself, but the customer was happy to give me ten and six.

My next job was to get the oil seal out of the differential of a customer's car. It is necessary to hammer hard in an awkward position under the car to get it out, and I missed the target several times, hitting various parts and hoping I did not do too much damage to them. I hope that customer's car ran again.

I was moved to the Langlaagte Depot and worked in the oil store taking stock and executing orders. I climbed the fuel storage tanks to dip them and work out stocks and calculate vapor and other losses. I dipped rail tank cars on arrival and decanted them into the storage tanks. I did a spell at the Jan Smuts Depot fuelling aircraft. South African Airways were using Viscounts on their internal services then. Because of the altitude, they had to boost their engines with a water-methanol mixture at take-off. Mixing the water and methanol had to be done in exactly the right proportions at 62 degrees Fahrenheit. The trouble was that every time water was added there was a temperature rise, and then the mixture had to cool to 62 degrees to see if it was now correct. It was seldom right at the first try, so it was quite a tricky operation requiring patience. I must say it was with considerable relief that I saw planes which I had refuelled take off successfully. It was just as well the passengers didn't know who had mixed the fuel!

After six weeks I was taken off the training course and was made transport supervisor for all the lorries in the Transvaal and Northern Free State. The main problem here was that the farmers never ordered their fuel till not only had a cloud appeared but, the rain had started dropping out of it. So a depot such as Delareyville which normally had a throughput of some thirty thousand gallons suddenly jumped to three hundred and thirty thousand gallons in a month when the rains came. This meant rushing in extra lorries from other depots in order to cope, provided of course that it was not raining everywhere at the same time. It was an interesting and quite responsible job, but I had to ask before my salary was adjusted. Then it went up to a hundred and thirty pounds.

At the end of a year, when my training program should have stopped, there was no prospect of my being "slotted" into the executive position I had been promised as the company was waiting on a reorganization being planned in America. The branch engineer was a Charles Pogson whom I had taught as a cadet in 1941 in the Officer Cadet Training Unit at Wouldham on the Medway. He, finding conditions unsatisfactory in Mobil, had recently transferred to Total. He had recommended to them that they should recruit me. I was offered the position of Branch Operations Manager either in Rhodesia or in Natal. The position was exactly what I had hoped for in Mobil and so I accepted with alacrity and chose Natal. I was to start on a salary of two hundred and fifty pounds a month.

In October 1959 I moved to Durban, and then began my three happiest years in business. The branch manager was Dick Morley, who had served in the Gunners during the war, the sales manager was Dick Frost, a delightful man who had served in the Natal Carbineers in the war. We all got on like a house on fire together, and it was a very happy branch. My senior operations man was Chris Klopper, the terminal superintendent at Island View, who had also served in Italy, and I relied on him a great deal while I was picking up the ropes. He subsequently became the superintendent of the government reserve storage scheme in charge of filling disused mines with fuel for strategic reserve purposes.

The company warned me that I might be moved later, and therefore it seemed best to send the boys to boarding school. The headmaster of Hilton College could not have been more helpful. He agreed to accept Chris for January 1960 without taking the entrance exam. John was to go in January 1961 and in the meantime would stay with a friend in Yeoville and continue in King Edward's Prep School till then. David was to go to Durban High Prep School until he was old enough to go to Hilton in 1964. My financial position had improved enough to make this program feasible.

I rented a very pleasant family house in Durban North, where the family joined me when the Christmas holidays began in 1959.

Win was soon given a teaching post in a nearby school and later was promoted to the matric class at Durban Girls High School. We could not have managed the school fees without the additional income she earned.

Being an operations manager in an oil company is rather like sitting on the top of a volcano. Anything can happen. A four thousand gallon tank truck can have an accident in West Street in central Durban, an accident can happen when discharging a ship at Island View Terminal, or in any depot.

My first crisis occurred only six weeks after arrival in Durban. In those days we were bringing in refined products, not just the crude oil. This meant that a tanker would bring to us up to five different products. To pump a ship, a slug of water would be put down the pipeline after each product to prevent the products mixing as they were pumped. The water soon settled to the bottom of the tank where it could easily be drained off. With diesel, one hour for each foot of product in the tank is allowed to give the water time to clear to the bottom. On this particular occasion we had forty feet of diesel in the tank after pumping, and so the water should all have dropped to the bottom of the tank in forty hours. But this time the diesel remained cloudy even after sixty hours. I took a sample to an industrial chemist, who found that the water had gone into suspension with the diesel and, although the quantity of water was minute and within specification, the cloudy appearance made the diesel unmarketable. We found in the laboratory that the water would clear if the diesel was passed through salt, or it would clear if its temperature was raised a mere 5 degrees Fahrenheit. But there were a million gallons to clear, and I needed the tank in another three weeks when I would have another ship to discharge. No one in the Head Office could give advice nor seemed inclined to get involved.

I decided to try the heating method. We emptied another tank and installed a two inch pipe heating coil in it. I hired a boiler which I had to put outside the tank farm and lagged the pipes from the boiler to the tank, a distance of some forty yards. Having supplied ourselves with a quantity of coke, Klopper and I started the fire going in the boiler. It is not all that easy to stoke a boiler, and I was so grateful that I had been taught how to do it when I was a young officer at Chatham before the war. Only the lube oil foreman, Bill Cole, Klopper, and I could do it. We tried to teach another staff member, but he could not get the hang of it. So the three of us stoked that boiler continuously day and night for a fortnight, taking it in four hour shifts. Without fail, as soon as we raised the temperature 5 degrees the product cleared, and we pumped it in 40,000 gallon lots through our heating system and into a third empty tank. I remember, when I relieved Klopper one morning, he looked up at me with his face all covered in smuts and eyes red from the smoke, saying, "What of my status now?" To which I replied as I took the shovel from him, "And what about mine?"

Our problems were compounded by rain several days on end. The cold rainwater running down the sides of the tank cooled the product further and also slowed down the heating process. It was clear that we were not going to get the whole tank clear in time and that the company would be faced with port charges while the tanker was delayed for several days. One morning, with the next ship only a few days away, I was stoking in the early hours when suddenly the product cleared after a temperature rise of only three degrees. I hastily dipped the remaining product in the tank and to my delight found that all the hundred thousand gallons remaining had cleared. No one has been able to offer me an explanation for this happy outcome. Whether the product would have cleared after a fortnight even if we had done nothing about it, or whether our successive reductions in the product level shook the remaining water out, no one can tell. But my relief was enormous.

All the road tankers are fitted with pressure vacuum valves which let air in or out as the day temperature varies, causing contraction or expansion of the fuel. But in the event of an accident in which the tanker rolls, the valves are supposed to shut off completely. I decided to test all our valves by upending them when fitted to a drum filled with product. Hardly any of them worked. Whereupon I required the supplier to replace the faulty

Back Again Mr. Begbie

ones. A year later, a tanker belonging to Transvaal Branch did roll, the valves had not been tested, the product ran in the gutter for four hundred yards down the street, someone dropped a cigarette, the product caught alight and travelled all the way back up the street to the tanker, setting fire to six cars parked en route and to the tanker and the house against which it had crashed. Although being an oil company operations manager is like sitting on a volcano, I thoroughly enjoyed it. I was constantly travelling, inspecting and checking the depots from Queenstown and East London in the Eastern Cape to Hluhluwe in Northern Zululand, involving round trips of 500 miles or more.

There were amusing moments as well. On one occasion we ran short of lubricating oil at the terminal at Island View. I rang Head Office for instructions and was told to send forty unmarked drums to the Wakefield depot, fill them with Castrol oil, and then decant them into Total Oil cans. In the meantime we had a service station in Durban North which was being run by one of our in-house operators. When I visited him one day to see how he was getting on, he said, "These Durban people are an amazingly conservative lot and insist on using Castrol oil. Don't tell anyone but fortunately the previous operator of this station left a lot of empty Castrol bottles at the back, and I'm putting our oil into them and they are selling like hot cakes." But I couldn't tell him he was merely putting Castrol oil back into Castrol bottles!

Win and I, and the boys when they were at home, together with two retired missionary ladies whom we took with us, used to worship at Christ Church, Pinetown. In those days, on arrival we just about doubled the very small congregation. The Rector was the Rev. Stephen Bradley, who later was consecrated bishop and became the Presiding Bishop of the Church of England in South Africa. As well as being the Rector, he was also the superintendent of all our mission churches, and he was frequently away. Somehow he knew that I was a member of the OCU, and so he asked me to preach for him when he was away while Mr. Bill Abraham read the service. For the first sermon I ever preached I chose for my text Psalm 42:11, "Why art thou cast down, O my soul? And why art thou disquieted within me? Hope thou in God: for I shall yet praise Him, who is the health of my countenance, and my God." After the service, when I greeted the people at the door, Miss Keeler, an elderly saint who had given the money to build the church, looked me very severely in the eye and said, "You've missed your vocation, young man!"

I don't know whether this started a subconscious train of thought in my mind, but it may have done. At any rate, after that I preached quite frequently when Bradley was away. As a matter of interest, the congregation attending that church, which has been enlarged several times, is now nearly a thousand, and there are several daughter churches of it.

Although in Total Oil Natal we had a smaller throughput than any of the other branches, we were the first branch to make an operating profit. As this was due to the efficiency of our operations, the Managing Director moved me up to Head Office in Johannesburg in September 1962. Houses to rent were difficult to find, but my sister found a large one in the far north corner of Bryanston with the open veld the other side of the fence, and that became our family home for the next eighteen months. It was just as well that the boys were boarders at Hilton College. David had to stay one more year as a boarder in Durban Prep before joining the others at Hilton in January 1964.

I soon became involved with the work of Christ Church, Hillbrow, where the Rev. Bernard Wright had taken over from Bishop Morris. I was quite soon licensed as a lay preacher and preached at various churches along the Reef when called upon to do so. I became a Sunday School teacher, working under Ralph Shaw, a first rate, dedicated Christian was who also Treasurer of the central funds of the denomination.

I used to ride Bob Grayston's horses for recreation, and Chris joined me riding during the school holidays. The three boys and I also used to play golf together in the holidays, and we had several caravan holidays down to the Cape coast. After a year we bought a lovely thatched house in Parktown North which was altogether more convenient. We all hoped, and especially Win, that we were going to put down permanent roots at last. We had a lovely secluded and spacious garden at the back, and much to the delight of the boys there was a separate front door to their end of the house. I also bought the boys a second hand Fynn yacht, in which we used to sail on Germiston Lake. Win found a post at a nearby school to continue to help with the school fees.

In the Head Office the Managing Director told me to work with a management consultant named McCaul who had been working in the company for some time to introduce a new system of cost accounting. I was to evaluate the system, and if I recommended that it was beneficial, I was to develop it further with a view to introducing it to the company as a whole.

I learned an enormous amount from McCaul, in particular how to code cost centres and the kinds of cost in a such a very logical manner as to produce an infinitely more efficient and meaningful management tool than that currently in use. In particular, it would enable management to spot immediately which operations were cost efficient and which were not. The computer would analyze the reasons for subsequent detailed investigation by line management and corrective action by those concerned.

However, added to the usual resistance to change, the facts that there was a change over of managing directors in mid-stream and that the system was beyond the understanding of the finance manager, ensured that the scheme never got off the ground.

In the end I joined a team of executives working under the same finance manager with whom I and others found it impossible to work. Happily for me, in April 1966 I was offered a huge promotion to the international staff of the Companie Francais de Petrole. This would require willingness to serve anywhere in the world for tours of duty of two years, with two weeks annual local leave followed by six weeks leave every second year, with paid flights for myself and my family to anywhere in the world. There was an attractive salary to go with it, free housing, and company car. The first appointment would be as Operations Manager of the Nigeria company with Head Office in Lagos.

But by this time I was so involved in the founding of Christ Church, Blairgowrie, that it was impossible to accept this offer. Having rejected such a senior promotion, I was in honor bound to resign from Total Oil. In fact, the managing director gave me a lengthy dressing down in French, of which I understood little.

So I had to start at the beginning again as a humble systems analyst with a fertilizer company. Within a few weeks I was promoted to become the long term systems manager to introduce a total computerized management information system for the company. Another man was appointed short term systems manager, and both of us were authorized to recruit our own teams.

I had never done a course on computers, and the art of programming remains a closed book as far as I am concerned. But the Lord has blessed me with an analytical brain, and all my life I have been trained to, and had to, think logically. Such a way of thinking is absolutely essential for anyone taking a responsible position in this field. The output of a computer is only as logical as the designer of the system on which it is to work. But without the knowledge I had gained from Mr. McCaul, I don't think I would have known where to start. My team was soon working enthusiastically within the parameters I had set.

At this stage the short term systems manager, who was a Jehovah's Witness and who had enlisted an entire team of Jehovah's Witnesses, launched a holy (unholy?) war against me. He wrote a paper to top management alleging that I didn't know what I was doing, knew nothing about computers, etc. Management had to call in a computer consultant to referee, and she reported that I did know what I was doing. As a result, the short term manager was fired, and his team then joined my team. It was soon evident to all of us that they were quite incompetent, and I had to fire them one after the other. At this stage management said I must not fire the last one, as the Head Office staff were getting the impression that I, the

Christian, was waging a war against Jehovah's Witnesses! So we kept the last one, whom we could really only use as a clerk, on strength as a sort of pet, rather as we had kept on the last Hindu at Risalpur to ensure Hindu holidays for ourselves as well as Christian and Mohammedan ones.

This job was by far the most onerous task, without any exception, that I have ever attempted. To develop a total system takes at least two years. To begin with, an in-depth study of line managers' requirements, from the managing director downwards, has to be made by a team of systems analysts, and all the company products, operations, and procedures have to be charted. In this process, a surprising amount of unnecessary activity is usually brought to daylight. Having done that, the flow of all information from the point of each operation all the way up through the levels of management has to be coordinated and simplified onto a logical flow chart which forms the basis from which the system is developed. Then all these types of information have to be incorporated into a sophisticated coding system and the computer files organized.

Only when this point has been reached after at least a year's work can the systems manager delegate the different parts of the total system to teams comprising systems engineers and programmers.

Whereas in all other fields of management the detail can be delegated, the systems manager can never divorce himself from the detail. If one of his teams hits a problem which he has not foreseen, only he can decide whether any adjustment will affect any of the other teams. In making such a decision, he has to remember why he made a detailed decision concerning thousands of different codes months or even over a year previously. I found this mental effort to be an enormous strain.

The whole problem was made worse still by conflict between the administration manager and the planning manager to whom I was responsible. The former did what he could to sabotage any project undertaken by the planning manager, including mine. So it was a most unhappy situation made even more complicated because we had two managing directors (!) who were quite incapable of resolving the senior staff problem. It ended by my company being taken over by a competitor — a fate richly deserved.

But meanwhile I had resigned to prepare for ordination as rector of Christ Church, Blairgowrie, a new church of which I had become a founding member. So ended my commercial industrial career ten years after the end of my military life.

Chapter Fourteen

The Birth Of A Church

During the latter part of 1964, when I was a member of the council of Christ Church, Hillbrow, in Johannesburg, the rector, the Reverend Bernard Wright, used to refer to "the hole in my bucket." Eventually he disclosed that the hole represented the constant drain of young marrieds from the flats of Hillbrow to the new suburbs to the northwest of Johannesburg.

In April he called a meeting of those members of the Hillbrow and Bramley congregations who lived nearest to the new suburbs. These included Bob Wagner, who lived in Hurlingham, Owen and Doris Smith, who lived in Greenside, and myself, who lived in Parktown, north from Christ Church, Hillbrow, and Ted and Ina Dell, who lived in the Johannesburg part of Blairgowrie, and Mr. and Mrs. Phillips and their sons Brian and Neil, who lived in Blairgowrie, from Holy Trinity Church, Bramley. I attended with the firm resolve not to become involved as I was, I thought, already doing enough, being a church councillor, lay preacher, and Sunday school teacher, as well as having a senior position in the head office of Total Oil.

Sometimes men speak with a special unction of the Holy Spirit, and it was so with Bernard that night. As he spoke, I could see the lights of the new suburbs twinkling in the darkness, but there were no street lights to show people the way. There was much need of more light, and I thought with a strange concern of the Spiritual light all those families would need. I knew then that, not only would I become involved, but that the Lord was calling me to the leadership of the new venture. I had never been so sure of a calling in my life, and Win recognized it in my face the moment I got home.

During May, we were all involved in an evangelistic mission conducted by the Rev. Bertie Rainsbury in Johannesburg, and it was not until July that we had all recovered sufficiently from the prodigious efforts we had all made to make the mission a success.

So as from mid-July, we began holding monthly meetings for prayer and planning in the home of Mr. and Mrs. Dale. At the first of these I was elected chairman, and I led the meetings from then on. Meantime we all continued with our commitments to Christ Church, Hillbrow, and Holy Trinity Church, Bramley respectively. Two new-comers to the first meeting were Dick and Audrey Brentley, who had been converted during the Rainsbury Mission. In fact we had all been so spiritually reinvigorated that it is not too much to say that the new church grew out of Bertie Rainsbury's ministry amongst us. Others who joined us early were Jack Brown and Mrs. Joslin from Christ Church, Hillbrow.

An ad hoc committee was appointed, consisting of myself, Owen Smith, Ted Dale, and Bob Wagner. Our numbers built up quite quickly, and we were already a group of about twenty by the beginning of August. I did a centre of gravity calculation to determine what site would be central to all the homes by then involved. It worked out at a spot a few hundred yards up Gordon Avenue, in Blairgowrie, from where the church now stands. So we looked for suitable sites as near to our centre of gravity as possible.

We also considered the factors which should influence our choice of site. These were, that it should not be on a main road because of noise and danger to children, nor should not tucked away in an inconspicuous side road. It should therefore be on a road used by local residents to go to the shops and to the schools. It should it be on high ground where it could be seen and from whence the church bell could be heard. It should be near a school to attract children to the Sunday School.

We found three possible sites. One was where the Methodist Church now stands on H.F.Verwoerd Drive, which we rejected because of traffic and noise. One was high up on Barkstone Drive, and the last was the present site on the corner of Gordon and Mackay Avenues. I remember going to the town clerk's office one day to see if there were any sites which we might have overlooked, and I saw on his map two large vacant areas. On enquiry I found that these were reserved for schools and that our third site would be exactly halfway between the two. That settled it, and I knew with absolute certainty that the Lord's choice of site was the third one. Jack Brown reached the same conclusion quite independently, perhaps with Irish intuition, saying, "There's only one place for the church, and that's on the corner of Gordon and Mackay Avenues. I'm telling you!"

Towards the end of August a crucial meeting was held in Mr. and Mrs. Phillips's home in Main Road, Bordeaux. Those present included Mr. Norman Levey, Mr. Ralph Shaw, Mr. Rudi Meijers, and the Rev. Bernard Wright from Christ Church, Hillbrow. I was by now absolutely convinced that the Lord was directing us to go ahead. Norman Levey was hesitant, and so was Ralph. But eventually I persuaded them to recommend to the Hillbrow congregation that we be given financial assistance to buy the site.

A few days later I addressed a special vestry meeting of Christ Church, Hillbrow, which endorsed the decision to give financial support and resolved to grant a loan of R3,000 to the new church.

We ascertained the prices of stands in Blairgowrie, and quarter acre stands were at that time selling for R800. As the two stands we wanted, being on a corner, were larger, the two together comprised three quarters of an acre. So the whole site was worth R2,400 plus about R100 for being on the corner. So I suggested we should offer the owner R2,500. But some of the others said that, seeing we were sure this was the Lord's choice, we should offer more to make sure we were successful. I forbade that because if it was the Lord's choice, He would ensure that we obtained it for what it was worth and no more.

Rudi Meijers sent off the telegram to the owner in Bulawayo on the Friday, and I asked everyone to remain in prayer till the answer was received. It came on Monday, and Rudi brought the good news to me at the Christ Church, Hillbrow, Sunday School sports at Bez Valley Farm. I was almost overcome with joy.

Our monthly meetings continued throughout 1964 and early 1965, with numbers increasing all the time, so that there were already thirty six of us plus children that autumn. In Bible studies I took the mission of the seventy and taught the people how to go visiting in pairs door to door when the time came.

Meantime the ad hoc committee, to which we had added Dick Brentley and Dennis Stewart, a quantity surveyor, considered what sort of structure we should build. We decided on a building of which the front half should be a church to seat about one hundred and twenty people, and the back half should be a hall into which the church could expand later. A separate hall could be built later. There were also to be some half dozen class rooms along the side, plus vestry, kitchen, and toilets. Mr. van der Ham, the architect of Total Oil, kindly agreed to design the building free of charge. We told him the cost must not exceed R20,000. This building was to have run parallel to Gordon Avenue where the rectory and the back half of the church now stand.

This structure would not have been nearly as attractive as the church we eventually built. The Lord over-ruled when Dennis calculated that this building would have cost at least R32,000, and that ruled it out.

But at this very time Dennis knew of another architect who had been working on a block of flats which, it so happened, the developers decided not to proceed with. So Mr. John Whitefield was immediately available to design a church for us. It turned out that he had previously designed two churches, and so he had the experience we needed.

Just previously, I had met the organist at Holy Trinity Church, Bramley. He was an architect's clerk, and we had a very constructive discussion on the way in which the design of a church ought to reflect its theology. Fresh from this discussion, I was able to brief Mr. Whitefield on exactly what we wanted. There must be no chancel. The table must run east-west, and there must be built-in flower boxes on either side of it to prevent it ever being turned north-south, in which position it could become an altar. The communion rail must be curved round the table to foster a feeling of family unity and love as we partook of the Lord's Supper. The Bible on a lectern must be in the most prominent position in the centre of the church and in front of the congregation. The pulpit must be to one side to emphasize that the preached word, however much inspired by the Holy Spirit, is still produced by fallen men and therefore not free from error. The choir and organ must be placed on the side opposite the pulpit where they can be heard without being obtrusive. The font, used, *inter alia*, to symbolize entry into the true church, which is the company of God's faithful people, must be near an entry into the building. To avoid the congregation having to turn round when there is a baptism, there must be an entrance near the front of the building. This would have the added advantage of encouraging people to fill the church from the front instead of from the back. (For this reason, the under floor heating only extends under the front half of the church). Above all, the design must somehow produce a feeling of awe, love, and warmth, even of the grace of the Lord Jesus Christ.

How well Mr. Whitefield designed to these specifications is evident to anyone who enters the building. The upward sweep of the roof above the Lord's Table lifts one's thoughts upward, and the downward curves of the roof along the wing walls either side of the Table seem to mirror the outstretched arms of the Saviour towards little children. The use of natural wood and rough, golden brown bricks, and the way in which the sunlight comes through the colored glass onto the Lord's table during morning service, all add to the beautiful simplicity of the building.

Gratefully we accepted the design which Mr. Whitefield estimated would cost no more than our limit of R20,000. To save money, we decided to sub-contract the work to the various trades, which Mr. Whitefield would supervise for the usual fee of 6% all told.

Meantime, as no sites in Randburg had been set aside for church use in the town plan, we had to apply for consent use. The Rev. Bernard Wright and I had to appear before the Management Committee, and I was asked what caused me to pick that particular site.

When I outlined how the Lord had led us to this site, I could see that the Committee were already won over. The chairman asked Bernard what he would do if a black man entered the church. Bernard answered extremely well. He said that, if he were to ask the man to leave, the *Sunday Times* might well have a reporter outside, and such an incident would be grist for their mill. On the contrary, he would welcome the man and advise him that if he wished to worship in his own language, he could do so either in Christ Church, Hillbrow, in the afternoon when services were held in Zulu, or in either of our churches in Soweto.

In the event, we were given consent use for a church for white use only. Reluctantly we accepted this, thinking it better to have a church for some people even if we couldn't have it for all the people. But we determined to take up the issue again if and when black people expressed a wish to come to this church.

In one of our regular monthly meetings we discussed the naming of the church. Emmanuel had been suggested by Christ Church, Hillbrow, Council, but we were unanimous that the church should be called Christ Church, Blairgowrie. We did not include Randburg in the name because we expected to build more churches in Randburg sometime in the future.

Early in 1965 we began to look for premises in which we could begin to hold services and start a Sunday School. We looked everywhere, but there were no halls built in Randburg at that time. We explored garages and new shop buildings which had not yet been let, but each time we found one a tenant appeared. There seemed to be absolutely nowhere to go.

Also early in 1965, we designed a leaflet to inform the residents of Randburg of our plans and that we were here to bring the Gospel of Jesus Christ to the town. It must be realized that we were the first English-medium church to open in Randburg. We said how we intended this to be a family church. The church service would be held at the same time as Sunday School so that the whole family could come at the same time. We included a tear off portion on which recipients could volunteer their services as chorister, organist, Sunday School teacher, canvasser to homes, sidesman, youth leader, typist, gardener, or offer financial help. We used the Randburg water rate address list for sending out the leaflet. I think there were about forty replies from people who promised support.

One of those who responded to the leaflet was Mrs. Joan Johnstone. She asked if arrangements could be made to baptize her baby, and I asked the Rev. Bernard Wright to come over from Hillbrow to call on her. "It so happened," (and there are lots of "it so happened" stories by arrangement of the Lord in the birth-pangs of this church) that on the day Bernard called, Mrs. Johnstone's friend was having coffee with her. This was the first time this friend had been in Joan's house, as previously Joan had always gone to the friend's house for coffee. So by the Lord's appointment the friend was present while Bernard explained the significance of infant baptism. At the end Joan asked, "When will you be starting a Sunday School, as I have a little girl who would like to come?" To this Bernard replied that the committee had looked everywhere for a hall, but there just wasn't one anywhere in the area. The friend, who it so happened was a Christian, said, "Oh, but I've got a hall upstairs in my house and you can use that!"

Without wasting a moment, the three went across to the friend's house, which backed onto Joan's house, and there upstairs was a hall sixty feet long and twenty feet wide, quite empty except for a ping-pong table and a darts board. It was light and airy, in excellent repair, and had a Marley tile floor. In addition, a large balcony led off it and access was by a separate door and staircase. Whoever has heard of a modern house being built with such a facility? Nothing will ever shake me in my firm opinion that the Lord had that house specially built for us, and specially arranged for it to have a Christian owner who would be put in touch with us. The address was 45 Susman Avenue.

This was in early April 1965. We had a certain amount of money in the funds by now, and Owen Smith was asked to become the superintendent of the Sunday School. We asked him to obtain quotes for miniature chairs and tables for the kids, Sunday School books, and other materials which would be needed. He found that equipment for forty children would just about use all our funds. Christ Church, Hillbrow, and Holy Trinity Church, Bramley, lent us some chairs for adults. We decided to provide for forty children and announced our intention to begin with a family service on Sunday 25th April 1965. We prayed most earnestly that the Lord would bless the occasion.

The great day arrived. Exactly forty children came, and I'm sure that if we'd had the faith to provide for sixty children, sixty children would have come. Some thirty adults were present. Bernard preached, and Owen and I led in different parts of the service. The Lord was manifestly with us, and it was a most blessed occasion. So some eight months after the church began, we were enabled to open the Sunday School and begin regular monthly family services.

From the last few letters from my father in England, it was evident that he was sinking rapidly. I would have gone to see him if this hadn't been such a vital period in the life of the church. But he died a little before his eightieth birthday on May 5th before I could get to him. I loved and admired my father above any other man and was absolutely devoted to him. Without fail, we had written to one another every week, both in war and peace. I was bitterly sad not to have been with him at the end. It was to be the beginning of the price I and my family were going to be called upon to pay in the years ahead. Being in the centre where I could see the Lord's hand at work in every aspect of the work, it was a price I could pay gladly, but it was not so easy for my family as my time was being taken up more and more.

Soon after my return from England, where I had attended the funeral of my father and stayed on for three weeks to comfort my mother, we were viciously attacked in his parish magazine by "Father" Matthews, the rector of St. Thomas's Church, Linden, of the Church of the Province of South Africa. He seemed to imagine that no other church had the right to operate within the unspecified borders of his parish, and accused us of being a schismatic church. The Rev. Dr. Jack Allen, Rector of Holy Trinity Church, Bramley, responded to this attack most fully and adequately in a letter to Matthews, with copies to all our members. The attack did us no harm and may have gained us a few families who were revolted by Matthews' behavior.

For the rest of 1965, we held a family service each month and a communion service once a month in the evening. The Revs. Bernard Wright, Jack Allen, Ernie Jump, and Len Flemming officiated at these services, as did Bishop Bradley whenever he was up in the Transvaal.

The Sunday School continued to grow all the time. As it grew, we prayed to the Lord to send us more teachers, and we were never short. But it has to be said that it became apparent later that several of these teachers were not sufficiently spiritually mature, and some were not even converted, for the task. But we were getting so many children that we just had to appoint whoever we could to look after them.

Meanwhile, I had frequent meetings with the architect as the plans developed and a fair amount of correspondence with Bishop Bradley, who was always available to give advice even from a distance. By the end of 1965 we had in the funds a loan of R3,000 from Christ Church, Hillbrow, a gift of R2,600 from Mrs. Bernard Price, a long term member of the Hillbrow congregation, and a grant of R2,400 from the Central Trustees of the Church of England in South Africa. I had also made an appeal to all the major business firms in Johannesburg. I reminded them that they made grants for education, but that it was at least as important for them to have staff whose reliability was based on religious convictions firmly held. In the result, the Anglo-American Corporation gave R1,000 and JCI R500. Contributions from other, mostly engineering, firms brought the total from this source to over R2,000. We had also generated a further R1,000 from amongst ourselves. After paying for the land, this left us with a little over R7,500. With this backing, I managed to raise a bond of R16,000 to finance the building of the church.

At about this time we received another shock when we discovered that, in a legacy, the two stands exactly opposite our site in Gordon Avenue had been left to the Church of the Province of South Africa. I dreaded the possibility that two Anglican churches might be facing each other across the road, and all the ill feeling which would be bound to arise. We prayed most earnestly and agonizingly that the Lord would intervene and over-rule in this situation. Thankfully to Him, we learned that the CPSA had decided to sell both stands, and it was with enormous relief that we saw two private houses built on them soon after.

I should mention that Owen Smith and I shared the visitation of Sunday School parents and of others who had joined us. By the end of the year 1965 the fellowship must have comprised some sixty adults and nearly one hundred children.

Early in the new year 1966, Mr. D.G. Mills, the Chancellor of the Church of England in South Africa, wrote to me from Cape Town to suggest that I put up a notice board on the site to advertise the fact that a church of the CESA was soon to be built there.

We had no sooner erected the board than I was tipped off that a massive attack was about to be launched on us by the CPSA. In this, members of that denomination were to be called in from all along the Reef to visit in pairs every house in Blairgowrie and Bordeaux to tell the people to have nothing to do with us. Having foreknowledge of this extraordinary attack, I could have preempted it. But I did not wish by any action of ours to appear to have provoked the quarrel. So I called on all our members to pray for the conversion of those who were going to come against us and to wait in their homes for these people and present them with the Gospel. The effect was amazing. Many of these people had not understood the true position, and, after being enlightened by our people, they were so ashamed of their actions that they went off home. Others got the impression that they had been sent to encourage people to go to the new church being built on the corner! The net result was that we gained another dozen families and twenty more children in the Sunday School. The Lord over-ruled this evil thing in a most amazing way, in fact, not by might, nor by power, but by His Spirit, just as His Word promises.

Meantime we had bought a Baldwin Model 26C organ for the church, and it was kept in the Hodson's house where our organist, Mrs. Ruth Hodson, could practice on it and become familiar with it. It cost about R2,500. Sometime that January 1966 the first sods were cut and building began.

At about this time, Brian Cameron and Thyra Anderson, who had been teaching in the Sunday School for some time, were led to found our youth group. We could not have had finer Christian leaders. They were joined amongst others, by Maureen Smith and my sons.

We now began making preparations for the laying of the foundation stone. This was scheduled to take place on Saturday, 12th March 1966. Bricks, the pre-stressed beams which would hold up the roof, and other materials would be on site by then, and we planned to "sell" these to raise funds. We also arranged to provide teas and cakes for the same purpose, and there was also a sale of work. The organ was moved across for the ceremony, and electricity for it was borrowed from the house next door.

We had a lovely sunny day for the occasion and were encouraged by the presence of many members from other CESA congregations in the Transvaal. The Rev. Bernard Wright officiated, and I was given the honor of laying the stone by the Presiding Bishop. I said, "Before having the great honor of laying the foundation stone, I want to make it quite clear who has founded this church.

"The Lord has done it and it is marvellous in our eyes. He gave the Rev. Bernard Wright the vision which began the work. Through 1964, God brought together a little group of Christians and caused then to dedicate themselves to the task.

"He found this magnificent site and ensured that it was bought for no more than it was worth.

"He blessed a leaflet which was given a wide distribution and through it added greatly to the band.

"In miraculous circumstances, He found us a hall to use for the Sunday School.

"He overthrew and turned to advantage an attack made on us by others.

"He blessed posters in shop windows and has caused the Sunday School to flourish beyond our wildest hopes. He has added Sunday School teachers as the number of children has grown to its present figure of one hundred and five.

"He has caused our youth group, which began only four weeks ago, to grow already to twenty five members.

"He has moved in peoples' hearts to cause them to give generously to enable the church to be built.

"He has found us a skilled organist. He has found us an architect to design this beautiful church and a builder to build it. May we pray continually for them, that they may build soundly and easily overcome any snags which may arise.

"He has worked in the hearts of a large number of men and women to bind them together in the unity of His Spirit.

"He has guided and provided at every step of our progress. He has blessed this work far above anything we asked or thought.

"Wherefore in the name of Almighty God, the Father, the Son, and the Holy Spirit, to His glory and for His worship and service, we lay this foundation stone of Christ Church, Blairgowrie. Here may spiritual sacrifices of praise and prayer be offered continually, and the sound of the glorious Gospel be heard. Here may true believers be built up in the faith and love, and sinners find salvation.

"And to God be all the glory through Jesus Christ our Lord, Amen."

I cannot now remember how much was raised that afternoon, but I am sure it was not less than R2,000. There was also a gift of R1000.

Each Sunday, many of us used to go up to the site after service or Sunday school to see how the work was going on. When the floor was cast before the walls were up it looked enormous. Then as the walls went up it came back to the size we expected. A thrilling day was when the main pre-stressed timber beams went up.

Although I had been very happy in Total Oil when I was operations manager for Natal and Border based in Durban, I had not been so happy in the Head Office in Johannesburg. It was at this time, in April 1966, that I was offered the promotion to the international staff of Total Oil, the C.F.P. But I realized that if I left now it would be bad for the church. So I started to look around for another job, since there would be no future for me in Total Oil if I turned down this promotion. But I could find nothing and began to feel that perhaps the Lord wanted me in Nigeria.

At this stage Owen Smith came round and pleaded with me, saying the whole work would collapse if I left now, and we prayed to the Lord for definite guidance. Next morning, the data processing manager in Total, Martin Birkenbosch, to whom I had previously confided my problem, accosted me on arrival and said that he had seen a vacancy for a systems analyst advertised in the paper, and I should apply for that. I was far above the age asked for, but nevertheless Martin insisted that I should apply. So I said that I would write. "No, ring them up," he said. So I did, and to my surprise I was hired that day and found myself in the computer business with very little previous experience. This was in a fertilizer company. The Managing Director of Total Oil was furious when I handed in my resignation and gave me a fearful tirade all in French, of which I could not understand a word. But I got the drift of it all right.

Almost immediately after joining the company, I was promoted to manager to plan and implement a comprehensive, computerized management system, with authority to recruit my own staff. I think it was the most exacting task I have ever done. I draw attention to this because it illustrates the pressure under which I was working at the time.

All sorts of problems kept cropping up in connection with the building of the church. At about this time we had the problem of getting the church spire up. I managed to borrow, at no charge, a Galleon mobile crane with a seventy foot jib, but that was still not high enough, and we had to build a ramp for the crane to climb up. So at last the job was done. I was still leading the Bible study and prayer meetings, visiting the sick in the lunch hour, sharing the pastoral visitation with Owen Smith in the evenings, and preaching periodically.

By the middle of 1966 a working party, led by Owen, was working on Saturday afternoons making the communion rail for the church. The party consisted of Dick Brentley, Ray Johnstone, Brian Sherratt, and myself. We spent hours and hours, I remember, sanding down the wood by hand.

At about this time I was approached by a number of members to accept ordination as they wanted me to be their minister. I had not quite realized that I had in fact virtually become such to them in all but name. I cannot be sure now who they all were, but I think they included Owen, Bob Wagner, Dick Brentley, and Brian Phillips. I had not expected this call and prayed deeply and at length for guidance. It would put a great strain on the family. Neither Win nor I had any formal theological training, and we thought it would be unfair on the boys to be called suddenly to adjust to life in a rectory. Oddly enough, I don't recollect that the cost in financial terms ever bothered me, except that ordination would have to be delayed till my boys were through Hilton College. A minister's stipend would certainly not pay for that.

Yet, particularly since ordination had not been my idea, but had come from several of God's people acting quite independently of one another, I came to feel that it was God calling me into the ministry, and we as a family would have to pay the cost whatever it might prove to be. Already God had given me a great love for the people of Randburg and a deep concern for their spiritual welfare. Also, the people were appreciating the expositions of Scripture which I was giving them.

I therefore wrote to the church council two letters, of which the second was not to be read until they had made up their minds about the first. In the first I offered myself to them for ordination. In the second I said it was already proving excessively time wasting trying to run the church from my house in Parktown North. If there was a unanimous call from them to enter the ministry, I would sell my house and lend the proceeds to the church to build a rectory.

All this was agreed to and referred to Bishop Stephen Bradley, the Presiding Bishop. He consented to this plan but said I ought to go for training. I would have loved to have done this, but I asked who would then look after the church and who would pay for my sons' education? The Bishop replied, "Two good questions to which there are no good answers. You will have to carry on as you are for the time being." On this understanding, I put my house on the market and began planning the rectory, for which I did the architectural drawings myself, and Jack Brown began building it in September 1966. The rectory had to be double story as space was limited, and I tried to make it match the church, although on a smaller scale. It contained a large lounge, separate dining room, small kitchen, two double bedrooms, two single bedrooms, and a double garage. Jack built it with the R8,000 from my house, a remarkable achievement.

We held the first family service in the hall at the back of the church in October 1966 as the pews were not then ready. But very soon thereafter regular Sunday services were held in the church. From then on I preached on every Sunday, either in the morning or in the evening, whenever a minister was not present. Sunday School was held in the hall and vestries, but unfortunately the partition between the church and the hall was by no means sound proof despite the insulating material with which it was constructed.

We moved into the rectory at the beginning of February 1967, and my sons and I worked feverishly to make the driveway round the church and in front of the rectory and spread chips over the cambered surfaces. Meantime my dear Win, having had a lovely garden in Parktown North, struggled with the dust and mud being brought into the house from the bare earth outside.

Appropriately, the landscaping of the garden in front of the church and the two heaps planted as rockeries were laid out by Mr. and Mrs. Heap, who lived lower down Mackay Avenue. They were wonderful Christian people and had two mongol boys. Mrs. Heap used to say she was so glad that the Lord had given them to her, as a non-Christian woman might not have looked after them properly. Mr. Seegers made the pulpit and Owen made the hymn boards. Other members of the congregation made the boards displaying the Ten Commandments and the Creed, and the lectern which is a trinity in timber. Win and I gave the font and the carpet round the Lord's Table. The congregation collected funds and gave the aisle carpet. The pews, Lord's Table, and prayer desk were made by a firm in Discovery.

On Saturday, 12th March 1967, Bishop Bradley came to dedicate the church to the glory and service of Almighty God. The church was packed to the walls with, besides our own people, clergy and representatives from all our congregations in the Transvaal. The congregation also included the Mayor and Mayoress of Randburg and ministers of other denominations represented locally, all of whom spoke words of welcome and congratulation.

During the service a heavy thunderstorm and torrential rain broke over Blairgowrie. When called on to speak, I said it was our prayer and hope that this church would be as a light set on a hill in a dark and stormy world. The service closed with the hymn which had become especially our own, "O for a thousand tongues to sing my great Redeemer's praise."

Meantime the Sunday School continued to grow phenomenally under the direction of Owen Smith. We had children everywhere, including even in the rectory, which added to my wife's burden as there was the cleaning up to do after them. In desperation, we bought a second hand marquee, erected it where the hall now stands, and divided it with hessian screens into six classrooms. By now, in mid 1967, there were some 200 children and some twenty Sunday School teachers.

Unfortunately, except for the monthly family service, only one or two of these teachers ever came to church, and in that service the sermon was necessarily no more than watered-down milk. Most of those teachers were not fully committed Christians, and one, who was a most gifted teacher, was actually a follower of Kirkegaard! With church service and Sunday School taking place at the same time, the church had developed into two separate fellowships, with each ignorant and increasingly distrustful of the efforts of the other.

The loss of twenty adults to the Sunday School also meant a corresponding reduction in the size of the worshipping congregation. It was a sad situation, but I could not see what I could do about it. So far from Christ Church, Blairgowrie, being founded on a Sunday School, the latter was a distinct handicap to the church's spiritual growth. In fact, it turns out that practically none of those children stayed on in the church when they grew up. Despite it all, the congregation continued to grow, conversions were taking place, and the saints were being edified.

In August 1967, Synod was held in Christ Church, Blairgowrie, for the first time. It was a great occasion for the church and was the first opportunity for the Central Executive and other members of the denomination to see what the Lord had been doing in our midst. I remember clearly they were quite amazed, especially Mr. D.G. Mills, the Chancellor of the denomination, who declared we were an example to the whole denomination. It will be appreciated how small the denomination was at that time as Synod was easily accommodated in the church for its sessions and in the hall at the back of the church for its lunches and teas. The founding of Christ Church really marked the beginning of the extensive growth in the denomination which was to take place in the ensuing two decades.

It had become our practice to begin every service with a chorus sung by the childrens' choir, in red cassocks, on the basis of the Scripture, "a little child shall lead them" (Isaiah 11:6). Mrs. Ruth Hodson trained them very well, and I used to think of them as my little robin red breasts. After the Synod service Mr. Mills said, "I say, old chap, never let them take away those red cassocks from you."

By this time I was getting very tired and run down. Each week I was preparing a sermon and a Bible study and taking three such studies in the evenings. I was visiting the sick in the lunch hour and doing pastoral visitation in the evenings on my way home. Also, my secular work had become very demanding. Just before Synod, I had to retire to bed with a thrombo-phlebitis in my leg and utter exhaustion. Win too was worried regarding my health and was herself overwrought.

At Synod, Bishop Bradley, knowing I was still unable to walk and that therefore my forthcoming holiday would have to be a motoring one, asked me to tour round Rhodesia as he had received letters from there asking for the CESA to extend into that country. He gave me a file of letters, and Win and I undertook the tour in September. But that is another wonderful story to be related in the next chapter. In addition to two trips to Rhodesia, the correspondence with folk in Rhodesia was added to my load until the Rev. Bernard Wright was transferred there in January 1969. It is not too much to say that the whole work in Rhodesia was the offspring of Christ Church, Blairgowrie. We had always thought in terms of mission, but the extent of our vision did not stretch beyond places like Weltevreden Park, a neighboring suburb. But the Lord had other ideas!

Towards the end of 1967, Brian Cameron and Thyra Anderson, who had led the youth group since its inception, were married. She was an exceedingly beautiful bride and a worthy first bride of the church. They moved to Pretoria and were greatly missed as committed Christian youth leaders and Sunday School teachers. My eldest son Christopher and Maureen, Owen Smith's daughter, who were both Sunday School teachers, took over the leadership of the youth group.

One evening there was a knock at the door, and a stranger, who introduced himself as Mr. Alan Hudson, was there. We sat down in the lounge, and he said he was a Jehovah's Witness and that he had had peculiar dream the night before and was greatly troubled. In this dream a voice had told him to go to Christ Church, and he was surprised to find that this was the church because, although he lived nearby and often passed the church, the Witnesses were taught that this was the church of Satan! I took him over to the church and we stood by the lectern. The discussion soon came to the Lord Jesus Christ, as it always must. I opened the Bible at Matthew 3:3, where the Apostle identifies John the Baptist as the one Isaiah prophesied would come to prepare the way of the Lord. Then I took him to Isaiah 40:3, where the Lord is identified as God. "So," I said, "here you have Jesus Christ clearly identified as God by reference to the Old Testament Scripture." This was enough for Alan, who had been taught to deny the deity of the Lord Jesus Christ. He thereupon accepted Jesus Christ as his own Saviour and Lord, and, being almost overcome with joy, we prayed and thanked God together for this wonderful deliverance. Alan immediately joined our mid-week fellowship for Bible study and prayer, and of course became a regular worshipper morning and evening on the Lord's Day.

The reaction of the Jehovah's Witnesses to this conversion of one of their members was quite awful and illustrates the horrid spirit which animates them. Alan showed me a circular letter which was sent to all the Witness Temples along the Reef, saying Alan had now been dis-fellowshipped, and that if he applied for work in any company in which Witnesses worked they were to do all they could to prevent him being employed. He was to be punished for his defection!

Meantime the ladies had been running cake sales, sales of work, and jumble sales under the devoted leadership of Yvonne Ellery to raise money for the building of a Sunday School hall. I think by the first half of 1968 there was rather more than R1,200 in the fund.

At this stage a strong wind blowing through the gap between the church and rectory ripped the marquee from top to bottom. We had no sooner got it repaired than the same thing happened again. I came to the church council and said I was convinced that this was the Lord telling us He didn't want His children accommodated anymore in a shabby old tent. I said we should go ahead in faith and use the money we had, which was just enough to buy a steel and iron sheet roof. The council agreed, and we committed the project to the Lord in prayer. Having done so, I said we should ask Brickor for a donation of bricks. "You'll never get a brick out of Brickor, I'm telling you," said Jack Brown.

Within two weeks of asking the Lord for help, the following three things happened. Brickor gave us all the golden brown face bricks for the interior of the hall. A builder, who was a neighbor of Koos Verwey, who worked on my staff in the fertilizer company, died and his widow gave us all the stock bricks which he had ready to build a house in Fontainbleau. On Saturday, Jack Brown and I were setting out the foundations of the hall with a dumpy level when a middle-aged man, a complete stranger, came and lent on the gate between the church and the rectory. Thinking he might have some need, I went over to him, but before I could say anything, he asked, "Is it true you are going to build a Sunday School hall?" "Yes," I said. "Well, I am a bricklayer and I lay bricks five days a week to provide for my family, but on the sixth day I lay bricks for the Lord. I have come to lay your bricks." His name was Mr. Richard Norman. So within two weeks of asking the Lord for help, we had face bricks, stock bricks, and a bricklayer. Talk about receiving "exceeding abundantly above all that we ask or think!"

The steel for the roof arrived, and I asked for volunteers to erect it on Saturdays. Those who helped included my three sons, Christopher, John, and David, Dick Brentley, Brian Sherratt, Ray Johnstone, Merry Hodson, and Bill Dowding. The wives, who were also sustaining us with refreshments, helped us heave up the portals. It was quite dangerous work for the men who had to balance high up on the portals while the steel purlins were passed up to them from below. Once the first two portals were fixed together by the purlins, it was not so bad as we had something steady to build onto. One who did the most tricky top work was Christopher. It took many weeks of Saturdays before all the iron roof sheets were up. I came home one evening when the sheets were up on one side and therefore unsecured at the top. There was a terrific thunderstorm raging and the wind was blowing underneath the sheets and lifting them at the top. I climbed up and held them down with my own weight. What with the rain, lightning, and the gale, it was quite terrifying up there. I yelled loudly for help, and Merry Hodson came up and we eventually got everything secured.

As soon as the roof was finished bricklaying began. Richard Norman laid all the face bricks perfectly while the rest of us concentrated on the stock bricks. Quite quickly the size of the working party diminished so that, for the next two years, it consisted of Richard Norman, Dick Brentley, and myself, assisted by young Roddy Baker from next door but one, and occasionally, and when he could, by Alan Hudson. By the end of 1970 the hall was virtually complete, and we had got it up, all 3400 square feet of it, for just over R5,000! But the additional commitment of the hall on top of everything else was proving too much. On one of his visits near the end of 1968, I said to Bishop Bradley that I must either go full time into the ministry or concentrate on my secular occupation, which was already suffering through my commitment to the church. I simply could not do both any longer. He agreed and decided that I should be ordained early in the new year.

In January 1969 Win and I went off on a holiday on our own and during it reviewed our situation. The strain on both of us had been enormous, and I had, perforce, neglected my boys when they really needed me most. This in turn had driven Win to distraction, and I came to the conclusion that for the sake of the family, who had already sacrificed enough, I must refuse ordination. I promised Win I would do so.

Immediately on our return to Blairgowrie, even before we had unpacked, Dick Brentley and Mike Lobley came round to see me to say that there had been disagreement in the church council over my ordination.

All except Owen Smith wanted me ordained. The rest of the council had put up such a resolute case on my behalf that they said I couldn't possibly let them down now. I never did discover what Owen's objection, was but I think he really wanted Bernard Wright in my place, which was a bit hard seeing that Owen was mostly responsible for putting me in the rectory in the first place. But the extraordinary thing was that through his opposition, I was prevented from withdrawing and forced into ordination whether I wanted it or not! In the light of the way in which the Lord has used me since, I have never doubted that He was over-ruling throughout this peculiar interlude.

Owen withdrew from the fellowship to our great loss, and Christopher and Maureen, who by now were married, also withdrew to my great sorrow, not wishing, I suppose, to take sides between Owen and myself. Sadly, with the departure of Christopher and Maureen the youth group went into temporary eclipse.

On Sunday evening, the 12th March 1969, I was ordained a deacon by Bishop Bradley assisted by Bishop Douglas. The service was marked for me by a most inspiring message read from the pulpit from the Rev. Richard Drake, the Baptist minister who had been such a help to me after my conversion in 1948. He remained a life-long friend. A particular joy for me was that my mother, who was on a visit from England, was present accompanied by my eldest sister, Joan. I was presented with a typewriter, with which I began typing this history.

With his extensive Bible knowledge, Alan grew quickly in knowledge and faith, and usefulness in the Master's service. So it was that on Owen Smith's withdrawal, Alan took over the Sunday School, which continued to grow under his direction. By the end of 1969 it reached no less than three hundred and twenty five children present on any particular Sunday. They were divided into three divisions, each with a supervisor in charge, and twenty eight teachers besides Alan and a secretary. It was sad that Owen missed this spectacular growth and blessing.

Amongst the congregation a real work of grace was going on. People were being converted and others built up in their faith. Some thirty people were meeting each week for Bible study and prayer. Besides the group in the church on Wednesdays, there were also home groups, of which two were in Blairgowrie and one was in Malanshof.

Amongst those whom the Lord brought to conversion was a Mr. Taylor from Birmingham in England. He was only with us for less than a year, but in that time he and his son Nicholas joined the confirmation class and were duly confirmed. His firm collapsed, and when he came to say goodbye, he said, "I want you to know that I am convinced that the Lord sent me to

South Africa so that I could find Christ here. I return to England quite content."

I was learning all the time and gaining pastoral experience. In an article entitled "One Thing Leads to Another" which I wrote for the CESA magazine at this time, I changed the names of those involved. I wrote, "Mr. White has been coming to church regularly every Sunday for the last two years and has signed the church membership register. When confirmation classes began he asked if his daughter, Alice, could join. We had never seen Alice in church up to that time. So when the class assembled for the first session, I explained the aim of the course as being that every candidate should be brought into a vital, living, and real relationship with Jesus Christ as Saviour and Lord before confirmation service was held. I added that I was sure that thereafter every new Christian would come to church every Sunday not only because God requires this but also because each one would want to take a weekly opportunity to praise God and to thank Him for His love in providing One by Whom sins could be forgiven, and through Whom lasting peace with God could be enjoyed. In token of this, membership of the confirmation class would be dependent upon regular church attendance throughout its duration.

"The next week, Alice brought her friend Betty Love. The week after that old Granny Austin died, and Mr. and Mrs. Austin, strangers to me, came to arrange the funeral. At the funeral I met Claire Austin who, after enquiry, said she would like to join the confirmation class. So I arranged to go to her home the next evening to bring her up-to-date on the two sessions she had missed. At her home that night, it transpired that Mr. Austin had not been confirmed either, so he and Mrs. Austin listened in. Now Claire and Mr. Austin have joined the class, and Mrs. Austin comes along as well because she finds the sessions so interesting. All the Austins have signed the membership roll and come to church every Sunday evening.

"At the next session Betty Love brought her sister Diana, and on Easter Monday evening I was able to bring Diana up-to-date on the sessions she had missed. The same day Mrs. Love rang up and asked if I would go round and see her as neither Betty nor Diana had ever been baptized.

"So I went round on Tuesday night and met Mr. and Mrs. Love for the first time. They are friends of Mr. White.

"After greeting one another, Mrs. Love said, 'Well, I'm a Catholic and my husband's a Presbyterian who sometimes goes to the Anglican Church. The funeral directors gave us Father Pope's name when mother died, and he was ever so good, so we went to St. Boniface's once or twice. I do think it's wrong to have all these different denominations, don't you?'

'Ah, there I agree with you,' I said, 'for if we have been baptized with the Holy Spirit, Who is the one Spirit, then we have all been baptized with the same Spirit, and have become all one in Christ Jesus. We have become members of the body of Christ, and the body of Christ is the Church.'

'But I still think there shouldn't be different denominations, but that all should come under the Pope,' she said.

'I think their separate existence is a good thing,' I replied. 'When our Lord Jesus Christ was on earth, men, women, and children came to Him in many different ways. Some were led, some were brought, and some came under their own steam. Some were told to repent and believe, some to believe and be baptized, some had hands laid on them, and some apparently needed no outward symbols at all. Likewise people have come to Christ in many different ways down the ages. To the extent that the denominations in this Twentieth Century represent those different ways, their separate existence is wholly to be commended — provided of course that they are leading people only to the Lord Jesus Christ.'

'I agree with you about there being different approaches to God,' said Mr. Love — 'I mean the Muslims, the Hindus, and so on. Confucianism was going long before Christianity, too.'

'The fact that one is older than another is not the point. We are only concerned with finding the truth, and Jesus said, I am the Way, the Truth, and the Life, no man cometh unto the Father but by Me. The Bible says...' But Mr. Love interrupted, 'Oh, surely you don't believe all that! How would you like that if you were a Muslim?'

'Well, to begin with, I wouldn't be a Muslim for anything, having spent some years in their countries and seen how their false religion leads them to behave. But more important, the Bible is the infallibly inspired written Word of God, and it is therefore true in every respect, since God cannot lie. So it is true that no man can come to the Father except by the Lord Jesus Christ. I found this to be true in my experience too. I couldn't find the Father till Jesus found me. Haven't you found this to be so too?'

'Well — er, ahem, I think I must come to your church sometime. Of course I shall be there when my daughters are baptized. By the way, my friend Mr. Good has two daughters whom I don't think have been confirmed. Is there still time for them to join the class?'

'Yes, indeed there is,' I said, 'if they come quickly. Do bring them along to the next session. But I must go now. Goodnight to you both.'" So I took my leave conscious of God's elective finger going before, and praying that one thing would lead to another.

Through a friend I was called to the home of a young man who was dying from kidney disease. He had a wife and two young children. The circumstances were desperately sad. They were not church going people, but over the weeks I was enabled to lead the young man to Christ before he died. The wife remained unconverted and not unnaturally desolated. I was with her when he died. I put my arms round her and wept with her at this moment. The only way to console in such circumstances is really to care and to try to bear some of the burden of sorrow before it is possible to pray to the Lord to come and comfort and strengthen.

She insisted on coming to the burial as well as the funeral service in church. She was utterly distraught and hysterical and tried to get into the grave with her husband at the end. For some reason the family did nothing, and it was left to me to restrain her. Eventually she came away from the cemetery with me, and I handed her over to the care of her parents. My back was no sooner turned than she was back at the grave again, and again I had to bring her away.

I mention this incident to describe the emotional strain which ministers often have to bear, especially if they have to deal with more than one tragedy at the same time. A minister is not like a doctor. He doesn't and cannot shut his mind to tragedy when he leaves a house of sorrow, because he is still going to uphold that family at the throne of Grace. He really does bear another's burden and he weeps with them that weep and rejoices with them that rejoice.

Another couple who joined the church were Ossie and Midge Baker. It was there youngest son who was helping so much in building the Sunday School hall. Ossie was second-in-command of West Park Commando, whose headquarters were in the old police station in the dip of Jan Smuts Avenue in the nearby suburb of Craighall. He approached the officer commanding, Wynter Prevost, who had me appointed as the commando chaplain. So in 1969 and 1970, West Park Commando had their annual church parade in Christ Church. The sight and sound of the Commando marching up Mackay Avenue led by the pipes and drums of the Transvaal Irish Regiment was great publicity for the church and of course a tremendous excitement for our Sunday School children. The church was packed and the congregation overflowed into the hall at the back. I think the pipers who gave us a recital after church in the garden were a little disappointed to be given only orange juice to refresh them!

I have already said that I made a big mistake in arranging for the Sunday School to take place at the same time as the church service. But I made another even bigger mistake. No one had warned me about the need to protect the church membership. As soon as people had become regular in church and were contributing to the funds, I allowed them onto the voting role of the church. I never first obtained from them a credible statement of their faith. Most of the people were from the Church of the Province of South Africa (CPSA), which is the Anglo-Catholic Church. By and by they were elected onto the church council, and, not being converted, they tried to introduce CPSA ways into our church. I now found myself in a majority of one on the council and it was a most miserable time. I wept tears over what was now happening. This caucus was even meeting behind my back to introduce wrong things into the church. I appealed to Bishop Douglas, who wisely advised me to do nothing but to pray and put the whole problem into the hands of the Lord. Over many weeks, I begged the Lord to intervene. I repented bitterly for having put the church into this situation. Then, without my doing anything except pray, the Lord sorted out the whole affair in a most remarkable way. Two of the men involved were found philandering with the other's wife and took themselves off in disgrace, and the other two were converted. So we had an all Christian council again, but it was a lesson I shall never forget.

We had confirmation classes in both 1969 and 1970, and one of those converted was Grahame Wray, with whom I had a vital talk while in camp with West Park Commando. He was later ordained and has since been used by the Lord in building up the work, especially amongst black people based in Fort Victoria, now called Masvingo, in Zimbabwe.

Each year we arranged Sunday School sports at Giloolies Farm in the eastern outskirts of Johannesburg. I'm not sure but that the main excitement for the children was the trip in two hired double decker buses! We also had an annual families outing to the Gibsons' Farm, Stonyridge, in the Magaliesburg Mountains. The great thing was to duck the rector in the swimming pool!

In October 1970 I was at last made presbyter and was presented with a lovely and very useful portable communion set for visiting the sick.

At the same time, we heard from the family in England that my mother was no longer able to look after herself and that none of the family there were able to provide a home for her. So it was decided that she should come to us. She came in late October, and it was very soon evident that her condition was such that we could not look after her as well as the church. In addition, Win and I were pretty well exhausted after seven years of very hard work. So I gave in my notice that we should have to retire in January. The Rev. David Streater, who was still in England, was available to succeed me and could have arrived in February, but there was delay and he didn't arrive till June. The unnecessary interregnum did not help the church.

It was agreed that the R8,000 which I had lent to the church to build the rectory should be returned to me. Because of inflation, it was no longer enough to build a house, so, like Paul who at one stage had to return to tent making, I now had to set about building a house myself at the age of fifty-one at Hogsback in the Eastern Cape, as will be related in a later chapter.

On the 19th January 1971, I was given a very moving farewell conducted by my great friend and pastor, Bishop Desmond Douglas. Now, when I visit Blairgowrie, and look up at those three roofs over the church, the hall, and the rectory, I know certainly that I could not possibly have done it but that the Lord had given me both the physical and the spiritual strength to do what He had purposed all along.

Chapter Fifteen

Rhodesia

At Synod in Christ Church, Blairgowrie, in August 1967, Bishop Bradley told me that he had had many letters from folk in Rhodesia over the last few years appealing for the Church of England to be established there. This was four years before I was ordained, but he asked me if I would be prepared to go there on behalf of the CESA and follow up these leads.

At the time, I was recovering from a bout of thrombo-phlebitis in my left leg which had kept me in bed for the three weeks before Synod, and I was due for a fortnight's leave from my firm. I consulted with Win, who said that, as I was not yet allowed to walk, our holiday would have to be a touring one and we might as well go to Rhodesia for it. Neither of us had been there before. So the Bishop gave me his file of letters from Rhodesia and sent a letter of introduction on my behalf to the Prime Minister of Rhodesia, Mr. Ian Smith.

I wrote to all those who had written to Bishop Bradley to tell them when I would be in Fort Victoria, Umtali, Salisbury, and Bulawayo.

At Christ Church, Blairgowrie, we spent much time in prayer over the last few weeks before departure, and I asked for prayer by all the CESA Churches to continue throughout my tour. As will be clear, those prayers were answered in a remarkable way, and I was made abundantly conscious of the fact that the Lord had gone before me to each place I went. It is sometimes in small ways that the Lord indicates His blessing upon a venture at its beginning. I had forgotten that it was holiday time, and we did not book in at hotels anywhere. I was at the time very tired from all the effort of getting Christ Church, Blairgowrie, going, and so we decided to spend a weekend at Tzaneen, in the beautiful mountains and forests of north eastern Transvaal, so as to rest and freshen up before going further. To my horror, we found the car park full of cars when we got to the hotel at Magoebaskloof outside Tzaneen. So with sinking heart I walked across to the reception office and with little hope asked for a room. The receptionist looked at me as if she'd seen a ghost, and said, "We've been turning people away all morning as we are full. I've just this minute put the phone down after a cancellation. By all means you can have a room." From that moment, I never doubted that I was in the Lord's will and that He would continue to go before me all the way.

The drive up from the Rhodesian border at Beit Bridge was quite beautiful. We passed through the flat country of the low veldt with large white owned ranches on either side. Roads off to the right led to extensive irrigation areas created by white initiative where big crops of sugar, cotton, and mealies were grown.

From Nuanetzi, a tiny trading post about halfway to Fort Victoria, the road climbed slowly through superb park-like country in which every now and then huge kopjies of granite rocks showed through the greenery of the trees. As we approached Fort Victoria, after some 200 miles the parkland gave way to more large cattle farms.

On arrival in Fort Victoria we found a Mr. Bryan Elvy waiting for us at the hotel. Bryan Elvy was in fact a retired major of the Royal Marines, a huge man who had played forward for the Royal Navy in the annual match against the Army at Twickenham. He was now commanding a territorial battalion of the Rhodesian Army and owned the Farmers Supply Store in Fort Victoria.

Elvy was somewhat surprised that I had not booked a room at the hotel, but he had managed to get one which looked out on to a blank wall about two feet away. He also said that it was so long since he had written that he doubted whether more than a handful of people would still be interested in seeing me. But he would try to get them together two evenings hence.

Fort Victoria was a small market town for the surrounding agricultural community. It had, I suppose, about 3000 white inhabitants and ten times as many blacks.

The following day, Win and I visited the ruins at Zimbabwe and then drove all the way round Lake Kyle, stopping for a picnic on the way. It was a lovely day, restful, and with beautiful scenery to enjoy.

When we arrived at the Presbyterian Church Hall the following evening, I found Bryan Elvy standing at the door clearly very deeply moved. He told me that he had never known God to work in his life before. When he had walked from his shop the four hundred yards to the bank the day before, he had met everyone he could possibly have asked to the meeting in those few yards and, "look, they are all here!"

So, instead of half a dozen, I found myself addressing some thirty people. I asked them to allow me to remain seated as my leg would not permit me to stand. I opened with prayer and readings from Ezekiel 34:1-12 and Matthew 9:35-38. As I spoke, I found the Holy Spirit gave me great freedom of utterance. I began by reading the attack which had been made in the Bulawayo Chronicle that day:

> Bulawayo Chronicle 6th Sept. 1967
> PRIMATE DID NOT BAN S.A. BISHOP
>
> Brisbane, Tuesday — The Anglican Primate of Australia, Archbishop Phillip Strong, denied to-night he had banned a South African bishop from preaching in any church in Brisbane because of his alleged pro-apartheid views.
>
> It has been reported that Archbishop Strong had imposed the ban because Bishop S.C. Bradley was head of a sect which "supported anti-Christian apartheid policies."
>
> "I only said it was unlikely he would preach in Brisbane," Archbishop Strong said to-night.
>
> UNOFFICIAL
>
> The Archbishop also said he had not expressed a wish that other Anglicans join in a ban on Bishop Bradley. Bishop Bradley, who was born, trained, and ordained in Australia, is on an unofficial visit here as a "Bishop of the Church of England in South Africa." Archbishop Strong said the name "Church of England in South Africa" had led to much confusion and misunderstanding. It was not recognized as part of the Anglican Communion by the Church of England in England, or by other parts of the Anglican Communion, he said. — Iana-Reuters.

I said that such attacks on the true Church of England in South Africa were not uncommon. The CESA was the historic and authentic Anglican Church in South Africa, having its origins in the congregations established in the Cape at the beginning of the last century. Some congregations broke away in 1870 to form the Church of the Province of South Africa, from which the Church of the Province of Central Africa was derived. In 1880 judgement was given in the Cape Supreme Court that the CPSA had separated itself "root and branch" from the Church of England, and this judgement was upheld in even stronger terms by the Judicial Committee of the Privy Council in London in 1882. Legally, the CESA remained the only true Anglican Church in South Africa to this day. It was a gross insult therefore to refer to the CESA as a sect. It was a fully fledged church which had more important things to do than to express political opinions. It was a church which had remained true to the doctrine of the Church of England as established by law in England as it is enshrined in the Book of Common Prayer 1662 and the Thirty Nine Articles of Religion which are printed therein. I continued after this manner:

"The Gospel is so simple a child can understand it, unlearned men were used by God to propagate it, and yet it can bring such power that it has used men to 'turn the world upside down.'"

"The message is just this: All men are sinful (Romans 3:23) and because of this they have been cut off from communication with God (Isaiah 59:2). They cannot by good works earn their way back to God because, in the sight of an infinitely good and holy God, the finite deeds of finite men are of infinitely little worth. In fact they are of no worth at all, 'for all our righteousness are as filthy rags' (Isaiah 64:6). Moreover, the Bible tells us that the 'wages of sin is death' (Romans 6:23). By this is meant the second death which goes on and on in a fire which shall never be quenched. (Mark 9:43-48)

"It was because of this frightful state to which all mankind has fallen that 'God so loved the world that He gave His only begotten Son, that whosoever believeth on Him should not perish but have everlasting life' (John 3:16). Jesus Christ achieved this salvation for each and every one of us who believes, by taking all our sins upon Himself (2 Corinthians 5:21) and then suffering the death penalty for them (1 Peter 3:18). But each one of us has to appropriate this salvation for himself by faith if it is to avail, for 'the Gospel of Christ is the power of salvation to everyone that believeth' (Romans 1:16). The Gospel call is therefore, 'Repent, and be baptized every one of you in the Name of Jesus Christ for the remission of sins, and ye shall receive the gift of the Holy Spirit' (Acts 2:38). It is only those who have wholeheartedly responded to this call who have within themselves that power and inner peace which flows from an assurance of being right with God, 'for the Spirit itself beareth witness with our spirit, that we are the children of God' (Romans 8:16). It is this same Spirit that enables us to communicate in prayer (Romans 8:26) with the risen Lord Jesus Christ who is the only Mediator between God and man (1 Timothy 2:5) and who one day is coming again (1 Thessalonians 4:16-17).

"The so-called modernists, Roman-Catholics, Anglo-Catholics, devotees of the ecumenical movement and of the World Council of Churches, or call them as you will, preach a very different doctrine. It is difficult to know why they do it, but one can only surmise that they have had no encounter with the Lord Jesus Christ and know nothing of the peace, joy, and power of the Holy Spirit indwelling their hearts. If they had, their lips would be full of praise for the sheer wonder of His presence and the divine love which made it possible. Knowing nothing else, their ministers rely on sentimentality and outward show. Knowing nothing of the risen Lord Jesus Christ, their more notorious bishops deny the virgin birth, the ascension, and resurrection. Knowing nothing of the supernatural they deny the supernatural, and so the miracles are 'explained' and well known stories of the Old Testament are written off as myths and fairy tales. Their god is a god of their own invention, just as are the effigies of Our Lord and others that they place above their altars despite the Second Commandment. They overlook the fact that Almighty God is not only a God of love, but also a God of justice, and a God of wrath. They overlook the fact that Almighty God alone is the law-giver defining His morality, which is not to be flouted without penalty even if, under the cloak of the catch-word 'new morality', it is given the sanction of men in the guise of bishops and priests.

"Not knowing the Lord Jesus Christ, these people propagate a gospel which seeks to set up the kingdom on earth without Christ. They seek to set up a paradise on earth to overcome social injustice and international tension but entirely ignore the fact that the first man fell in paradise!"

I went on to say that if they took a stand against all this nonsense, they would be constantly attacked and vilified as we were in the CESA. But such opposition often helped to weld a team, as Rhodesia well knew, and in any case there was no need to worry over what men might say. I gave proof from personal experience of how God does answer prayer, of what joy and privilege it is to share in the Lord's work, and of what a marvel it is to find constant evidence of His guiding hand and bountiful provision for our labors. I spoke of the countless blessings we had received at His hands in the growth of Christ Church, Blairgowrie, from beginning with six dedicated workers with an income of R30 per month three years previously, to the current situation with a mailing list of 250 homes, an adult congregation of seventy-five in the mornings and twenty in the evenings, a Sunday School of over 200 children, and a lovely church and rectory representing a total investment of some R40,000.

I went on to remind those present that ours was a mighty, omnipotent, and omnipresent God who would most certainly work through people dedicated to Him anywhere. What had been achieved at Blairgowrie could most certainly be achieved in Fort Victoria.

I spoke for about an hour, questions went on for another half hour, and individual discussions took place over tea for a further half hour. The interest and evident keenness which had been aroused was to me quite overwhelming. The sort of comment was, "This is the first Bible based sermon or talk we have had in years." "But we haven't seen the Thirty-Nine Articles of Religion for more than twelve years." "How do we start?" And so on. I felt so sad about the years the CPCA had wasted, and so grieved at its failure to lead those people into the way of Truth, that I determined that the CESA should help them in every way that the Lord would show us. The opinion of the meeting was to challenge the CPCA to give it one more chance. None thought the CPCA would mend its ways, and in that case they would leave it and form their own church to be affiliated with the CESA.

I suggested that they meet with like minded people at other centers and adopt a constitution modeled on that of the CESA, and that they elect Bishop Bradley as their first bishop. I warned that it was essential to adopt such a constitution immediately and lodge it in the proper quarters to safeguard from the CPCA any property which they might acquire.

Mr. Elvy was convinced that between Fort Victoria, Triangle, and Bulawayo they would be able to support a minister by the beginning of next year. If they achieved this, I committed the CESA to supplying that minister.

When I arrived in Bulawayo eight days later, I found a letter from Mr. Elvy which included the following which speaks for itself:

"That your visit was God ordained, I have little doubt. I have around me eight or ten men and women of like mind to myself, and we are to meet again for prayer, study, and thought on Thursday at our house. We want to decide what to do now for the benefit not of us, but of the Church as a whole. We pray we may be used aright.

"In the ignorance into which we have been subtly led over the years, we have so much still to ask, to find out. It's a bit difficult without guidance from a minister, but we are trying and no doubt will have many doubts to clear up. However, I think you have left behind a little nucleus of determined people who are determined, under God, to put forward a true interpretation of His word.

"Pray often for us. Send us any people who can help us."

We left Fort Victoria for Umtali with a song in our hearts praising God for what He had graciously enabled us to do. We drove through country which was ablaze with color which we thought at first was some kind of blossom. But it wasn't. It was the new spring leaves of the Msasa trees which grow everywhere there. The young leaves are a glorious pink which looked absolutely magnificent set against the peerless blue sky and the mountains in the distance. Soon we saw a silver structure set against the blue looking like a miniature Sydney harbor bridge. It was the Birchenough Bridge and we stopped at the cafe, which was adorned with bright red bougainvilla, for a cold drink there.

Thereafter the drive up to Umtali was through black owned land. The inefficient and destructive subsistence farming being carried on was in stark contrast to the productive white managed farms we had passed through.

We spent the 7th to 9th of September based in Umtali. Umtali lies a few miles from the Mocambique frontier and is the main entry town for goods arriving by rail from Beira. It had then about 3000 white inhabitants.

Unfortunately, my only contacts there were all away. We drove for miles over pretty rough dirt tracks in the general direction of the Mocambique frontier to find Mr. and Mrs. Helby, who had written to Bishop Bradley some years before. I left some 1662 Prayer Books and other literature for them at the farm. On their return they were so impressed that a retired colonel had travelled so far to try to help them spiritually that they got a group together who, in liaison with Bryan Elvy in Fort Victoria, founded St. Stephen's Church, Umtali. So our visit there was by no means in vain.

We met a number of Rhodesians in Umtali, and we were tremendously impressed by them. In the face of their betrayal by the British Government, their spirit was exactly like the defiant spirit of England when threatened with invasion by the Nazis in 1940. There were no people more loyal to England during the Second World War: they had supplied the highest percentage of volunteers into the armed forces of any country in the Commonwealth, and many of them fought in the Battle of Britain. Their cheerfulness and tremendous morale made a deep impression on us. My growing disgust with the policies of successive British Governments, which will have become apparent from these memoirs, reached its peak in Rhodesia, and I became a naturalized South African in case I got called up to fight for the wrong side.

From the 9th to the 13th September we were in Salisbury. A small group got together, but there was no recognized leader as in Fort Victoria. Though I gave a similar address to the one I had given in Fort Victoria there was little response. There was no real spiritual hunger, and the folk there were merely dissatisfied with the CPCA because of its left wing politics. I was certainly not crusading for a right wing church! But one of their number arranged an interview for me which was broadcast by the Rhodesian Broadcasting Company. By God's grace this resulted in the conversion of a young lady in Gwelo who subsequently became a missionary.

The reaction of the people in Bulawayo was something between the Fort Victoria and Salisbury position. Some had already broken away from the CPCA and had formed an independent Anglican Church under the ministry of the Rev. Len Gunter. Unfortunately he was away at the time of our visit, but I asked the folk to report my visit to Mr. Gunter with the recommendation that they liaise with Mr. Elvy in Fort Victoria. Mr. Gunter subsequently transferred to the CESA, bringing his congregation with him.

On our return to South Africa, Christ Church, Blairgowrie, became the liaison church for the work in Rhodesia, and we supplied the leaders there with literature and every help of which we were capable. We kept up a constant prayer for them at all our meetings and services.

For the remainder of the year 1967 and throughout 1968, Bryan Elvy and I were in constant correspondence as he sought my advice and encouragement in his labors for truth in Fort Victoria. The first matter was to prepare for the meeting with the CPCA rector of Fort Vic. Bryan's letter of 18th September included this:

"I have had more real pleasure and happiness than for many years in reading and studying the Scriptures. I have had hours and hours of pleasure and inspiration in this. I have seen more truth in these hours than in all the years since I came here. If you have done nothing else, you gave me that!

"So, Dick, we need the prayers of all your people. Pray for the few of us, who could I think become many. Pray for our Rector that he may come to understand. Pray that we may receive the guidance of the Holy Spirit in which we have got to trust implicitly."

On October 5th Bryan reported to me on his confrontation with the Rector, of which the following are extracts:

"Then he got onto Colonel Begbie! According to him you had been asked to come to Fort Victoria. I hadn't asked you (though I thank God that you came when you did). That fell somewhat flat. Then you were pulled to pieces for using Christian Laymen (which you did not!) and for an unpardonable attack upon the faith and practice of the CPCA. Then we had a vague and rather inaccurate attack upon the CESA and its 'unacceptability' to other Anglicans, with various not very accurate mentions of Colenso, Lambeth Conference, Archbishop Fisher, and Bishop Bradley in Australia. As regards the latter, it was more than fortuitous that I had in my hand the copy of Bishop Bradley's letter which you kindly sent me. (It so happened!).

"Anyway, the outcome, when we were able to speak without offence, was a long argument — all in a pleasant humor until the poor harassed Rector got too hot under the collar with the indirect criticism of his ministry. I was well armed from my studies, and I fear the Rector was put to confusion, but never did he give one inch or a single sign that he would even consider our request that FAITH and TEACHING might replace the endless and meaningless ritual of our weekly 'Mass' which so effectively masked off from our people the Truths handed down for us by the Disciples.

"The result is that none of our little group wavered one inch but all are rather confirmed in the rightness of what we seek. One — Alan Heasman — has resigned as a Church Councillor, but this I will not do — yet! I still believe that for my fellow lost souls in the church, I must go on to the very limit of my ability to try to convince the Rector that he is wrong and must have the courage to admit it. I may not win, but I believe that this is God's will for me however inarticulate I may be and however unlearned."

Some days later the rector sent for the Bishop, and Bryan gamely took them both on. He reported to me on October 31st, of which extracts are as follows:

"I have argued for hours with Bishop and Rector that the CPCA is hiding the reality of Christ, which must be our aim, in a froth of symbolism and ritual. Our children, whose very future as young men and women beloved of Christ depends upon their understanding of the means of grace open to them through faith in Christ, are denied this and are tortured by a weekly 'Eucharist' that means nothing to them but constant kneeling, and an emptiness within their hearts, for they are denied the very teaching which alone can point them to the way to the Cross.

"I am terribly conscious of the prayers and the encouragement coming to me from you and the many wonderful Christians who have written to me.... Dick, I wish I could say that we ARE now an entity of your Church, but I still remain very conscious of the fact that there is a wider and greater Church than any single congregation. I dare not do what I like. I must always be guided by the Comforter who I am convinced will show me the way. In my heart I am wholly with you, but I know that I must continue to drift in a sort of no-man's-land, in conflict with many but unable yet to let myself be embraced into the love and fellowship which you all offer me. God alone must direct me. Rest assured that I seek His direction and guidance unceasingly. That, I believe, is exactly as you would have it. Just pray that I am never blind to His directions. I may have little distance to go or I may have many months ahead seeking out my fellows to show them a Way which you and I know is the only way of Truth. This we MUST find of our own volition and through the Spirit. All the help and prayer of our friends in your church helps enormously — so beg them to keep it up even if they get frustrated from my apparent inaction.

"We all remember you with great affection whenever we meet and would love nothing more than to have your own Spiritual strength here with us, but we realize this is OUR battle for God."

Then on the 3rd November came news of the decisive step which had virtually been forced on him:

"A line which follows very closely on my last. It is intended just to tell you that today I have tendered my resignation as Church Warden and Councillor to the Rector and I feel like a new man — free and unfettered!

"As you know well, I have delayed this step for many weeks in the fond hope that it might be God's will that I should be used to reconcile the Anglican Church here to the personal convictions that I hold and which I know to be right. May be I have been presumptuous in even hoping, but anyway events have proved my hopes false.

"I have advised all Anglicans in the parish of my reasons through the attached letter...

"Incidentally UMTALI, where you appear to have drawn a blank, is now coming through loud and clear and claim to have a little group of twelve. This is Mrs. Helby for whom you left notes. I have been on to her by letter, but you might find it worthwhile following up as, frankly, at the moment I am pretty deeply involved here."

At about this time Bryan and I had to disclaim any connection with some group in Salisbury who advertised in the press for any who would support an Anglican Church of Rhodesia. This group was merely trying to found a church with right wing politics instead of the decidedly left wing political stance of the CPCA. The CPCA were making the most of this to belittle what we were doing in Fort Vic and Umtali.

On 9th November came the great news that Bryan had started regular services of Morning Prayer in his house with five families already committed and another six families likely to join them soon. The Presbyterian minister had undertaken to administer the Lord's Supper for them once a month, but according to the rites of that church, of course.

On 17th November Bryan wrote again:

My Dear Dick,

I think the time has now come when your proposal that Archdeacon Douglas should come to us, should be put into effect.

We are now in the unenviable position where we ARE a CESA congregation but have no official status and are consequently nameless and without a constitution. It is now essential that we should be able to speak from a recognized base and be constituted as a parish in Fort Victoria under Bishop Bradley's oversight....There are many people just waiting and watching before they will commit themselves....They will not commit themselves until they know what they are asked to commit themselves to.

The most extraordinary aspect of the approaches I have had is that they are from so many people who have for years been thought by our Rector here as "dead" spiritually. I give unceasing thanks that we seem most able to help these who have suffered the most in the past from almost deliberate spiritual starvation. They are very far from indifferent to the Word of God and this is a revelation to us.

As a temporary measure I have now arranged with the Rev. Gunter to come through, starting in January, from Bulawayo to minister to us when he is able to. This will give us a fillip and enormous strength but our aim and object is to be able to support a minister of our own before many months pass.

Over the weekend 25th-26th November, Win and I were delighted to have Bryan to stay with us in the rectory. Bryan and I attended a meeting of the Central Trustees and Executive at which Bryan gave a comprehensive report on progress in all the centers in Rhodesia. Bryan wrote on 14th December, "I can't tell you how much that weekend meant to me or what impressions I got into my head of the love, kindness, and happiness of your parish and of your home particularly (around which the parish revolves anyway!)." On his return to Fort Victoria, it was decided to name the church there Christ Church partly to mark the link with Christ Church, Blairgowrie. At my suggestion, the Blairgowrie Church Council resolved to present the church at Fort Victoria with an inscribed set of Communion Plate to commemorate forever the link between our two churches. On the 12th December 1967, the presentation was made by Mike and Lee Lobley, our Church secretaries, who were visiting Rhodesia at the time.

My correspondence with all three centers in Rhodesia continued well into 1968, and I visited Fort Vic once again to preach in July of that year. From then on the Rev. Bernard Wright from Christ Church, Hillbrow, in Johannesburg visited Rhodesia once a month, and so now my part in this wonderful work of God gradually faded. I shall always be grateful that I was given the joy and the privilege of sowing the seed and watering it with the prayers of my congregation and of myself during its first months of tender growth.

Chapter Sixteen

Army Chaplain

Soon after I was ordained in March 1969, a member of the Christ Church, Blairgowrie, congregation, Mr. Osie Baker, asked me whether I would be interested in becoming the chaplain of West Park Commando. The Commando is somewhat similar to a Territorial Army battalion. Osie had served as a parachutist during the Second World War.

On arrival at the HQ, I had to fill in a form in which details of my previous military service were asked for. This record seemed to guarantee my acceptance, and I was welcomed to the Commando by the OC, Commandant Wynter Prevost. In the South African Army, commandant is a rank of the same seniority as a lieutenant-colonel. Wynter had served towards the end of the war in Italy as a Gunner and was now also the Chairman of the Johannesburg Branch of the Gunners' Association.

Within a matter of weeks I went into camp with the Commando at Mapleton, about halfway between Johannesburg and Heidelburg in the Transvaal east of Johannesburg. There was far too much drinking amongst the officers and sergeants, but otherwise the Commando was reasonably efficient. A high proportion of the national servicemen were Jews from Witwatersrand University. These had to come to "padre's hour" with me the same as everyone else. I told them all straight out that I believed absolutely that both the Old and New Testaments were the infallibly inspired Word of God, that they didn't just contain the Word of God, but that they were the Word of God from beginning to end. In deference to the Jews present I would base all my Bible studies on the Old Testament. The Jews must understand that inevitably I would give a Christian understanding of the Old Testament and asked them for their permission to proceed. With this approach I never had any difficulty and consistently preached Christ and Him crucified from the Old Testament. Often the Jews would express appreciation, saying that they had never heard a Christian explanation of their Scriptures before. One young Jew, who was training to be a lawyer, was deeply affected, and I gave him a copy of Frank Morrison's book, *Who Moved the Stone*; Morrison was a lawyer who had tried to disprove the resurrection but ended up proving it and becoming Christian in consequence. I do not believe in instant conversions as a general rule, for my own experience had been otherwise, and I saw my task as one of sowing the seed for another to reap. Very, very few of the officers and men gave the impression of being true hearted Christians.

I also relieved the Rev. Len Flemming of the chaplaincy of the State President's Guard, who were stationed at Wonderboom just North of Pretoria, for a couple of months. I used to drive over from Blairgowrie early on Tuesday mornings to take a padre's hour there at 8.00am. After several weeks I received a phone call and a voice said, "You don't really know me, but I am one of the soldiers you speak to on Tuesday mornings. My name is Derrick Dickenson, and my brother, Barry, had a terrible accident last night and he will die unless there is a miracle. He had a few beers after preparing for the Wits Rag Procession last night and on the way home crashed his beetle into a tree in Jan Smuts Avenue. Please will you come and pray for him?" I said, "Are your parents happy that I should come? Shouldn't there be a minister from the family church?" "No, we all want you to come." I said, "Alright, I will meet you in the General Hospital as soon as I can get there. Please ask your parents to come too."

The Dickensons had arrived first, and I was introduced to them in Barry's room. Barry was lying paralyzed from the neck down but perfectly conscious and in no pain. After introductions and small talk, I said to him, "You remember that Jesus used to say to a sick person, will you be made whole, not will you be patched up. So do you want to be made whole? By this I mean do you want to be healed spiritually as well as bodily? Do you want to *know* Jesus as your Saviour and to follow Him as your Lord as best you can for the rest of your life?" "Yes, I want to be made whole," said Barry. "Then," I said, "we can pray for you." I then led the family in prayer and said I was sure we would all continue to pray for Barry every day.

I visited Barry daily till he was transferred to the HF Verwoerd Hospital in Pretoria. Thereafter, I visited him each week, opening up the Scriptures to him sometimes when he was lying flat out on his stomach in some awesome contrivance. I found it very hard to restrain my tears as I contemplated the waste of this boy who only a few weeks previously had been playing hockey for Wits. One day when I was with him a team of doctors came to see him and one pricked Barry's leg and he winced. "Why did you do that?" asked the doctor, "You can't feel anything." "But I can," said Barry. "This is extraordinary," said the doctor. "It will be possible to operate after all." I am certain that the Lord had answered our prayers.

Some two years later, the whole Dickenson family called to see us at Hogsback, in the Eastern Cape, where we moved at the beginning of 1971. Barry actually ran with the aid of callipers and sticks to meet me. They had come to thank me, and this made me embarrassed and I said, "No, this is the Lord's doing, not mine." I prayed that they would continue as His faithful followers and bid them Godspeed as they left.

The camp was again at Mapleton in 1970, and both my younger sons, John and David, were in camp with me. One of those deeply affected during padre's hours was Graham Wray, who asked if he could come to me to be prepared for confirmation. He came and brought his younger brother, Christopher, to join our confirmation class at Blairgowrie.

After a few months Graham also brought his elder brother Peter and Peter's wife Janet, to evening prayer one night. The very next week Peter had to be operated on for a malignant growth at the top of his spine. Unfortunately, it was so close to the spinal nerve that the surgeons couldn't get it all away. I used to visit Peter every week in the Johannesburg General Hospital and continued to do so after we moved to Hogsback in January 1971 whenever I was up in Johannesburg, which was quite often. During these visits Peter was wonderfully converted, and he became a magnificent example of Christian fortitude to all the doctors and nurses and to anyone else who visited him. Soon after his admittance to hospital Janet bore him a baby daughter, but Peter said he would like to delay the baptism until he could attend it and it could be combined with a thanksgiving for his recovery. There were several further attempts to remove the malignancy, all of them unsuccessful.

The awful thing was that Peter's mother also developed the same disease, and it was feared that it was hereditary. I had several vital conversations with Mr. and Mrs. Wray which I trust the Father used to draw them to Christ. Although both Christopher and Graham were pronounced clear of it, Graham would not marry for many years in case he passed it on to any children he might have.

In July 1971 I attended the Number 1 Chaplains Course at the Army college at Voortrekkerhoogte outside Pretoria. The chaplain general, Major General van Zyl, attended most of the course but seemed to assume that moral preparedness was the same thing as Spiritual preparedness. I met several future friends on the course including Chaplains Moore and Bothman and Chris Noorde, the future chaplain general. During this course there was a debate as to what rank army chaplains should have. The chaplain general wanted us all to be given the status of full colonels. I opposed this as I thought the gold on our cap peaks and the purple collar patches would create an unnecessary barrier between us and the men. The counter argument was that, particularly in these days the dignity and authority of the Church needed emphasizing in this way. I think this was right and, provided one makes oneself accessible, the rank with its trappings is no barrier. But in camp and on active service, I insisted on my tent or bivouac being amongst the mens' lines and not the officers'.

Towards the end of 1971 Peter Wray's father rang me up to say that Peter was sufficiently recovered for me to come to Johannesburg to baptize the baby. By the time I arrived a few days later, Peter had gone into a terminal decline. He was lying on the sofa at home, and he asked me to go ahead with the service exactly as we had planned it but I was to give thanks for his eternal life, though not for his mortal life which was clearly soon coming to an end.

The church was full, and I gave, said Mr. Wray, an inspired address which had helped them all. The Holy Spirit must have just used my lips, for even soon afterwards I had little idea of what I had said. But I do remember it was hard to keep back the tears all through. The family then came to the home with me, where I baptized the baby while Peter lay on the sofa. Peter and his mother went to be with the Lord not many weeks later.

Meanwhile, although I had moved to Hogsback in January and been posted to Midland Commando with Headquarters at Grahamstown, West Park Commando refused to appoint any other minister and retained me. So I did a three week camp with West Park and another with Midland Commando each year, with frequent weekend camps as well. I also spent a month on active service on the Angolan border in each of the years 1976, 77, 78, and 80. This meant that I often had to leave Win alone in a half built house in a half cleared forest and half a mile from the nearest habitation. As a good soldier's wife she put up with it all, sleeping behind locked doors with an automatic within reach and the two dogs in the bedroom with her.

Through Wynter Prevost, the national chairman of the Gunners' Association, Ramsay Addison, asked me to officiate at the unveiling of the Gunner plaque to be fitted to the Cenotaph in the centre of Johannesburg. Part of the service had to be in Afrikaans, and I hastily had to learn the Lord's Prayer in that language. But I have always been hopeless at languages, perhaps through laziness, and I found even this modest requirement almost beyond me. However, I was assured by friends at Hogsback who were helping me to learn that once I started, the congregation would take over and no one would notice my stumblings.

So on St. Barbara's Day (St. Barbara being the patron saint of Gunners) 1972, I found myself robing with the Mayor and Corporation of

Johannesburg in the mayor's parlor of the City Hall. There were many other dignitaries present, including the Director of Artillery from Defence Headquarters, Major General Robertse, and Brigadier Meintjies, the Commander Witwatersrand Command. As far as I remember, I, together with a very elderly but delightful chaplain who had served with the Gunners during the war and who would assist in part of the service, led the procession from the City Hall out into the sunshine. There the Transvaal Horse Artillery were drawn up in full strength together with the band of the Transvaal Irish and detachments of several other units, and a large crowd of retired Gunners and the wives of both serving and retired Gunners.

A dais had been prepared for me with a public address system with speakers fixed high up on the surrounding buildings. The slightest whisper into this thing sent my voice booming round the square, and there was no way that the combined voices of the congregation would take over from mine when it came to the Lord's Prayer in Afrikaans. As it happened, all went so well that Graham Wray, who arrived late on the scene in the middle of the Lord's Prayer, thought the Afrikaans was so good that it couldn't possibly be me, and so he thought he must have come to the wrong place!

When the service was over General Robertse said to me, "I want that sermon." I said, "It's only written out in rough." He said, "No matter I will take it as it is and have my secretary type it out, and I will see that it is published in the next issue of *Paratus*." *Paratus* is the official magazine of the South African Defence Force, and so far as I know this is the only sermon in English that has ever been published in full in it.

As a result of this occasion I was made an honorary life member of the Gunners' Association, which I feel would have pleased my long dead Gunner father. Each year from then on till we left Hogsback in 1981, the Gunners used to fly me up to Johannesburg to say grace at the annual dinner held in the Rand Club. I used to spin out the grace as long as I reasonably could in order to include a message however brief in it. One year a brigadier said after dinner, "That grace was far too long. It is quite enough to say, For what we are about to receive, thank God!" I said, "Having flown me up 560 miles all this way, you must at least expect me to sing for my supper." The branch chairman, Dr. Butch Matthias, who had overheard this exchange, said, "Don't take any notice, Dick, just you carry on as you have been doing. That is what we want."

Down at Grahamstown, the Officer Commanding the Midland Commando was a quite useless drunken oaf who set the most appalling example to the national servicemen, who were almost all young students from Rhodes University. They had already been indoctrinated with left wing and pacifist ideas, and the example of the OC tended to confirm them in their opinions.

I used to take padre's hours for them in groups while they were waiting to shoot on the range at East London. On the first such occasion the Rhodes students asked how I could justify military service with Christianity. I said, "If you are prepared to listen for three quarters of an hour, I will tell you." To this they agreed, and at the end of the time there were no further questions. The company commanders, who were all worthy farmers who had served in the war, said they'd never seen this "bolshie" lot so effectively silenced.

When all the groups had been through me, I walked up to the firing point for old times' sake and soon saw all the miss flags being assembled at one of the targets. So I wasn't surprised when in a short while I was invited to have a shoot. I hadn't touched a rifle for nearly twenty years nor ever handled an R1 rifle before. Nevertheless, to my own surprise, and everyone else's, I was one of twenty out of over two hundred who qualified as a marksman that day and wore a marksman's bronze rifle badge on my uniform from then on. Some said, "We'd better go to church now in case we get shot." But others said, "We'd better not in case we do!"

At a later camp in about 1974, the OC set such an appalling example that we would have had a mutiny but for the well judged intervention by the sergeant major. It was so bad that I formed up with the second in command to advise the OC to resign rather than disgrace his office further. But he had powerful friends who enjoyed the shooting on his extensive farm and nothing came of it.

Fortunately the Midland Commando was split up shortly thereafter, and the Alice Company, in whose area I lived, became part of Winterburg Commando. That had no sooner happened than the Alice Company became a commando on its own and I became its chaplain.

At the annual camp in 1975 I asked the minister of the Alice Dutch Reformed Church if I could borrow his church for the annual commando service. "This is excellent news," said he, "I need to take my wife to Port Elizabeth to see a doctor, and I shall be most grateful if you will take my service in the church and combine it with your commando service." "But I can't speak a word of Afrikaans," I said. "That doesn't matter. It will do my people good to hear the Gospel in English for a change." So I, a British immigrant, found myself taking morning service in a Dutch Reformed Church in English! I must say I found it a bit daunting, for when I arrived I was shown into the vestry where the assembled elderly deacons, all wearing their dark suits and white ties, greeted me with no little suspicion. After prayers in Afrikaans, I was ushered into the church and up into an enormous high rostrum where I felt completely isolated. We had half the hymns in Afrikaans and I managed the Lord's Prayer in my Afrikaans, which must have sounded as bad as Churchill's French. However, all went well, and I could tell I had the congregation with me as I led and preached.

In August 1976 I followed West Park Commando up to the Caprivi in Southwest Africa (now Namibia) for border duty. I drove to Johannesburg and stayed the night with my sister Joan, who took me over to the Air Force station at Waterkloof near Pretoria soon after dawn one morning. From there I flew in a C130 Hercules aircraft to Grootfontein. The Hercules, although very reliable and requiring a short landing strip is quite the noisiest plane I have ever been in. In the military version it is also pretty uncomfortable as one sits in four rows lengthways down the aircraft on net seats slung from the roof.

After some delay in Grootfontein I flew on to Mapsha in a C160, which is similar to the C130 but only has two engines. The captain of the aircraft very kindly invited me to sit in the cockpit for the flight. The cockpit was spacious with a padded bench at the back on which I sat with the wireless operator/navigator sitting on another bench to the right facing his radio. The captain and first officer sat beside one another on a level some two feet below me. I was surprised when soon after take off the captain, first officer, and navigator all went to sleep.

Eventually I saw the Mapsha airstrip in the distance, and as I was about to wake the party up, the captain stirred and stretched himself saying, "We must be about there by now," and immediately began the descent. None too soon I thought. The Commando ration truck was there to meet me, and we drove along a dusty and bumpy earth road, which the troops called "The Golden Highway," some 170 miles westwards and then turned north along an appalling track to Kwando Camp.

I really thought the camp looked like something from the wild west as we approached it through the surrounding bush in the dusk. The last 100 yards to the camp had been cleared of bush. The camp itself was surrounded by a high earth bank in the form of a rectangle. There were heavy machine gun emplacements at each corner, and these and other weapon positions along the bank were all manned as the garrison was standing too, it being last light. Only the tops of the tents were just visible inside the wall, and the South African flag was flying from a pole in the centre.

On arrival I was warmly welcomed by all my friends in the commando and was allotted a tent to myself. I was amazed to find that everyone had proper beds with mattresses and that there were seats over the earth toilets. Times had indeed changed since the Second World War!

During the camp, I held Bible studies each evening at which we also sang the popular religious choruses. I went out frequently on patrols with the chaps, either on foot or in the armoured cars of a troop of the Natal

Mounted Rifles who were also in camp with us. Sometimes I went out with a patrol carried in a Hippo, a most ungainly mine-proofed vehicle. On one such occasion we came upon five cheetahs together, two adults and three fully grown cubs. They wandered across the track only a few yards ahead of us and quite unconcerned by our presence. In fact the Caprivi bush teamed with game of every sort, and droppings covered the ground everywhere.

I took morning service each Sunday, followed by a communion service for those who wished to stay. For this purpose I had written and had printed some 500 copies of a service book. In it I printed only those parts of Morning Prayer and Holy Communion in which the congregation join, with a brief description of what the minister is doing or praying for in between. This all went on to three pages, and I included twelve hymns which I was sure I could lead unaccompanied.

A future leader of the work at Waterfall in Natal and a young Greek soldier who joined a mission in the southern suburbs of Johannesburg were both converted as a result of this camp. I often held services for small groups on guard in isolated places in the bush and made much use of the 139th Psalm in my ministry to them, "Even there shall Thy hand lead me, and Thy right hand shall hold me."

I was up on the border again in November 1977, this time to Ovambo. It is very hot at that time of year, with the temperature going up to 50 degrees Celsius. So one has to rest in the middle of the day. Even so, it is terribly hot in the tents.

Owing to the left wing policies of the South African Council of Churches, churches affiliated to that organization had discouraged or forbidden their ministers to serve as chaplains in the Defence Force. The result was that on this tour and at later subsequent ones, I was either the only English speaking minister in Ovambo or there was sometimes one other. So I was told to visit as many units and sub-units as possible in the time available.

In general outline, I spent three or four days with each regiment or battalion and from the HQ visited different companies and platoons each day. In practice I soon found it didn't really pay to visit down to platoons. There I could only speak to ten or twelve men because sections were out on patrol, and this at the expense of a great deal of travelling time. I could speak to more people in the same time by going only to the company HQ where the reserve platoon was also located. In such places I spoke to up to sixty men. Depending on the distances I had to travel, mostly at slow speed in mine protected vehicles along very rough dirt tracks, I usually fitted in between three and five services or talks each day. Whenever there appeared to be a number of the Lord's people desirous, I administered the Lord's

Supper with army biscuits and fruit juice. Each Sunday I usually managed a voluntary early communion service, then the parade service, and an evening service at a second unit, plus a couple of talks to other groups in between.

One evening I conducted a communion service to the accompaniment of thunder and pouring rain, mortar, and small arms fire! We were in a partly buried tent, but none of us flinched, being certain of the Lord's protection. It was for all of us a deeply moving service because we knew God was with us.

In all I spoke to nearly 4000 men and never to more than 300 at a time, sometimes to only six, but usually to about sixty at a time.

Everywhere I went the emphasis of my preaching lay on:

(a) The ultimate and absolute authority of the whole Bible as being the very Word of God revealed to man, and how it should be accepted and submitted to as infallibly inspired on the authority of and by the example of the Lord Jesus Christ.

(b) The sovereignty of Almighty God and the binding nature of His Holy Laws on Church, State, and the individual.

(c) The imperative need for individual repentance and faith in the Lord Jesus Christ and His finished work, and that such trust is not an optional extra but essential if judgement is to be avoided both in this world and the world to come.

(d) Humility as being the hallmark of a true hearted Christian, but that assurance and confidence in the Lord were also the birthright of all true Christians. Holiness of life was essential to enjoy the latter.

(e) The menace of false and unscriptural teaching and practice. I warned of the evils of the ecumenical movement, of the W.C.C. and S.A.C.C., and urged everyone to bring pressure on their churches to return to their own doctrinal standards. I also warned of the pitfalls of relying on experience divorced from doctrine and that such misplaced trust left one wide open to the insinuations of syncretists, Christo-Marxists, etc.

Wherever I went, I was most kindly and gladly received by all ranks up to the most senior. The Commander of the Military Area ordered himself and his entire staff at Oshikati to hear me.

Though there seemed to be very few true hearted Christians, it also seemed that I was able to "get through" to a large percentage of those whom I addressed. Unfortunately, the very nature of my mission prevented any kind of follow up. My duty was to scatter the seed widely, in the faith that the Word does not return unto God void, but accomplishes that which He pleases. I could but pray wherever I went that He would water the seed.

Because of constant moving there were few opportunities for individual conversations. Those that I had were almost all with true hearted Christians who were going through a period of spiritual doubt and depression, caused I think through lack of fellowship with other Christians, lack of an English medium ministry, and through much misplaced trust in religious feelings. To such, I explained that assurance depended more on trusting in the faithfulness of God to His Word than on personal feelings, important as these were. I also tried to get the men to continue in Bible study and prayer together after I had gone. I often distributed copies of Lt. Gen. Sir Arthur Smith's *Hundred Days Bible Study*, published by the Officers Christian Union, to help them.

I shared in all the experiences and discomforts of the men, always insisting that I be given a tent in the troops lines and not amongst the officers so that I would be the more accessible. I found the heat more trying than anything I had experienced elsewhere, perhaps because of my age (I was by far the oldest man on the border). The courage, good humor, endurance, and keenness of the young men were quite magnificent. They travelled for hours along tracks never knowing from minute to minute when they might be blown up by a mine. Although if properly strapped in one was unlikely to be seriously hurt, it was nevertheless an uncomfortable feeling. Where the tracks were too dangerous, I was flown by helicopter at tree-top level to give the terrorists the least chance of shooting at us.

The need was enormous, and my reward was to see the gratitude on the faces of those boys on the border who were being deliberately starved of a Christian ministry by their own churches.

It was also a joy to meet the Rev. Peter Kalangula in Oshikati and have a time of fellowship with him. He was not only the leader of the Church of England in Ovambo, he was also at the time the minister of education for the territory. His life was constantly threatened by SWAPO, the marxist terrorist organization, which the United Nations eventually forced into power in Southwest Africa. SWAPO had already murdered his cousin in mistake for him.

I spent another month in Ovambo in December 1978, at the height of the hot weather. Again I was the only English speaking chaplain with the Defence Force in Ovambo. Again I toured round all the camps, but now the mine-proofed vehicles, called "Buffels," were much more efficient and safer than what we had before. Previously one often just sat on a layer of sandbags on the floor of a Unimog four wheeled drive lorry.

On 14th December I found myself in camp with 21 Maintenance Unit, a citizen force unit, at Ondongwa. The OC, a Comdt Viljoen, was a farmer from northern Natal. He had the habit of making a provocative remark to anyone who was introduced to him. He greeted me with, "Oh, of course you English speakers know nothing about the Day of the Covenant!" The Day of the Covenant is a remembrance of the vow taken by the Boers to serve God if He would give them the victory at Blood River some hundred years before. I replied, "Oh, yes we do." "Oh no you don't," came the immediate, aggressive reply. "I can assure you we do, and at Christ Church, we regularly observe the Day of the Covenant as a religious holiday and hold a remembrance service that morning." "Alright then, you will conduct our Covenant Service the day after tomorrow."

I was well prepared for this, knowing that I would be with the army on 16th December, and had the words of the covenant with me and details of the circumstances of its inauguration after the Battle of Blood River all those years ago. At the service, we had the Lord's Prayer in Afrikaans and the lesson was read by an Afrikaans speaking officer. In my sermon I switched from the covenant sealed at Blood River to the covenant sealed in the Saviour's blood and preached a challenging Gospel message. We finished by singing "Die Stem" (the South African national anthem), the words of which had a deeply stirring appeal there on the border. The OC came up to me afterwards with tears in his eyes, saying he'd never heard such a meaningful Day of the Covenant Service. By contrast, the occasion generally is used in South Africa for a political address set in a religious setting instead of bringing a message from the Word of God.

I was with the Maintenance Unit for five or six days and held a Bible study in my tent each evening which was well attended. I was amused after the first day to find outside my tent a nicely painted notice that read "Soul Tiffie." I've been called a "Sky Pilot" or "God Botherer," but to be acknowledged as a soul artificer was a new one to me. I was deeply touched at the end of my visit when the young artificers came and presented me with an engraved ball point pen made out of two R1 rifle rounds. I still treasure this in my desk. I also ministered to the Air Force and the "Parabats" while I was at Ondongwa.

At Ombulantu I was with an infantry company and a troop of mounted infantry. The flies from the horses were awful, and we had to get under a net to have our meals. From there I had to catch a convoy to Ruacana. There was to be no more travelling on my own as in previous years, as SWAPO had penetrated more deeply. This convoy had to pick up some water engineers about twenty minutes along the road. They were constructing a pipeline to carry water from the Kunene River at Ruacana to Oshikati.

However, the water engineers were not ready when we arrived at their camp, and so we had an hour's wait in the blazing hot sun, which annoyed me as time was precious to me. I went to cool off in more ways than one under what little shade there was under a baobab tree.

I had no sooner sat down than a civilian man appeared from the other side of the tree shaking water off his hands which he had evidently been washing. His name was Mr. Jansen and he had a caravan the other side of the enormous trunk of the baobab tree. As soon as he saw me he spotted the chaplain's insignia on my shoulders and said, "How can you, a Christian minister, be in uniform and carrying an automatic pistol on your belt?" I said, "If you will come and sit down, I will tell you." At the end of a considerable dissertation, he said, "I'm sure my wife would like to see you because she also believes that the Bible is the Word of God." I promised I would call on them as soon as possible after we arrived in Ruacana.

A day or two later I called at the Jansen's house and had a long conversation with Mrs. Jansen, at the end of which we prayed together and she repented of her ungodliness and put her trust in Christ and His finished work. But Mr. Jansen was in bed with a high fever, and we could do no better than kneel and pray by his bedside.

Back in the Eastern Cape, the Alice Commando was disbanded and I became the chaplain of the Amatola Commando with HQ in Stutterheim. I went into camp with them two years running, but I have to confess that I never really thought my ministry was successful amongst them. Generally, I think Evangelical Christianity was entirely strange to them. Many of them had dropped out of their churches altogether because of their disenchantment with their left wing political stance.

In 1980 I was up on the border again, but this time in the winter, which made it easier for me. I was flown up to Ruacana in a little two seater airplane, and we flew low to keep out of trouble as much as possible. Whenever the pilot saw people on the ground, he circled round them in a steep turn to make sure they were not terrorists. There was a company stationed on the airfield at Ruacana, and I ministered to them for the first few days. The OC said, "You are the first padre I've seen to whom the troops actually run to hear you!"

Then I went on to another company camped right on the border and while with them had the opportunity of going over the hydroelectric power station. It is all under ground in three huge galleries dug out of the rock. It could produce power sufficient for the southern half of Angola and most of Southwest Africa but was out of action thanks to the activities of SWAPO.

In Ruacana I went to call on the Jansens. But the house was empty, and all I could do was to pray for them as I sat in my Land Rover outside the house. When I returned home to Hogsback, there was a letter for me from Mrs. Jansen, now resident in the Orange Free State, to say that her husband had at last been converted. It seemed that this had happened at the exact time I had prayed for them all those hundreds of miles away the week before.

Then I went on to the battalion HQ and the reserve company who were stationed in Ruacana as the town guard. So there was a large congregation for Sunday morning service. There was communion for those who wished to stay afterwards. The OC told me that he had a company in a new base at the Concor Dam, which was back on the road to Ombulantu. It had been sited there because it lay on a favorite terrorist incursion route, and so far no chaplain, either Afrikaans or English speaking, had visited it. I determined to go there that Friday.

So I had to return to the airfield in order to catch the convoy to the Concor Dam camp. At the airfield an Apostolic Faith Mission chaplain had arrived, and we were introduced. "I'm so glad to meet you," he said, "the whole camp is talking about you." "Oh, no," I said, "don't tell me I've been commending myself." "On the contrary," he said, "they are all saying you brought Jesus Christ to the camp." I thanked God, for only the Holy Spirit can enable anyone to do that, and my prayers had been graciously answered.

I travelled in the convoy to the Concor Dam, and when we came off the tarmac on to the dirt road the Buffel in front of us was blown up on a mine. Fortunately all the chaps were properly strapped in and no one was hurt and only two were deafened for forty-eight hours.

As the camp had only recently been established, the defences had not been completed and the surrounding earth wall was still very low. The OC was only a lieutenant, and he had no other ranks higher than corporal. The army had to expand so much that there was an acute shortage of medium senior officers and of warrant officers and sergeants. I thought the young men were doing exceedingly well.

That night after I had gone to sleep the sentries heard the screams of a man being murdered somewhere outside the camp. It turned out that a deserter from the Ovambo Battalion had been surprised by a SWAPO gang which had got away with his R1 rifle and a suit of "Browns" (the bush uniform we all wore). The gang had then gone on and murdered the headman of a nearby kraal for no other reason than that he was the headman.

The OC said, "We are going after these murderers in the armoured cars, would you like to come with us?" "Certainly," I said. I was then given a ten minute lesson on the 90mm gun and went as the gunner in the second armoured car. When we reached the kraal, we found the poor little villagers all in a state of shock. The headman's body was quite shattered as SWAPO kill in a foul way, emptying a whole magazine into a body, and there was blood everywhere.

We chased the gang through the bush all day as their tracks were easily visible from the turrets of the cars. But we failed to catch up with them. Next day was Sunday, and I suppose because I had gone out with them the whole camp came to communion service that morning, and we had a wonderful service with the Holy Spirit manifestly present.

I spent much of that year at Oshivello and at Oshikati with my own Amatola Commando. They became the town guard for Oshikati that year, and I gave Bible studies for each guard before they went on duty. This kept me busy throughout the day, and I also made time to minister to the Sapper squadron who were often out searching for mines. In both units there were opportunities for chats and answering questions by individuals.

Soon after returning to Hogsback, I was rung up by the chaplain general and asked if I would stand in for two months as the chaplain at the Military Academy at Saldhana. I leapt at the opportunity. Win came with me and we were allotted the flatlet in the officers' mess used to accommodate VIPs!

On our arrival there, Win and I were rather surprised to see that a large number of officers were gathered on the steps of the main building to welcome us. It turned out that a certain Rev. Cedric Begbie had been prominent recently, taking part in SACC demonstrations in the streets. There was immediate relief when it was seen that we were white!

This appointment was a tremendous opportunity as the English speaking chaplain was also the English speaking chaplain for the Naval Gymnasium at Saldhana, the Air Force College at Langebhan Road, and the Air Sea Rescue detachment at Langebhan, whereas there were Afrikaans speaking chaplains at each of the three larger establishments. In addition to the Sunday morning service at Saldhana, there was an evening service at Langebhan Road and short mid-week morning services alternately in Afrikaans and English at all four places. After taking the first mid-week service at Langebhan Road, the tubby little Afrikaans Air Force chaplain came rushing up to me, saying, "But that was my doctrine!" I said, "Be assured, my brother, you have no monopoly of the Reformed Faith." "In that case you take the mid-week service here every week for so long as you are here."

Before my time was up the OCs of the Academy, the Gymnasium, and the Air Force College, and all three Afrikaans speaking chaplains, appealed to the chaplain general to post me there permanently but agreement was not forthcoming. Brigadier Muller, the OC of the Academy, said one day that this was a battle he was determined to win. I gather there was also a deputation of student officers asking for me to stay.

Sadly it was not to be. The retiring age for permanent force chaplains was sixty. As I was already over sixty and only a citizen force chaplain, it was not possible for the chaplain general to keep me on, especially as there was dissatisfaction already amongst permanent force chaplains with the early retiring age.

In 1981 I was called to Scottburgh in Natal and became chaplain of the Oribi Commando with HQ at Warner Beach. They seemed to me to be quite ineffective, and my relations with them never became fruitful. Perhaps it was that I was becoming old. So after being presented with the Pro Patria medal for active service on the border and the De Wet medal for ten years service, I resigned in 1982 two years after the retiring age for army chaplains.

"Wickits," the home we built at Hogsback
in the Amatola Mountains of the Eastern Cape, South Africa 1971-1981.

Members of West Park Commando in camp
at Mapleton near Heidelberg, Transvaal in 1970.
Myself between John, aged 22, and David, aged 19.

Christ Church, Blairgowrie, Randburg, Transvaal.

Holy Trinity Church, Scottburgh, Natal.

Chapter Seventeen

Builder And Church Planter

Soon after it was decided that I should be ordained, Win and I went on holiday in January 1969 touring along the Garden Route beside the Southern Cape coast. This is one of the most beautiful parts of South Africa, with miles and miles of glorious beaches on the one hand, the rugged Outeniqua and Tsitsikama Mountains on the other, and in between a narrow coastal plain in parts thickly wooded with either indigenous forests or pine plantations, and in others occupied by lovely, productive mixed farming. The mountains, beaches, and forests are a Godsend to hikers who appreciate the scenery and display of all manner of wild flowers.

We decided that, as I was about to take this substantial drop in income, we had better do something about securing our future. We resolved to buy a plot of land on which to build a house for our eventual retirement which we could use as a cheap holiday base in the meantime. Being by the sea, it would make, we hoped, an attractive holiday rendezvous for our sons as well. We had R3,000 available to buy a plot, and there would be R8,000 returned to us from the rectory with which to build a house. Because of inflation our R8,000 was not worth as much as when we had loaned it to the church, and so I would have to build the house myself.

We saw one small farm we should loved to have bought near Knysna. It was a pipe-dream, really, and anyway it was ruled out by the fees of Hilton College, where our three sons were being educated. Other suitable plots were beyond our means. So we more or less gave up the idea.

One evening, while staying at the Tsitsikamma Forest Inn, we mentioned to a couple staying there how much we had enjoyed the mountains and forests in Pakistan. So they suggested that, instead of driving directly back to Johannesburg across the Karoo, we should go back via Hogsback in the Amatola Mountains of the Eastern Cape, where we would find the sort of scenery we so much admired.

So we drove back via Port Elizabeth and Fort Beaufort. By the time we reached Grahamstown we were in such mist that we couldn't see much of the countryside. In fact, we arrived at the Ambleside Hotel at Hogsback hardly aware that we had climbed a pass, so thick was the mist. We were rather disappointed.

But next morning dawned fresh and sunny, with a few clouds swirling around the magnificent cliffs of the mountains. Below them were pine forests, and below them a second series of cliffs with extensive indigenous forests at their feet.

Win and I were immediately so attracted to this scenery that we asked the manager of the hotel if there were any plots to sell. "Yes," he replied, "In November I divided the land across the road from the hotel into ten plots, each of four and a half acres. Eight have been sold already, but there are two fronting onto the road which I can show you. In addition, someone who took an option on another plot has written in the post just received this morning that he wishes to surrender his option. So I can show you that one as well."

He took us first to the two plots on the road. Both received a lot of dust from the road and neither had any view. He took us to the third plot with some difficulty as the whole area was so thickly infested with wattle that we had to hack our way through with axes. But there was a small cleared area at the far end of this site which was known locally as "The Look-out." Standing there at an altitude of exactly four thousand feet, we had the most magnificent view imaginable. At our feet was a cliff which dropped vertically nearly a hundred feet into the indigenous forest which fell steeply to the Tumie Valley some two thousand feet below. We could see a village of thatched Xhosa rondavels almost at our feet, then down the valley almost to Alice some twenty miles away with, in the distance, the hills above Grahamstown nearly eighty miles away.

The cliffs on which we stood extended round to the left in a horseshoe so that they also faced us across the ravine about a quarter of a mile away. We could hear a waterfall round to the left. The whole of the ravine was covered, with indigenous forest consisting, as I later discovered of yellow woods, iron woods, assagai trees, knobbly bark trees, Cape chestnuts, and a host of other trees, bushes, and ferns.

Above the cliffs there were extensive pine forest plantations reaching back to a further set of cliffs. Over the latter a waterfall known as "the Kettlespout" was clearly visible. When the wind blew strongly from the southwest all the water was blown back up over the cliff in a spray which sometimes froze in winter onto the surrounding pine trees, making a fairyland scene.

Above this second set of cliffs there was open veld sloping up to the cliffs of the three Hogsback mountains. The highest one was the one on the right immediately in front of us and had an altitude of six thousand four hundred feet.

So from where we stood we had, right in front of us, no less than four thousand feet of mountain, two thousand feet down to the valley floor and two thousand feet up to the peaks of the mountains. I asked the manager how much he wanted for the plot, and he replied R2,500. I calculated that my three thousand would just cover this together with transfer costs. I looked at Win, who was standing behind the manager, and she nodded. So we bought the site.

The manager then took us to meet some of the other residents. These included Brigadier Peter Cook, on whose staff I had served in 1940, and Mrs. Cook, Charles and Lexie Elliott, whose brother, then Lt Col G. McMullen, had commanded the Depot Battalion, Royal Engineers, at Chatham when I joined there in 1939 as a second lieutenant, John and Bobby Gray, whom I had met when she was in the Women's Auxiliary in Nanyuki, Kenya in 1946, the two sisters Peacock, with whose cousin I had served in the War Office in 1950, and Dick Bomford, whose sister had been one of my eldest sister's friends at Blackheath High School in the twenties.

It seemed to me that the Lord meant us to come to Hogsback because He had this site made available for us on the very day we arrived and at the price we could afford, and by there being such a remarkable number of people in that small community with whom I had a previous connection.

During subsequent holidays we used to engage laborers to help us clear the wattle off enough of the site to begin building and start a garden. Eventually we engaged a builder to build us one room and a bathroom onto which the rest of the house, which I had designed to be built by stages, could be added.

Peter Cook was at this time chairman of the border branch of Toc H. He used to stay with us in the rectory at Blairgowrie when he came up to Johannesburg for the annual general meetings of Toc H. He used to join us in worship at Christ Church, and on the first such occasion he took my hand in both of his and said with tears of gratitude in his eyes, "Dick, you've taken me back to the Church of England as I knew it in my youth."

I was being given wonderful opportunities to witness through my army contacts. One such was to officiate at the opening of the GEM (Gunners Engineers Moths) Homes in Northcliffe in Johannesburg by the Mayor of Johannesburg, Dr. Kin Bensusan. I don't know whether this was his first contact with the Church of England in South Africa, but it was the beginning of a lasting friendship with one who subsequently became an ordained minister of the denomination.

In a later holiday at Hogsback, Peter insisted that I preach in the little rondavel chapel there which is owned by the Church of the Province of South Africa but which they allow other denominations to use.

Win and I arrived at Hogsback to stay after I had resigned from Christ Church in January 1971. We had just one room to live in while the village shop owner kindly undertook to store most of our furniture. I immediately set to work to add another room so that we could accommodate my mother, who was staying temporarily with my sister Joan in Johannesburg. I finished the room in February, and Joan brought my mother down by car. My mother's mind had gone very badly, and she often didn't know where she was or who I was. One of us had to be by her all the time. I think she was reasonably happy watching me laying bricks in those lovely surroundings.

Unknown to me, Peter and other churchgoers had approached the Bishop of Grahamstown to ask him to appoint me as the resident Anglican minister at Hogsback. They had not realized that there were two separate Anglican Churches in South Africa. At first the rector of Alice, "Father" Tim Stanton, who came up to Hogsback once a month, had tried to dissuade them, even going to the extent of warning the residents to have nothing to do with us church-wise or socially because, in his opinion, we belonged to a schismatic church! But he had not reckoned on my long-standing acquaintance with so many of the residents, and they had the more insisted on my appointment.

Bishop Bill Burnett asked me to go to see him in Grahamstown soon after our arrival. After exchanging pleasantries I suggested that we should commit our meeting to the Lord in prayer, but the Bishop said this was unnecessary as we could pray afterwards. He offered to give me his general licence and was rather surprised when, after thanking him for his offer, I said I could not accept it until I had permission to do so from Bishop Bradley my Presiding Bishop. At the end of the meeting he prayed in tongues, which rather took me aback, and I suppose I should have asked him to stop as there was no interpreter present (1 Corinthians 14). Subsequently, Bishop Bradley gave his approval to my accepting the licence, and so I became the first minister in 104 years to have a licence from bishops of both churches simultaneously.

It was agreed that I should take the service on alternate Sundays, and the Methodist minister from Fort Beaufort and a retired blind Presbyterian minister should share the other two.

Unfortunately the Rector of Alice did not keep to the agreement and continued to come to Hogsback once a month, thus splitting the congregation into a pro-Begbie element and a pro-Stanton element. So at the request of several worshippers, I used to take an early communion service on the Sunday Stanton came up in addition to the one morning service a month I retained. Some years later, Stanton was put in prison for six months for refusing to testify in a terrorism trial.

In May my poor mother had a severe stroke which weakened her mind even further. She spent some weeks in hospital in Alice, and my brother Denys flew out to sit with her. The hospital was unwilling to look after her indefinitely, and the doctors were adamant that it would not be possible for Win and I to look after her any more. Joan and Denys thought the best thing to do would be to fly my mother back to England to have her admitted into a home there, and I rather reluctantly agreed. In the event, the flight from East London to Johannesburg proved too much for her, and so Joan managed to find a place for her in a home in Johannesburg where she visited her daily. I used to go up to stay with Joan for a week each month so that I could sit by my mother each day to relieve Joan a bit. My sister Lorna also flew out for a month to do her bit. This terribly sad pattern continued for the next eighteen months. I think my mother was most distressed on the occasions when her mind was sufficiently clear for her to realize what her condition was. She died just before her eighty-fourth birthday in October 1972. Bishop Desmond Douglas officiated most beautifully at her funeral.

In between these engagements and spells of duty with the army which I described in the previous chapter I continued building our house. With Win's help I did everything with only my gardener, Jerry Lingani, working with me. I reckon it took two years of forty hour weeks spread over the four years till 1975. In this time, we completed a house containing a double and a single bedroom (large enough in fact to take two beds), lounge, dining room, study, kitchen, one and a half bathrooms, and entrance hall. We also completed a rondavel in the garden big enough for use as a double bedroom, and a block containing a double garage, workshop, generator room, and fuel store.

Towards the end of this program a beam fell on my head through my own carelessness. It concussed me, and I ended up with four stitches in my head. A few days later I developed a high temperature, and over the phone our doctor in Alice insisted that I be admitted to hospital immediately. Win with a kind neighbor had the greatest difficulty in getting me off the property because of incessant rain which had made the track impassable without chains. They fitted the chains to the wheels in pouring rain and drove me up to the road, where Dr. Hood was waiting to take me in his car to hospital in Alice. I was suffering from a severe attack of tick-bite fever which gave me the most terrible headache and a quite frightening depression. I was out of hospital after a week, thirty pounds lighter and very weak.

In that condition I was driven down to East London to attend a rather important Christian meeting, and I stayed the night with some friends. That night I had an unforgettable dream or even vision, for I cannot tell at what point I changed from sleep to wakefulness. At any rate I saw on the dressing table at the far side of the room a light and illuminated by it a stack of books which I knew to be theological ones. Fallen off the top of the stack but still leaning against it was my Bible. A voice coming from above me and to my left said, "Read my Word." Again the voice said, "Read my Word." By this time I knew it was the Lord, but I was ashamed to look up. In His presence my sin and guilt were overwhelming. I was overcome and wept that the Lord should come to such a one as I. A third time the voice said, "Read my Word." I knew I had not been reading the Bible as much as I should but instead had been neglecting it while I studied theological works. By the time the voice came the third time I was awake. The light had gone, the dawn was breaking, there were no books on the dressing table, and my Bible was on the bedside table where I had left it before going to sleep. I remained with my head bowed for a long time, meditating on what I had been told, sure that this had been a message from God because it was true to the teaching of Jesus. I was and remain inexpressibly thankful to Him for so lovingly deigning to put me right.

When I had regained my physical strength we upgraded the servants' quarter so that it contained a bedroom, sitting room, shower, hand basin, toilet, and a hall-cum-kitchen, all served by electric light. Jerry used to call it No 1 Hogsback because it was so superior to the quarters of all the other servants at Hogsback.

We also created a lovely garden, and I was especially proud of our display of dahlias, fuschias, and Hogsback lilies which grew to heights of over six feet with several blooms of long white trumpets on each stem. We grew all our own fruit and vegetables. In the orchard we had apples, plums, nectarines, and peaches, as well as bushes of red and white currants and proper English gooseberries. We also grew enormous quantities of raspberries and had strawberries and cream twice daily from October to March each year. Win made jam and bottled enough fruit to last the full year, which was a very arduous task with the anthracite stove in the heat of summer. The potatoes also lasted the year, and my only failure was with lettuces which went to seed before they hearted.

The old Presbyterian minister, who took one service a month and had been blind from birth, accepted the liberal theology of the last century and so did not accept large portions of the Bible, including some of the words of Jesus, as being the infallibly inspired Words of God. He never preached anything remotely resembling the Gospel, and one got the impression that he believed one could contact God through nature without any intervention by the Lord Jesus Christ. He was white with rage with me one day after service for preaching on the text, "There is none other name under heaven given among men, whereby we must be saved" (Acts 4:13). When I quoted the words of Jesus recorded in John 14:6 he angrily refused to admit that these were correctly reported. At which point there was clearly no purpose served in continuing the discussion.

Shortly after, in October 1974, I preached in the chapel on Reformation Sunday. I referred to the trials of our Church of England martyrs and how they lived if they would admit that the bread and wine became the body and blood of Jesus and how they died in agony in the flames if they refused. I explained how the blasphemous practices of the mass had crept in again to various sections of the Anglican Church thus leading people away from a true understanding of the Gospel. This was too much for the Church of the Province members, and in consequence I was ejected from the chapel by "Father" Stanton, who said, "But don't tell anyone that we have forced you out!" I felt rather like Paul ejected from the synagogues.

I spoke to Mr. Herbert Hammond, the then Registrar of the Church of England in South Africa, saying that my ministry at Hogsback, such as it was, was now over and so I was available. He said Fort Victoria in Rhodesia would like to have me. This, the Church Warden, Major Bryan Elvy at Fort Victoria, confirmed to me in direct correspondence.

So I set off by road for Rhodesia, leaving Win to follow later. During the eleven hour journey to Johannesburg I became more and more unhappy. The further I travelled the further I seemed to be going out of the Lord's will. It was a miserable but growing conviction. When I arrived in Johannesburg I called on the Rev. Norman Dunning at Holy Trinity Church in Bramley and shared my burden with him. He rightly said, "Only the Lord can tell you what to do, Dick, no one else can. Wait on Him."

I left Norman and drove up to the top of Corlett Drive, where I could either turn left to Rhodesia or right back to Hogsback. I stopped the car and prayed, "Lord I don't know which way to turn, please help me to do what You want me to do." After a while the conviction grew on me that I must go on up to Fort Victoria and tell them of my misgivings. After all, I had said I would come to them, and I must tell them the truth face to face.

So I drove on and arrived at Fort Victoria to an enthusiastic welcome due to my previous relationship with the people there. I was no less pleased to see all my friends again, especially the Elvys. After supper I said I had some news which I feared might turn out to be a disappointment to them. I told them how this unhappy feeling had developed that I was not in the Lord's will; but I was not sure. Bryan Elvy was quite wonderful. "Don't distress yourself, Dick, we shall all pray about this right now, that unless the Lord gives one or more of us a clear indication that you are to stay with us by twelve o'clock tomorrow morning, we shall take it that you are to go back to South Africa."

I spent an unhappy morning, much of it spent in prayer. A few minutes after twelve, Bryan came to me and said, "Get back into your car, Dick, and God go with you."

When I arrived back at Hogsback a deputation consisting of Dr. Cedric Cooper, Mr. Fran Hunter, and Mr. John Bowker came to see me. They had decided, as the Gospel was never preached in the chapel, to form the Hogsback Evangelical Church, and they had come to call me to be their pastor. As I had nothing whatever to do with this development nor had it even entered my thoughts, I felt the more convinced that this was what the Lord required me to do and was the reason for my unhappiness during the long drive to Rhodesia.

We began services at once in October 1974 and soon had a congregation which varied between two and three dozen, and in holiday time sometimes grew to fifty or more. By and by, by the grace of God every member of the church became converted. I never wish to serve a more united and loving fellowship. It was pure joy to be with them. Fran and Vi Hunter, Edward and Muriel Bean and her sister Phyl Main, were all weaned out of the charismatic movement to a lively understanding of the doctrines of grace. Edward and Muriel later became the founders of St. James's Church meeting in Kenton-on-Sea and Port Alfred. All three of the Bean daughters joined Church of England churches.

Often ordinands or recently ordained ministers who had been trained in Grahamstown would attend our church. On several occasions they came for long conversations with me. Some said that Dr. So-and-so had destroyed the Old Testament while Dr. So-and-so had destroyed the New. Another said he would not have known what to believe or reject from Rhodes had it not been for the presence of a Bible Institute student on the course. It was tragic to see the damage the liberal theology of Rhodes University was doing to the souls of so many in the ministry of so many denominations.

The years at Hogsback were essential for my own growth in Biblical knowledge and spiritual maturity. I accumulated a moderate theological library and was able to make up for my lack of formal theological training.

In fact, some of the ministers who had been trained at Rhodes used to say that they envied me for my Bible knowledge!

During these years, and on frequent visits to the Transvaal, I became involved with the Christian League of South Africa founded by the Rev. Fred Shaw, a Methodist minister. I thought it would be a counter to the politicized and Marxist inclined South African Council of Churches. I soon discovered that it was little more than a right wing political movement masquerading as a Christian movement. But in it I met Mrs. Dorothea Scarborough, a most remarkable and courageous Christian lady with whom I became close friends. When we discovered that the Christian League was also being funded by the Government as part of the so-called information scandal we immediately resigned.

But we were both convinced that there was a crying need for an inter-denominational fellowship which would stand to defend the Gospel in a far more militant way than churches which still adhered to Evangelical Christianity were doing. So we decided to found the Gospel Defence League, of which Mrs. Scarborough became the spokeswoman through the monthly circular letters which she began to write. In addition to the Gospel Defence League letter, she also typed and distributed to every minister and theologian in Germany *Vox Africana*, a circular letter exposing the Marxist activities of the WCC and SACC. I believe that largely through her writings the West German churches, previously the biggest contributors to the WCC, halved their contributions.

One of the few Evangelicals remaining in the Church of the Province, the Rev. Warwick Seymour, was rector of Fort Beaufort. He was also responsible for the churches at Seymour and Post Retief. Warwick and I enjoyed a close friendship together, and he often asked me to preach in his three churches. If the sermon was appreciated at Post Retief I would sometimes be given a leg of mutton! To get there we had to drive down the precipitous Mitchell's Pass, then up the Catberg Pass, and finally down the Devil's Bellows Pass. It always seemed an odd way to go to church!

One Sunday when we were in church at Seymour, Warwick shared the communion service with the Rev. Harwood Dixon from the CPSA in Graaf Reinet in the Karoo. Harwood at that time was an Anglo-Catholic, wearing vestments and in the communion service hanging on to the chalice like grim death, it being inappropriate for the sinful laity to handle the "blood" of Christ.

Subsequently, he and his whole family used to come to church with us at Hogsback during their holidays. I don't know whether it was the simplicity of our 1662 Prayer Book service which struck him, but eventually he made enquiries through me to join the Church of England. It was my privilege to introduce him to the Church at a General Synod a few years later.

I was often away with the army during our years at Hogsback, but the Evangelical Church congregation had become quite spiritually mature and able to fend for themselves during my absences. The Baptist ministers from King Williams Town, fifty miles away, frequently kindly stood in for me while I was away.

It was for this reason that in March 1976 I felt able to offer myself to help at Christ Church, Hillbrow, in Johannesburg as they were about to face an interregnum following the resignation of Bishop Douglas as their rector. Bishop Douglas said on the phone that had they known I was available, they would certainly have called me as their rector. I said I would rather come up "on appro" for six months or so while we adjusted to city life again and the congregation had the chance to get to know us. In the same month we went up to Johannesburg and ferried up the minimum amount of furniture we would need in our VW combi and beetle, making two trips of it so that there was no charge to the church. I must say we rattled round the large rectory in Bristol Road like two peas in a pod, as we left most of the rooms devoid of furniture. It was freezing cold in that house in winter.

I found the congregation at Hillbrow in a very distressed state and riven by divisions. The dear old treasurer was now too old for the job, the books were in an awful mess, and the accounts had not been audited for the last two years. Within weeks of arrival a deputation of Sunday School teachers presented me with an ultimatum that unless the superintendent and his wife, who was in charge of the primary children, were asked to resign, they would all pull out. I pleaded for time, which was granted. After a few weeks, I found that the superintendent, who was a real "holier than thou" fellow, was impossibly rude to the teachers, as was his wife, despite warnings by me. This of course put him at daggers drawn against me, and he looked for faults in me and Win. He fastened on the fact that Win and I, though not totally abstinent, are very moderate in the use of wine and never touch spirits. I am convinced that our Lord made the best alcoholic wine at Cana, am aware of "wine that maketh glad the heart of man," and take to heart the admonition to "take a little wine for thy stomach's sake." I am also careful not to take wine in any company which is likely to stumble when I do so. I find that insistence on tee-totalism is often by those who think nothing of such matters as unpunctuality and disobeying the traffic laws, which is tedious to say the least. In the army we would have called such people "nit-pickers."

After a few weeks of trying to get this man to treat the teachers with reasonable respect, there was nothing for it but to take the church wardens with me to his house to ask for the resignation of himself and his wife from the Sunday School. Unfortunately, the wardens left me to do the talking even though they were in agreement with the action we were taking. The wife flew into a rage, shrieking, "Don't you know I am an epilectic?" This only confirmed her unsuitability to be left in charge of little children.

Matters were made worse by the fact that the chairman of the church council, whom I deeply respected, had a very sick wife and, presumably for that reason, never attended church or council meetings while I was there.

Over the ensuing months the atmosphere gradually improved, a new church treasurer was appointed, and the groups who met with me for prayer and Bible study grew both in numbers and spiritual understanding.

Bishop Douglas told me of a Portuguese family he used to visit who lived in a little flat near the church. So I, following his example, used to visit them as often as possible. They were Roman Catholics but always welcomed a reading and exposition of Scripture. I chose Scriptures which pointed clearly to the unique sacrifice and priesthood of the Lord Jesus Christ and of the need to be joined to Him by faith rather than to a church.

By and by the husband died although still comparatively young, and the family asked me to officiate at the funeral in the crematorium chapel. I had no sooner begun the service than the widow and her sister began to weep and cry hysterically. I had to stop and quiet them and no one else would help. I hadn't proceeded much further with the service when they started again, and again I had to interrupt the service. The reason for this terrible sorrow was that, despite everything I had told them they were still not convinced that there is no condemnation to them, that are in Christ Jesus. Their terrible anxiety was due to the fact that they believed their loved one was now enduring the flames of purgatory. I have never hated the Roman Catholic system more than at that moment. After the service, the undertakers took it upon themselves to express their sympathy with me, saying that they had never experienced a worse occasion than this.

For years previously there had been endless debate as to what to do with the very valuable property which adjoined the church. I pressed the church council to come to a decision on this. I recommended that the church be extended back into the existing Sunday School Hall; that the existing kitchen be converted into a stairway leading up into a tower which would give access to a gallery to be constructed in the extended church. This would increase the seating capacity of the church from about 120 to some 400.

I further recommended that the adjacent, very valuable property be developed or sold to a developer to provide a multi-story block of flats and shops. Part of the underground parking and sufficient accommodation for the Sunday School and a curate would then be leased back to the church or be bought by the church under sectional title. The council gave its provisional approval, and Wynter Prevost of West Park Commando, who was a leading architect in Johannesburg, undertook to draw up the plans *pro Deo*. He had a connection with the church, having been confirmed in Christ Church when he was a boy before the war.

This plan, which would amply provide for all the church's accommodation needs, would have brought so much income to the denomination that it would have been possible to build at least one new church debt-free in the Transvaal each year for the foreseeable future. However, my successor persuaded the church council to abandon this plan and to erect most unattractive buildings which made wasteful use of the site, and a literally golden opportunity was lost.

Sometime in the second half of 1976, I invited Mr. W.D. Chalmers, who was the religious organizer in the South African Broadcasting Corporation, to preach in Christ Church and his name appeared in the usual church notices in the press. In the week before he came, I was rung up by a woman who said she was the religious reporter of the *Sunday Times*. "How can you have a man like Chalmers to preach in your Church?," she asked. I felt like saying it was nothing to do with her whom I asked, but instead I said, "I have invited him because we appreciate the stand he is taking for Biblical Christianity on the radio." "Don't you know of his attitude towards the Jews?" I said as I did not read her paper, I was unaware of what he might or might not have said about the Jews, but we admired his stand for Biblical truth. I was attacked on the front page of the *Sunday Times* for admiring the stand taken by Mr. Chalmers, but the words "for Biblical truth" were left out. The media both in South Africa and the United Kingdom are resolutely hostile to Evangelical Christianity and will only permit a watered down version of Christianity, which is more damaging than useless, in their publications. They will answer for this on the Day of Judgement.

Peace and harmony now reigned at Hillbrow and the congregation was slowly increasing. Those who were attending Bible study and praying with me wanted me to stay on as rector, and I intimated that I would accept such a call. However, the Presiding Bishop was insistent that a well-known evangelist should become the rector and asked me to carry on until he was available early in mid-1977. This I was not prepared to do, and so Win and I left Johannesburg in January of that year and returned to Hogsback, where my friends in the Hogsback Evangelical Church were delighted to have us back.

During the years 1977-79 I was writing my book, *Freedom under Authority*. In this I warned that freedom without authority only led to licence and a collapse of moral standards. True freedom could only be enjoyed under the authority of the Word of God, which meant that the State had to be as much under His authority and laws as the individual.

Whilst admitting that the Bible, the infallibly inspired Word of God, did not specify what system of government men should adopt, the system should itself be conformable to Biblical principles. I attempted to show how democracy ought to be remodelled on those principles to ensure that power remained in godly and responsible hands. During the writing of the book I came under the influence of the Rev. Rousas Rushdoony and his Chalcedon Foundation, and have remained so ever since.

In a foreword to the book, Bishop Bradley, the Presiding Bishop of the Church of England in South Africa, wrote: "At a time when real values are being eroded it is necessary, and good, to have a book such as this that attempts to set out the real positive values. 'There is a way that seems right unto a man, but the end thereof is the way of death' is as true today as when it was first written. It seems that people will not realize that God is still the Judge in His universe, as he was in the days of Judah and Israel; if He is ignored, His Word, His commands, His promises, then judgement must follow....I believe you should read this book."

I sent copies to the State President and to every Member of Parliament in South Africa. The world would be a happier place today if this book had been heeded. The book nevertheless enjoyed a wide circulation, and many have been helped by it. Mrs. Scarborough kindly typed the book for me, which also helped her into a clear understanding of the Reformed Faith.

These years till the end of 1980 were my busiest years with the army, and I spent nearly a quarter of each year away from Hogsback. The fact that I had a small, mature congregation made it possible to fulfil these engagements.

One of the greatest highlights of our years at Hogsback was the wedding of David and Sandy Muller, which took place on the 12th February 1980. David and Sandy came to stay with us for a week before the wedding so that I could have marriage counselling sessions with them. Sandy was already a Christian from St. Stephen's Church, Claremont, Cape Town, of the CESA. Sandy had been prayerfully trying to lead David to Jesus, but he was still a seeker when they came to me. During counselling he was wonderfully converted. The wedding took place in the oak avenue where the upper branches of the tall trees make a natural cathedral and logs laid in rows are the pews. It was such a wonderful occasion, with the Holy Spirit almost tangibly present. It was a glorious day, and the reception was held in the beautiful garden of our home. The whole fellowship joined in, attending the service and helping with the food, and all agreed it was a most happy and memorable occasion.

For many years I had been an avid reader of the *English Churchman*. In one issue a very one-sided report appeared concerning conditions in Southwest Africa. I wrote to the editor in protest and invited him to tour

Southern Africa to ascertain the truth. I undertook to finance the tour provided he came with an open mind and would report fully on his visit in subsequent issues of the paper. In the event, the Rev. David and Mrs. Judith Samuel came in his place, and I arranged finance through a friend I had made in the Blairgowrie congregation. I arranged their entire itinerary, part of which I conducted for them myself. They met the minister of finance in the Transkei and other officials throughout their tour. They stayed with us at Hogsback, and David preached for me in our church. We took them along the Garden Route to George, where they took the plane to Cape Town and then on to Southwest Africa. There they met the Rev. Peter Kalangula who had been excommunicated from the Church of the Province because he had refused to follow the subversive policies of their bishop there. When David told Peter about the Church of England in South Africa, Peter was immediately keen to join up with us. David reported this to Bishop Bradley, and in the result Peter and all his thousands of followers joined the Church of England. God works in mysterious ways, and I little thought that my letter to the *English Churchman* would be the means by which such a large contingent would join the CESA.

Folk who visited Hogsback from East London asked me to try to begin a Church of England work in that town. So for six months at the beginning of 1980, I used to take a morning service at Hogsback and drive the ninety miles to East London to take an evening service there and do it the other way round on alternate Sundays. Services in East London were held in the YWCA hall, but we never had a congregation of more than a dozen or so and usually less. So I abandoned this through lack of support. At about the same time others who had visited Hogsback from Port Elizabeth, or who had heard me on the radio, asked me to start a work in that city. I undertook to go and stay down there for three months early in 1981 to investigate the possibilities.

At about this time I was bitten by a poisonous spider. Our doctor warned me that this was at least as toxic as a snake bite. He was right, and I then endured no less than thirty-one abscesses and carbuncles over the next two and a half years, two of which required going to hospital for operation under general anesthetic. One such was in the worst possible place on my posterior. When I came to, I found myself lying in a pool of blood and rang for the night sister. Being up-ended by her, she had the unpleasant duty of removing yards of elastoplast off an unshaved bottom, the owner of which found it so painful that there was only one thing to do. That was to make a joke of it. "You are really shaking the church to its foundations tonight," I said, and then added, "This is the last time I shall tear a strip off anyone." Anyway it kept the rest of the ward amused.

The Hogsback work was clearly coming to an end. Cedric and Jesse Cooper had died, and Fran and Vi Hunter had returned to East London for health reasons. Ed and Muriel Bean were about to move to Kenton-on-Sea, and the McFerren family were about to be posted to a forestry station in Zululand. On top of this, Win was having to drive me down the ninety miles to East London for treatment for my abscesses every two or three weeks. It seemed therefore that we should have to leave Hogsback both in order to continue to serve the Lord and because my condition meant that we ought to be nearer medical help.

It was a terrible wrench to leave Hogsback after the beautiful home we had created. I took one more film of the flowers and the butterflies in the garden to give a permanent reminder of the happy years we had spent there with a Christian fellowship such as I doubted we should see again this side of heaven. But having done almost all the work with our own hands, we managed to sell the property at such a price as to secure our financial future.

One of the great things about serving the Lord is that you never know what He is going to do with you next. What he did do with us will be related in Chapter 19 and following.

Chapter Eighteen

Broadcaster

After I had invited Mr. W.D. Chalmers, who was doing his utmost to support Biblical Christianity in his post as religious organizer in the South African Broadcasting Corporation, to preach in Christ Church, Hillbrow, in 1976, he invited me to join the panel of broadcasting ministers.

Over the next ten years, from 1976 to 1986, I broadcast on occasion Morning or Evening Prayer and sermon from Christ Church, Hillbrow, and St. Stephen's Church, Claremont, Cape Town. I took part in broadcast panel discussions with two other ministers, usually the Rev. Rex Mathie of the Baptist Church and the Rev. Jack Dazell of the Presbyterian Church. I also broadcast some twelve messages, in groups of three a year, either in evening epilogues which were quite short or in mid-week fifteen minute morning services.

Anything up to fifty letters would come in response to each group of three broadcasts, and I was hardly finished with these before I was preparing the next group of three broadcasts. The letters were mostly from Christians who sent me much encouragement. I remember particularly one letter from a travelling representative who, he said, made a point of stopping his car wherever he was in order to listen to me. I reproduce here a selection of extracts from letters received in response to my broadcasts during those years, not to advertise myself but in order to illustrate how people appreciate hearing the Gospel preached, as it were, straight from the shoulder.

315

From Durban
I just want to thank you for that beautiful preach we all listened to. It was too beautiful for words. I feel so blessed and enjoyed every minute. It will be an eye opener for many, especially the prayer we had to repeat at the end.

From Howick, Natal
We turned on our radio and heard your most excellent sermon. May I say how much we enjoyed it. Please let me have a copy. May you be spared to serve your people for many years.

From Rondebosch, Cape
I wish to thank you for the lovely broadcast this evening, and I pray that many will be led to our Lord and Saviour.

From Chaka's Kraal, Zululand
Both my husband and I were so impressed by your inspiring address on Sunday night to us and your congregation, — we truly thought we were with you and could envisage you all through the service. If only all who call themselves Christians could take a look at themselves in the sight of God, — they would see how far from being a Christian they are. You spoke so plainly about our wrongdoings — this is essential in God's work for men and women do not know at what they stumble.

From Durban
We have just listened to your message coming over the air to us in our home here in Durban, and would just like to say what a wonderful blessing it was to us. It just thrilled our hearts to hear God's Glorious Gospel preached in this way; this Gospel that sets the prisoner free. This is the message we need in our churches today, the message that should be broadcast throughout our land.

We say, God richly bless you, as you continue to proclaim this miracle working Gospel, and we know that many souls will find Christ as their Saviour, for has He not declared, My Word shall not return unto me void, but it shall accomplish that which I please and it shall prosper in the thing whereto I send it. Thank you once again.

From Cape Town
We listened into your service and were greatly blessed by the whole atmosphere and particularly your sermon. We were so impressed that you gave such an outspoken Evangelical message without mincing the truth; giving all a clear exposition of the Gospel — being born again — and giving an insight into the dangers of drug addiction, then inviting the seen and unseen congregation to take a definite decision in view of the Lord's near return. Thank you very much indeed for such a broadcast sermon and may many respond to your appeal, and thereby encourage you to continue preaching in that strain.

From Pretoria
I turned on the radio to listen to the broadcast service. So often one is very disappointed, but my heart thrilled, as you so faithfully preached the way of salvation. The Lord will bless you mightily as you so clearly preach the Gospel, and I am sure there must be souls in the

Kingdom to-day and rejoicing among the angels of heaven for sinners who have repented. My prayers and good wishes to you in your ministry.

During those years, I broadcast from studios in Johannesburg, Port Elizabeth, Cape Town, and Durban. Most often the controller in the studio was also a Christian, and knowing this made me feel more at ease as I broadcast. Only in Cape Town was this not the case, the controller being better known for reporting cricket matches. I could sense his hostility to the Gospel as I delivered my message.

I had been appointed directly by the SABC, but henceforth the ministers were to be appointed by their own denominations. But by now the CESA had shifted considerably from its conservative evangelical position, and the minister appointed wasted no time in taking me off the list of broadcasting ministers.

As I had grown older, broadcasting and the voluminous correspondence associated with it had become quite a burden. So I was not altogether sorry when I was so abruptly taken off broadcasting, but, in view of the letters I had been receiving, I did wonder whether the Lord's will was being frustrated by this action.

Chapter Nineteen

Church Planter And Author

I feel I must introduce the next part of my story with a text from Acts 16:6-9:

> Now when they had gone through Phrygia and the region of Galatia, they were forbidden by the Holy Spirit to preach the word in Asia. After they had come to Mysia, they tried to go to Bithynia, but the Holy Spirit did not permit them. So passing by Mysia, they came down to Troas and a vision appeared to Paul in the night. A man of Macedonia stood and pleaded with him, saying, "Come over to Macedonia and help us."

> Now after he had seen the vision, immediately we sought to go to Macedonia, concluding that the Lord had called us to preach the gospel to them.

At Synod in October 1980, Bishop Joe Bell, who was the Assistant Bishop for Natal and Kwa-Zulu, asked me, "Dick, would you care to go get yourself a sun tan on the Natal south coast for a month?" "What on earth are you talking about?," I asked. "Well," said the Bishop, "There is a small group of a dozen or so elderly people at Scottburgh who are mad keen to have a CESA church established there. I don't really think there is a future for us in Scottburgh, but will you go there for a month and then tell me what you think? There is a fully furnished cottage a few miles down the coast at Pennington where you and Win can stay free of charge." I agreed to go for a month in November.

Scottburgh is about twenty miles down the coast from Durban in Natal, and we arrived there at the beginning of November 1980. We were given a great welcome, particularly by Neil and Madge Wright, whom we had known when I used to go to take the service at St. Stephen's, Krugersdorp, when I was rector at Blairgowrie. Neil was now the licensed lay reader in charge, and he had exercised a fine pastoral ministry and was greatly loved by all. Amongst the others there was Mary Jump, widow of our old friend the Rev. Ernie Jump who had helped me when I was still a layman in charge at Blairgowrie. Ernie and Mary had retired there, but Ernie had exercised a fruitful ministry amongst these people for two or three years until he died in 1977. Thereafter this fellowship was provided with ministerial assistance from Christ Church, Pinetown, where Bishop Bell was the Rector.

Mr. Errol and Mrs. Ros Davey, who lived in Scottburgh, also had a holiday cottage in a beautiful garden in Pennington, a small village five miles down the coast from Scottburgh. This they very kindly made available for Win and me.

This small group of CESA members met in the Roman Catholic Church hall in Scottburgh. I was somewhat disconcerted to have to preach with the Virgin Mary looking over my shoulder and in the pervasive smell of incense and candle smoke from the Mass which had been celebrated there the evening before. There were only thirteen in the group, all of whom were elderly. At the end of the first service they gathered round and said, "You are not leaving, you know, you are going to stay with us!" I said that I was committed to investigating Port Elizabeth first and only after that would I be able to say where the Lord wanted me to be. So we stayed the month of November with them, and we warmed to them as they did to us.

After Christmas, Win and I went down from Hogsback to Port Elizabeth where a flat was put at our disposal. Supporters included David and Sandy Muller, who had been married from our house at Hogsback, David having been converted during counselling sessions, and Aston and Jean Tainton, who had been influenced by my book *Freedom under Authority* from Addo, and Aston's sister Nan Tainton, who was a nursing sister in Port Elizabeth. There was also another who had been church warden at St. Mark's church in Plumstead, Cape. Unfortunately, the latter and his wife were to be transferred back to Cape Town and the Mullers to East London. So there didn't seem to be any future at the time, though the Taintons and Owen and June Phillips, who had been influenced by my broadcasts and who moved from Tarkastad to Port Elizabeth, became founder members of the church established some years later under the ministry of the Rev. Ernie du Plooy. So the Holy Spirit did not permit us to go either to East London or Port Elizabeth but to other places which the Holy Spirit had in mind.

In any case, it was clear to me that if anyone was going to be used to plant a church in Scottburgh it would have to be someone in my age group. Win and I were by then just sixty-one years old. I also thought, and still do, that there is no community so much in need of the Gospel as a community of old people who will so soon have to meet their Maker.

Back at Hogsback I wrote to Bishop Bell saying I thought there was a future for the church in Scottburgh, that the people there had called me, and that I believed this was a call from the Lord.

So we put our house on the market, and it was let until it was sold a few months later. At Scottburgh, Ros Davey had bought an acre corner site on the corner of Williamson and Arbuthnot Streets. It had a lovely but much over-grown garden and a much neglected cottage and garage. With an enormous amount of hard work, they were getting this property ready for use as a rectory, and it would be ready for us to occupy in May 1981. So that month we said goodbye to Hogsback and moved with all our possessions to Scottburgh.

When we arrived at Scottburgh the rectory was not ready for occupation and we had to find ourselves temporary accommodation in a chalet in a caravan park in Park Rynie a few miles down the coast. We were far from comfortable there and fortunately our furniture was delayed by heavy rain so that the pantechnicon had been unable to negotiate the Hogsback roads.

At the rectory, there was as yet only a tap on the wall in the kitchen with no kitchen units, and bare concrete floors in the kitchen and bathrooms. The contractors were not getting on with the work, and so I became the colonel all of a sudden and these deficiencies were soon put right. But I had to buy some second-hand wardrobes as there were no fitted cupboards in the bedrooms.

The income of the church was R90 per month, to which Christ Church, Pinetown, added R400 per month, reducing by R40 per month to nil in ten months time. I was given a stipend of R150 per month (The rate of exchange at that time was about R3 to the £1). Mrs. Davey let the property to the church for R250 per month. So most of the assistance from Pinetown went towards paying the rental.

Gradually the congregation built up, despite a tragic number of deaths. The first year was quite heart-breaking as during it I buried nine members, including some of the most active. In addition, because Madge's health deteriorated so, Neil and Madge Wright had to move to an old age home in Durban. They were a great loss although they continued to visit us whenever they could. There was an old age home at Renishaw a mile or two up the hill behind Scottburgh with a devoted Christian lady as matron. By her influence I was invited to lead a weekly meeting for Bible study and prayer which was well attended, and I also administered the Lord's Supper there once a month. Mary Jump also arranged an interdenominational coffee morning once a month in one of the rooms of the town hall to which she invited a variety of speakers and sometimes myself.

We all wanted to have our own building as soon as possible. By gifts, by jumble sales, and by sales of work and of cakes, funds were gradually being built up. Ros Davey graciously offered to sell the property to the church and advanced a loan of R60,000 at 5% interest to enable us to buy it. We had by this time an elected church committee, all of whom came to our weekly meeting for Bible study and prayer. At their request I designed and did the working drawings for a chapel to seat about a hundred people. We could just afford a very small kitchen which would also served as a robing room for me. This was to be connected by a covered colonnade to the main door at the back of the chapel. The rear wall was to be built of breeze blocks which could readily be demolished so that the chapel could be enlarged later on.

I would have preferred this chapel to be built at the front of the site alongside the rectory where there was also room for it to be extended in due course. However, Ros Davey particularly, who was also putting up most of the money, insisted that it be erected at the back of the site so that the space alongside the rectory could be reserved for a full size church later on.

My plans were approved by the local authority, and work began at the beginning of 1982. A member of the Pinetown congregation who was a construction engineer kindly put in the footings and floor slab free of charge. To save money, it was decided that I should supervise the work, which would be done by directly employed labor. As this labor consisted of bricklayers and other tradesmen in full-time employ during the week, the work could only be done at the weekends. I had to decide whether it was lawful to carry on working on Sundays. Remembering that our Lord taught that it was legitimate to carry out essential work on the Sabbath day and that this was the only way to get the chapel built, I and the committee decided that we were in order.

We all agreed that Ros Davey should have the honor of laying the foundation stone, and this was done in a simple ceremony on 3rd October 1982.

After some discussion, I managed to persuade a Dutch builder living nearby to loan us some scaffolding free of charge. I noticed that he had in his yard four rather handsome pillars lying there, and I asked him if he would give them to me. He absolutely refused. Then I asked where about in Holland his family had come from. He said Meijel, and I said my division liberated that town during the war. He said his uncle lived in Aspen, and I said we liberated that town too. "So now," I said, "what about liberating those columns for my church?" So they were duly liberated, as can be seen by anyone who visits the chapel today.

When the walls reached the right height, I pop-welded the semi-circular frames on to the tops of the window frames. I made all the chancel furniture myself, including the pulpit top and lectern. I dedicated the chair for the bishop in memory of Commander John Carter and had a brass plate inscribed for it. John was a veteran of the Battle of the Atlantic. Although well into his eighties, he used to read the lesson without glasses and most beautifully. He also used to nod and raise his hand when he appreciated points in the sermon. He had died during the year, and I missed him greatly. I also did the signwriting by hand for the Ten Commandments, which took me three hours per line to do. In accordance with the enactment of King Edward VI, these are displayed above the Lord's Table. Wing Commander Len Preddy made the lectern and Mrs. Elsie Kinsell donated the Bible in memory of her husband, David. Errol Davey made the window sills, kitchen cupboard and table, and the holders for the books on the backs of the chairs, which was a long and laborious task. We did not have pews because, there being no funds to build a hall, we needed to be able to move the chairs for informal meetings. There were curtains to shield off the chancel when these were held. We used to have a quarterly social with a finger supper and a visiting speaker. Mrs. Zoe Waldegrave made the frontal for the pulpit lectern and the offertory bags and her husband Jack made the handles although they had emigrated to the UK before I had arrived.

So altogether, the building and furnishing of the chapel was a real team effort, and that, with the socials, drew us together in a truly loving fellowship.

Bishop Bell came to dedicate the chapel in October 1983, and with visitors from Christ Church, Pinetown, and local dignitaries, there was a large company present, and we all enjoyed tea in the garden afterwards. As soon as we moved into the church the congregation doubled and grew to three dozen or more, with over fifty on the lists.

Over the years it has grieved me to the heart to find the extent to which people have been led astray by falsity in the churches or have become disillusioned altogether. They have become unaware that they need to be saved, being confused by blurred truth or blinded by dead ritualism. All these poor souls, and many who have passed on, are lost because of the ministry of false shepherds! Knowing the truth one would be callous indeed not to have a deep, deep concern for all these poor people. How thankful they are, too, when they are finally led to Jesus as their personal Saviour and Lord! Typical of the comments I have received was one from an elderly lady who said, "All my life I have known 'churchianity,' but now I know Christ." What joy it has been to me to return thanks to the Father for translating these people out of darkness into the Kingdom of God's dear Son!

I arranged to take St. Luke's Church, Mid Illovo, which was one of our Zulu speaking churches, under our wing. The rector there was the Rev.

Lucas Radebe. The church and rectory were perched high up on a ridge near a bus station and a Zulu trading store. Lucas had five other churches to care for, each of which was under the immediate supervision of a catechist. These were scattered in Kraals on mountains round about with deep valleys in between. It took Lucas the best part of a day to reach those of his churches which were inaccessible by car.

I was shocked at the state of his rectory. It was just a five roomed, mud brick house with cement rendering on the walls and a low corrugated iron roof and no ceilings. The heat in summer must have been like an oven and the cold in winter no less uncomfortable. We raised enough money to put ceilings in three of the rooms, and Eric Jackman, my churchwarden, and I put up the ceilings ourselves, taking about four Saturdays to do it. I rather wish a photograph could have been taken of us at work and published in the overseas press to counter some of the vicious propaganda against white South Africans. We left it to Lucas to paint the ceilings. Two years later he had still not done it, and I wish a photograph could have been taken of that too!

Major Malcolm and Mary Begg, with Rowena and Andrew, joined us at this time. Malcolm was a Sapper who had taken early retirement. He remembered me from when I was DAA&QMG at Chatham and he a young officer in 1954. That connection of long ago brought him and his family to our church. He now ran a school for teaching aspirant security guards. I used to lead Bible studies in his house. One Saturday evening he was converted and was so transparently happy that it brought tears of joy to my eyes. The following Sunday he had to leave after church for East London, where he was due to have a business meeting on Monday morning. Driving across the Transkei he ran into a bullock which ran across the road and Malcolm was killed. On Monday morning I had to break the news in succession to Mary, Rowena, and Andrew. Mary knew what it was as soon as I walked up to her, and I held her in my arms as we both wept. I think the children guessed when their respective school heads sent for them to see me. It was a terribly harrowing time, and poor Mary was desolated. Before the funeral Mary wanted to see Malcolm in his coffin, but I had to prevent that as he was very disfigured. At least at the funeral it was possible to bring some words of comfort as I knew that Malcolm was with the Lord. How thankful I was for that, but I don't think I felt well for at least a fortnight after doing what I could to support the family through this tragedy. I felt Malcolm's loss very keenly myself because he had become such a strong support to me and taken the finances of the church well in hand.

During 1984, I preached a course of sermons right through the Thirty Nine Articles of Religion. The congregation were unanimous that the sermons should go into a book. Thus my book *The Anglican Faith* was produced later, and it has become prescribed reading for lay preachers in the Church of England in South Africa and in two of the Anglican denominations in the United States. Now in its second reprint, it is being used in the Sudan of all places to train Sudanese ministers and catechists in the basics of the Christian Faith. In his foreword to the first edition, Bishop Foord wrote, "All Christians need a clear grasp of the great central themes of the Bible in order to discern truth from error. The Reverend Dick Begbie has done just that for the layman today. We are furnished with a manual that will enable us to study systematically the key doctrines of the faith.

"The Thirty Nine Articles express superbly the substance and spirit of Biblical Christianity and also provide a model of the way to express the Christian faith in today's confused world.

"The Anglican Church is the poorer for its neglect of its Biblical heritage as set out in the Thirty Nine Articles. They are of permanent relevance as a test of true Biblical Christianity and all Christians need to study them carefully and rediscover in them a definitive declaration of the truth of God's Word.

"I really cannot say that I have always liked the Church of England throughout the world as I find it today, but I remain an Anglican by conviction, for in the Thirty Nine Articles, I possess a priceless heritage - a true and clear expression of Biblical Christianity.

"I commend to all a careful study of these Thirty Nine Articles and of the Reverend Dick Begbie's exposition of them. His book throbs with the desire and prayer that people will discover 'This is eternal life, that they may know you, the only true God, and Jesus Christ, whom you have sent.'"

By the end of 1984 the church had grown to the extent that a considerable part of the debt had been paid off and more promised under the wills of the members of the congregation so that only half the debt remained unaccounted for.

Throughout the whole of 1981, 1982, and well into 1983, I continued to suffer from the effects of that poisonous spider bite. A new abscess or carbuncle would come up every ten days or so. As soon as one had cleared up another was on its way. It was cured at last with penicillin, but the long period of ill health had rather pulled me down and I felt the need for a lay-off.

The income was now such that a full stipend could be paid. Accordingly, I resigned at the beginning of 1985 and the Rev. Bernard Wright came to take my place. Win and I moved into a flat in Scottburgh which we had bought with the proceeds from the sale of our Hogsback house. Bernard and I being old friends, it was no embarrassment to him to have us in his congregation as we continued to worship at Holy Trinity Church.

I was also, at the request of Bishop Dudley Foord, using the time to write a handbook of procedures for the Church of England in South Africa, which had not had one before. This handbook was to be based on the handbook of Sydney Diocese which needed to be modified to suit South African practices. To establish these I had to research all the Synod, Central Executive, and Central Trustee minutes throughout the previous hundred years. After a few amendments agreed by the Central Executive, this book was subsequently approved by Synod and taken into use.

One day in March, Bernard told me that at a Bible study he was holding in the home of a Mr. and Mrs. Law at Beasley further down the coast the Laws told him that their son-in-law had refused to have his three children baptized. He was insisting that no one but a certain Dick Begbie should baptize them. But the problem was, he did not know where this minister was. Did Bernard know? The son-in-law, whose name was Brett Sephton, was farming near Maclear, and Bernard gave me his telephone number.

It so happened that I was about to leave on a journey all the way down the coast to Cape Town to persuade booksellers to buy my book. So I rang Mr. Brett Sephton, told him who I was, and asked him if I could help him in any way. He sounded delighted to hear my voice and said that I had a conversation with him in 1978 in Oshikati in Ovamboland when I was there as a chaplain and he was a sergeant in First City Regiment from Port Elizabeth. Although he had never forgotten the conversation, I could not even remember what he looked like. When I offered to visit him during my trip, he welcomed the idea at once, and I said I would arrive at his farm at 5 pm the following Sunday.

Before setting out, I committed my whole journey to the Lord, praying that the Holy Spirit would go before me preparing the way. The Sephtons were suitably impressed when I arrived at their farm precisely at 5pm as I had promised. Brett immediately introduced me to his wife, Sue, and their three children, Craig, Katherine, and Mark, and I was most warmly welcomed by them all. Soon Brett suggested that we should meet his parents, whose farmstead was only a few hundred yards away. As we walked over Brett said that his father had served in the war in Italy with 6th South African Division and was rather proud of the fact that 24th Guards Brigade had been attached to them.

In the homestead we found the parents, Aubrey and Althea Sephton, Brett's younger brother Graham and his fiancee Phyllis, and Mrs. Sephton's mother. After a few pleasantries all around, I said to Aubrey, "I've got something in common with you, I was in 24th Guards Brigade Group in 1941." In this way an immediate rapport and lasting friendship was established. Very soon Aubrey said, "There's one thing about you ministers that I've never understood, and that is your emphasis on the writings of Paul, which I am not sure are part of the inspired Word of

God." I guessed at once that Aubrey had been exposed to British Israelite doctrine, and so, without letting on, I initiated a lengthy discussion to show that salvation was by grace alone through faith in the person and work of the Lord Jesus Christ, and consequent commitment of one's life to Him as one's Master. I backed up my discourse with references to both the Old and New Testaments, and especially John 1:12-13 which shows that God's people are not those born into any particular nation, but are those called by God into fellowship with His Son, the Lord Jesus Christ.

Brett and Sue had to leave to see to the children before I had finished. It was quite dark when I did so, and Graham and Phyl offered to show me the way back in the dark. As soon as we were outside they asked me what they must do to be saved.

I replied, "Give up leading your lives as if God does not exist, that is, repent, believe that the Lord Jesus Christ has paid the penalty for your sins in full, and vow to obey Him as your Lord. He will give you the Holy Spirit to help you if you ask Him just as Jesus has promised to do." Whether they were converted that night or not I do not know, but they certainly were converted later. Very, very sadly, Graham died in 1996 after a long battle with cancer, but at peace knowing that he would soon join His Lord in glory.

Back with Brett and Sue, I asked if I could phone Cecil Murray, who was caring for a small CESA group in Queenstown, to make an appointment to meet him next morning. Brett and Sue kept me going with questions till late into the night, and we finished with prayer. Before retiring I said I was on my way to Cape Town and would be returning in two weeks time at Easter. Would they like me to come again to Maclear to baptize their children and hold an Easter communion service? They welcomed this idea enthusiastically and were sure they would be able to assemble a congregation of two dozen or so. There were a number of people in the district who had left the Methodist and Church of the Province churches because of the involvement of those churches in politics. I told them I would need time with the children on the Saturday beforehand.

Next morning Cecil escaped from school in Queenstown to meet me at his home, where he introduced me to his lovely wife, Eileen. To our mutual surprise, we found that we had both been in Maclear the previous day where Cecil had been meeting with Alden and Ernesta Lake and Trevor and Jennifer van Coller, who had all expressed great interest in the CESA. We were amazed that the Lord had arranged for both of us to be in Maclear for the first time on the same day, and this convinced us that the Lord was about to do a new thing in Maclear. I told Cecil I would be in Maclear on Easter Sunday, and we arranged for me to take a communion service in Queenstown on Good Friday, and then for me to go on to Maclear.

Booksellers in Queenstown, East London, Port Elizabeth, and Cape Town all accepted my book, but not Grahamstown, which is such a stronghold of liberal and unreformed theology.

On my way back from Cape Town, I administered communion to a small congregation in Queenstown on Good Friday and then drove on to Maclear, where I was again warmly welcomed by Brett and Sue. I had a lengthy session with Craig, Mark, and Katherine to explain to them the meaning of baptism in terms of the Covenant. I forget their exact ages, but they must have been about twelve, ten, and eight, and were old enough to understand the promises which would be given by their godparents on their behalf. I think they understood the Gospel but were really too young to make a firm commitment at that stage, nor did I press them to do so.

Easter Sunday was quite unforgettable. The Sephtons had cleared their lounge and arranged chairs in rows with a table and rostrum for me. Lovely flowers had been arranged, and a silver-plate bowl had to serve as a font. I had brought prayer books and hymn books with me, and Sue provided a suitable silver chalice. Althea Sephton played the piano to accompany the lusty singing of the congregation. We held the baptism first, followed by the communion service. There were some three dozen present, including Mr. and Mrs. Law, Sue's parents who were visiting from Natal. I am incapable of describing the atmosphere, but the presence of the Holy Spirit was almost tangible throughout the morning. It was an infinitely moving and joyful occasion.

After the second service we all adjourned to the step, where a tremendous spread of food had been laid out. After everyone had been refreshed, Aubrey called everyone back into the lounge. Without more ado, and without me in any way suggesting it, the company unanimously decided to found a congregation of the Church of England and asked me what it should be called. My suggestion of St. John's Church was adopted, and so that church was founded on Easter Day 1985. A committee consisting of Aubrey as chairman, Trevor van Coller as treasurer, Brett as secretary, and Alden Lake and his father Clifford, was unanimously elected. Aubrey, who was a member of the divisional council, was soon to retire to Maclear and leave his farm to Graham. Trevor was the town clerk of Maclear. They wanted me to be their resident minister, but I said I could only undertake to visit them for two Sundays and the week in between once a quarter. Alden Lake had been a Methodist lay preacher, and he would take morning service each Sunday in the hall of the school. I also undertook to tape my own sermons and to send them up to help Alden, who was a very busy schoolmaster.

This procedure was followed throughout the years 1985 to 1988. After that the Rev. Harwood Dixon, who had moved to Umtata, which is only an hour's drive from Maclear, visited Maclear for one weekend each

The Council of St John's Church, Maclear, Eastern Cape 1987. Alden Lake (Lay Preacher), Trevor van Coller (Treasurer), self, Clifford Lake, Aubrey Sephton (Chairman), and Brett Sephton with whom I had spoken at Oshikati on active service in Ovamboland in 1978.

month. He administered the Lord's Supper for them and visited them on their farms, and his ministry, owned by the Lord, bore much fruit in the lives of all the fellowship.

In April 1986 Win and I moved to Cape Town, partly because Bishop Foord wanted me to be his administrative officer or chaplain and partly because the humidity at Scottburgh was not suiting the health of either of us. We stayed temporarily in a rented flat in Mowbray and soon found a very pleasant flat in Kennilworth where I would be an easy train ride from the Bishop. However, we had no sooner bought the flat than my possible appointment with the Bishop was cancelled.

At this stage I was approached by the wardens of Holy Trinity Church, Gardens, Cape Town, with a view to being called as the rector of that church. The church had been without a rector since the Rev. Murray Hofmeyr left about a year before. In the interregnum, the Rev. David Streater, our lecturer at the Bible Institute at Kalk Bay, had filled in part-time, and he was now leaving for a post in England. So at the end of May I became the rector of the mother church of the denomination. As I was now sixty-six and the retiring age for ministers is sixty-eight I undertook to serve for two years, after which the position could be reviewed. Having only just moved Win twice in as many months, I declined to move yet again into the rectory in Orangezicht. This did make visitation in the vicinity of the church difficult for me as our flat was about eight miles from it but I did what I could.

I was sad to find the mother church of the denomination with a small congregation of forty or so and overdrawn at the bank by some R3,000. Apparently there had been a good deal of discord before my arrival, but this soon dissipated. I think my insistence that there should be no votes in the church council but that we should always wait on the Lord to bring us to one mind on any issue helped to heal old quarrels. Knowing that "the devil, is a roaring lion, walketh about, seeking whom he may devour." As was my usual practice, I introduced the congregation to the practice of praying for one another regularly by name instead of only when someone was sick. To do this, I gave everyone a prayer cycle so that everyone was prayed for by at least one other person every day of the week.

My ministry there was appreciated particularly by the Tuesday morning Bible study and fellowship and by the Ladies Christian Home nearby. But I was always conscious of the handicap of living so far from the church. Nevertheless, by virtue of the rectory being let and by my only accepting a small stipend, the church finances gradually improved and a very substantial bank balance was built up.

Donald Irwin, who had been a member of the Church Council for some forty years, and latterly a Churchwarden, also produced a monthly Church

Rector of Holy Trinity Church, Gardens, Cape Town, the mother church of the Church of England in South Africa, 1986-1988. Photographs of our three sons taken in their early twenties in the background.

magazine called *Trinity Chimes*. I wrote the rector's letter for this and also a series of articles on the history of the Church of England. In these I showed how the Gospel came to England very soon after the Resurrection and some 600 years before Augustine came to Canterbury with his Roman Catholicism which was to usher in a dark age until the great Reformation in the sixteenth century. I showed how the Church of England services had evolved on lines similar to the synagogue services approved by our Lord by his presence at them and by the early Christians until they were driven out of the synagogues.

Donald insisted that these articles be put together in a booklet, which he typed out and which I called, *Our Church of England Heritage*. This was published by the CESA with a foreword by Bishop Desmond Douglas which included these words: "The Reformation was a re-discovery of God through His Word. Immediately His majesty and mercy began to be reflected in the lives and outlook of believers, in the furnishings of the Churches, the appearance of the clergy, and in the liturgies. Bible in hand the Reformers searched the writings of the fathers and discovered much treasure with which they enriched and strengthened the Church. A great deal of it is in our Prayer Book.

"Dick Begbie's booklet is very timely. Apostasy is assuming runaway proportions, and a great dividing of the ways lies ahead. We cannot afford to neglect anything that will educate and equip God's people to discern error and follow truth."

Subsequently, an American edition of this booklet was published by Providence Reformed Episcopal Church in Corpus Christi, Texas, which is a local Church of the Reformed Episcopal Church of America. The Rt. Rev. Royal U. Grote, Missionary Bishop of the Special Jurisdiction of North America of the Reformed Episcopal Church, wrote in the foreword, "This timely work by the Rev. Dick Begbie is being issued at a very crucial time in America's religious history. Having just passed through a period when God has shaken the Church and called her back to her original roots, many are now returning to traditional values and looking for a Church which focuses its worship on Almighty God and not man.

"Although the Rev. Begbie is from South Africa and the specifics of the booklet reflect the views of a different Anglican body from our own, we feel that this work can be helpful to anyone who is beginning to take the first steps in learning the principles and ideas of worship which are common to the liturgical expressions found in the different versions of the Book of Common Prayer. It is my prayer that God will use it to that end."

Holy Trinity Church has always been a difficult church. It is located in a small side street well off the beaten track. It is a church which, despite change elsewhere in the denomination, has kept faithfully to the reverence and dignity of liturgical worship, and its architecture and furnishings reflect that ethos.

The suburb in which it is located is populated by people of limited means and education. Despite all efforts by my predecessors and myself, very few of the people who live there have ever worshipped in that church. A mission hall with an informal type of service might provide a more effective means of attracting the local people. Attempts to do so in the hall beneath the church have also come to nothing. The result is that almost all the members live in suburbs some miles from the church. In my time the congregation did begin to build up slowly, but with hardly any of the local people.

I was also rector of three and, for a time, five daughter churches. I suppose I was functioning as a rural dean though without the title. The main burden was to have all these people on my heart and to pray for them and their needs each day. They were St. James's Church, Kenton-on-Sea where Ed Bean, formerly of the Hogsback Evangelical Church, was the lay reader, St. Stephen's Church, Queenstown, where Cecil Murray was the lay preacher, and St. John's Church, Maclear where Alden Lake was the lay preacher. I used to visit them every quarter for ten days, including two Sundays, in a road journey on my own of over 1600 miles which included visiting members on their farms. The second Sunday was always the busiest. I used to take the communion service in Maclear in the morning, drive 400 miles to Kenton, and take the communion service there in the evening. I was very thankful to the Rt. Rev. Desmond Douglas and Mr. Herbert Hammond, who gave excellent sermons during my absences, and to Messrs. David Hall and Richard Daly, who led the services. Later the Rev. Claude Mitchell pulled out of the Church of the Province at Hermanus with most of the congregation. These formed Christ Church, which met in the scout hall at Hermanus. It became yet another daughter church, and either I, Bishop Douglas, or Mr. Herbert Hammond preached there at least once a month.

All in all it was a very busy time, not helped by the fact that in 1986 I had to undergo a prostrate operation which went wrong and from which I took a long time to recover.

In my travels to the Eastern Cape churches, I passed through Knysna and Plettenberg Bay. At the former were Charles and Gwen Hibberd, who used to worship at Holy Trinity Church in Bramley, Johannesburg, and at the latter were Alan and Letitia Versfelt. Alan had been on the Central Executive of the Church and had been largely instrumental in the founding of St. Stephen's Church, Krugersdorp, in the Transvaal, and Trinity Church, Hilton, in Natal. I used to call on these folk, who said there was no English speaking church preaching the full counsel of God anywhere between George and Plettenberg Bay, and they began to urge me to think about planting a Church of England church in the area.

Eventually in April 1988, a meeting was held in the home of John and Rosemary Walters, who had been members of Holy Trinity Church, Salisbury, in Rhodesia. I little knew at the time that Rosemary had been pressing Bishop Foord some years before to start a work in George. He had in fact stayed a few days with the Walters and promised that he would do what he could to get a work started. He also had come to the conclusion that no English speaking church between George and Plettenburg Bay was preaching the Gospel. Some two dozen people were present at the meeting, including Alan and Charles. It was agreed that I should hold a service when I next came through in June. I reported these developments to the Holy Trinity Church council, who supported me with their prayers and advice, as indeed they did for all the daughter churches for which we had been made responsible.

In June the service was held in the George Town Hall with some three dozen present. The number included several Church of the Province people who attended out of curiosity rather than with any intention of becoming involved. Many pressed me to become their resident minister, and this pressure was intensified by the Walters, with whom I was staying the weekend. They showed me what lovely country and beaches there were round about. In particular they took me to a retirement village called Genevafontein which I had to admit was most attractive.

I went back and inspected some of the cottages on the Monday morning before leaving for Cape Town. The feeling was growing on me that I was being called to undertake this work, but all the time as I drove back to Cape Town I was asking myself how I could possibly ask Win to move yet again.

I told Win all this on my return, and to my surprise, she said, "I rather like the idea of living in George." I kept the Holy Trinity Church council informed of these developments, and they, like me, were waiting on the Lord to show what should be done.

So on the Thursday, we drove over to George and stayed the night with John and Rosemary Walters. A two bedroom cottage in Genevafontein Village with the very best view of the mountains and forests was still available. It almost seemed that, like that lovely property at Hogsback, the Lord had this one waiting for us. So we bought it. On the way back to Cape Town, Win said, "You'd better put our flat on the market without delay, otherwise we shall have two places." On arrival in Cape Town I rang the agents at 3.45 pm and the flat was sold to a doctor at 5.15 pm at our price! The doctor was happy to wait three months while I served out my notice at Holy Trinity. It almost seemed as if the Lord was ejecting us from Cape Town to take up what was now clearly His calling for us to go to George.

The Holy Trinity Church council recognized that the Lord was calling me to George and so agreed, though perhaps a little reluctantly, to our move. It was agreed that I should come back to Cape Town on alternate weekends until my successor as rector there arrived.

We moved to George at the end of September 1988 and began services in the Seventh Day Adventist Church on alternate Sundays. On the intermediate Sundays I drove back to Cape Town to take the services there and hold Bible studies on the Mondays and Tuesdays there as before. We soon built up a congregation of three dozen or so at George, and I continued to drive once a quarter to visit the churches in the Eastern Cape. Early in the New Year 1989, a successor for me as rector of Holy Trinity Church, Cape Town, was appointed, and from then on responsibility for the Eastern Cape fell on him.

Later in 1989 we were visited by the Registrar of the Church of England, who suggested that we should buy the SDA church, which was on the market.

In February 1990 Win and I celebrated our seventieth birthdays by inviting some two dozen close friends to dinner at the Far Hills Hotel outside George. I had invited Herbert Hammond, who was one of the Central trustees of the Church of England in South Africa to propose a toast to us. In the course of his speech, he said that the Central trustees had decided to give R150,000 as a birthday present to enable us to buy the SDA church! I am rather ashamed to say I was completely overcome and wept openly for joy. The Central Trustees had never given anything towards my work before, apart from a grant of R2,600 to help build Christ Church, Blairgowrie.

In the course of negotiations, it transpired that the Seventh Day Adventists were asking far too high a price for their property, and in any case it was situated in an area which was rapidly being converted from residential to commercial use.

In the meantime, we had accumulated enough money in our George building fund to buy a piece of land. Charles Hibberd, Alan Versfelt, and I visited the town planner, who informed us that development of residential properties in George would be by extension of the eastern suburbs in 1991 and 92, towards the south after that, and then perhaps some up-market suburbs to the northwest after that.

So I began to look for a suitable site in the east. This must not be on a main road where noise and danger to children would be excessive, nor must it be tucked away in a side road where no one would see the church. A site on a feeder road to a suburb was what was required. I found such a site which had the added advantages of being on the opposite side of the road to a small park and on the same side of the road upon which a school was

Win and myself taken at Knysna Heads, soon after our 70th birthdays, when I was still minister-in-charge of St Philip's Church, George.

to be built later on. It was also near a large suburb of colored people which gave promise for a multi-racial congregation. But it has to be said that most of the colored people speak Afrikaans, so that only a small proportion would be likely to attend an English speaking Church.

I designed a church to seat a hundred with space for later extensions or on which to build a hall and Sunday School accommodation. But I considered that future development in George would require a second church later on in the western half of the town. I arranged with none other than the building inspector to produce the final working drawings. The Lord led us to a Christian builder who gave us an excellent quote, and it was good to be able to pray with him before work began.

Meantime a magnificent site had been acquired for a nominal sum for a church at Maclear to be built at the top of the hill overlooking the town. The church, which I designed, was built with dressed stone recovered from abandoned farm buildings in the district. Aubrey Sephton was the resident engineer. They gave me the honor of laying the foundation stone when the Church was consecrated at a service in 1990 at which Bishop Bradley officiated. Both the churchwardens of the mother church, Holy Trinity, Cape Town, Donald Irwin and Les Powell, as well as my successor as rector, the Rev. Billy Farr, attended. I continued to visit very occasionally as once the Lord has put the love of people into your heart, that love and concern remains, always.

It was decided to call the church at George St. Philip's Church, and the building was completed in July 1992. Again I made the boards for the Ten Commandments, but this time I only had to stick plastic letters on. Jack Brendon made lovely carved hymn boards and fixed a clock to the wall at the back of the church, I think so that I could watch the time as I preached! John Walters made the lectern, and the members paid for the pews, each of which cost over R600. One way and another, the funds raised by the local congregation doubled the sum provided by the Central Trustees of the CESA.

I was given the honor of laying the foundation stone on Sunday, 28th July 1992, in an inset in the wall as the church was already built by then. This was done in a short ceremony after Morning Prayer. I paid tribute to all the members and others who had done and given so much to complete the work. I also testified to the fact that the church had turned out better than I had pictured it in my mind, and I felt sure this was the work of the Holy Spirit. After I had spoken to this effect, Herbert Hammond said, "In a catalogue of thanksgiving there is one person who stands under God above everyone else, and that is the Reverent Colonel Dick Begbie. And I think that, in fact I know that, but for his vision, his energy, knowledge, leadership, and so on and so on and so on, that none of this would have

Nathia Gali Community Church, Pakistan.

St Philip's Church, George, South Africa.

happened. And I think that we must not part this morning without saying thank you to Dick for what he has done."

Throughout these years from Hogsback time onwards, my heart had been giving warning signals that all was not well. Recently it had not always been possible to disguise the fact, especially when I had dizzy spells while conducting services. At my age I really could not manage to provide an evening service nor do anything special for youngsters. By this time the congregation was reaching as many as fifty at Morning Prayer. The monthly income had reached a point that only R1,500 more was needed to finance a curate not yet cumbered with a family. Remembering that Christ Church, Pinetown, had subsidized the Scottburgh Church with R400 per month, decreasing by R40 a month to nil ten months later in 1984, I thought it not unreasonable to ask Central Funds to subsidizes to the extent of R1,500 per month, decreasing by R100 per month to nil in 1994.

The expansion of the work in George would require the services of a much younger minister to go calling on the young families moving into the houses that were springing up like mushrooms in the neighborhood of the church.

So in September 1992, I gave three months notice of my retirement to the church committee. I consulted with Bishop Frank Retief, the Area Bishop for Cape Province, and he gave me the names of several men who would be available for a call to George. From these, I recommended two to Charles Hibberd, the chapel warden. One of these whom we interviewed together was entirely unsuitable, but the other we took to at once and we invited him and his young wife to George. Both they and the committee felt that the Lord was calling them to George. But to our surprise and chagrin, this clear call from God was over-ruled by the Presiding Bishop!

With the consequent delay, the chapel wardens were becoming increasingly worried about my health, and because of this, and despite the reservations of the council of the mother church, Holy Trinity, Cape Town they called a man commended by the bishops but who was known not to have had a successful ministry in the Transvaal and to be one who had little use for the Prayer Book. So this man was required to sign a contract which was drawn up by Herbert Hammond of the mother church and approved by the bishops which required him to keep to the Prayer Book.

I handed over to him in May 1993. Almost at once he broke his contract, saying that the Lord had told him to break his promise! I attended one of his evening communion services, and it was quite the most shockingly irreverent and undignified performance it has ever been my misfortune to witness. Knowing apparently nothing of "submitting himself to others in the fear of God" (Ephesians 5:21), he split church down the middle and one by one the original members of the church left in disgust. They were replaced by those who required informality but who also came from humbler backgrounds and were unable to provide for the church financially. So after three agonizing years he left because there was no longer money to support him. I was terribly sad to see a work which the Lord had blessed so abundantly laid in ruins by this man.

For some time I had been concerned about mysterious pains in my chest. These became quite bad after walks on the beach, particularly while negotiating the soft, dry sand on my way back to the car. The doctor gave me a static ECG which, as previously, indicated nothing amiss. So I was diagnosed as having an infected wind-pipe (I cannot remember the technical name) and given antibiotics. One evening very soon after my retirement, I had what must have been a minor heart attack, because there was no permanent damage, but the pain was almost intolerable. In response to my phone call, my doctor's partner, no doubt seeing the diagnosis and not suspecting a heart problem, merely told me to take some painkillers and to call him again if the pain didn't go away in a few minutes. If the attack had been more severe I could easily have died that night!

Herbert Hammond happened to be visiting a few days later, and, seeing me not looking at all well, arranged for me to be admitted into hospital at Cape Town immediately. In fact he and his family virtually kidnapped me in order to get me in!

Three attempts were made with an angiogram to unblock an artery, which had been shown up by a dynamic ECG, but without success because, apparently, my aorta was so convoluted that they couldn't get into my heart. So I was discharged to see how I got on, and after six months the dynamic ECG registered all clear! I was told the heart had created its own bypass as local capillaries expanded and took over. I was told that happens very rarely, and I am sure it was the Lord's doing in my case.

I was very worried about all God's people who had virtually been driven out by my successor and were now without a spiritual home. Long enough had now elapsed for me not to be accused of splitting the church. So when I was approached, I immediately agreed to provide a ministry for these folk. Bob Labrum, who had been converted through my ministry earlier, and his wife Fay offered their lounge as a venue, and so we began in October 1993 with services every Sunday except the last each month and a weekly meeting for Bible study and prayer. The regular members were, besides Bob and Fay, who played the piano for us, Win of course, Charles and Gwen Hibberd, Pieter and Trish de Villiers, Bokkie and Helm Coates, Eddie and Mirl Lincott and Dennis Hill; occasional attendees would make us up to fifteen or sixteen and occasionally when members or others brought visitors we were up to a little under thirty. This, especially through the Bible studies, became a very close knit and loving fellowship, and we all became the closest of friends, with frequent outings to one or another's home or to a nearby picnic spot.

Meantime Holy Trinity Church in Cape Town had suffered a similar disaster from a disloyal and divisive minister. The sad thing was that in both cases, Bishops Frank Retief and Joe Bell took an equivocal if not hostile attitude, and the damage in both cases was thereby unnecessarily prolonged. To help fill in during the subsequent interregnum, I was asked to preach in Holy Trinity Church from time to time and used to stay the weekend either with the Irwins or the Hammonds.

This gave the opportunity for discussions with Herbert Hammond in which we wondered whether the time had come to form some sort of fellowship of like minded CESA members throughout South Africa interested in trying to maintain the identity of the CESA as a distinctly Church of England Church. So, on Herbert's advice, I went to see Dr. David Broughton Knox, the principal of our theological college. David had been principal of Moore College, Australia, and was a very dear Christian man with a brilliant and incisive mind. He advised that he did not think that the situation in the CESA had deteriorated so much that a fellowship on the lines I was considering was necessary. He described to me the *Australian Church Recorder* and suggested that I should found and edit a similar journal which, whilst friendly to the denomination, would air developments which were causing concern.

Talking the matter over further with Herbert, he said, and I agreed, that the matters concerning us were common to all denominations in South Africa and, from what we knew, throughout the world as well. So we decided that this journal should be interdenominational in character in so far as we could make it so.

On further reflection, I was conscious of the vast amount of Christian literature from Reformed and Evangelical bodies and from missionary societies which passed over my desk each month. These contained excellent material which is not seen by the majority of the laity. So I hit on the idea of condensing selected articles from this material and producing a *Christian Digest*. The *Digest* would be produced bimonthly and should be quite small so that it would not be too much for busy people in secular employ to read. As far as possible, condensed articles should be reduced to not more than a thousand words, with "shorties" in between to keep it light. The whole would fit onto eight pages of A5 paper.

With the support of a Board of Reference consisting of Bishop Desmond Douglas, the Rev. Drs. Jack Allen and Kin Bensusan and Herbert Hammond of the CESA, the Rev. Martin Holdt of the Baptist Church, and latterly of the Rev. Douglas Cranston of the Church of Scotland, and myself as editor, the *Digest* began publication in February 1993.

Our intention is best described by quoting from the editorial of the first issue.

"We are living in an era of attack on the person and work of the Lord Jesus Christ such as there has not been since the days of the sub-apostolic Church. The attack is directed by Satan and takes two forms. The first is an internal attack within our Protestant denominations leading to the substitution of entertainment for worship and to centralization of authority at the expense of the autonomy of the local churches. (The latter has historically always been at the expense of the Gospel as witness for example what has happened in the Church of Rome). The second is an external attack by secular authority aided and abetted by the World and South African Councils of Churches and often by denominations associated with them. This external attack is already evident in the United States of America and the United Kingdom amongst many others and is threatening in the New South Africa.

"Our only offensive weapon against this attack is 'the sword of the Spirit which is the Word of God' (Ephesians 6:17). When the visible Church was last in error and confusion comparable with her condition today, she was reformed by the grace of God mainly by laymen to whom the Word of God was made available. There is, today, a vast amount of good exposition of Holy Scripture but it is scattered amongst a number of periodicals and books, and not generally available to lay people.

"So the purpose of this digest is to bring, in condensed and clear form, such information as is relevant to our situation today to a much wider, and particularly lay, readership. The policy of the *Digest* will be to avoid criticism as far as possible but to present the truth in positive and telling style. Care will be taken to keep well clear of political bias one way or the other."

Circulation has depended entirely on the readership encouraging others to subscribe to the *Digest*. Although readers write frequently to support me, their efforts to enlist new subscribers has been very disappointing. The result is that circulation has never increased to the point that it has been able to influence events in the slightest.

In the meantime, developments in Church and State have continued to deteriorate to levels never before imagined, with segments of the Church even condoning sodomy, the sin which God says is a sign of a society under JUDGEMENT.

Chapter Twenty

Service In Scotland

When, largely as a result of external pressure, particularly by the US and UK Governments, Nelson Mandela and his atheistic Marxist associates came into power, it was quite evident that Christian standards, law and order, and responsible government would soon breakdown in South Africa as they have done throughout Africa. In this prognosis I was sadly not wrong, as subsequent developments have proved.

But I was concerned, in view of my heart troubles, at the probability of leaving my widow in such conditions. So towards the end of 1995, I made the agonizing decision to leave South Africa after thirty-eight years there and so many dear friends. We settled in a flat in Kilmacolm, not far from Glasgow, to be near our youngest son and his family. They could not have been more caring and helpful in getting us settled in.

Soon after arrival, I walked round to the local Episcopal Church to find a large notice outside announcing prayers for "His Holiness the Pope." That was enough to cause me to about turn immediately! It turned out that the local vicar, though a likeable man, was a committed Anglo-Catholic with, hardly surprisingly, a minute congregation. Equally not surprisingly, the Episcopal Church counts for nothing in Scotland.

So Win and I attended public worship at "the Old Kirk" in Kilmacolm once, which was enough to see that the minister there was a liberal of the most harmful kind. His ministry was so harmful because his message was lacking any sort of challenge to commit oneself to Christ in a meaningful way and was therefore popular.

So we found our way to St. Columba Church where the minister is the Rev. Douglas Cranston. Here we have a godly man fearlessly proclaiming the whole counsel of God. It has made him unpopular amongst the ungodly but deeply appreciated by all those who love and obey the Lord Jesus Christ and yearn to know more of Him. We are greatly blessed to have such a man in a relatively small community.

So we have been accepted as members of the Church of Scotland, but we do miss the liturgical worship of the Church of England. We miss the rich Biblical content of the 1662 Book of Common Prayer, and the dignity and reverence and the opportunity for congregational participation which it provides.

The Christian Digest has suffered a fall in circulation consequent on our leaving South Africa. But circulation outside South Africa is showing signs of picking up and we now have subscribers in Scotland, England, Ulster, USA, Canada, Hong Kong, New Zealand, and Nepal.

My heart was giving trouble several times a day, either beating too slowly down to forty per minute, or too fast up to two hundred per minute, or completely erratically. So early in 1997 I was fitted with a pacemaker which stopped it going too slowly and was put on several pills a day to deal with the other conditions. The result is that to my enormous relief I have been able to forget that I have a heart for the first time in years.

The result is that, in addition to continuing the editing and distribution of the *Digest*, I am able to assist Douglas Cranston with the ministry here. He has been appointed moderator for a Church in Port Glasgow which lacks a minister. So I am currently involved on alternate Sundays, taking the service either in Port Glasgow or here at St. Columba. I also conduct a weekly Bible study for a devoted group of seven or eight members of the church. I have also been called upon to conduct services for various ex-service organizations, particularly the Normandy Veterans Association in Glasgow.

Over the years, I have produced a course of one hundred Bible studies, and these are in use in George and Cape Town, and I use them here in Kilmacolm. I am being encouraged by the users to have these published as a book, but whether or not that comes to anything remains to be seen.

So will end an active life of twenty years in the British Army, ten years in business, and thirty years in the ministry in which the Lord has given me the immense privilege of working for Him. Though there have been buffetings as well as blessings, I have found that His service is indeed perfect freedom. His service is never a drudgery because His Holy Spirit causes one to want and enjoy doing the things which He wants one to do. At the end of it, one can only thank God for His infinite patience and long-suffering with a man who has made many mistakes and is a far worse sinner than even his closest friends know. Our God is indeed a God of amazing grace and infinite mercy to those who by His grace alone are united to Christ as their personal Saviour and Lord. To Him therefore be all the praise for ever and ever, Amen.

Mabws

by H.J.G.S and R.J.G.B.

The Mabws Estate was situated about ten miles south down the coast from Aberystwyth. It included almost all of the village of Llanrhystyd and eighteen farms situated in the valleys of two trout streams which joined just below the house and then ran on down to the sea about three quarters of a mile beyond the village. Part of the shoreline was included in the estate. It had a steeply sloping pebble beach, and all the pebbles were flat shaped. The ones at the top were the largest, and they gave a lovely ring as you walked on them.

The house was approached by a windy lane which climbed up fairly steeply for two miles from the village, and by a drive about half a mile long. The house consisted of three floors in an L shape, but owing to the slope of the ground, there was an extra lower floor with cellars on one side, and at the end a very dark kitchen with a basement window. As a little girl, I found the passage and kitchen dark and rather frightening. I used to run down the stairs from the ground floor past the "old" unused kitchen and into the "new" kitchen, which was full of light and bustle. Outside that lower floor, there was a lovely yard to play in which was paved with enormous, flat, grey stones with beautiful short grass growing between them. On one side of the yard were some outhouses which were used as a dairy, ironing room, and stores. When our father was a boy, he fell out of a window into this yard and, miraculously, was not seriously injured, although he had to spend several months on his back. Across the yard were stables which housed a horse and an old grey pony which was used, amongst other things, to tow the lawn mower. There was a pony trap, a cart, and an open carriage.

Beyond the outhouses to the side of the house, there was a large walled vegetable and fruit garden with gorgeous gooseberries and raspberries. Our mother used to work hard at making jam on an oil stove in one of the unused maids' rooms. There was no electricity, and all lighting was by means of oil lamps.

The old outside toilets, still in use, quite fascinated me. They were built over an underground stream and were divided in the middle by a high, old, brick wall. On one side of the wall was the maids' toilet and on the other that belonging to "the gentry." Each room had a long bench with three different sized holes, and you sat over whichever you preferred. They would have suited Goldilocks and the Three Bears! I was a little scared of falling through; there was quite a drop below!

There was a large croquet lawn in front of the house and a greenhouse with a rookery behind it away to the left. There was a hill sloping down to the croquet lawn where we could see rabbits hopping around. My nurse used to pull me down the slope in a hip bath, which was great fun.

Below the stables was a barn for hay, and a swing was fixed up inside for me. There were some other rather spooky outhouses, one certainly full of bats. Down below the buildings, my father dammed up the stream so that I could frolic around in it. Sometimes I went trout fishing with him. All I ever caught was an eel. If he couldn't catch a trout any other way, he would tickle one.

From outside, it could be seen that certain windows were blocked up, owing to windows being taxed at one period. All the rooms were quite big, and both the drawing room and the dining room had three very tall windows facing north up the slope to the park beyond the lawn.

There were two smaller rooms in the short arm of the L which had been converted by our grandfather — the downstairs one to a cloakroom with toilet and the one on the first floor to a bathroom and toilet. I cannot remember if the water was heated, as the bathroom was far away from the "new" kitchen. Certainly all drinking water had to be fetched from a well at the top of the drive.

This shorter arm of the L, which was added at a later date, was mainly for service. It was also quite old, as I remember. It had a stone flagged kitchen with a big old-fashioned stove and a wooden high backed bench at one side. Mrs Jones, the post mistress, having walked up from the village, could be found sitting there exchanging gossip over tea with the cook.

By the entrance door of that wing, there was a larder and scullery all stone flagged. There was a back staircase in the wing leading up to two or three maids' bedrooms on each floor. I had a bedroom which I adored up a short flight of stairs from the main staircase, but in the new wing. It had two deep windows at each end and a locked door into the maid's room beyond it. In the evenings I used to watch the rooks coming home to roost and the last rabbits gambolling on the hill.

We used to be quite a large house party in the summer with, besides our parents, our grandfather, two of our aunts and uncles, and three of our cousins. I remember going out sometimes with my cousins with Nancy, the old grey pony. I fell off once, and this so upset my cousins that I had the pony for the rest of the afternoon. Occasionally, we had an expedition to the sea. This was a great excitement as we went by pony trap and carriage. The horse and Nancy did not like to work, and they really had to be urged to the sea. Coming back was a different matter, and David, the coachman and handyman, used to get very nervous trying to hold the horse, especially on steep downward slopes.

I remember once being in the pony trap with Mummy and Dick. She got very agitated trying to avoid getting stuck in a ditch with something coming the other way, as all the lanes were very narrow by today's standards. I can still smell the honeysuckle growing in the hedgerows and hear the bees and wasps buzzing — not to mention the gnats! Still, when I hear water trickling over stones, I can see the little waterfall behind David's lodge.

David had two boys a little older than I, and the last summer I was there, we went mushrooming together before breakfast several times. Ivan, the eldest, could speak a little English, the younger one only Welsh. We also used to visit David's old father who was bedridden and who had worked at Mabws. He lived in a little cottage on the way to Ty-hen, which was one of the eighteen farms on the estate. I got chased by geese once on the way to the farm. I also visited New Mabws Farm at the top of the hill with my nurse, where I was given a glass of milk and also — very precious — an old Welsh jug which I still treasure.

The estate originally extended up into the mountains as far as a pretty little lake called Llyn Eiddwen. So there used to be eighteen sheep farms in addition to the valley farms still remaining. Our grandfather bought out his sister-in-law's interest in the estate, and her son lived in a house called Athlywdd, a little way south of Llanrystyd. I remember him as Uncle Lloyd, a big tease. His wife came from "The Red Lion" public house in Llanrystyd, so she was not acceptable at home, though I thought she was very nice.

There were white owls living in the attics at Mabws. It was a little frightening for a ten year old girl and a little boy of three to be taken through the attics to the new wing. On one occasion I met an owl face-to-face around the corner of a chimney stack! There was a legend that if the white owls left Mabws, Mabws would be burnt down. They used to snore on the window sills, and they were still there when Mabws was sold.

There was a ghost cupboard, which was more like a small room, off the drawing room. It had been bricked up by our great-great-grandfather after his wife had been murdered there. They slept in the room directly above the drawing room, and one night, hearing a noise, she went down to investigate. She discovered the butler stealing the silver from the silver room which was this cupboard. He hit her over the head with a silver candlestick and killed her and made off with the silver. Subsequently, the silver was found in a sack under a hedge about three miles from the house, and the butler was caught and hung for his crime.

Ever since then dogs have howled if left in the drawing room at night, and only members of the family can sleep undisturbed in the bedroom above the drawing room. Our father tried to catch a ghost once, but it was only an old rat going *plomp-plomp* down the stairs.

I enjoyed going down with David in the cart to buy bread — lovely hot, flat, white loaves straight out of the oven. There was a general shop where you could buy sweeties in three-cornered paper bags. Sometimes Dick would be given a bag because he was the young master. I think there was a Miss Jones there who crocheted lace for my petticoat. When we went to church, some of the service would be in English in our honor.

I can still feel the excitement of arriving for the summer holiday at Aberystwyth. David used to meet us in the carriage, and we thought it was very grand. It took four people, sitting two back to back. Then there was the excitement of arriving at the Mabws gates with the lions on top of the pillars on either side, and then around the laburnums to the main entrance where the staff were waiting. What heaven!

H.J.G.S = Helen Joan Glynn Stead, the last being the married name of my beloved eldest sister who passed away on August 5th 1990.

R.J.G.B = Me, i.e., Richard James Glynn Begbie

List of Abbreviations

AAQMG Assistant Adjutant and Quartermaster General

ADMS Assistant Director of Medical Services (The Senior M.O. in a Division)

ADOS Assistant Director of Ordnance Services (The senior officer for replacing guns and equipment in a Division)

APO Army Post Office

ARP Air Raid Precautions

AVRE Armoured Vehicle Royal (A Churchill tank modified for engineering)

BEF British Expeditionary Force

Bigot Officer privy to top secret papers with regard to forthcoming operations

Capt Captain

CBE Commander of the Order of the British Empire (one rank below Knighthood)

C.S.M. Company Sergeant Major

CB Companion of the Order of Bath (one rank below Knighthood)

C.O. Commanding Officer (of a battalion or regiment)

CRA Commander Royal Artillery (The senior artillery officer in a division)

CRASC Commander Royal Army Service Corps (The senior officer for supplying ammunition, rations, and transport in a division)

CRE   Commander Royal Engineers (The senior officer in a division)

CRENE Commander Electrical and Mechanical Engineers (The senior officer for recovering and repairing tanks, guns, and vehicles in a division)

DAAG Deputy Assistant Adjutant General (Responsible under the AAQMG for personnel and reinforcements)

DAAQMG Deputy Assistant Adjutant and Quartermaster General (Responsible for all administrative matters where there is no AAQMG)

Div   Division (Infantry or Armoured or Panzer)

DMP   Director of Manpower Planning

DMS   Deputy Military Secretary

DRA   Director Royal Artillery

DSD   Director of Staff Duties

DSO   Distinguished Service Order (Second highest decoration for gallantry)

FBE   Folding Boat Equipment

GC   Gentleman Cadet

GOC General Officer Commanding

GSO General Staff Officer (Grade I, II, or III)

IORE Intelligence Officer Royal Engineers

Lt   Lieutenant

Lt Col Lieutenant Colonel

L of C Line of Communication

L/Cpl Lance Corporal

LCV   Lorried Command Vehicle

LST   Landing Ship Tank

MBE   Additional Member of the Order of the British Empire (one rank below an OBE)

MC   Military Cross (Third highest decoration for gallantry)

MGO Master General of the Ordnance

MI   Medical Inspection

MO   Medical Officer

MT   Mechanical Transport

NCO Non-Commissioned Officer

OBE Ordinary Officer of the Order of the British Empire (one rank below CBE)

OC   Officer Commanding (a company or squadron)

OCTU Officer Cadet Training Unit

OCU Officers Christian Union

OTC Officer Training Corps (in universities and schools)

QMG Quartermaster General

QNSI Quartermaster Sergeant Instructor

RA   Royal Artillery

RCB Royal Commissions Board

RE   Royal Engineers

RSM Regimental Sergeant Major

SME School of Military Engineering

SMI   Sergeant Major Instructor

SSM   Squadron Sergeant Major

T.A.B. Combined anti-tetanus & typhoid injection

VAG   Vice-Adjutant General

VC   Victoria Cross (Highest decoration for gallantry)

Acknowledgments

I wish to acknowledge that without the urging by my sons and a number of close friends, I would never have had the patience to write this story of my life. In particular, I want to express my gratitude to Mr. Herbert Hammond, MA, of Cape Town, for the thoroughness with which he has checked the manuscript and made numerous corrections and suggestions, almost all of which I have accepted. I owe a debt of gratitude to Mr. Jonathan Ruffer of Ugley Green, Hertfordshire, England, for his attempts to find a publisher in England. Apparently the really hard fighting round Caen does not catch the popular attention as does, for instance, the events of D-Day itself or the defence of the bridge at Arnhem. Similarly, the religious publishers want the record of a new "victorious life" rather than the still small voice I have to offer. I also wish to thank Mr Francis Redelinghuys of FIO Computers, Box 2514, George, South Africa, for printing the master copy of the manuscript with such a clear font, free of charge, on a fast laser printer; Mr. Hennie van Zyl of Nashua, Box 1275, George, for photostating the master copy on very favourable terms, and Mr Bennie Kleynhans and Blitsdruk Printers, Box 1670, George, for their kindness in binding the original book so inexpensively.

About the Author

The author served in the Royal Engineers from July 1939, being mentioned in Despatches in 1944, made an MBE in 1945 and an OBE in 1958, until retiring as a Lt Col in 1958.

He was converted in 1948 through the ministry of the Officers Christian Union and has been an active Christian worker ever since. Since emigrating to South Africa in 1958 he has been active in the Church of England in South Africa and was ordained in 1969. He has been used to found several new churches and has served as a volunteer chaplain in the South Africa Army for 12 years. He has been awarded the Pro Patria medal for spells of active service on the border between South West Africa and Angola.